BROOKINGS PAPERS ON EDUCATION POLICY

1998

Diane Ravitch
Editor

Sponsored by
the Brown Center for
Education Policy

D1051281

BROOKINGS INSTITUTION PRESS
Washington, D.C.

EBROOKINGS PAPERS ON EDUCATION POLICY

1998

Introduction   *1*
DIANE RAVITCH

An Examination of American Student Achievement from an
International Perspective   *7*
HAROLD W. STEVENSON *and* SHINYING LEE
Comments   38

An Assessment of the Contemporary Debate over U.S.
Achievement   *53*
LAWRENCE C. STEDMAN
Comments   85

The Effects of Upgrading Policies on High School Mathematics
and Science   *123*
ANDREW C. PORTER
Comments   164

Uncompetitive American Schools: Causes and Cures   *173*
HERBERT J. WALBERG
Comments   206

Radical Constructivism and Cognitive Psychology   *227*
JOHN R. ANDERSON, LYNNE M. REDER, *and* HERBERT A. SIMON
Comments   255

The Use and Misuse of Research in Educational Reform   *279*
TOM LOVELESS
Comments   304

Standards outside the Classroom   *319*
LAURENCE STEINBERG
Comments   343

Remediation in Higher Education: Its Extent and Cost   *359*
DAVID W. BRENEMAN
Comments   371

BROOKINGS PAPERS ON EDUCATION POLICY contains the edited versions of the papers and comments that were presented at the inaugural Brookings annual conference on education policy, held on May 29–30, 1997. The conference gives federal, state, and local policymakers an independent, nonpartisan forum to analyze policies intended to improve student performance. Each year Brookings will convene some of the best-informed analysts from various disciplines to review the current situation in education and to consider proposals for reform. This year's discussion focused on "The State of Student Performance in American Schools." The conference and journal were funded by the Herman and George R. Brown Chair in Educational Studies at Brookings. Additional support from the Miriam K. Carliner Endowment for Economic Studies and from the John M. Olin Foundation is gratefully acknowledged.

The papers in this volume have been modified to reflect some of the insights contributed by the discussions at the conference. In all cases the papers are the result of the authors' thinking and do not imply agreement by those attending the conference. Nor do the materials presented here necessarily represent the views of the staff members, officers, or trustees of the Brookings Institution.

1998 Subscription Rates

Individuals $19.95
Institutions $34.95

Standing order plans are available by calling 1-800-275-1447 or 202-797-6258

For foreign orders add $6.00 surface mail and $14.00 airmail

Send subscription orders to The Brookings Institution, Department 037, Washington, D.C. 20042-0037. Or call 202-797-6258 or, toll-free, 1-800-275-1447.

Visit Brookings online at www.brook.edu

Conference Participants

J. Duke Albanese, *Maine Department of Education*
Carla Asher, *Dewitt Wallace–Readers' Digest Fund*
David Baker, *Catholic University*
Gail Hawkins Bush, *Philadelphia Education Summit*
Mary Cassell, *Office of Management and Budget*
Phoebe Cottingham, *The Smith Richardson Foundation*
Christopher Cross, *Council for Basic Education*
Liston A. Davis, *U.S. Virgin Islands Education Commission*
Joseph F. Dominic, *The Heinz Endowments*
Denis P. Doyle, *Denis Doyle and Associates*
Marjory Dugan, *Philadelphia Education Summit*
Diana Finnerty, *Seattle Office for Education*
William Galston, *University of Maryland*
Lawrence Gladieux, *The College Board*
Mario Golden, *U.S. Virgin Islands Education Commission*
Connie Goldman, *Maine Department of Education*
Janet Hansen, *National Academy of Sciences*
E. D. Hirsch, *CORE Knowledge*
Christine Johnson, *Colorado Board of Higher Education*
Vinetta Jones, *The College Board*
Phyllis Krutsch, *Wisconsin Board of Regents*
Leon Levesque, *Maine Department of Education*
Stanley Litow, *IBM, Inc.*
Anthony McCann, *House Appropriations Committee*
Daniel McMurrer, *The Urban Institute*
Brud Maxcy, *Maine Department of Education*
Hans Meeden, *House Education & Workforce Committee*
Tracy Meller, *The Smith Richardson Foundation*
Fritz Mosher, *The Carnegie Corporation*
Yas Nakib, *University of Delaware*
Ellen Pechman, *Policy Studies Associates, Inc.*
Susan Perles, *Academy of Leadership*
Thomas Rudin, *The College Board*
Isabel Sawhill, *The Urban Institute*
Roberta Schaefer, *Worcester Municipal Research Bureau*
Kathy Stack, *Office of Management and Budget*
Donald Stewart, *The College Board*
Kent Talbert, *House Education & Workforce Committee*
Thomas Toch, *U.S. News & World Report*
Craig Wacker, *Senate Labor & Human Resources Committee*

Introduction

DIANE RAVITCH

A CENTURY AGO, a Connecticut editorialist (no, not Mark Twain) wrote that everybody talks about the weather, but nobody does anything about it. Regarding schools, everybody talks about them, and almost everybody seems to have ideas about how to fix them. Education is an issue in which everyone can lay claim to a certain expertise, because they went to school and so did their children or the children of their friends. Educators used to complain about public apathy; this is no longer a problem, however, for education has moved to the front burner as a national issue that engages the attention of the president, the governors, and the public.

Changes in the national and global economies, not whim or fashion, have made education an important issue. Education is broadly understood as a critical investment, both for society and for individuals; without such investment, societies and individuals limit their prospects, their economic and technological progress, and their developed intelligence. Recognition of the importance of education has fueled the national movement for higher academic standards and higher student performance. In a modern society, those who hope to succeed must be well educated; as technological change advances, those who lack a solid educational foundation will be left behind. Poll after poll has demonstrated that every segment of the American public, including parents and students, agrees that the schools should expect more of students.

The current movement for improved education and higher standards provides common ground for those who seek excellence and those who seek greater social and economic equality. Without constant pressure to strive for excellence, young Americans will not be prepared for the ever-increasing demands of a competitive world economy. Without relentless efforts to improve the educational achievement of those stu-

1

dents in the bottom half, the social inequities in American society will become yawning and unbridgeable chasms as economic and technological change continues and perhaps accelerates.

In this inaugural issue of *Brookings Papers on Education Policy,* a varied group of scholars considers different dimensions of student performance. The fundamental requirement of good policy is accurate information about the current situation. Several contributors to this volume try to offer a clear picture of how American students are performing, as compared with their international peers and as compared with the past.

Harold W. Stevenson and Shinying Lee of the University of Michigan examine American students' achievement from an international perspective. Stevenson and his colleagues have spent most of the past two decades studying the comparative performance of students in the United States and various Asian nations. In this essay, the authors review the findings of major international assessments, in which American students generally perform poorly, and gauge the criticisms that have been made of these large-scale tests involving many nations. They also discuss their intensive case studies of student achievement in schools in Asia, Canada, Europe, and the United States. Stevenson and Lee's case studies lead them to conclude that American students and American schools are functioning less effectively than they should or could. The U.S. educational system needs repair and rejuvenation, they believe, and lessons should be learned from the successes and failures of other nations in solving similar problems.

Lawrence C. Stedman of the State University of New York at Binghamton reviews historical and contemporary evidence about the current state of student achievement in the United States. During the 1990s, a vigorous debate has taken place about whether student performance is in decline, has stabilized after a decline, or is better than ever. In seeking to answer this question, Stedman considers a wide range of evidence, including the results of then-and-now studies, the Scholastic Aptitude Test, the National Assessment of Educational Progress, and commercial standardized tests. Stedman has to pick his way through a mountain of contradictory data, while avoiding the political minefields on the left and right of educational policy debates. He concludes that student performance is not currently in decline, that it has been flat for a long period of time, and that it is far below what it should be. His findings will give comfort neither to those who believe that student performance is in a free fall nor to those who insist that the schools today are better than ever. But they should provoke educators and policymakers to think hard about how to set real academic standards and persuade students that what they learn in school will determine their ability to succeed in life.

Andrew C. Porter of the University of Wisconsin reports on studies that addressed several critical issues: Will higher graduation requirements in hard subjects such as mathematics and science cause dropout rates to increase among poor and minority students? Will higher graduation requirements cause teachers in advanced courses in mathematics and science to water down the content of their instruction? Do transitional courses exist that will help low-performing students who enroll in rigorous courses in mathematics and science? In these in-depth studies of school districts that set out to raise standards and to get students to take more credits in mathematics and science, Porter found that dropout rates did not increase among poor and minority students. He also determined that teachers did not water down the content of instruction when weaker students joined their classes. And he identifies specific transitional courses that help weaker students succeed when they take advanced courses in hard subjects. Porter's carefully detailed studies will be valuable to every school district that is trying to bring large numbers of students from varied backgrounds into a rigorous curriculum.

Herbert J. Walberg of the University of Illinois contends that American schools, compared with those in other nations, are markedly deficient in terms of students' cognitive growth from grade to grade. He devotes his essay to considering what schools must do to increase achievement and the obstacles that prevent them from succeeding. Walberg recommends that schools focus on their core mission, which is learning, and that they adopt uniform curriculum standards. He suggests that the current poor performance of the schools is caused by the conflicting demands that are placed on them by layers of government controls, and most especially by federal categorical programs, which increase regulation and bureaucratic constraints, thereby undermining effective schooling. Walberg recommends deregulation, incentives, and privatization, within a context of clear and uniform curriculum standards.

John R. Anderson, Lynne M. Reder, and Herbert A. Simon of Carnegie Mellon University bring to bear the perspective of cognitive psychology on some of the most popular reforms in American education today, especially the radical constructivism that seems to dominate much of mathematics education. Many of these reforms claim to have the authority of science, but Anderson, Reder, and Simon hold that they are usually based on ideology, not science. The oft-heard claim that children must construct knowledge for themselves, say the authors, is not supported by modern science; instead, students need instruction. Cognitive science, they say, points to the value of active learning and deliberate practice, in which the teacher knows what is to be taught and devises thoughtful strategies to teach it.

Tom Loveless of the John F. Kennedy School of Government at Harvard University inquires into the use and misuse of research by policymakers. Loveless maintains that educational researchers sometimes overstate the evidence for their claims, to see their agenda adopted as official policy, and that state-level policymakers have inappropriately imposed reforms on teachers and schools despite an inadequate research base. Loveless refers to two examples to make his argument: the official endorsement of constructivism in the California mathematics framework of 1992 and the official endorsement of detracking policies by various school districts. He reaches no judgment about whether such policies are good or bad but contends that both are grounded in ideology, not validated research. His primary plea to policymakers is to leave instructional decisions to those who must implement them—schools and teachers. Then, if mistakes are made, they can be corrected quickly by those who are closest to the classroom and likeliest to recognize what needs to be done.

Laurence Steinberg of Temple University explores the importance of standards outside the classroom. Steinberg is particularly concerned with the incentives and disincentives that youngsters encounter, inside and outside of school. He considers the impact on student performance of parental attitudes and behavior, peer influences, postsecondary institutions, and student employment after-school and on weekends. Steinberg finds that American teenagers are surrounded by friends, relatives, and institutions that encourage them not to work hard in school. He contends that society's emphasis on well-rounded children is used as a rationale for low academic standards and is counterproductive, because American children experience unusually high levels of anxiety, depression, delinquency, and substance abuse. The best-adjusted youth, he holds, are those who are most academically successful. He identifies specific policies that can change these negative dynamics: higher academic standards in school; performance-based examinations for promotion and graduation within all schools; informative transcripts for parents, employers, and postsecondary institutions; greater attention to parental responsibility and greater efforts by schools to draw parents into school programs on a regular basis; hiring by employers and admittance by postsecondary institutions based on students' performance in school; complete abolition of remedial education in higher education; and revision of child labor laws so that students are not permitted to work more than twenty hours each week. Steinberg argues that important linkages run between standards inside the classroom and standards outside the classrooms, and both must be changed to stress the value and importance of schooling.

David W. Breneman of the University of Virginia reviews the scanty evidence of the cost and extent of remediation in higher education. According to a recent federal study, 29 percent of first-time freshmen enter college in need of remedial work in mathematics, reading, or writing. In one sense, this kind of remediation is a burden imposed on institutions, students, and taxpayers by low standards in precollegiate education. Additional remediation is required for adults who are returning to college after a hiatus in their education, as well as for recent immigrants who are upgrading their language and mathematical skills. Because few states have attempted to tally the full costs of remediation, Breneman roughly calculates the annual cost at $1 billion, acknowledging that this figure may be an underestimate. One clear implication of his overview is that remedial education—or developmental education, the term preferred by its advocates—has become a sizable sector within American higher education. The question remains as to whether this sector will become a permanent feature of higher education, or whether states will attempt to make a distinction between first-time freshmen and returning adults. The latter group will clearly need academic support of a developmental nature to upgrade their skills. Remediation for first-time freshmen, however, raises serious questions about the hidden costs generated by low standards in high school, as well as whether such remediation reduces high school students' incentives to meet certain standards for admission to college.

Taken together, these essays have certain points of agreement: Student performance is improving in some areas but is still far from satisfactory. Education policy can support high standards or it can contribute to a student culture of getting by with as little effort as is necessary. Conflicting policies at different levels are likely to erode education standards. American education is not in crisis, but student performance undoubtedly must be considerably improved. It will not happen merely by hoping or wishing. It will happen when federal, state, and district policymakers, as well as parents, teachers, and employers, recognize that incentives and sanctions must be aligned to support high standards of teaching and learning in schools, communities, higher education, and the workplace.

An Examination of American Student Achievement from an International Perspective

HAROLD W. STEVENSON *and*
SHINYING LEE

T HE THIRD INTERNATIONAL Mathematics and Science Study (TIMSS) brought attention once again to comparative studies of students' academic achievement. As the largest and most comprehensive study of academic achievement ever conducted, it was based on representative samples of more than 500,000 students from a total of forty-one nations at grades three and four, seven and eight, and the final year of high school. Results for the middle school students, for which the analyses were most complete, were published first. Those for the elementary school students were published in June 1997, and the results for the high school students will be released in the spring of 1998.

Eighth Grade Results

The only countries that American eighth graders outperformed in both mathematics and science were Cyprus, Iran, Lithuania, and Portugal. Although U.S. scores in science for the middle school students

Data reported in this paper were collected with funds from the National Institute of Mental Health (Grant No. MH30567), the National Science Foundation (Grant MDR 89564683), and the W. T. Grant Foundation. Collection of the Taiwan data from eleventh graders was supported by grants from the National Science Council of R.O.C. (Grant No. NSC–0301). We wish to thank the many persons who worked with us on these studies—the teachers, children, and parents, and especially Liu Dawei.

7

were eighteen points above the international average, they fell seventy-three points behind top-ranking Singapore and forty points behind the second-place Czech Republic.[1] In mathematics, the differences were even greater—143 points behind Singapore and 107 points behind second-place Korea. The U.S. students were thirteen points below the international average.[2]

Another way of looking at the data is to consider the percentage of students from each country who would qualify for inclusion in the top 10 percent if students from all forty-one countries were combined. In mathematics, 5 percent of the U.S. eighth graders would be selected; in science, 13 percent. These percentages are in sharp contrast to the 45 percent of the Singapore students who would be in the top 10 percent in mathematics and 31 percent in science as well as to the 32 percent of Japanese students who would be in the top 10 percent in mathematics and 18 percent in science.[3]

Comparisons of the differences between seventh and eighth graders offer an index of what students learned during their first and second years of middle school. The increase in mathematics scores between seventh and eighth grades by American students was twenty-four points, compared with forty-two points for Singapore and thirty-four, thirty, and twenty-four points for students in the other top-scoring nations: Japan, Korea, and Hong Kong, respectively.[4] A similar hierarchy was obtained for science, with a sixty-three-point difference between seventh and eighth graders' scores in Singapore, forty-one in the Czech Republic, forty in Japan, twenty-seven in Hong Kong, and twenty-six in the United States.[5]

Policymakers and educators in the United States and in some of the European countries responded to the low scores of their students as important stimuli for reexamining the structure and functions of their systems of education. How could students, not only in the United States but also in countries such as England and Germany, perform so poorly in comparison with students in East Asia? The results cannot be attributed to differential sampling, whereby the samples in some countries become more and more elite as students drop out of school. In the case of TIMSS, the percentages of students in secondary school in Singapore, Hong Kong, Japan, and Korea were, respectively, 84 percent, 98 percent, 96 percent, and 93 percent, and for the U.S. sample, 97 percent.[6]

Fourth Grade Results

Although forty-one nations participated in the study of eighth graders, only twenty-six countries tested their fourth graders.[7] Moreover, nine of the twenty-six countries experienced difficulties in meeting the criteria for inclusion in the study. For example, some excluded too great a percentage of the population from the study. More detailed analyses of the fourth grade results will be necessary before precise findings can be determined; nevertheless, the results for mathematics are in close accord with those found for the eighth graders.

The average U.S. score of 545 in mathematics was above the average of 529 for all countries but far below the average scores for Singapore (625), Korea (611), Japan (597), and Hong Kong (587). Nine percent of U.S. students would be included in the top 10 percent of students from all countries. In contrast, the percentages for Singapore, Korea, Japan, and Hong Kong, would be, respectively, 39 percent, 26 percent, 23 percent, and 18 percent.

The results for science were much more favorable for the U.S. fourth graders, whose average score of 565 points was surpassed at a statistically significant level only by the 597 points received by students from Korea. Scores for the three other East Asian locations ranged from 533 (Hong Kong) to 574 (Japan). The U.S. fourth graders outperformed their peers in both math and science in nine countries: Cyprus, England, Greece, Iceland, Iran, Norway, Portugal, New Zealand, and Scotland, only a few of which would be considered economic or political competitors of the United States.

The discrepancy between the poor performance of American students in mathematics and their more successful performance in science is one of the most notable findings of the fourth grade data, especially in view of the similar trends obtained for the eighth graders. The results of the TIMSS material will be analyzed more thoroughly to discover if the difference is a consequence of mode of instruction, textbooks, laboratory facilities, relative difficulty of the tests, or other factors.

Second International Mathematics Study

The second International Association for the Evaluation of Educational Achievement (IEA) study was conducted in the early 1980s and yielded conclusions similar to those of TIMSS regarding the poor performance of American students in mathematics. Japan at the eighth grade and Hong Kong and Japan at the twelfth grade were the top scorers among the countries participating in the study (twenty countries at grade eight, fifteen at grade twelve). One analysis included only students from countries with similar twelfth grade enrollments in mathematics classes.[8] The median percentage of items correct in algebra for all countries was 57; the American percentage was 43. Corresponding percentages for geometry were 42 and 31; for a test of elementary functions and calculus, 46 and 29. In none of the analyses did the U.S. students achieve as well as the international average. American students' scores were generally among those at the bottom one-fourth of the countries in the six tests given. The U.S. students who were enrolled in calculus classes, often considered the nation's best mathematics students, were at or near the average levels of achievement attained by their counterparts in the fourteen other countries.

The First IEA Study of Science

The first IEA study of science was completed in the early 1970s with ten- and fourteen-year-olds and students in the last year of secondary school.[9] Japanese students received the highest scores at the elementary and middle school levels with means of 21.7 and 31.2 points. Mean scores for the American students at the comparable grades were 17.7 and 21.6 points. Japanese high school students did not participate in the study. The highest average for the high school students from the remaining countries was 29.0, obtained by New Zealand students; the average for the American students was 13.7. Relative to the top scorers, the performance of the American students declined as their grade level increased.

The First IEA Study of Mathematics

Results for the first IEA study of mathematics were reported in 1967.[10] This initial study dealt with two age groups, thirteen-year-olds (twelve countries) and students in their final year of high school (ten countries). Again, the Japanese were the top scorers for the thirteen-year-olds, and the American students' scores were markedly lower. Among the twelfth graders, however, students in several European countries (Belgium, England, France, and the Netherlands) and Israel received scores as high as or higher than those of the Japanese students. Looking at students studying mathematics in their final year of secondary school, the mean score for the Japanese students was 31.4 and for the American students, 13.8 points. For students not studying mathematics, the scores were lower, but the differences between the averages were of similar magnitude: 25.3 and 8.3 points. Among thirteen-year-olds, the average score for Japanese students was 31.2 points, and for American students, 16.2 points.[11]

Reading and Other Subjects

The question is often raised as to why so many studies of mathematics are conducted and so few of achievement in reading, history, and geography. The imbalance in testing subject matter is partly the result of the greater difficulty of constructing reliable, culturally relevant, and comparable materials in these subjects when the languages and cultural backgrounds of students differ so greatly from nation to nation. What aspects of geography should be shared by students in Canada, Indonesia, Israel, and Romania? What historical materials could one expect students in these countries to have mastered to an equal degree? Mathematics and science are much more uniform disciplines among different societies. For example, all elementary school children must cope with the mastery of fractions; all high school physics students must understand heat conduction. The major question in mathematics and science is not whether but how and when these concepts will be introduced.

Constructing comparable tests of reading achievement in different languages poses especially difficult problems because reading requires mastery of different writing systems and different grammars in addition to familiarity with different cultural phenomena. East Asian and Western cultures offer extreme examples of these difficulties. During the six years of elementary school, Chinese children must learn about three thousand characters that, when combined, represent more than seven thousand words; Japanese children are faced with the task of learning only approximately one thousand Chinese characters, but they also must master three other writing systems: two syllabaries (hiragana and katakana) and one alphabetic system (romaji). Readers of English learn an alphabet that makes possible sounding out words not yet explicitly encountered. In Chinese and Japanese, few cues are available within the characters that provide the information necessary for learning both their meaning and pronunciation. These differences do not mean that reading tests for cross-national studies cannot be constructed; they do mean that the interpretation of the findings of studies of reading in different languages is much more difficult than in studies of mathematics and science.

American children fared well in comparative studies of reading, especially during the elementary school years. Best known is the study of reading sponsored by the IEA and conducted between 1988 and 1990.[12] Of the thirty-two countries participating in the study, American nine-year-olds were found to be second only to their Finnish peers in reading scores. The mean score for the Finnish students was 569 and for the American students, 547. Among fourteen-year-olds, American students did less well. Finland again attained first place with an overall score of 560, but the American students' scores dropped to 535. Average scores for the Hong Kong and Singapore students, where English is the language of instruction but not necessarily of everyday speech, were 517 and 515 among nine-year-olds and 535 and 534 among fourteen-year-olds, respectively. China, Japan, Korea, and Taiwan did not participate in the study.[13] Wide differences exist in the reading ability of students from different countries and, at least for beginning readers, American students performed much better in reading than they did in mathematics and science.

Other Studies

The studies of mathematics and science sponsored by the IEA are the best known and most comprehensive of the comparative studies, but they are not the only large-scale studies that have explored students' academic achievement. The International Assessment of Educational Progress studies conducted by the Educational Testing Service have included an assessment of achievement in mathematics, science, and geography. Their second study, conducted in 1991, tested nine-year-olds from fourteen countries and thirteen-year-olds from twenty countries. Among the younger groups, Korea, Hungary, and Taiwan had the highest percentages of correct response: 75 percent, 68 percent, and

68 percent, respectively. Korea and Taiwan led the countries at the thirteen-year-old level, each with averages of 73 percent correct responses. The nine-year-old American students were correct on only 58 percent of the problems and the thirteen-year-olds, on 55 percent.[14]

The conclusions running through all of these studies are consistent: American students tend to be at or above average in science but receive low scores in mathematics. Their reading scores, especially during the elementary school years, give them a high place among other countries. So few studies have been conducted in other subject matters that no clear conclusions are possible.

Criticisms of the Large-Scale Studies

While the eighth grade results for TIMSS were widely accepted as reliable conclusions derived from "the most rigorous international comparison of education ever undertaken," as described by the U.S. project director, Lois Peak, a small group of highly vocal critics began probing immediately for its weaknesses.[15] Their purpose seemingly was to introduce doubt in the minds of their readers about the implications of the apparently poor performance of American students in comparison with that of their peers in other countries.

In contrast to those who interpret the TIMSS results as indicating weaknesses in American schools, these critics claimed that America's schools are better than ever and lashed out at those who have accepted the poor performance of American students as valid reflections of American education. D. C. Berliner and B. J. Biddle, for example, charged that those who take seriously the results of the comparative studies "have been prepared to tell lies, suppress evidence, scapegoat educators, and sow endless confusion."[16] G. W. Bracey, one of the most prolific of those who have rejected the comparative studies, continues to derogate the studies and refers to those who disagree with him as "school bashers."[17] R. M. Jaeger, disregarding the usefulness of criticism and evaluation as bases for improvement, writes: "School bashing enjoys a long and rich tradition in this country. It appeals to the public, it grabs attention, and it doesn't cost anything."[18] In an odd twist of politics, Americans who express dissatisfaction with their school systems and display an eagerness to see changes are paradoxically labeled by these critics as ''conservatives.''

One can understand the reluctance of some citizens to acknowledge the seriousness and pervasiveness of American students' deficiencies in achievement. The United States spends 4.02 percent of its gross national product on primary and secondary education—a higher percentage than the governments of the Czech Republic (3.75 percent), Korea (3.43 percent), Singapore (3.38 percent), Japan (2.82 percent), and Hong Kong (1.34 percent), the top-scoring countries in TIMSS.[19] Hearing, year after year, of still another study revealing that U.S. students are not competitive with their peers in many other industrialized countries is not pleasant.

The principal argument offered by critics of comparative studies is that American students generally are performing at a much higher level than that attained by their peers in previous decades and that American schools have never been better. While this argument may or may not be valid, it is largely irrelevant. The question is not whether U.S. schools are better or worse than they used to be, but whether they are graduating students who can be competitive as adults with their peers in other advanced countries. By dismissing the international comparative studies—though unable to counter with research of their own—the critics attempt to reduce the credibility of the bearers of the news. Because they are dealing with the data of others, and these data do not provide clear support for their views, they refer to casual conversations with friends or acquaintances and to news stories in magazines and newspapers and on television to bolster their argument that the results of comparative studies are invalid indices of the accomplishments of American students.

These critics will undoubtedly continue their harsh assessments of comparative studies, as they have done since the late 1980s, primarily in publications by professional societies in education, such as the *Phi Delta Kappan*. The time has come to dispel the negative implications of their criticisms by demonstrating that their arguments have little statistical validity and typically are not based on sound research or rigorous observations.

One of the most frequent criticisms challenges the comparability and representativeness of the samples of students from the various countries included in the studies. For example, I. C. Rotberg has suggested that, whereas the U.S. samples have represented the full range of the population, other countries have included only samples of elite or unrepresentative schools.[20] This criticism has proved to be ill informed, primarily because the critics either have lacked firsthand knowledge and experience in conducting comparative studies themselves or have failed to read the research reports carefully. These critics imply that researchers in the United States and other countries are unaware of or are unwilling to abide by the rules for obtaining representative samples of students.

The retention rate of American students in secondary school does not depart greatly from that of youths in locations such as Hong Kong, Japan, and Korea, and attendance at elementary schools is compulsory in these locations, as well as in Singapore. Moreover, continuous improvement has taken place in sampling, so that in the TIMSS study, for example, clear and uniform criteria were developed for a country to be included in the study, and exceptions to these criteria are noted in the footnotes of each table presenting the results of the study.

The second most frequently cited criticism has been an alleged failure to use tests that were equally relevant for all cultures being compared. The answer to this criticism is that items were chosen by agreement among multinational panels and were deemed by participants from each country to represent students' exposure to the words and concepts included in the achievement tests.

These critics implicitly accept that American students exhibit deficiencies in their academic achievement, but they accept other purported differences among the societies as explanations for the low achievement. Some of their suggestions for explaining American students' low scores include the following:

—Motivation of students. American students are assumed to take the achievement tests less seriously than do more intensely motivated students in other cultures, who view their participation as important for their country and who acknowledge the general importance of test scores for their own future opportunities.

—Cultural emphases on mathematics and science. Members of other cultures are assumed to place more emphasis on mathematics and science than do Americans, who are more likely to emphasize other subjects, such as reading and social studies. Moreover, American students' exposure to mathematics and science is less than what occurs in countries that require more years of mathematics and science in high school than do American schools.

—Homework. American students are assigned less homework than are students in other countries and are thereby deprived of opportunities to review and practice the content of their lessons.

—More time spent in school. The school year and school day are shorter in the United States than in many other countries, thus providing an unfair advantage to students who are given greater opportunities to learn.

—Heterogeneity of the populations. The overall variability of cultural, ethnic, and socioeconomic status is assumed to be greater in the United States than in many other cultures, and overall averages are lowered by the over-representation of less able students.

—Divorce and poverty. Many American students lack the harmonious and healthy home lives that exist in other societies and that facilitate school performance.

Some of these explanations can be made because they are impossible to evaluate. How, for example, can differences in motivation be accepted as a credible explanation when it cannot be determined whether motivation underlies achievement or the reverse? What indices are to be used in attesting to a country's degree of emphasis on mathematics and science? References to homework are appropriate, but consideration only to assignments made by the teacher may give an incomplete picture of the time students spend studying. In Japan, for example, homework (shukudai) is seldom assigned to students in high school, for students are expected to study (benkyo) on their own, reviewing the day's lesson and anticipating the lesson for the next day. Other explanations are more amenable to investigation, but their interpretation is questionable. Differences in the amount of time students in different countries spend in school do exist, but is it the amount of time spent in academic instruction or are content and quality of instruction more important determinants of academic performance? Poverty and single-family homes may influence academic achievement, but the mechanisms by which they influence academic achievement are unclear.

A more persuasive response to the critics may come from the smaller-scale studies that we conducted at the University of Michigan. They include a smaller number of countries than the larger-scale IEA studies, but the total number of students involved in the studies was more than thirty-two thousand. Because fewer countries were included, we could control variables in ways that are impossible or extremely difficult when studies are conducted with as many as forty-one different countries and may involve hundreds of thousands of students, as was the case with TIMSS.

The Michigan Studies

Large-scale studies have many advantages, such as yielding information about representative samples of whole nations and providing opportunities to compare the operation of variables over a wide variety of cultures. Smaller-scale studies, meanwhile, make it possible to construct true curriculum-based tests of academic achievement and to gain greater control over the sampling and testing procedures. The two approaches complement each other, and the results from both types of study are in strong agreement.

We conducted seven comparative studies of the academic achievement of elementary and secondary school students in mathematics and reading since 1980. Some of the studies included cross-sectional samples of students and others were longitudinal in design. The cross-sectional samples were studied at kindergarten, first, fifth, and eleventh grades. The longitudinal studies included all these same grades except kindergarten.

The studies with various replications were of four Western cultures and three from East Asia: three U.S. metropolitan areas—Chicago (Cook County), Illinois, Fairfax County, Virginia, and Minneapolis, Minnesota; the province of Alberta, Canada; Leipzig, Germany; Szeged, Hungary; Beijing, China; Sendai, Japan; and Taipei, Taiwan.

The primary sampling unit was the school. The samples of schools were chosen through reference to demographic information about each metropolitan area and through consultation with school authorities and professional colleagues in each city. The samples represented the full range of schools in these large metropolitan areas. In the United States, the samples included schools from inner cities, from middle-class neighborhoods, and from some of the most affluent communities in the country. Once the cooperation of representative samples of schools was obtained, the desired number of classrooms was randomly chosen at each of the relevant grades.

The same sampling procedures were applied in each of the locations. Care was taken at each step of the sampling process not to introduce bias into the sampling of students.

Because attendance at elementary school is compulsory in all of these societies, comparably chosen, representative samples of elementary school students in each culture could be obtained. During high school, students may attend different types of school, necessitating the inclusion of public and private schools, academic high schools, and technical and vocational high schools.

The Minneapolis metropolitan area was selected as the site for our first studies because of its homogeneous population of native-born, English-speaking families. The Chicago metropolitan area subsequently was chosen as a research site because it represents a more typical large American city given its racial, ethnic, and socioeconomic diversity. Schools in the city of Chicago have been described as being among the least effective in academic achievement in the United States, while schools in the northern suburbs of the city are often considered to be among the nation's finest.

Fairfax County, a suburb of Washington, D.C., was included as an example of an area of high socioeconomic status. The low scores in Chicago and Minneapolis prompted us to determine whether similar low scores would be obtained among an even more privileged group of students. Fairfax County has the highest median household income among all counties in the United States, and a high percentage of adults in Fairfax County hold a four-year college degree. The sample from Fairfax County included students attending a magnet school that is generally considered to be one of the most outstanding high schools for students interested in mathematics and science in the country. The average Scholastic Aptitude Test score in 1994 placed Fairfax seniors in this school in the 97th percentile for the United States.

Taipei, the capital of Taiwan, was the only large Chinese-speaking city where this type of study was feasible when we began our research. When mainland China adopted a more open policy, it became possible to include Beijing, the capital of China, as a second Chinese-speaking site. Sendai, a large city 350 kilometers northeast of Tokyo, was chosen on the recommendation of Japanese colleagues as the Japanese city most comparable to Minneapolis in socioeconomic and cultural status.

In Canada, the students were from a representative sample of schools in Edmonton, Calgary, and nearby communities. Hungary was chosen as a Western country because of its fame for producing world-class mathematicians and scientists, and on the advice of colleagues, we chose Szeged, a cultural center located 150 kilometers southwest of Budapest, as our Hungarian site. Selecting a typical German city was difficult because of the large differences in educational practices among the various states. Leipzig is a city of great culture and one that retained the general-purpose high schools that were common throughout former East Germany.

Ethnic status was a major variable only in the American samples. The most heterogeneous population was in Chicago, where 55 percent of the subjects were European American, 24 percent were African American, 15 percent were Hispanic American, 4 percent were Asian American, and 2 percent were Native American. Depending on the year the study was conducted, the percentage of European Americans in the Minneapolis sample ranged from 82 percent to 95 percent; up to 6 percent of the students in Minneapolis were African American. In Fairfax County, where 73 percent of the students were of European American backgrounds, 4 percent were African American, and 14.3 percent were Asian American.

As a result of these careful sampling procedures, the students included in our studies constituted groups representative of their peers in the various cities in which the studies were conducted.

Mathematics Tests

Instead of relying on tests constructed in one culture and in one language and then translated for use in other cultures, the mathematics tests were based on detailed analyses of mathematics textbooks. The potential thus exists for all students (with the exceptions to be noted) to be exposed to the mathematical skills and concepts included in the tests. Other than by observing every classroom every day of the school year, knowing with certainty that the teachers covered each of the topics included in the textbooks would be impossible. Even teachers' reports of what was covered, a commonly used measure of opportunity to learn, do not convey information about the manner or extent to which the concepts were presented. Thus, reliance on the topics included in the students' textbooks is a reasonable basis for including items in curriculum-based tests of mathematics achievement.

Another precaution necessary in studies of children of elementary-school age is to administer tests to children individually instead of as a group. One-on-one testing allows the examiner to read the questions to the child, thereby ensuring that an inability to solve a problem was not the result of the child's inability to read the problem correctly. Group testing in the high schools was done under the supervision of trained examiners, except that teachers in some classrooms administered the test.

Because our primary concern in initiating the studies was with American, Chinese, and Japanese students, the mathematics tests were based on analyses of the textbooks used by those three groups of students, tapping skills and concepts common to textbooks used in each of the locations. This procedure guaranteed the potential exposure of students to the information covered on the tests and eliminated the possibility of a differential match between curricula and test items in the different cities. The tests were reviewed by professionals in each of these locations, and their comments and criticisms were taken into account in developing the final versions of the tests.

However, because the textbook analyses did not include Canada, Germany, and Hungary, the possibility existed in those countries that some of the items on the test might have tapped concepts not covered in their textbooks. To examine possible effects of this differential procedure in selecting test items, we sought the advice of mathematics educators in Canada and Hungary. Their reviews of the test pointed out few discrepancies, and most of these occurred at advanced levels of the test where they would have little effect on the overall score.

All items in the mathematics tests required students to come up with their own solutions, but advanced levels of the reading comprehension test were assessed by multiple-choice items. None of the tests for elementary school students was timed. Students were allowed to proceed at their own pace, and all items were read by the examiner in addition to being placed in a written form in front of the child. For high school students, however, the necessity of fitting the testing into an academic period required that the length of the test be limited to forty minutes. The various versions of the tests used in the different countries differed only in the language in which the tests were written and in the use of the appropriate notation system and units of measurement.

Test items were presented in order of difficulty within successive grade levels. Testing continued for elementary school students until the child missed a predefined number of consecutive problems. At the high school level, students were allowed to respond until the forty-minute time limit had elapsed.

Reading Tests

The reading tests were constructed according to a procedure similar to that followed in constructing the mathematics tests. All words appearing in the students' textbooks were entered into a computer file, along with the grade and semester in which the word first appeared. The tests for the first three grades were constructed using only those words that occurred in the children's textbooks in all three languages. The words, sentences, and stories were selected and written simultaneously in Chinese, English, and Japanese following discussions held by bilingual members of the research team.

The words that are common among cultures begin to diverge after the first three years of elementary school, so words were matched by the semester in which they appear in the children's textbooks and according to compilations of the frequency of usage of words in written materials for children. Although the tests in the three languages after third grade are not identical, the themes and grammar for the stories as well as the grade levels and frequencies of the words were matched as closely as possible. For example, a story in the American test about repairs to the Statue of Liberty was matched in the Chinese version with a story about the repair of the Great Wall.

This procedure for constructing the reading tests ensures that the potential exists for the American, Chinese, and Japanese children included in the study to have been exposed to all the words appearing at and before their current grade level. Constructing such a test is an arduous task that would be nearly impossible when a large number of languages is involved. No attempt was made to develop German or Hungarian versions of the reading tests.

The Michigan Results in Mathematics

Results from the Michigan studies follow a common theme: Students in the United States are outperformed by their counterparts from other countries.

'At-Grade' Performance

Because we knew the grade level at which the various mathematical operations and concepts appeared in the East Asian and U.S. textbooks, and because we included in the tests only those that were covered within one semester of each other in the four sets of textbooks, we can determine the percentage of students who performed "at-grade" on the mathematics test. That is, we can determine, for example, whether a fifth grade student is capable of answering problems that appeared at or before the fifth grade. Because the tests were given on average two to three months before the school year ended, the percentages slightly underestimate what the students might have been able to accomplish at the end of the school year.

A much smaller percentage of first and fifth grade students in the Chicago metropolitan area were at-grade in mathematics than in Beijing, Sendai, or Taipei (see figure 1). The percentages in all four cities declined during the elementary school years, but the decline was greater for the American than for the Chinese and Japanese students.

The same pattern appeared at eleventh grade. The test included items tapping knowledge of arithmetic, algebra, geometry, trigonometry, and advanced math. By eleventh grade, students in all countries should have mastered the rudiments of applying arithmetical solutions to problems and should have learned basic operations in algebra. No indication exists that either is the case (see figure 2).

Remarkably small percentages of the American eleventh graders were able to solve either the arithmetic or algebra problems that would place them at the eleventh grade level. Much higher percentages of

**Figure 1. Percentage of Students 'At-Grade' in Mathematics,
in First and Fifth Grades in Four Metropolitan Areas**

Percent of students

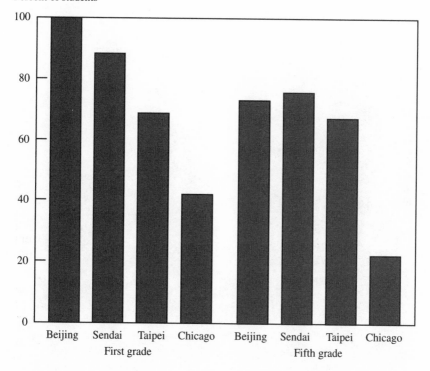

Note: First grade: $N = 801$ for Beijing, 750 for Sendai, 1,037 for Taipei, and 976 for Chicago. Fifth grade: $N = 831$ for Beijing, 808 for Sendai, 954 for Taipei, and 999 for Chicago.

students in Taipei, Sendai, and Beijing functioned at this level of proficiency than in Minneapolis.

Developmental Trends

The best answer to anyone who objects to the choice of any particular age level for a cross-sectional study is to describe developmental trends derived from studies conducted over the span of the primary and secondary school years. The performance in mathematics of primary and secondary school students in each city in relation to that of students in the same grade in the other cities is depicted in figure 3. The simplest way to interpret this graph is to consider a z score of 0 as the 50th

Figure 2. Percentage of Eleventh Grade Students Competent in Arithmetic and Algebra, in Four Metropolitan Areas

Percent of students

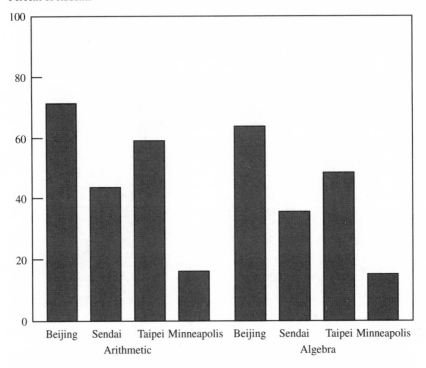

Note: N = 994 for Beijing, 1,119 for Sendai, 1,475 for Taipei, and 1,052 for Minneapolis.

percentile for all students at that grade level, a score of 1 as equivalent to the 84th percentile, and a score of -1 as equivalent to the 16th percentile.

The Japanese kindergartners performed at a relatively high level, and Japanese students continued to receive average scores above those of the American students at grades one, five, and eleven. The scores of kindergartners in Taipei were not much higher than those in Minneapolis, but the Taipei students demonstrated notable improvement throughout their years of schooling. The American students received the lowest scores during kindergarten and their relative status declined even further.

Not only did consistent differences turn up in the performance of the

Figure 3. Mean *z* Score in Mathematics for Kindergartners, First, Fifth, and Eleventh Graders

Mean *z* score

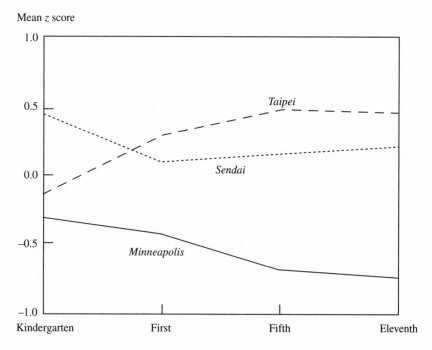

Note: Score is based on 1,970 kindergartners, 718 first graders, 723 fifth graders, and 3,646 eleventh graders, obtained from cross-sectional samples of students. The mean *z* score was derived from determining the distance in standard deviation units each child was from the mean score for all three cities adjusted for the unequal *N*s at each grade level combined; the average of these scores was then determined for each city. *N* = 2,115 for Sendai, 2,868 for Taipei, and 2,074 for Minneapolis.

groups of students in the three cities, but the level of performance was also consistent for individuals within these groups from the first through the eleventh grades. Relying on the results from a longitudinal sample of students who were tested at grades one, five, and eleven, the correlations between scores in first and eleventh grades were .60 for Minneapolis, .52 for Taipei, and .69 for Sendai. A strong tendency was evident, therefore, for students who received high scores during first grade to receive high scores in mathematics when they were in high school.

Figure 4. Mean Percentage of Correct Responses Made by Eleventh Graders in Seven Countries on Five Domains of Mathematics

Mean percent correct

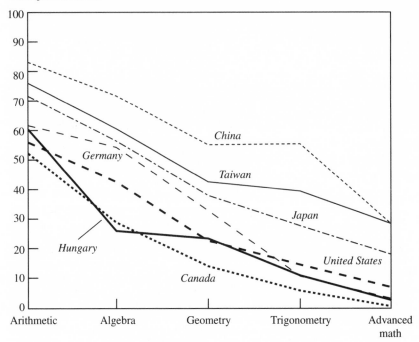

Note: *N*s for all countries ranged from 503 to 2,264; total *N* = 8,238.

Within-Child Variability

Perhaps, as some have suggested, American students perform un-evenly, doing well in learning and applying some types of concepts more effectively than others. This possibility can be evaluated for the eleventh graders by determining the percentage of correct responses for the five components of the test. The results of this analysis appear in figure 4. American students were not any more effective in one domain of mathematics than in any other. Higher percentages of the students from China, Japan, and Taiwan were correct in each domain than was the case in Canada, Germany, Hungary, or the United States.

Another way of looking at this suggestion is to compare the perfor-mance of groups of elementary school students who were given a battery of tests covering a wide range of mathematical concepts and skills. To permit comparisons of performance across different tasks, all scores were converted to *z* scores. The Chicago students were not competitive with the Chinese and Japanese students in nearly all instances (see figure 5). The weakness of the American students was widespread and was not limited to any particular domain of mathematics.

Diversity

If the argument that the diverse U.S. population results in a pile-up of scores at the lower end of the distribution is valid, plotting the frequencies of correct response should yield asymmetrical curves. This is clearly not the case according to the data in figure 6, where the percentage of fifth grade students receiving each score appears in the upper graph for three of the Western societies and in the lower graph for two of the East Asian societies.

Data from the eleventh graders are plotted in the same fashion in figure 7. Again, no indication exists of a disproportionate percentage of low scores by the American students. The asymmetry in the plots of the U.S. students' scores, as well as in those of their Canadian and Hungarian counterparts, is a result of the high level of performance by some students. The bimodality of the scores for Beijing and Taipei results primarily from the lower scores of the vocational school students and the higher scores of the students enrolled in academic high schools.

The Best in the World

Another argument made about American students' performance is that the best American students are able to compete with the best students in any country. Some evidence for this is found in the frequency distributions in figures 6 and 7, but strong evidence against this proposal appears in figures 8 and 9. In figure 8, the mean score for each of twenty schools in the Chicago metropolitan area and thirty-one schools in East Asia are plotted for first and fifth graders. Some overlap between the scores from Chicago and from East Asia is evident for the first graders, but by fifth grade the mean for only one of the Chicago schools is as high as that for the least successful East Asian schools. The same procedure was followed for the eleventh graders in plotting figure 9. The U.S. students' performance is more like that of East Asian voca-

Figure 5. Average z Score for Nine Subtests in a Battery of Mathematics Tasks Given to First and Fifth Graders

Mean z scores

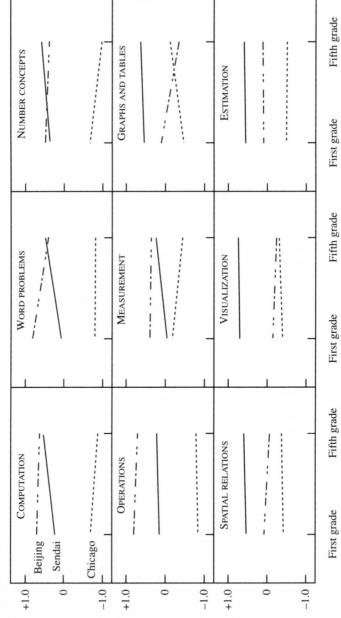

Note: First grade: N = 116 for Beijing, 120 for Sendai, and 236 for Chicago. Fifth grade: N = 119 for Beijing, 120 for Sendai, and 235 for Chicago.

Figure 6. Distribution of Scores in Mathematics for Fifth Graders

Percent of students

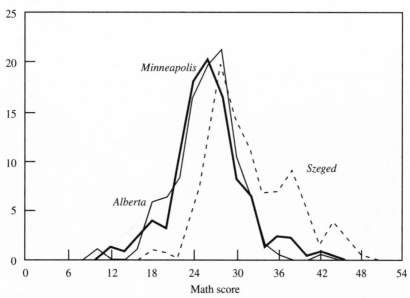

Percent of students

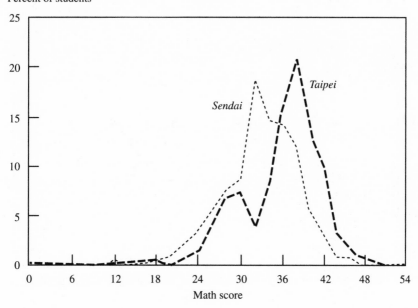

Note: *N* = 202 for Alberta, 241 for Minneapolis, 264 for Szeged, 273 for Sendai, and 242 for Taipei.

Figure 7. Distribution of Scores in Mathematics for Eleventh Graders

Percent of students

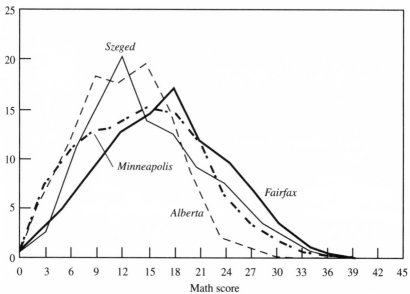

Math score

Percent of students

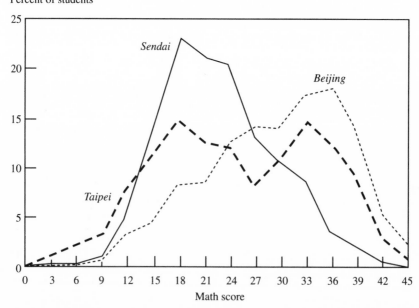

Math score

Note: N = 794 for Alberta, 1,566 for Fairfax, 1,052 for Minneapolis, 1,072 for Szeged, 994 for Beijing, 1,119 for Sendai, and 1,475 for Taipei.

Figure 8. Mean Scores for Elementary Schools in Beijing, Sendai, Taipei, and Chicago

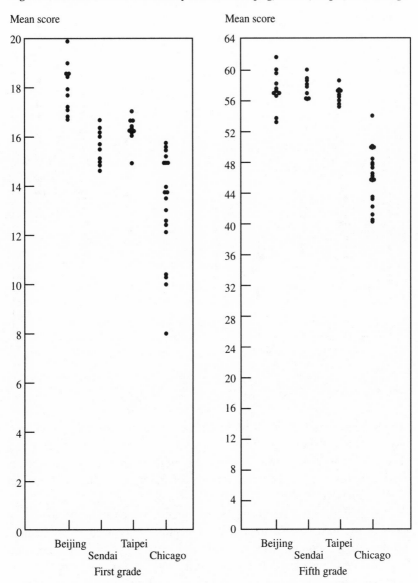

Note: Scores are for eleven elementary schools in Beijing, ten in Sendai, ten in Taipei, and twenty in Chicago. *N*s for all countries ranged from 750 to 1,037 for first graders and from 808 to 999 for fifth graders; total *N* = 8,132.

Figure 9. Mean Scores for Schools in Eight Cities

Mean score

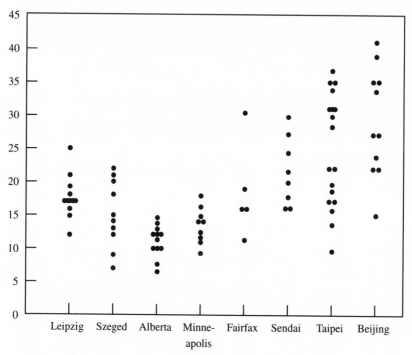

Note: Total *N* = 8,238.

tional school students than for students from the East Asian academic high schools. (The large number of schools was sampled in China and Taiwan because of the need to include both academic and vocational high schools, and in Taiwan, because of the need to include boys' as well as girls' schools.)

Another way of responding to the suggestion about the competitiveness of the best American students is to look only at the performance of the college-bound students. This was done separately for the male and female eleventh graders (see figure 10). The most distinctive features in comparing the various curves are the high level of performance of males and females in Beijing and Taipei, the lower level of performance of females in Sendai, and the marked differences between the American and Chinese students in the performance of both males and

Figure 10. Distributions of Scores on Mathematics Tests for College-Bound Male and Female Eleventh Graders

Percent of male students

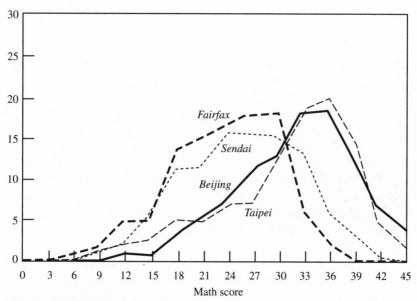

Math score

Percent of female students

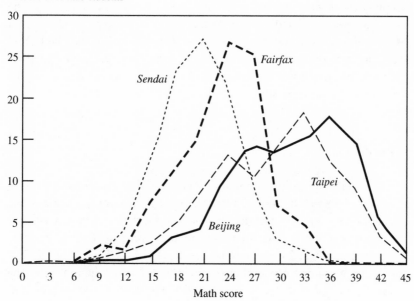

Math score

Note: Male students: $N = 411$ for Beijing, 140 for Fairfax, 560 for Sendai, and 459 for Taipei. Female students: $N = 391$ for Beijing, 137 for Fairfax, 284 for Sendai, and 465 for Taipei.

females. Students attending Fairfax County schools are not the peers of the Chinese students.

A final comparison was made of the students attending Fairfax County's highly selective magnet school in science and technology with students attending the highest ranking schools in Beijing. The mean score on the mathematics test for students from the top Chinese high schools was 35.2, a score significantly above the average of 30.4 for the students attending the magnet school in Fairfax.

Summary of Mathematics Results

In figure 11, the results of the comparative studies, derived from the longitudinal sample, depict the median (horizontal lines in the box), the 25th and 75th percentiles (outer lines of the box), and the 5th and 95th percentiles (extent of vertical lines). At each grade, the median score for the Minneapolis sample falls behind that of the students from Taipei and Sendai. After the first grade, the 75th percentile for Minneapolis is in the region of the 25th percentile for the two East Asian cities.

The methodology used in the studies of mathematics achievement meets many of the criticisms that have been made of comparative studies, such as those dealing with the comparability and representativeness of the samples, the content of the tests, and the grade levels employed. The results are consistent and at times dramatic: When compared with the East Asian students, even students from some of the best schools in the United States are not competitive. The results from the larger-scale and smaller-scale studies are in close agreement and offer convincing evidence of the weaknesses in the U.S. students' knowledge of mathematics.

Reading

As we have suggested, conducting cross-national studies of reading achievement is much more difficult than is the case for mathematics or science. Our results do not dispute the finding that, overall, American elementary school students are more capable at reading than are students from other countries. For example, the scores of the U.S. first and fifth graders on a reading comprehension test were higher than those of the Chinese children (see figure 12). But if one looks only at the questions

**Figure 11. Median Scores in Mathematics, Represented in Box Plots for
Longitudinal Samples of Subjects**

Percent correct responses

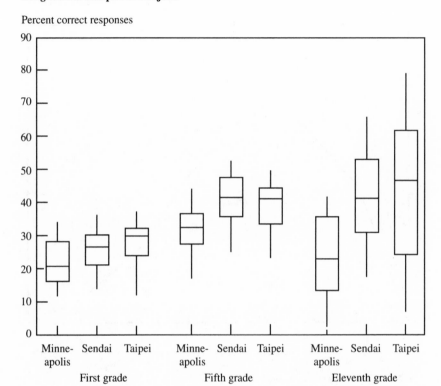

Note: First grade: $N = 237$ for Minneapolis, 240 for Sendai, and 241 for Taipei. Fifth grade: $N = 118$ for Minneapolis, 165 for Sendai, and 164 for Taipei. Eleventh grade: $N = 198$ for Minneapolis, 82 for Sendai, and 156 for Taipei.

at the first or the fifth grade levels, Chinese children surpass the American children. The Chinese children are very effective in reading and understanding the words they have been taught; American children do less well with the words they have been taught, but a higher percentage are able to read new words, presumably by sounding them out.

A further indication of the difficulties in attempting to characterize the reading abilities of American and Chinese children are the scores on a reading vocabulary test, plotted separately for each of the Beijing and Chicago schools in figure 13. The height of the lines indicates the average score obtained by the first graders in two randomly chosen classrooms in each of twenty schools in Chicago and in eleven schools

Figure 12. Reading Comprehension Scores for First Graders

Percent of subjects

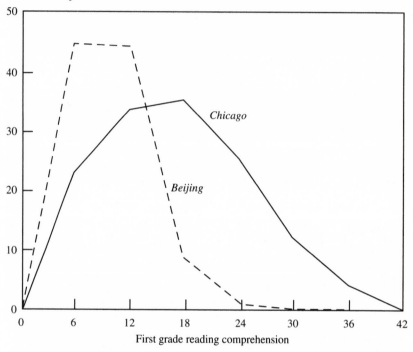

First grade reading comprehension

Note: N = 801 for Beijing and 240 for Chicago.

in Beijing, yielding a total sample of forty classrooms in Chicago and twenty-two in Beijing. The range of scores within each classroom (in terms of the mean ± 1 standard deviation) is denoted by the length of the line.

A great variability exists within and between the Chicago classrooms; some students in some classrooms read very well while others are very ineffective. These data are strikingly different from those of Beijing, where the scores are generally lower than those in Chicago, but little variability is evident in the children's scores either between or within classrooms.

Figure 13. Average Scores on Vocabulary Reading Test

Mean score

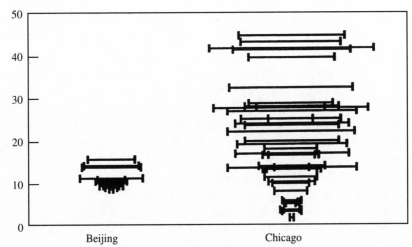

First grade vocabulary test

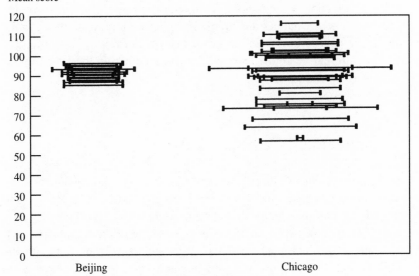

Fifth grade vocabulary test

Note: Average scores ±1 standard deviation on the vocabulary reading test for each school. First grade: *N* = 801 for Beijing and 228 for Chicago. Fifth grade: *N* = 831 for Beijing and 217 for Chicago.

Conclusion

On the basis of the data and arguments reviewed, American students—and, in turn, the schools they attend—are generally functioning less effectively than they should or could. Arguments about interpretation and explanations are likely to continue, but the time has passed for reliance on apologies, rationalizations, and lashing out at critics in defense of a system that needs repair and rejuvenation. The comparative studies have served their purpose in demonstrating weaknesses in the U.S. educational systems, and the time has come to move on to other, more productive discussions. Using the results of past comparative studies, time can be spent more profitably by learning from the successes and failures of other nations to improve American educational systems than by trying to justify where the United States stands in comparison with the nations that are or will be its competitors in the world economy of the twenty-first century. By considering the educational systems of other countries as laboratories where various practices have been tried out, the United States can gain large amounts of new information about what is possible in educating its children and youth. The question of what is transferable from one culture to another continues to be asked, but it serves as an insufficient reason for failing to explore alternative approaches and innovative ideas in the education of American students.

Comment by Catherine Lewis

Because Harold W. Stevenson and Shinying Lee did a wonderful job of painting the differences between Japanese and U.S. education and of proving that they are real, I am not going to address those issues. I am going to give two examples that show some of the richness as well as some of the complexity of trying to understand and apply in the United States what goes on in other countries. They are examples in which, I fear, the United States may be marching off in the wrong policy direction, based on a misunderstanding of Japanese education.

The first issue is the importance the Japanese place on children's emotional attachment to school. I argue in *Educating Hearts and Minds* that Japanese elementary education succeeds because of its emphasis on helping children develop positive emotional bonds to school.[21] When children develop strong emotional bonds to school, they come to care about the school's values, including values such as hard work, persistence, and the importance of learning. This process is called internalized motivation and is at the heart of some American school reform approaches, such as the Child Development Project.[22] Internalized motivation means you do something because you believe in it as a long-term value. You may not find it immediately enjoyable or get something for doing it, but you believe it is in your own long-term self-interest or in the interest of the group that you care deeply about.

For example, I went into a Japanese elementary school about two years ago to make a videotape. I hired a professional crew to film some student-led class meetings, where children talk about what kind of class they want to be and how they are treating each other, and they discuss any problems that have arisen in their class.

I arrived at the school to find that the teacher, who had agreed to be filmed, had been called out to a sudden family emergency. There was no teacher. Typically, Japanese elementary schools do not hire substitute teachers, except in cases of long absences. The principal said to me: "You are interested in student autonomy and student-initiated learning, so why don't you just film anyway, without the teacher?"

So, I took the film crew into the fourth grade classroom, where a math lesson was going on. Students had composed word problems about long division with rounding, which their classmates then solved. About seven problems could not be solved because they had been poorly written by the students—for example, not enough information had been provided. The students were trying to figure out whether these problems could be solved, and why or why not. They got into an energetic but orderly discussion, with no designated student leader. I was puzzled by how the students managed such a fruitful discussion with no teacher or student leader.

After the discussion, I asked the students how they had decided who would speak. The students said: "Last week we had a class meeting. We decided that, as a class, one of our problems is that some students tend to dominate the discussion. Therefore, we agreed that whenever two students want to speak at once, the one who typically speaks least in the class will have the floor first. When more than one person wanted to talk, we looked at each other, and let the student who speaks up least have the floor.''

This is just one example of the many kinds of student-led discussions that take place in Japanese classrooms. Sometimes two students will lead a discussion. Sometimes students use different hand signals to show whether they want to agree, disagree, or add to what has been said. Such hand signals are used so that the student leading the discussion might take the agreements first, and then the disagreements, and then the additions or whatever.

In a Japanese classroom, an amazing infrastructure exists for the exchange of ideas. Student-led class discussion is one example, I think, of what Thomas Rohlen means when he says, ''It is not just mathematics that is going on here.'' Great internalized motivation undergirded that class discussion. The students did not have a teacher present, but they actively pursued the lesson. They cared about the values of school, such as communicating in a respectful way with each other, including the quietest class members, and getting to the truth about the math problems.

As I documented in *Educating Hearts and Minds,* for Japanese elementary teachers, the key to elementary education is to get children to develop strong, positive emotional bonds to school. For example, teachers explicitly work to build students' friendships; they avoid competition and any kind of external rewards or sanctions that would lead children to view one another as competitors. An emphasis is placed on small groups where children learn to be like families together, to take care of one another. These heterogeneous groups stay together for a long time. Japanese students typically are with the same teacher for two years. There is complete social promotion.

About thirty days of the longer Japanese school year are devoted to festivals, whole-school activities, school trips, community service, sports day—activities that build shared enjoyment, school spirit, and a strong emotional connection to the school. Roughly one-third of the required instructional hours in Japanese elementary school are nonacademic—art, music, physical education, homemaking, and so on.

Discipline is not focused primarily on getting kids to follow rules made by adults, but on helping the obstreperous kids form friendships and thereby develop emotional bonds to school. Discipline also is focused on getting all kids to help shape the promises and goals they will live by at school.

But, when the Japanese example is held up, the inferences drawn from it are hardly ever "Follow Japan's example and use no ability grouping, less competition, complete social promotion. Have strong focus on nonacademic subjects and schoolwide activities such as sports day." Yet the effect of these practices is to make school a fulfilling place for Japanese children. Japanese elementary schools feel much more like summer camp with interesting academic lessons added than they do like the American image of "school." I once asked a Japanese teacher, "What is your most important job as an elementary teacher?" She said, "My job is to create happy memories."

As I argue in *Educating Hearts and Minds,* emotional bonding to school is likely an important factor in Japan's academic achievement. Japan's edge in achievement emerges during the elementary years when the focus is on a noncompetitive, familylike school environment. The achievement gap emerges in samples—including those studied by Stevenson and colleagues—where few children are attending cram schools. Something is happening in Japanese elementary education that attaches children to school. And that attachment underlies children's motivation to work hard in school.

This is not just a theory that works in Japan. The Child Development Project operates on the same basic theory. As articulated in the United States by Marilyn Watson as well as J. P. Connelly and J. G. Wellborn, when children's basic needs—for friendship, for meaningful work at school, for autonomy—are met, they will attach to school.[23] When school is a place that meets children's needs, they are motivated to maintain their attachment to school and to care about the values that are being promulgated, such as hard work and treating one another in a respectful fashion.

Thomas Sergiovanni said, "The more the school cares about students, the more students care about matters of schooling."[24] That is a simple way of describing the importance of children's attachment to school.

The portrait I have given of Japanese elementary education is dissonant from what the media report. The media reflect much more the American assumption that, if Japanese schools are doing so well academically, it must be at the expense of social development. Those familiar with Japanese schools know this is not true; academics and emotional attachment to school are not in a hydraulic relationship. Emotional attachment to school and academics can be combined. It may well be that this kind of thoughtful, deep academic learning can be achieved only by building a collaborative, friendly, supportive social environment.

For example, in a Child Development Project classroom, the teacher had worked hard to create a caring community of learners by establishing strong friendships among students, avoiding competition, and emphasizing the intrinsic satisfaction of learning, instead of handing out rewards and punishment. During a math lesson, students pulled ten marbles from a bag containing black and white marbles and predicted from their ten marbles what the distribution was of black and white marbles in the bag of one hundred. What the teacher wanted them to notice was that, if only one student's sample of ten marbles was examined, the data were not as reliable as when all twenty class members took samples. The students, working in pairs, drew ten marbles. They compared their estimate with the estimates of their classmates. They quickly got the point.

I saw this lesson repeated in another school, a similar, upper-middle-class school nearby. Again, the children were drawing the marbles in pairs. They made predictions based on their own marbles. But when the time came to revise their predictions based on classmates' data, they spent the rest of the period arguing and trying to justify their initial predictions. They said things such as, "You did not put your hand all the way into the bag, so your estimate is no good." They were more committed to competition—to showing that they were right—than to learning. Learning was prohibited by the amount of competition that was going on.

The lesson drawn from the Japanese education system that the United States should concentrate more heavily on academic competition is both ironic and troubling. Promoting children's emotional bonds to school should be more heavily emphasized, while effective academic approaches are sought that do not undermine those bonds. The message of the Japanese experience is that everything about schooling affects children's social and emotional development. Techniques should not be chosen that boost children's academic performance in the short run if they undermine children's attachment to school in the long run.

The second issue is the need for a more top-down, centralized curriculum, with greater accountability. Since about the late 1970s, Japanese elementary teachers have shifted science education from lecture-centered to more hands-on, student-centered inquiry. It is precisely this transition that most U.S. science specialists believe educators must make. When I tell my colleagues that I am studying the change in science education in Japan, they say: "Why would you study this in Japan? It is a top-down centralized system. Teachers are told to do it, and they do it."

But changing one's teaching or shifting from lecturing students to promoting active problem solving and inquiry is not easy. Often students have been socialized for years to guess the right answer that is in the teacher's mind. To get a lively discussion going, to get students to look carefully and critically at their experiments, is daunting. However, some evidence exists that this shift has happened successfully in Japanese classrooms. Japanese elementary and middle school science achievement is among the highest in the world.

I have identified many of the puzzle pieces of how this shift occurred in Japan. They do not look like the pieces that the United States is trying to put into place in its reform efforts.

First, Japan has a frugal national curriculum. Japan's national Ministry of Education strongly limits the required content taught in Japanese elementary schools. The committee that examines textbooks does not approve them if they include too much information. For example, one elementary science textbook submitted for review included an experiment in which students linked together three batteries. The committee rejected the textbook; two batteries, not three, was regarded as the limit of what elementary students should be expected to study. Someone is making the hard decisions about what not to teach.

In discussions about standards in the United States, reference to a way of limiting content is rarely heard. The usual dialogue is about ensuring that things are taught, not limiting what is taught. The Third International Mathematics and Science Study (TIMSS) analyses show that Japanese standards expect eighth graders to study eight topics in science, whereas U.S. standards expect youngsters to study more than thirty topics.[25]

Second, the national standards in Japan are focused on social, emotional, and character development. For example, the major national goal for Japanese elementary science is to "nurture hearts that love nature, the ability to solve problems, and the acquisition of scientific ways of thinking."[26] For mathematics, a major goal is for children to spontaneously apply principles of mathematics to daily life. At issue are big, social, motivational, and, often, ethical character development goals, not narrow academic standards.

Third, Japanese national goals are abstract, with the expectation that they will be brought to life in the classroom by teachers. National guidelines do not try to specify what is going to happen in the classroom. They include broad, general goals such as initiative, autonomy, problem solving, and love of nature. They assume that the classroom is where these goals are brought to life. And a system is set up for doing just that—a system of teachers' professional development with real, shared classroom research lessons at its core.

In these research lessons, teachers at a particular grade level work together. They say, "Let's take the goals of initiative, autonomy, and problem solving and apply them to how we teach, say, solar energy." The teachers all rethink together their teaching of solar energy, try lessons in their classrooms, and then do a lesson for the whole school to watch. It is a real lesson, not a staged lesson, with real students. The faculty has a lively discussion afterward: Did students show initiative during this lesson? Did they actively generate and solve problems? Or did the teacher tend to lecture?

Teachers discuss the lesson they experienced together. Here is an exchange that took place between two teachers after they had seen a lesson designed to increase children's initiative and to teach about solar energy. One teacher said: "I felt sorry for the students when Mr. Horita concluded the lesson with his own summary statement, rather than using the students' own words to summarize the lesson." Another teacher said: "I do not agree with several teachers who think that the students' ideas were, somehow, stifled by the teacher's summary. As someone who does not know much about electricity, I found the teacher's summary very helpful. Students who, like me, have limited knowledge about solar energy may have found the teacher's statement helpful after hearing such a wide variety of opinions expressed by their classmates." The teachers discussed how the goal of having students take initiative could be balanced with the need to learn certain content knowledge about solar energy in the context of a real lesson in a real classroom.

Imagine how different things might be in the United States, if, for example, teachers who were grappling with ideas such as constructivism and higher-order thinking had the opportunity to jointly plan lessons with other teachers and to talk about whether and how these ideas came to life in lessons they all witnessed and whether students grasped the intended subject matter.

Instead of the expected centralized control with carrots and sticks in Japan, I found professional development led by teachers, focused on real, shared classroom lessons and yet connected to major national goals such as students' initiative. No standardized testing is done in Japanese elementary schools. When the Ministry of Education tried to introduce it in the 1960s, Japanese teachers put their jobs on the line and said: "We won't permit achievement testing. It is the first step toward privileging high-achieving students." Several Japanese teachers lost their jobs over this refusal.

About every ten years, a representative sample of six hundred Japanese schools is assessed by the national Ministry of Education to check whether the curriculum is accomplishing its aims. The individual schools' results are not disclosed. It is truly an assessment to see how the national curriculum is doing.

The kinds of puzzle pieces discussed in the context of school reform in the United States—detailed guidelines, assessment, accountability—are absent in the Japanese case. Instead, observers find general statements of educational philosophy; thin, spare textbooks; and a lively system of teacher-directed professional development focused on improvement of real classroom lessons.[27] The examples of students' emotional attachment to school and of the reform of Japanese science teaching provide a caution about the ways that cross-national comparisons are often used to derive policy implications for the United States.

Comment by Thomas Rohlen

Many people have studied Japanese education over a long period of time. Research has revealed the system's strengths and weaknesses as well as the reasons for Japan's notable successes and failures.

As understanding advances, a context of knowledge is created that is far richer than simple measures of math and science achievement. The aggregate outcomes that Harold W. Stevenson and Shinying Lee underscored in their research raise many issues of interpretation, especially in a comparative perspective.

This paper underscores the need to reexamine American education in light of the accomplishments now well documented for East Asia. To those working on East Asia, this point is well substantiated in numerous other studies, including many based on firsthand observations. Whether preschools or junior high schools, education in Japan up through the ninth grade gets high marks from virtually all those doing empirically based comparative work.

What makes East Asian schools successful? Of what relevance is this success for American schools? These are two burning questions raised by Stevenson and Lee. It would be wonderful if a few critical practices could be identified with confidence that explain Japanese—or East Asian—achievement levels. Better would be if such practices were readily transferable to the U.S. system. Some items stand out in practical terms, such as high standards and effective classroom instruction, which undoubtedly are of considerable relevance. But the foundations of those and other notable elements of the East Asian success story are historical and administrative. In other words, they do not stand alone but are part of whole systems. It would be oversimplistic to conclude, on the basis of narrowly defined math and science test results, that what America needs is one or another aspect of the East Asian system—without grasping the basic thinking and set of values involved. Many significant differences exist between the East Asian approach and the United States' at every level, from the classroom to the school administration to national policy. Differences also show up longitudinally over the course of the K-12 sequence.

Does this mean that America cannot learn from the success stories of other educational systems, such as those in East Asia? Hardly, but no one should expect to find one or two proverbial silver bullets.

A few less obvious aspects of Japanese educational success are relevant and instructive, especially given the present atmosphere of heightened national frustration and political debate.

All studies of Japanese compulsory education show schools focused on much more than math and science. Considerable evidence is available that Japanese students, on average, are getting more music and art than American students. Japanese students receive significant encouragement in matters of self-government, small-group communication, and other skills of a civic nature. Instructional practices emphasize discovery, not rote, in the elementary years, and the United States— not Japan—pushes cognitive skill development and testing in the early grades. Moral issues are attended to routinely, and one of the world's most complex writing systems is taught well enough so that literacy in Japan is universal. In sum, teaching is inclusive, ambitious, effective, and does not ignore social or emotional development. The schools keep nearly all students learning together at least through the sixth grade and well into junior high school. Large skill gaps do not emerge before the end of compulsory education.

The dichotomy of equality and excellence in education is not something the Japanese are troubled by. The Japanese do not discuss the issue as if one or the other option should or inevitably will prevail.

Instead, according to data on reading and math, such as that presented by Stevenson and Lee, the range of variability in the student populations of Japan and China decreases over time in some respects. Classes are kept together. They do not track in Japan until the end of the ninth grade. Excellence and equity are both maintained compared with the United States.

In the matter of reading, however, an underlying difference in language may be intractable. That is, learning to read East Asian languages as a child is far less confusing than learning to read English. The child learns a manageable number of characters each year, and school texts are geared to this. As a result, classes can progress as a whole without the necessity of tracking, special reading programs, individual tutoring, and all the other responses developed in the United States to the challenges of written English. Differences in writing systems do not encompass the entire story. But tracking in the United States is much more likely given the peculiarities of English. Not surprisingly, compared with East Asia, Americans spend a large proportion of class time in elementary school on learning to read. This activity dominates the curriculum and is the greatest challenge faced by U.S. teachers.

What other differences of a fundamental kind need to be mentioned to put Stevenson and Lee's data in proper context? Relatively few Japanese children grow up in single-parent families. Few suffer serious poverty. Virtually none is an immigrant or the child of immigrants. Few grow up in neighborhoods devastated by crime and drugs.

Another contextual difference is the much higher regard for education, especially for high standards, found in Japan and the rest of East Asia. Sports, peer popularity, teen romance, and so forth are much less central than they are in the United States; academic effort is widely emphasized. Schooling and the popular imagination connect in a different and more positive manner in East Asia.

One reason for this is the national preoccupation with university entrance examinations found in East Asia. Parents and teachers focus on this ultimate reality. Does this preoccupation distort learning as is often asserted in the United States? Yes and no. Yes, because teaching to exams and cramming for exams dominates the year or two before college; no, because the idea of preparation is general enough before that time so that good educational practice, not rote, is emphasized.

Nor are the Japanese much interested in a topic that captivates the American public politically: the local control of schools. Half of public teachers' salaries in Japan are paid by the central government, for example. National standards and guidelines are taken for granted, but not enforced by constant testing. Entrance exams are a more powerful motivating force. Standards and guidelines are largely embedded in textbooks and the professionalization of teaching. Leadership of the system, in other words, is clear and authoritative, even if, as everywhere, educational policy gives rise to much public dissatisfaction.

The amount of time students are studying, not just doing homework, also differs considerably. Several years ago, I calculated that between fifth and twelfth grades—seven years—the average Japanese student studied about 3.2 times more than the average U.S. student. That is, when school time, homework, average attendance, instructional time per class hour, and attendance at cram schools were added up, Japanese students spend remarkably more time on learning.

On the other side of the equation, they do much less of other kinds of things, including socializing with one another. Except for watching a notable amount of television, they are far more focused on the crucial task of learning in an academic sense than are their American counterparts.

Given all these advantages, one might ask: Why are the Japanese not doing even better yet? International achievement tests measure only a part of what schools are about. Japanese teachers are concerned with more than just math and science. They are doing a great deal with the children's general development. This clearly shows up in the general behavior of the population later on. The Japanese are law abiding, polite, and, in numerous other ways, highly socialized. Japanese teachers also are intentionally slowing down the pace of their classes. They are concerned with slow learners and unwilling to leave them behind. Many parents are uncomfortable with this. They send their kids to cram schools because the public schools are not willing to favor the above-average students' pace.

These differences raise related questions. Given the challenges American teachers face, for example, are they not doing as well as can be expected? Many are making extraordinary efforts, especially in the inner cities and poor rural districts. But sacrifice and effort are not the whole story. American teachers can learn from the classroom practices of their Japanese counterparts.

Can other lessons be learned from Japan? The United States cannot afford to enter the twenty-first century without national standards and greater national leadership. The economic imperatives are clear in an increasingly global world.

This raises the question of whether the Japanese focus on international comparisons of this sort and to what effect. At present, surprisingly, they are not looking at international tests as particularly relevant. They spent the twentieth century catching up with the West in general, and instead of sitting on their laurels, they now are focused on the flaws they see in their system—inflexible and uninspired higher education, lack of diversity, and so forth. In other words, the international context is different for the two nations—focusing the United States on the basics and Japan on issues of innovation and research and development.

While East Asia is worth paying attention to in defining the scale of problems in American education, the fundamental solutions will be by necessity of the United States' own making. The set of challenges to be faced is large.

Although comparisons of the sort brought on by international tests are important, they can readily lead to a dangerous skewing of focus. Math and science do not equate to education.

Finally, yes, Japanese education is centralized, relatively standardized, and competitive, but this hardly justifies the stereotypes of severe school regimentation and conformity. Yes, Japanese students study hard for entrance exams, but they do much less rote memorization than critics imply. Yes, the Japanese media are attentive to school bullying and student suicides, but American teenagers suffer from these problems to a much greater degree. Yes, Japanese education is impressive, but it also faces serious problems and should not be idealized.

Instead of exaggerating the merits or demerits of East Asian education in the U.S. debate about reform, the challenge illustrated by the data Stevenson and Lee presented should be soberly accepted as the evidence that American education can do much better.

Notes

1. A. Beaton, M. Martin, and others, *Science Achievement in the Middle School Years: IEA's Third International Mathematics and Science Study (TIMSS)* (Boston College, TIMSS International Study Center, 1996), p. 22. To aid comparisons among the various International Association for the Evaluation of Educational Achievement (IEA) tests, raw scores were transformed into standard scores with an average of 500 and a standard deviation of 100.

2. A. Beaton, L. Mullis, and others, *Mathematics Achievement in the Middle School Years: IEA's Third International Mathematics and Science Study (TIMSS)* (Boston College, TIMSS International Study Center, 1996), p. 22.

3. L. Peak, *Pursing Excellence: A Study of U.S. Eighth-Grade Mathematics and Science Teaching, Learning, Curriculum, and Achievement in International Context* (Department of Education, National Center for Education Statistics, November 1996), pp. 25–26.

4. Beaton, Mullis, and others, *Mathematics Achievement in the Middle School Years*, p. 29.

5. Beaton, Martin, and others, *Science Achievement in the Middle School Years*, p. 29.

6. Beaton, Mullis, and others, *Mathematics Achievement in the Middle School Years*, p. 14.

7. L. Peak, *Pursing Excellence: A Study of U.S. Fourth-Grade Mathematics and Science Teaching, Learning, Curriculum, and Achievement in International Context* (Department of Education, National Center for Education Statistics, June 1997), pp. 20, 21, 24, 25.

8. C. C. McKnight and others, *The Underachieving Curriculum: Assessing U.S. School Mathematics from an International Perspective* (Champaign, Ill.: Stipes, 1987), p. 23.

9. L. C. Comber and J. P. Keeves, *Science Education in Nineteen Countries: An Empirical Study* (New York: Wiley, Halstead, 1973), p. 159.

10. McKnight and others, *The Underachieving Curriculum*, p. 23.

11. T. Husen, ed., *International Study of Achievement in Mathematics: A Comparison of Twelve Countries*, vol. 2 (Wiley, 1967), pp. 22–25.

12. W. B. Elley, *How in the World Do Students Read? IEA Study of Reading Literacy* (The Netherlands: International Association for the Evaluation of Educational Achievement, July 1992), pp. 14, 24.

13. M. Binkley and T. Williams, *Reading Literacy in the United States: Findings from the IEA Reading Literacy Study* (Department of Education, National Center for Education Statistics, 1996), pp. 4–5.

14. A. E. Lapointe, N. A. Mead, and J. M. Askew, *Learning Mathematics* (Princeton, N.J.: Educational Testing Service, 1992), pp. 18, 84.

15. Peak, *Pursing Excellence: A Study of U.S. Eighth-Grade Mathematics and Science Teaching, Learning, Curriculum, and Achievement in International Context*, p. 9.

16. D. C. Berliner and B. J. Biddle, *The Manufactured Crisis: Myths, Fraud, and the Attack on America's Public Schools* (Reading, Mass.: Addison-Wesley, 1995), p. xii.

17. G. W. Bracey, "Asian and American Schools Again: Research," *Phi Delta Kappan*, vol. 77 (May 1996), pp. 641–42; and G. W. Bracey, "Many Visions, Many Aims, One Test," *Phi Delta Kappan*, vol. 78 (January 1997), pp. 411–12.

18. R. M. Jaeger, "Weak Measurement Serving Presumptive Policy," *Phi Delta Kappan*, vol. 74 (October 1992), pp. 118–28, especially p. 124.

19. Beaton, Mullis, and others, *Mathematics Achievement in the Middle School Years*, p. 15.

20. I. C. Rotberg, "Myths about Test Score Comparisons," *Science*, vol. 270 (Dec. 1, 1995), pp. 1446–48.

21. Catherine Lewis, *Educating Hearts and Minds: Reflections on Japanese Preschool and Elementary Education* (New York: Cambridge University Press, 1995).

22. C. Lewis, E. Schaps, and M. Watson, "The Caring Classroom's Academic Edge," *Educational Leadership*, vol. 54 (September 1996), pp. 16–21.

23. J. P. Connell and J. G. Wellborn, "Competence, Autonomy, and Relatedness: A Motivational Analysis of Self-System Processes," in M. R. Gunnar and L. A. Sroufe, eds., *Self Process and Development: The Minnesota Symposia on Child Development*, vol. 23, pp. 43–47 (Hillsdale, N.J.: Erlbaum, 1991).

24. Thomas J. Sergiovanni, *Moral Leadership: Getting to the Heart of School Improvement* (Jossey-Bass, 1992), pp. 138–39.

25. W. H. Schmidt, C. C. McKnight, and S. A. Raizen, *A Splintered Vision: An Investigation of U.S. Science and Mathematics Education* (Boston, Mass.: Kluwer Academic Publishers, 1997).

26. MONBUSHOU (Ministry of Education, Science, and Culture), *Shogakkou Gakushuu Shido Youryou* (Course of Study for Elementary Schools) (Tokyo, Japan, 1989), p. 58.

27. Catherine Lewis and Ineko Tsuchida, "Planned Educational Change in Japan: The Case of Elementary Science Instruction," *Journal of Education Policy*, vol. 12 (1997), pp. 313–31.

An Assessment of the Contemporary Debate over U.S. Achievement

LAWRENCE C. STEDMAN

A RE TODAY'S STUDENTS as literate and well informed as those of earlier generations? Are they learning as much as those of several decades ago? Are they mastering fundamental knowledge and skills? These questions are at the heart of a fierce public debate over the quality of today's schools and how they should be reformed. For two decades, a diverse set of educators—from across the educational and political spectrum—has called attention to a decline of achievement.[1] They have pointed to the Scholastic Aptitude Test (SAT) decline, deteriorating reading performance, and poor historical knowledge. They have blamed the decline on a lowering of academic standards, specifically the watering down of textbooks, the expansion of electives, the relaxation of discipline, social promotion, and a reduced emphasis on reading and writing. Several have called on the public schools to restore their commitment to Western cultural values and knowledge.[2]

Two major accounts of the decline have circulated—a widely publicized version claims that a general decline began in the mid-to-late

Portions of this essay were adapted from several of the author's earlier works, particularly Lawrence C. Stedman, "An Assessment of Literary Trends, Past and Present," *Research in the Teaching of English,* vol. 30, no. 3 (1996), pp. 283–302; and Lawrence C. Stedman, "Respecting the Evidence: The Achievement Crisis Remains Real," *Education Policy Analysis Archives,* vol. 4, no. 7 (1996), available via the World Wide Web at http://olam.ed.asu.edu/epaa/. The author thanks his graduate assistant, Christopher Lopez, for his skilled work helping collect and graph National Assessment of Educational Progress race data.

53

1960s that continues today, and another, more refined version holds that this general decline ended around 1980 and was followed by a partial recovery in the 1980s and 1990s as a result of the imposition of higher standards.[3]

The notion of a decline has been vigorously disputed in recent years, however. Some researchers contend that school achievement is at historically high levels and that the reports of a decline were greatly exaggerated or even fabricated.[4] The new perspective originated with the Sandia Report, a controversial assessment of education by analysts with the Department of Energy.[5]

The debate often has been mired in educational and political hyperbole. The 1983 *Nation at Risk* report, for example, decried a "rising tide of mediocrity that threatens our very future as a Nation and a people."[6] C. Sykes asserted that educators have been "dumbing down the texts" and "dumbing down our kids."[7] A. Bloom and others blamed the decline on the egalitarian policies and social upheavals of the 1960s.[8] In response, unfortunately, have come equally sweeping claims by those who argue the public schools are not in a tailspin but are doing well. The leading voice of these revisionists, Gerald Bracey, maintains that the educational system is performing "better than ever" and that student achievement has "climbed to record levels."[9] In releasing its national standards, the National Council of Teachers of English pronounced that "students today read better and write better than at any other time in the history of the country."[10] Does the evidence justify such broad assertions about achievement gains? The revisionists have gone so far as to argue that the educational crisis has been "manufactured" by right-wing forces wishing to discredit public schooling.[11]

The debate has enormous implications for school reform. The revisionists have argued that school critics and politicians are ignoring the needs of the poor and urban areas; in turn, the revisionists have been faulted for fostering complacency and undercutting needed general reform. On the one hand, if student achievement truly has been declining, then resurrecting the education policies of an earlier era—strict pedagogy and no-nonsense discipline—may make sense. On the other hand, if the schools are generally succeeding, sweeping changes—such as restructuring and vouchers—may be unnecessary, and targeting students and schools with low achievement may be more effective.

Four major types of evidence shed light on the debate over achievement trends: national assessment data, SAT trends, test renorming studies, and then-and-now studies.[12] Both sides in this debate have frequently misrepresented the evidence and ignored contradictory information. Participants have rarely discussed the limitations of the data they are using. Although the debate often seems to fall along ideological lines, educators of widely differing political and educational beliefs have worried about the decline of excellence. Concerns about U.S. achievement cross the conservative-liberal and traditional-progressive divides.

Defining and Measuring Achievement

Assessing achievement trends is no easy matter. The data often seem precise, yet achievement can be hard to define and measure properly. Established measures have often portrayed academic performance as a hierarchical, unidimensional skill, but it is complex and multidimensional. In recent decades, new understandings of cognition and learning have emerged. Simplistic definitions have given way to an understanding that learning involves both knowledge and skill and varies by task and context. In the realm of reading, educators now routinely describe different types of literacy—prose, document, quantitative, academic, job, and functional.[13]

Assessments since the mid-1980s have better reflected these new appreciations, but in reviewing historical data, the earlier definitions and measures impose limitations. Nevertheless, the older data are useful because they provide evidence of long-term achievement trends and have figured prominently in national discussions of the achievement decline. Some of the most reliable measures of long-term trends, such as those from the National Assessment of Educational Progress (NAEP), have used modern conceptions of learning and measurement.

Researchers' interpretations have been heavily dependent upon which measure they focused on—NAEP, SAT, or standardized test trends; which statistics they used—standard scores, percentiles, or percentage correct; and how careful they were about accounting for changes in test populations and the relevance of test content.

Achievement Trends

The best measure of U.S. achievement trends comes from the National Assessment of Educational Progress, a federally funded program run by the Educational Testing Service. Every couple of years since 1969, NAEP has tested large, nationally representative samples of students in various subjects and has repeated items to establish trends. The test frameworks and objectives have been developed with contributions from curriculum specialists, parents, teachers, business leaders, and policymakers; they reflect a broad consensus of what students should know and be able to do. Results are reported on a scale that runs from 0 to 500, with performance levels defined at five points from 150 to 350.[14] This trend series is focused on ages nine, thirteen, and seventeen. NAEP also conducts a second, parallel assessment at grades four, eight, and twelve that incorporates new developments in curriculum content and testing methods. It reports the percentages of students at three new competency levels—basic, proficient, and advanced—as well as average scores on the 0 to 500 scale.

NAEP's tests embody rich conceptions of knowledge and skills and, from the earliest days, included elements of what is now called performance assessment. The math assessments, for example, have required students to plot data, use calculators, interpret graphs, and read charts and tables. The reading assessments have asked students to interpret and evaluate different types of authentic materials: short stories, poetry, newspaper articles, graphs, ads, and so on. The tests have frequently used open-ended questions requiring students to construct their responses.

NAEP has distinct advantages over the other measures because it involves nationally representative samples, it tests school content, and it uses diverse testing methods. By contrast, SAT trends are based on a measure of aptitude, not school content, of a self-selected population of college-bound students that changes annually. (However, the SAT-taking pool is an important group, not only because it represents those preparing for elite colleges but also because—by the early 1990s—it included more than 40 percent of all high school graduates.) Commercial standardized tests have been affected by the practice of teaching-to-the-test and by the district's familiarity with the tests after repeated administration of the same forms. Then-and-now studies have been hampered by changing school populations and changing curriculum content that limit comparability and by small local samples that limit generalizability.

What have the trends been on NAEP's assessments? With some fluctuations, student achievement has been essentially stable for a generation (see figure 1).

Some minor improvements have occurred. Science achievement at age nine and math achievement at ages nine and thirteen gradually rose during the 1980s and into the 1990s.

Writing performance can be traced back into the 1970s. (The data do not appear in the figure because earlier assessments used somewhat different procedures.) In spite of some declines on certain tasks in the 1970s, overall writing performance remained roughly stable at all three age levels across the decades. NAEP analysts reported, for example, that the "levels of writing performance in 1988 appeared to be substantially the same as in 1974."[15]

In spite of these generally flat trends, some revisionists and others have characterized NAEP scores as being at "all-time highs" and showing statistically significant increases.[16] In a strictly numerical sense, this is true for certain ages and subjects, but it paints a rosy and misleading picture. NAEP reading scores, for example, were a few points higher in 1994 than in 1971 but generally stable or flat scores would be a fairer description. NAEP's samples are also so large (about thirty-one thousand students in 1994) that even small score improvements, of little educational importance, have been statistically significant.[17]

An important exception to the general pattern also should not be overlooked. Seventeen-year-olds' science scores declined substantially between 1969 and 1982 and have not yet fully recovered. The decline was 22 scale points, which corresponded to a drop to about the 32nd percentile. Judged by the performance of thirteen-year-olds, this was almost a two-year decline. Expressed as percentage correct, the science decline seems more modest—about 7 percentage points in thirteen years.[18] Seventeen-year-olds' science scores improved steadily from the early 1980s to the early 1990s. This particular trend matches the formulation that a decline occurred in the 1970s followed by recovery.

NAEP also has assessed civics achievement several times, although it has not been included in its formal trend studies. An analysis of common items shows that seventeen-year-olds' civics performance declined in the early 1970s and was likely lower in 1988 than in 1969 (see table 1). Thirteen-year-olds' performance declined a modest amount in the early 1970s (2 to 3 percentage points), then improved slightly in the 1980s.

Figure 1. Reading, Math, Science, and Writing Achievement, 1969–94

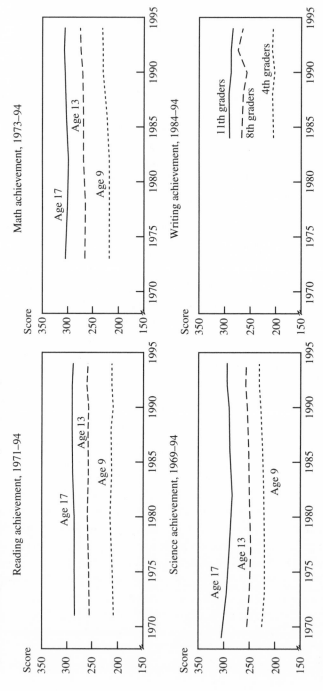

Source: J. Campbell and others, *NAEP 1994 Trends in Academic Progress* (U.S. Department of Education, 1996), p. v.

Note: The axis range in this and later figures reflects a compromise. Using the full scale for individuals—0 to 500—would have been inappropriate because few students score below 150 and the figures display group, not individual, achievement. Age groups do not average at the extremes—0 to 150 or 350 to 500—so the full scale would have left much of the figures blank and improperly flattened trend lines. However, graphing programs, by default, can exaggerate fluctuations because they scale the axis to the range of scores and separate the lines to fill the graph. So I chose instead a compromise axis of 150 to 350 because that spans 4 standard deviations or most of the scale (about 95 percent of individual scores) and represented well group differences. The most recent National Assessment of Educational Progress (NAEP) trends report used a similar approach, graphing scores for the three ages against a 170 to 320 axis, or 3 standard deviations. In figures 3 and 4, where I graphed achievement at only two ages and grades, which span less of a range, I used a 220 to 320 scale as the best compromise to fairly depict differences and reveal fluctuations over time.

Table 1. Civics Achievement, Seventeen-Year-Olds, 1969–88

Percent correct

Civics area	1969	1972	1976	1982	1988
Citizenship knowledge	73		65		
Social studies knowledge		64	59		
Civics proficiency			61.7	61.3	59.6

Sources: National Assessment of Educational Progress, *Changes in Political Knowledge and Attitudes, 1969–76,* Citizenship/Social Studies Report No. 07–CS–02 (Denver, Colo.: Education Commission of the States, 1978), p. 69; and National Center for Education Statistics, *Digest of Education Statistics 1991* (Department of Education, 1991), p. 122.

Part of the concern over the decline in excellence has pertained to a loss in high-scoring students. On the SAT, there was a drop in verbal scorers above 600 in the early 1970s (from 11 percent to 8 percent), with basically flat trends since then.[19] (The absolute numbers dropped substantially from more than 116,000 in 1972 to around 66,000 by 1983 and 79,000 in 1994, or 7.6 percent of the total.[20]) The proportion of top math scorers also declined substantially but has been recovering and by the late 1990s was above early 1970s levels.

Other indicators showed less change at the top than the SAT and full recovery from whatever declines occurred. On the American College Testing Program (ACT), the proportion of top scorers (26 or above) was stable in the first half of the 1970s, was down by only 1 percentage point in 1980, then recovered in 1985 and has been rising in the 1990s.[21] The proportion of seventeen-year-olds reaching the highest proficiency level (350) on the NAEP tests has been roughly stable for several decades.[22] The percentage of twelfth graders demonstrating math proficiency has risen in the 1990s from 12 to 16.[23]

Other signs point to stable or improving general educational performance. High school completion rates have hovered in the 82 to 86 percent range for several decades (see figure 2). Enrollments in college preparatory math and science courses rose during the 1980s and early 1990s.[24]

SAT Decline

The SAT decline is the most publicized and disputed indicator of the achievement decline. SAT scores dropped dramatically—verbal scores, for example, fell more than 50 points to 424 between the mid-1960s

Figure 2. High School Completion, Twenty-One- and Twenty-Two-Year-Olds, 1972–91

Percent

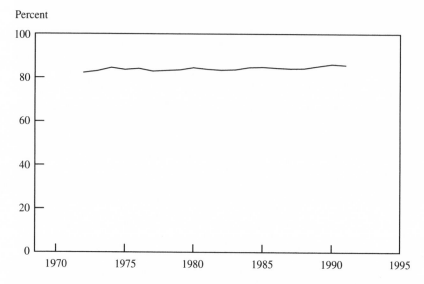

Source: National Center for Education Statistics, *Dropout Rates in the United States 1991* (U.S. Department of Education, 1992), p. 97.
Note: See note in figure 1.

and 1980. Since then, verbal scores have fluctuated, rising a bit in the early 1980s, dropping to an all-time low of 422 in 1991, then rising again slightly. Math scores, at their trough of 466 around 1980, have been rising fairly steadily but remain below their 1970 level.

Revisionists have attributed the entire SAT decline to demographic changes in the pool of test takers and thus argued that it does not indicate a decline in achievement. Bracey pointed to the dramatic growth in minority and academically weaker test takers and concluded that "no decline exists or ever existed."[25] The Sandia analysts argued that "the reason for the decline is not decreasing student performance," but increases in students from the bottom half of their high school classes.[26] By contrast, school critics generally accept the SAT decline at face value, either ignoring or discounting demographic effects, and believe that it reflects a real decline in the quality of U.S. schooling.[27]

The evidence suggests that much of the SAT decline—though clearly not all of it—was compositional.[28] The historic expansion of educational opportunity, particularly during the 1960s, helped change the test-taking group dramatically. The SAT was normed in 1941 on about eleven thousand students, most of whom were white, male, middle-class students bound for Ivy League colleges. Today's SAT is taken by more than a million students, of whom almost a third are minority, and even more have lower socioeconomic status and high school class rank.[29] Given these students' weaker preparation and the often poorer condition of minority schools, today's scores are understandably below the 1941 norm of 500.

The demographic changes and their impact were complex, however. During much of the 1970s, the pool of test takers did not expand, yet scores still declined. The tremendous rise in minority test takers cannot explain the large decline in white students' SAT scores during the 1960s and 1970s.[30] Their social composition, however, also changed, as a greater proportion of students with weaker academic skills and poorer socioeconomic backgrounds took the SAT and more often headed for nonselective colleges.[31]

The most comprehensive analysis of the SAT decline—the College Board's special Advisory Panel on the Scholastic Aptitude Test Score Decline study in the mid-1970s—concluded that much of the 1960s decline, from two-thirds to three-quarters, but a smaller part of the 1970s decline, from 20 percent to 30 percent, resulted from demographic changes in test takers.[32] If one considers the additional effects of changing family size and birth order (later-borns score more poorly), up to 40 percent of the 1970s decline may have stemmed from compositional changes.[33] More recent analyses suggest that about half the recent fluctuations in verbal scores can be accounted for by demographic changes.[34]

As the Advisory Panel observed, arguing that the inclusion of lower-scoring students caused the decline is deceptive. The real cause lies in the poorer education of minority students and others in the expanded group of test takers. Instead of celebrating it as an indicator of expanded opportunity, as some revisionists have, the SAT decline is a disturbing reminder that educational equality and widespread excellence have not been achieved.

Class Rank and the SAT Decline

The class rank explanation of the SAT decline has had such currency—even appearing in a major educational research book—that it deserves a separate assessment.[35]

The Sandia analysts presented a graph showing that average SAT scores have been stable for students from the different fifths of their classes.[36] They argued this meant that a changing mix of students, not a worsening in performance, had produced the decline. Other revisionists echoed this claim, both about class rank and minority group changes.[37]

Their graph, however, covered the years 1976–90, a period when average SAT scores changed little. It ignored the mid-1960s and mid-1970s, when most of the decline happened. The changes in class rank were also relatively minor. The proportion from the bottom two-fifths of their classes rose only from 2 percent to about 5 percent between 1976 and 1990. By focusing on the average, they masked fluctuations in verbal scores for different class rank groups. All class rank groups had declining verbal scores in the late 1980s and early 1990s that mirrored the general verbal trends. The top two-tenths also lost ground verbally in the late 1970s. In other words, the recent verbal decline, albeit minor, partly resulted from declining performance and not simply a changing class rank mix.[38]

The similar argument about a changing mix of minority students also depended on average scores and the post-1976 period. White students' verbal scores, however, fell between 1976 and 1990, while several minority groups' verbal scores declined in the late 1970s and again in the late 1980s, paralleling the national verbal trends.

Size of the SAT Decline

Even the size of the apparent SAT decline has been disputed.[39] Several revisionists have noted that average SAT scores declined only about 5 percent between 1970 and 1990, although this ignored the late 1960s decline and the larger verbal decline.

Expressed as changes in standard deviations and percentiles, the SAT decline seems dramatic. The verbal decline was about one-half a standard deviation, meaning that college-bound students of the 1990s are performing at about the 32nd percentile of those of the mid-1960s. Math performance had declined to the 38th percentile by 1980. Percentiles, however, indicate the relative standing among individuals instead of the actual amount of change in performance. As the Advisory Panel asked: "But *how much* worse are students doing now than their counterparts used to do?"[40]

Analyses of raw score changes suggest that the decline was more modest than has been suggested. D. Berliner and B. Biddle were right to raise this vexing, yet largely hidden, issue. The SAT has been composed of about eighty verbal and sixty math questions. Each question corresponds to about 10 scale points in the middle of the scale.[41] The drop of 54 verbal scale points thus corresponds to a loss of about five-and-one-half questions, or about 7 percentage points; the math decline of 36 points corresponds to about three-and-one-half questions, or 6 percentage points. Part of this, perhaps as much as 40 percent, resulted from changes in test takers. The overall raw score decline, therefore, may have amounted to only a couple of questions, or 3 to 4 percentage points.

The SAT and School Performance

What caused the remaining portion of the SAT decline may never be known. Although the Advisory Panel pointed to television watching, changing family structures, and social-political disruptions, it also implicated a lowering of academic standards.[42] Several researchers have laid out the case for a weakening of textbooks, grade inflation, expanded electives, reduced homework and assigned reading, and so on.[43] While considering several of these explanations plausible, C. Jencks cautioned that hard evidence on them was often lacking, such as about homework, or was contradictory, such as about textbook difficulty.[44]

Some suggestive counterevidence should be noted. In a background study for the Advisory Panel, G. Echternacht compared educational changes in high schools with stable SATs and those with declines worse than the nation's.[45] Principals in the two sets of schools reported similar increases in truancy and discipline problems. Their schools had expanded pass-fail grading and nontraditional offerings to the same extent. English curricula and enrollments in academic courses were similar. The decline in SAT performance was not linked to what the schools had been doing. In a separate background study, R. Jackson found that a set of traditional and experimental high schools showed similar drops in SAT scores, suggesting that educational innovation was not a major factor in the decline.[46]

Such limited school effects should not be surprising. The College Board has strongly warned against using the SAT to measure school quality and effectiveness.[47] Educators of diverse political and educational persuasions have expressed similar concerns.[48] The SAT is an aptitude test designed to predict college performance. Although the math section includes some algebra and geometry problems, the SAT does not measure most of the knowledge found in the high school curriculum—no sciences, foreign languages, English literature, or U.S. history. The test is a speed and endurance one—with more than two hundred problems in three hours or more than one per minute.[49] Such a rapid-fire processing of test items is hardly a good way of judging the quality and depth of students' K-12 learning.[50]

Indications exist that high school achievement among some of the college-bound did not decline in certain important academic areas. Evidence comes from the College Board achievement tests, which do cover high school subject matter. During the period of the greatest decline in SATs, 1967 to 1976, students improved their performance on six major achievement tests, including English composition, the three high school sciences (biology, chemistry, and physics), and the two major languages (French and Spanish).[51] About 20 percent of those who take the SAT also take achievement tests, so this is a select, but important, subset of high school seniors. These students had lower SAT scores than their predecessors but had higher achievement scores in these areas. The Advisory Panel speculated that the SAT was changing in its relevance to high school education.[52]

Performance on the ACT natural science exam—which measures students' ability to read and interpret materials from biology, chemistry, physics, and earth sciences—never did decline.[53] Performance has been gradually rising over the past two decades.

Furthermore, the average high school student has not lost whatever skills are tested by the SAT. A short version of it, the Preliminary Scholastic Aptitude Test (PSAT), was given to nationally representative samples of high school juniors five times from 1955 to 1983. Although the trends were not uniform, scores in the early 1980s matched those of the 1960s.[54]

Trends on Nationally Normed Tests in the 1970s and 1980s

The revisionists generally reject the idea that any significant decline occurred in test scores. Berliner and Biddle, for example, claimed that there was "only *one* test, the SAT, that ever suggested a decline" and attributed that decline entirely to demographic changes in test takers.[55] Such assertions, however, overlook declines on nationally normed standardized tests, during the 1970s.

From 1970 to 1978, scores on the leading secondary school tests experienced a striking downturn.[56] This decline has been presented in dramatic statistical guises.[57] P. Copperman argued that the average high school student of the late 1970s ranked at only the 39th percentile of his 1965 counterparts.[58] On several tests, eleventh and twelfth graders lost a year or more in reading achievement during the 1970s.

Care must be taken in judging this decline, however. The stark descriptions are problematic. First, standardized tests are constructed in such a way that small shifts in test performance can produce large changes in percentiles and grade equivalents. On the Science Research Associates (SRA) test, for example, twelfth graders dropped a whole grade level in reading between 1971 and 1978, which sounds alarming, but their percentage of correct answers fell only from 72 to 68, or a 4 percentage point drop. Other tests also showed small changes.[59]

Second, compositional changes caused part of the decline on these tests just as they had on the SAT. Immigration from low-scoring groups increased, more black students stayed in school, families were bigger (later-born children score lower), and single-parent families increased. These factors may have accounted for as much as 30 to 50 percent of the score decline.[60]

Third, standardized test renormings are not reliable measures of national trends.[61] The renorming samples are usually not nationally representative; only a few school districts or a fraction of the national sample are given the old and new tests. Sometimes two different groups take the tests, or only parts of the tests are given. Even test publishers have warned against using the data to infer national trends, citing changing samples and relevance of test content.

Fourth, the decline needs to be put into a historical context. Even after they had fallen during the 1970s, several standardized test scores remained around or above early 1960s levels.[62] Iowa Tests of Educational Development (ITED) scores for tenth through twelfth graders, for example, improved in the 1950s and 1960s, then fell back in the 1970s to around 1962 levels. When compared with the gains in educational attainment, the decline seems less substantial. The median educational level of the adult population (twenty-five years and older) rose two full years between 1960 and 1980, from 10.5 to 12.5. Between 1940 and 1980, it rose nearly four years, from 8.6 to 12.5.[63] A skill decline of a few percentage points, or one-half a year (adjusting for compositional changes), appears modest compared to these substantial gains.

Finally, extensive evidence contradicted a 1970s decline. Secondary students improved their reading and math performance from five months to a full year in a comparison of results on the Metropolitan and Stanford Achievement Tests. Thirteen- and seventeen-year-olds maintained their NAEP reading scores while nine-year-olds improved theirs slightly.[64] Seventeen-year-olds' functional literacy improved, and several of their writing skills remained stable or improved. Junior and senior high school students improved their Stanford achievement scores between 1973 and 1982 in diverse areas, including reading, math, science, and spelling. College Board achievement scores rose in several key areas. ACT scores in the natural sciences remained stable, as they have for several decades.

The best evidence, therefore, suggests that a score decline occurred in the 1970s on nationally normed tests, but it was a modest one and not universal. Claims that scores did not decline go too far when several at the high school level did.

In the 1980s, renormings of several commercial tests suggested improvement, particularly at the elementary level. Composite scores on the Iowa Tests of Basic Skills (ITBS), for example, reached all-time highs. The news was not all good, however. High school trends were mixed, with declines on several tests at several grades. The amount and duration of the improvement have been exaggerated and misrepresented. The standards report from National Council of Teachers of English (NCTE) claimed that, since the mid-1970s, reading scores at grades one through nine had been improving at a 2 percentile per year rate on five of six major tests.[65] The renorming data, however, only covered through the mid-1980s and the rate of increase on the five tests was 1.4 points, with three tests around 1 percentile point.[66] Berliner and Biddle claimed "virtually all" commercial tests would "show that today's students are out-achieving their parents substantially," but they presented little generational evidence and selectively graphed recent renorming data, omitting all SRA and high school scores, which showed some declines.[67] The major historical reviews of renorming studies refute their claim.[68] The best that can be concluded is that this generation of students generally performs about the same as earlier ones, but the patterns are complicated, and some of the evidence is contradictory.

The rosy accounts also assume that all the recent improvement was genuine, yet the gains were partly caused by test familiarity and districts' repeated use of the same tests. The 1980s back-to-basics movement also helped to artificially raise scores by frequent testing and skill-drill approaches. These factors probably created part of the apparent gains by minority students during that decade as well, meaning that their achievement did not improve as much as supposed.

Then-and-Now Studies

Then-and-now studies provide a longer-range perspective on the contemporary achievement debate. In these studies, researchers assess the achievement of contemporary students on a test given years or decades earlier. This is not a new idea. Throughout the twentieth century, school critics have questioned whether schools have lost their way, and educators have turned to such studies to determine whether or not achievement has been declining. In one of the earliest studies, J. Riley found that ninth graders in Springfield, Massachusetts, in 1906 outperformed their 1846 counterparts in spelling, arithmetic, and geography.

The results of such studies can shed light on competing perspectives of historical trends in student achievement. Some critics of progressive education have argued that a historic transformation of the school earlier in the twentieth century—from an academically oriented institution to a social and vocational one—contributed to a major decline in academic performance.[70] They contend that the rise of child-centered education and a life-adjustment curriculum dramatically reduced disciplinary content, particularly in high schools. At the elementary school level, E. D. Hirsch, Jr., argued that the schools had reduced their teaching of traditional cultural information, while R. Flesch blamed the literacy decline on the abandonment of phonics.[71] Other critics argue that achievement and literacy improved steadily from early in the twentieth century through the mid-1960s, but that the advent of open education, relaxed standards, and a weakened curriculum in the 1960s and 1970s produced the "first major skills decline in American educational history."[72] In contrast, the revisionists have used then-and-now studies to argue that the current generation of students is doing better than earlier ones.[73]

Most then-and-now studies have focused on reading achievement. Research by Roger Farr and his colleagues suggests that modern students are better-skilled than earlier ones. After adjusting for age differences, they found that Indiana students in 1976 had outperformed those of 1944–45.[74] Their comprehensive review of then-and-now studies also indicated that students' reading skills had improved over the century. They concluded that "anyone who says that *he knows* that literacy is decreasing is . . . at best unscholarly and at worst dishonest."[75]

In the 1980s, Carl Kaestle and I updated their research and expanded it to functional and job literacy, NAEP trends, and renorming studies.[76] We were struck, however, by the limited nature and poor quality of the then-and-now data. Few studies were nationally representative. Many were limited to a single city or town or to midwestern states with few minorities and no major cities. Few researchers accounted for changing social composition, yet ten to twenty years had passed between city testings and twenty to thirty years in the typical state study. The tests often measured skills other than reading comprehension, illustrating the nature of earlier conceptions of literacy. The Indiana study, for example, involved speed reading tests and short-term memory tests (students had to answer ten questions in two minutes about reading passages they could no longer see). On the one test that measured what is typically regarded as reading comprehension, tenth graders in 1976 showed no gain even after researchers adjusted their scores upward because they were younger. The soundest conclusion is that Indiana students in the 1970s were probably reading about as well as their counterparts had in the 1940s. Still, this finding is important because it suggests that, even in the trough of the decline, modern students were doing as well as those of an earlier generation.

In spite of their limitations, then-and-now studies are subject to sweeping claims. In the 1990s, several revisionists asserted that "almost all the results" on then-and-now studies showed improvement.[77] The claims were even more specific in the new NCTE standards document: Of "several dozen studies of this nature, all but one conclude that more recent students outperform earlier students."[78] Of the thirteen local then-and-now reading studies that have been done (covering through the 1960s), five showed no real change and two showed declines. Two of the three studies done in the 1970s suggested student reading had deteriorated somewhat since the 1920s and 1950s.[79] Overall, across the century, more studies showed gains than declines, but the gains were small and several trends were stable. The changes, up or down, were usually half a school year or less—well within the margin of errors Kaestle and I unearthed. We concluded that reading performance had been stable throughout most of the twentieth century but cautioned that then-and-now studies are "fraught with design and interpretation problems."[80] Little hard evidence exists, therefore, that the rise of child-centered education or the supposed abandonment of phonics over the course of the century harmed national reading achievement. Researchers have yet to systematically assess how the transformation of the high school into a mass institution affected subject matter achievement.[81]

Interpreting Trends

The four types of achievement evidence thus reveal fairly stable performance on several important indicators, but also some fluctuations and declines, particularly in the 1970s. Summarizing such complex achievement trends is a tricky business. Too often, the data have been forced into pat, neat stories of decline or improvement. The actual evidence is messy and trends are mixed. Student performance was stable in several cases—for example, on the NAEP reading assessments, then-and-now studies, and the ACT natural science test—or showed gradual, small rises such as on the NAEP math assessment at lower ages and the NAEP science assessment at age nine. Other indicators fit the scenario of decline and partial recovery—for example, NAEP science scores at age seventeen and SAT math scores; while some stagnated after declining—for example, SAT verbal and NAEP high school civics scores.

Trendlines for college-bound students showed more striking declines, but also some mixed patterns. SAT verbal and ACT composite scores remain down, though the declines were partly related to demographic changes in test takers. SAT math scores have recovered to early 1970 levels. By the late 1980s, ACT English Usage scores had returned to their 1970 level. Other college-bound indicators showed stability or improvement such as the ACT natural science exam, the percentage at the top on the ACT composite, and the College Board achievement tests.

In spite of this complex portrait, the evidence is clear and strong enough to reject the conventional wisdom or popular view that achievement and schools are currently declining. Nearly all indicators have been level or rising since the mid-1980s. The evidence also refutes the revisionists' claims that a decline never occurred and that performance is better than ever. Although the declines were often modest, as on nationally normed standardized tests, they appeared on several leading indicators in the 1970s, particularly at the high school level. To be sure, the decline was not universal—important contradictory evidence is available, including stable NAEP reading scores and rising elementary math achievement—but the indicators that are higher than a generation ago typically are only marginally better than they were before. Overall, the average student's performance in the 1990s is not that much different from that of the 1970s, but that is partly because some scores recovered after declining in the 1970s.

How should the stable performance that appears on some of these key indicators be interpreted? At one level, given the major changes in school populations and societal conditions over the past several decades, it suggests an unrecognized resilience by the schools. Schools in the late 1990s face more diverse populations; students face more difficult circumstances. More minority students are enrolled in school; childhood poverty rates have risen; and single-parent households, teenage suicide, and juvenile arrest rates for violent crimes just about doubled between 1970 and 1990.[82] Students are more likely today to have both parents or the sole adult in the household working.

Several social changes during this past generation, however, should have made the work of schools easier and improved achievement. Parents of NAEP test takers are more educated than they were before—a substantial majority now have some post–high school education and more than 40 percent of NAEP's high school students have at least one parent who is a college graduate.[83] A quarter century ago, 20 percent of high school students came from families in which no parent had graduated from high school; that has dropped to only 7 percent.

Reported drug use dropped dramatically during the 1970s and 1980s.

Table 2. Math Achievement, Twelfth Graders, 1990–96

Level	1990 (percent)	1992 (percent)	1996 (percent)	1990–92 (rate)	1992–96 (rate)
Advanced or better	1	2	2	.5	0
Proficient or better	12	15	16	1.5	.25
Basic or better	58	64	69	3	1.25
Below basic	42	36	31	3	1.25

Source: C. Reese and others, *NAEP 1996 Mathematics Report Card for the Nation and the States* (Department of Education, 1997), p. 47.

In the early 1990s, former secretary of education and drug czar William Bennett reviewed the data and concluded that "overall drug use among Americans is down more than 50 percent from its peak in the late 1970s." He continued, "Among adolescents, drug and alcohol use is at its lowest point since monitoring began in 1975."[84] (Marijuana and alcohol use has risen since the early 1990s, however.) High school students also reported feeling safer in school in 1990 than they had in 1980.[85]

Contrary to popular impression, teenage birth rates declined steadily from 1960 through the mid-1980s, dropping almost in half.[86] After rising in the late 1980s, they are once again declining and in the late 1990s are about the same as they were in the early 1970s.

Two important educational measures improved. Per pupil expenditures almost doubled during the period, and pupil-teacher ratios became smaller in both elementary and secondary schools.[87]

Such changing circumstances, many for the better, suggest that maintaining academic performance is not that impressive. Achievement may be better interpreted as having stagnated on several leading measures, particularly since the mid-to-late 1970s. Several scholars argue that increased expenditures coupled with flat scores means that the educational system has become less efficient.[88]

The case should not be overstated, however, as student performance did improve in the 1980s on NAEP math and high school science measures. Still, even in those areas, progress has slowed (see table 2). At the rate of math improvement between 1992 and 1996, it will take another generation before all seniors reach the basic level and until the year 2132 before even half achieve proficiency.[89] Other indicators, such as the age-trend data, showed little or no math and science improvement in the 1990s.[90]

Figure 3. Achievement Gaps by Race, Selected Years, 1990–96

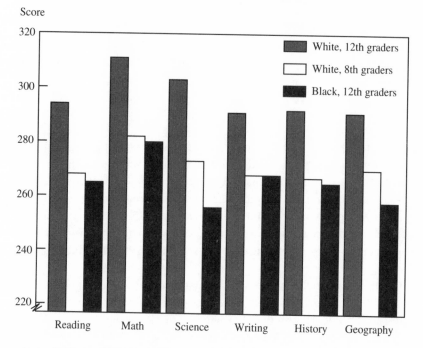

Sources: Reading data (1994), J. Campbell and others, *NAEP 1994 Reading Report Card for the Nation and the States* (Department of Education, 1996), p. 27; math data (1996), C. Reese and others, *NAEP 1996 Mathematics Report Card for the Nation and the States* (Department of Education, 1997), p. 33; science data (1990), L. Jones and others, *The 1990 Science Report Card* (Department of Education, 1992), p. 10; writing data (1992), A. Applebee and others, *NAEP 1992 Writing Report Card* (Washington: National Center for Education Statistics, 1994), p. 102; history data (1994), A. Beatty and others, *NAEP 1994 U.S. History Report Card* (Department of Education, 1996), p. 19; and geography data (1994), H. Persky and others, *NAEP 1994 Geography Report Card* (Department of Education, 1996), p. 17.

Note: See note in figure 1.

Trends in Equality of Opportunity

The revisionists have argued that the real achievement problems lie in minority and urban schooling. Strong evidence confirms their concern. The NAEP results reveal large, lingering achievement gaps among different racial and ethnic groups. Although black students' reading achievement, academic course taking, and high school completion have improved, the 1996 NAEP assessments show that twelfth grade black students are performing at the level of white eighth graders (see figure 3).[91] These students are about to graduate, yet they lag four or more years behind in every area that NAEP tested—reading, math, science, writing, history, and geography. Latino seniors do somewhat better than eighth grade white students in math and writing but, in the other areas, are also four years behind white twelfth graders.[92]

What is striking is how large this gap has been over time. Black seventeen-year-olds have seldom performed better than thirteen-year-old white students in a generation of testing (See figure 4). Still, an eighth grade reading level in the mid-1990s is an improvement over the 1970s, when black students lagged well behind thirteen-year-old whites.

Progress in black achievement generally slowed or ceased in the late 1980s and early 1990s (see figure 5). Racial gaps in achievement in most subjects and ages are as large or larger than they were in the late 1980s.[93] In reading, the achievement gaps between blacks and whites at ages thirteen and seventeen are 45 to 67 percent larger than they were in 1988. Nine-year-old black students are as far behind white students as they were in 1980. In math, about a third of the racial achievement gap has been bridged during this past generation, but the gap has been increasing at ages thirteen and seventeen in the 1990s. In science, about one-tenth of the gap at ages thirteen and seventeen was closed in twenty-five years; at that rate, it would take 250 years to totally close the gap. The gap also has grown larger since the mid-1980s at all three ages. In spite of fluctuations, black students lag as far behind in writing as they did in 1988.

The conclusion is distressing, but unavoidable. The progress that was once made toward equality of opportunity has stalled. The patterns raise troubling questions about efforts to achieve equality of opportunity and social justice. The concerns go well beyond the schools themselves as a recent report on the condition of black education makes clear:

> Black children are at an educational disadvantage relative to white children for a number of reasons, including lower average levels of parental education, a greater likelihood of living with only one parent, fewer resources in their communities as a result of income-based residential segregation, and, especially, a greater likelihood of experiencing poverty. In 1992, 46 percent of black children, as opposed to 16 percent of white children, lived in a family with an income level below the poverty line.[94]

A generation has passed and the achievement of educational equality

Figure 4. Reading, Math, Science, and Writing Achievement, by Race, 1969–94

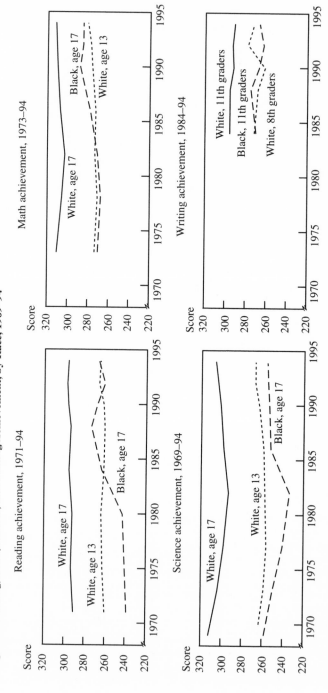

Reading achievement, 1971–94

Math achievement, 1973–94

Science achievement, 1969–94

Writing achievement, 1984–94

Source: J. Campbell and others, *NAEP 1994 Trends in Academic Progress* (U.S. Department of Education, 1996), pp. A-6, A-9, A-68, A-71, A-136, A-139, A-202, A-205.
Note: See note in figure 1.

Figure 5. Reading, Math, Science, and Writing Achievement, by Black Students, 1969–94

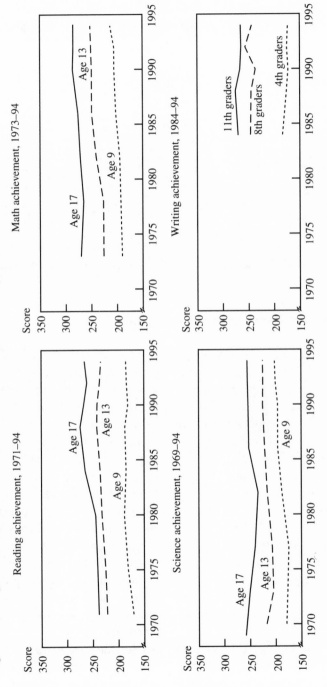

Reading achievement, 1971–94

Math achievement, 1973–94

Science achievement, 1969–94

Writing achievement, 1984–94

Source: J. Campbell and others, *NAEP 1994 Trends in Academic Progress* (U.S. Department of Education, 1996), pp. A-3, A-6, A-9, A-65, A-68, A-71, A-133, A-136, A-139, A-199, A-202, A-205.
Note: See note in figure 1.

Table 3. Achievement on the 1994 and 1996 NAEP Assessments, Twelfth Graders
Percent

Subject	Below basic	Basic level	Proficient or better	Advanced or better
Geography	30	43	27	2
History	57	32	11	1
Math	31	53	16	2
Reading	25	39	36	4

Sources: Geography data (1994), H. Persky and others, *NAEP 1994 Geography Report Card* (Department of Education, 1996), p. 28; history data (1994), A. Beatty and others, *NAEP 1994 U.S. History Report Card* (Department of Education, 1996), p. 33; math data (1996), C. Reese and others, *NAEP 1996 Mathematics Report Card for the Nation and the States* (Department of Education, 1997), p. 47; and reading data (1994), J. Campbell and others, *NAEP 1994 Reading Report Card for the Nation and the States* (Department of Education, 1996), p. 44.

Note: NAEP = National Assessment of Educational Progress. "Proficient or better" includes students at the advanced levels. Basic percent was found by subtracting proficient or better from basic or better in the original data sources.

remains an elusive dream. Schools and society remain divided into two different worlds, one black and one white, separate and unequal.

Persistent Problems in Student Achievement

Characterizing the achievement problem as one of minority education or educational malaise would be a mistake, however. The debate over both racial performance and achievement trends has obscured a more fundamental and pressing issue: the low levels of achievement that repeatedly show up in national assessments.

NAEP analysts have contended that the two highest proficiency levels, 300 and 350, reflect the knowledge and skills needed for higher education, business, and government.[95] Unfortunately, only around half of U.S. high school students reach the 300 level and few—3 to 10 percent—reach the 350 level in the major high school subjects.[96] In recent years, the National Assessment Governing Board (NAGB) has developed a second set of standards based on what students should know and be able to do at the fourth, eighth, and twelfth grades. Scores are now reported for three new achievement levels—basic, proficient, and advanced. Recent assessments using these new standards have shown that most students are not proficient and that large percentages cannot even make the basic level in each subject tested.

The data for high school seniors provide the best overall assessment of K-12 performance (see table 3). Only 16 percent of seniors were proficient in math and only 2 percent achieved the advanced level. In reading, the figures were 36 percent and 4 percent, respectively. Almost a third of the seniors failed to reach the basic math level, which reflects only partial mastery of fundamental skills and knowledge.[97] One-fourth fell below the basic level in reading. Student performance was poorest in history. Only 11 percent of the seniors demonstrated proficiency and more than half were below the basic level. These findings suggest that there is a serious educational problem.

Concerns have been raised about the construction and interpretation of these levels, however.[98] Their predictive validity is undetermined— the connection between a given level of performance and future academic or economic success is likely more tenuous than claimed in the NAEP reports. The original NAEP proficiency levels were arbitrarily set; that is, the 300 and 350 levels were set at 1 and 2 standard deviations above the mean. This predetermined that only a small percentage of students would initially reach the 350 level, which produced serious misunderstandings and misrepresentations. School critics and the media have reported that the system is doing poorly because few students are reaching this top level, yet this was psychometrically predetermined.

Recent reports from the General Accounting Office and the National Academy of Education have questioned the procedures that established the new NAGB levels and their reliability, validity, and utility.[99] NAGB's own technical report found substantial and troublesome variability in how panels defined the basic level. The advanced level apparently exceeds world-class standards with the result that few students, even of high ability, can achieve it. The extent of these problems, however, has been disputed.[100]

The 1996 NAEP report cards clearly label the standards as "developmental" and indicate that "the process for setting them remains in transition."[101] The system probably will be revised in the future. Nevertheless, both the commissioner of the National Center for Education Statistics and the National Assessment Governing Board believe the levels are "useful and valuable" in reporting on student achievement.

Good reasons exist for taking the NAEP findings seriously. That so few students reach the upper levels is troubling when the problems that define these levels are not particularly difficult. The 300 level in math, for example, includes simple decimal problems, and level 350 includes "routine problems involving fractions and percents."[102] In history, many of the problems at the 350 level required nothing more than simple recall of basic factual information.

Although the level-setting procedure initially limited the proportion of students at the top, it did not prevent this proportion from growing. The levels were designed explicitly to reveal improvements, yet the percentages of high school students at the highest level in the various subjects have remained about the same for two decades.

NAEP releases some test items that allow educators and the public to evaluate student knowledge directly. Careful reviews of individual items and sets of items have avoided many of the scaling and level-setting problems but still confirm that a serious achievement problem persists and that many students struggle with basic material.

High school juniors and seniors have trouble with material that was covered in middle school general math courses—simple algebra and basic math such as estimations, finding area, and percents. Less than half have "a firm grasp of seventh-grade content."[103] They do not know elementary, yet important, information from U.S. history courses such as the purpose of the Monroe doctrine, the names of leading muckrakers, that the Scopes trial dealt with evolution, or that U.S. foreign policy was isolationist after World War I.[104]

Many lack critical reading skills and are not well read.[105] They are not conversant with major women and African American writers or classics by Shakespeare, Conrad, and Whitman. Few have performed well on NAEP's writing assessments, even though a "finished performance" was not expected.[106]

Their geographical knowledge is limited. Many seniors—more than a third—have trouble with the basic concepts of latitude and longitude.[107] Given the Vietnam War, it is unsettling that almost two-thirds could not locate Southeast Asia on a world map. Most also could not find Saudi Arabia. Less than half knew that slavery was a major reason that many Caribbean people are of West African descent.[108] Only about a third recognized a description of a rain forest and could identify a country that had one.

In addition to the NAEP studies, a 1988 assessment of college seniors found "significant gaps" in students' knowledge.[109] A majority could not identify the *Federalist Papers*, the Missouri Compromise, Reconstruction, or major works by Shakespeare, Joyce, Eliot, and Austen.

They also did not know Ellison, Wright, or the "Letter from Birmingham Jail" by Martin Luther King, Jr.

Although the achievement evidence should be interpreted cautiously, it is reasonable to conclude that much of the curriculum is not being learned. U.S. schools spend several years on such basic material, but with limited success. At issue is not challenging material from Advanced Placement (AP) classes or even second year algebra.

To be sure, there have been bright spots. High school students have done well on basic math operations such as adding whole numbers and reading a line graph. Most are competent with the basic mechanics of writing—spelling, grammar, and punctuation—and so additional whole-class drill and practice in these areas is considered unnecessary.[110] They are familiar with some major documents and figures from U.S. history and can identify several leading countries such as the Soviet Union (92 percent), Canada (87 percent), and West Germany (76 percent). But, on the whole, achievement is at troubling low levels. The results are unimpressive for twelve years of schooling. The tests measure much of what schools are teaching and show they are not succeeding. An NAEP review in 1990 concluded that "very few students demonstrate that they can use their minds well."[111] Student achievement may be worse than the data imply. The NAEP results do not include dropouts, who presumably would score lower.

Issues of Interpretation

The revisionists have never dealt directly with the evidence of low achievement. Instead, they have offered a series of arguments designed to discount or dismiss the findings. Berliner and Biddle, for example, wrote that the "standards against which America's schools are to be judged and found wanting are arbitrary and can be made up as one goes along."[112] Historically, this is untrue. The major studies have relied strongly on school- and curriculum-based measures—the textbooks that are most widely used, teacher consensus about what is important to be tested, and citizen panels that decide what students should know and be able to do.

The revisionists have argued that the standards for knowledge are unrealistic and are those of academics, classicists, historians, and test designers.[113] It is easy to be critical of seventeen-year-olds' lack of knowledge. Many people acquired knowledge on their own or after high school—reading biographies and popular histories, traveling, taking history and literature courses in college, and following the news. The problem, however, is not unrealistic adult standards (or harsh judgments by ivory tower academics). One wishes it were so simple. Even some revisionists acknowledge that the material at issue is basic.[114] Most people would reasonably expect high school seniors to be competent in seventh grade math and basic social studies information, but they are not.

Student motivation to do well on the NAEP assessments is an important concern.[115] At present, students have no stake in the outcome; they are not even told how they did. NAEP performance probably would be better if the tests were high-stakes, but compared with that of the SATs, the burden on students is negligible. NAEP tests take only forty-five to fifty minutes. To reach a given level, students have only had to answer correctly 65 to 80 percent of its problems.[116] Such a low standard provides a fudge factor that partly accounts for motivation. (One could reasonably argue that the standards should be stricter. It would mean, however, that even fewer students have mastered basic material.) Placing NAEP items into "moderate" stakes settings—such as the Georgia assessment program—has not changed the results. Direct evidence from schools mirrors that from the tests. In 1992, the first national assessment of classroom writing portfolios showed that students' best writing was not that good. Only between 4 and 12 percent of the eighth graders achieved high marks (5 or 6) on the six-category evaluation scale. About one-fourth to more than 40 percent received low marks (1 or 2), depending on whether informative or narrative tasks were being considered.[117]

Standardized test evidence also has been faulted because it does not measure real-world problem solving. Standardized tests, however, do give some indication of real-world problem-solving ability; a marked correlation exists between scores on traditional tests and those on performance assessment measures.[118] The NAEP tests also have directly measured performance on real-world tasks and materials. Results from authentic, performance-based assessments will likely provide little comfort. When students' understanding of a subject is probed, surprising gaps and confusions often appear.[119] The 1992 NAEP reading assessment, for example, found a marked drop-off in performance as reading questions became more open-ended—from around two-thirds correct on multiple-choice problems to only around a third or less on questions requiring an extended response.[120] This suggests that as districts and states begin adopting authentic assessment, they will find that student performance is even poorer than previously thought.

Historical Evidence

The problem with academic achievement goes back at least half a century. In the middle of World War II, the *New York Times* surveyed seven thousand students in thirty-six colleges and found "a striking ignorance of even the most elementary aspects of United States history." Even though they were an elite—college attendance was then rare—they knew almost nothing about many important phases of this country's growth and development.[121] The test involved straightforward questions of basic material. The *Times* found that only 16 percent of the students could name two contributions by Thomas Jefferson. Only 20 percent could name two figures connected with trusts or two areas purchased by the United States and the nations that sold them. Only 13 percent knew that James Madison was president during the War of 1812. These startling findings even produced congressional calls for an investigation of the nation's schools.

High school seniors were also doing poorly. In 1943 a national sample averaged only around 34 percent correct on the kind of popular knowledge found in U.S. history textbooks.[122] The geography problem also is not of recent vintage. Although a Gallup then-and-now study found adults, age eighteen and older, knew more in the 1940s than they did in the 1980s, it also showed that performance was weak then.[123] Respondents could identify only half of the European countries—and that was just after World War II.

Surveys by national polling organizations in the 1950s and 1960s suggest that general knowledge has been weak for decades. In the late 1950s, for example, high school graduates, ages twenty-five to thirty-six, averaged only 34 to 65 percent correct on items dealing with domestic public figures and events, foreign figures, history, humanities, geography, and science.[124] Many surprising gaps existed. In domestic politics, only about a third knew their U.S. representative; less than half knew which party held a congressional majority. In foreign affairs, only about a third knew who Adenauer was and only about half knew Nehru. In literature and art, only 8 percent knew that Rubens was a painter, one out of five who composed the *Messiah,* and 37 percent who wrote *A Midsummer Night's Dream.* In geography, only about half knew that Montana bordered Canada or that Mt. Everest was the highest mountain in the world. Unexpectedly, only 6 percent knew which planet is nearest the Sun, 13 percent the major language of Brazil, and 42 percent how many feet are in a mile.

Several recent national studies have shown that civics knowledge in the 1980s was at the same modest level it had been going back to the 1940s.[125] In spite of increases in educational attainment and expanded media, the public still has trouble with basic political and economic concepts; U.S. government structures; and the people, countries, and U.S. policies involved in major events and issues.

The evidence suggests a persistent problem in academic achievement; it does not mean that the achievement trendlines have been flat for fifty years. The data show definite fluctuations, with some indicators going up in different periods and others going down, particularly in the 1970s. Even before the 1970s declines, however, student achievement and general knowledge were not that strong. This reinforces the notion that persistent low achievement rather than a decline in achievement should be of major concern.

Technological Progress and Mass Knowledge

Without examination, some revisionists have rejected the historical evidence of low achievement out of hand, arguing that it is incompatible with U.S. military and scientific accomplishments—victory in World War II, space exploration, advances in medicine, and computer inventions. They write:

> We find it ludicrous that anyone should claim that "academic and general knowledge have been at low levels for decades" in this country. If this were actually true, how on earth did our nation ever manage to win World War II, send astronauts to the moon, create a plethora of new

pharmaceuticals, and invent the transistor and virtually all the computer technology now used world wide?[126]

Such accomplishments, however, did not depend upon the mass of U.S. students and adults being well informed and knowledgeable. Instead, they exemplify the prowess of the U.S. military-industrial complex, the skills of a narrow technical elite, and the inventiveness of an individual or group of individuals. It took a Jonas Salk to develop the polio vaccine, for example. The transistor was invented by John Bardeen, Walter Brattain, and William Shockley (the same Shockley who later espoused racially charged ideas about intelligence being genetically determined). The microcomputer revolution can be largely credited to three school dropouts—Steve Jobs and Steve Wozniak, who developed the Apple II computer, and Bill Gates, who founded Microsoft.

U.S. citizens' lack of knowledge of civics, history, geography, and literature had little bearing on the outcome of World War II or getting a man to the moon. Several major pharmaceuticals were developed by researchers from other countries or by those who were educated well before World War II. Penicillin, for example, was developed by Alexander Fleming, a Scottish biologist. Streptomycin was discovered by Selman Waksman, who was born in Russia in 1888. The oral form of the polio vaccine was developed by the Polish American Edward Sabin, born in 1906.

Conclusion

Persistently poor academic achievement for more than fifty years is disturbing news. It raises troubling questions about long-standing institutional arrangements for education and social commitments to learning. It calls into question the historical, bureaucratic school structures and teaching practices that have dominated education for much of the twentieth century.[127]

The enduring large gap between minority and white students' achievement is alarming and, so, the revisionists' call for a renewed focus on the poor and inner-city schools should be heeded. School financing systems must be overhauled and quality education should be provided for low-income rural and urban students. A danger arises, however, that the revisionists' message will be misconstrued as a call to abandon general reform. The schools are not collapsing, but the deep, long-standing academic problems that plague U.S. schools need to be addressed.

Reform is needed for many reasons—educational, political, and humanistic. It need not be predicated on the supposed economic consequences of low achievement levels.[128] A complex, democratic society needs a well-read and knowledgeable citizenry, but this is far from being realized. As M. Schudson points out, the late twentieth century U.S. democracy, with its ballot propositions, weak political parties, nonpartisan elections, and widely available political information, requires a better-skilled and more informed citizen than did nineteenth century politics.[129]

Students also need to be well informed about the key events and people, social struggles, and literary works that have shaped this multicultural society. In a society torn by debates over immigration and affirmative action, alarms should go off about how little students know of world cultures and how poorly informed they are about the United States' tortured racial history. NAEP testing in the late 1980s showed that the vast majority of high school students did not know that Jim Crow laws segregated blacks, what the Three-Fifths Compromise was, or what the Emancipation Proclamation did. Substantial percentages did not know what *Plessy v. Ferguson* or *Brown v. Board of Education* were about. They lacked basic information pertaining to the Civil War, one of the nation's epochal events and a key force in shaping race relations. Sizable majorities were unfamiliar with the Missouri Compromise, nullification, the *Dred Scott* decision, and the dates of the Civil War and Abraham Lincoln's presidential term. Such ignorance is not an artifact of obscure psychometric scaling procedures. Knowledge does matter.

The achievement data represent only part of the picture. For two decades, high school profiles have revealed that students are often disengaged, teachers' work factorylike, and intellectual life poor. Students seldom read on their own and report little intellectual activity outside of schoolwork.[130] These conditions have spawned restructuring movements such as the Coalition of Essential Schools and led to calls for national standards and reform reports in English, science, math, and history.

Ignoring such evidence or arguing that it is the product of a right-wing misinformation campaign stands in the way of needed reform. The educational crisis is not manufactured; it is real. Such persistent failure strengthens the case for a fundamental restructuring of schools. There is no simple fix, however. A return cannot be made to an illusory golden age of education. Teaching methods must be revolutionized, intellectually challenging materials and standards developed, and personal support for students provided. The historical practice of sorting students into tracked programs and emphasizing life-adjustment education should give way to a common focus on academic and intellectual activities. Families and students need to reorder their priorities. Reading books should take precedence over watching TV, doing schoolwork over aimless Internet surfing.

Reforming schools is important, but the problems originate deep within the society. Educational reform efforts must be part of a broader social and political agenda, one that addresses social inequality, inadequate health care and housing, economic insecurity, and a commercial culture that devalues education and learning. In this, I share much common ground with the revisionists. Schools are not solely responsible for the educational system's problems, nor can they be held solely responsible for fixing them. To succeed educationally, deeply rooted social, economic, and cultural problems must be solved.

Comment by Ina V. S. Mullis

As Lawrence C. Stedman contends, the poor quality of achievement for many students is a matter of serious concern.

Some encouraging news about eighth grade student performance in mathematics has been forthcoming from both the Third International Mathematics and Science Study (TIMSS) and the National Assessment of Educational Progress (NAEP). Stedman makes the important point that, in measuring long-term trends, educators and scholars are essentially prisoners of past ideas and technologies. To address this issue,

NAEP initiated new assessments in the 1990s in a number of subject areas, including mathematics. These assessments incorporate more recent measurement methods and are based on frameworks generally consistent with the work being done in developing standards in various subject areas.

Somewhat different from the general pattern of stability in educational achievement shown by NAEP's long-term trends, results from the more newly developed national assessments in mathematics show relatively steady improvements in achievement between 1990 and 1996 at grades four, eight, and twelve. This is good news.

One of the United States' national goals is to be "first in the world in mathematics and science achievement by the year 2000," as President George Bush and fifty governors declared in 1989. The TIMSS results for fourth grade students show promise toward reaching this goal. In science, U.S. fourth graders were outperformed by students in only one country—Korea. In mathematics, fourth graders achieved above the international average but were outperformed by students in seven countries—Singapore, Korea, Japan, Hong Kong, the Netherlands, the Czech Republic, and Austria.

In interpreting stability, however, Stedman put the NAEP gains in mathematics achievement into context by calculating the rate of improvement. According to his calculations, it will be the year 2132 before half the twelfth graders reach the proficient level on the NAEP mathematics scale.

The TIMSS mathematics data for seventh and eighth graders provide another way of putting the performance of U.S. students into context. Compared with the other countries participating in TIMSS, the relative performance of eighth graders in the United States was well below that of U.S. fourth graders. Even though the average achievement of U.S. eighth graders resembled that of other major industrialized nations such as Canada, England, and Germany, by and large, the international performance standards in middle school mathematics and science are being set by Singapore, Japan, and Korea (see exhibit 1).

The TIMSS mathematics results provide several perspectives from which to view the overall performance of U.S. eighth graders.

—The United States is not among the top-performing countries. Besides top-performing Singapore, Korea, and Japan, Hong Kong also performed very well in mathematics at both grades, as did Belgium (Flemish) and the Czech Republic.

—Twenty countries had significantly higher average achievement than the United States at grade eight, thirteen countries had average achievement about the same as the United States, and only seven countries had mathematics achievement lower than the United States. At grade seven, seventeen countries had higher achievement, twelve countries similar achievement, and nine countries lower achievement.

—In contrast to the findings at grade four, U.S. students at both grades scored below the international average, which is the mean achievement at each grade of all the participating countries.

—Eighth graders in Singapore, Japan, and Korea outperformed those in the United States by more than one hundred points on the TIMSS mathematics scale. This difference is substantial, especially considering that the difference in performance between grades seven and eight was only twenty-four points in the United States, one of the smaller gains shown by the TIMSS countries between those grades.

Considerable speculation exists about why the United States seems to have lost its relative advantage in mathematics achievement between the fourth and eighth grades, especially because this pattern also occurred in science. One explanation centers on the nature of the U.S. curriculum. For example, the TIMSS results indicate that the U.S. mathematics curriculum is similar to that of other countries in the lower grades but is less advanced than that of the top-performing countries by the eighth grade. This is reinforced by the achievement results. When the concepts were more specialized, such as in measurement or geometry, U.S. eighth graders had particular difficulty. The example shown in exhibit 2 requires an understanding of important concepts in perimeter and area and of the properties of rectangles and triangles. Forty-four percent of the eighth graders in the United States compared with three-fourths or more of the students in Singapore, Korea, and Japan answered this question correctly.

The curricular effects could also be seen in performance on the algebra items. U.S. students had difficulty with traditional algebra items such as those that required simplifying, evaluating, and writing expressions. For example, in contrast to 86 percent of the students in Singapore, only about half the U.S. students were successful in identifying the correct expression to represent a simple problem situation (see exhibit 3).

U.S. students, however, also had particular difficulty with items requiring basic mathematical reasoning. For example, a group of items involving proportionality were analyzed separately, and all were difficult for U.S. eighth graders. Only 24 percent of the eighth graders in the United States correctly answered a problem involving basic proportional reasoning, compared with 83 percent of the students in Singapore (see exhibit 4).

Stedman notes that looking at the results of individual test questions allows educators and the public to evaluate student knowledge directly. Discussing the persistent problems in student achievement, he observes that NAEP has found that many students lack critical reading skills.

Similar to the procedure used for the mathematics assessments in 1992, NAEP initiated new reading assessments, which represented an innovative effort regarding the content assessed and the types of questions asked. The NAEP *Reading Framework* encompassed a forward-looking view of reading as a dynamic, interactive process that involves reading a variety of different kinds of materials for different purposes. The assessment was based on naturally occurring reading materials that provided a longer, more realistic reading experience than previous reading assessments, and the questions primarily required students to construct their own written responses.

As Stedman explained, compared with 1992, NAEP's *1994 Reading Report Card* found no significant changes in average proficiency in the national population of fourth or eighth graders and significant declines at grade twelve for the nation and across a broad range of subgroups. As one of the authors of NAEP's *1992 Report Card* and one familiar with the 1992 results, I found these results disappointing because I had anticipated improvement in achievement. Students need to be able to make inferences from texts and draw conclusions such as those demonstrated by this NAEP task.

For example, eighth grade students were given a brief biography of Anne Frank that explained about her experiences and that her diary is read throughout the world. They were given a fictional short story written by Anne Frank about a young Christian girl in Nazi Germany who watched her Jewish friends being taken away. Students also were given a poem with a related theme by Edward Hill, entitled ''I Am

One.'' The spirit of the poem is that one cannot do everything, but everybody should try to do what they can. The task asked students to explain how the poem helps to understand Anne Frank's life.

To respond to the question beyond a cursory level, eighth graders needed to understand both the poem and the information about Anne Frank's life sufficiently to perceive and communicate connections between them. Responses were scored on a 4-point scale, from unsatisfactory to extended. Unsatisfactory responses exhibited little or no understanding of the poem or of Anne Frank's life (see exhibit 5). Partial responses provided some evidence indicating that the student understood the relationship between the poem and Anne Frank's life but did not include any explanation or examples (see exhibit 6). Essential responses explained the relationship between the poem and Anne Frank's life in terms of some straightforward aspects of the war, Anne's reactions to it, and her inability to stop it (see exhibit 7). Extended responses showed evidence of richer understandings by discussing the larger significance of Anne Frank's life, such as how she preserved history through her writing (see exhibit 8). These students understood that Anne's writing and her diary were how she did everything she possibly could.

This extended-response question was one of the most difficult in NAEP's 1992 assessment (see exhibit 9). Students were asked to demonstrate intertextual understanding and go beyond specific ideas and to consider more global interpretations. Still, 62 percent of the eighth graders provided unsatisfactory responses, indicating essentially only a literal understanding of the material. Only 11 percent provided essential or extensive responses.

Stedman noted that few students have performed well on NAEP's writing assessments, which is an understatement. The low level of performance was so distressing that, even more than usual, the assessment methods came under attack as the root of the problem. Thus, to complement its more traditional assessment approaches and provide some context for the writing assessment results, NAEP began to study classroom-based writing by conducting a pilot study in 1990 and a more ambitious data collection effort in 1992.

As part of the 1992 writing assessment, NAEP asked nationally representative subgroups of the fourth and eighth graders who participated in the standardized writing assessment to work with their teachers and submit three pieces of writing from their language arts or English classes that represented their best writing efforts. Students were asked to give preference to pieces developed using writing process strategies such as prewriting activities, consulting with others about the writing, and revising successive drafts—in other words, to all of the processes that can benefit writing but are difficult to implement in large-scale writing assessment. To parallel the NAEP writing framework, students also were asked to select pieces, if possible, that represented different kinds of writing. That is, they were asked to submit papers representative of the three types of writing covered in the NAEP *Writing Framework*—narrative, informative, persuasive. The majority of students each submitted at least three pieces of writing. More than ten thousand papers were evaluated in all.

Teachers were contacted and notified in advance that some of their students would be participating in the portfolio study. They were given a brief description of the study and a copy of the report on NAEP's 1990 pilot portfolio study so that they could see how their students' classroom-based writing would be analyzed and evaluated. More than three thousand students participated, representing a 90 percent response rate. In particular, 1,650 of the eighth graders who were asked to participate submitted portfolios. For 57 percent of the papers, students had spent more than fifty minutes; the median length at grade eight was 166 words.

The results for informative and persuasive writing were as follows:

—At grade eight, about half of the papers submitted (47 percent) were classified as informative writing.

—The papers were evaluated by trained readers according to a specially designed 6-point scale. In reading and evaluating the informative papers, the scoring guide development team focused on the presentation of information and ideas for the purpose of informing an audience. In general, differences between levels 1 through 4 focused on the degree to which the writer established relationships or coherence among pieces of information and the difference between levels 5 and 6 pertained to the degree to which the writers conveyed a sense of audience and purpose. To receive a 6 rating, the paper needed to demonstrate mastery of the conventions of written English (grammar, usage, mechanics) and employ a clear and effective organizational structure. There was a high degree of agreement in the ratings (adjacent agreement 91 to 98 percent, exact agreement 51 to 67 percent).

—Forty-three percent of the papers were judged to be of low quality—consisting of lists of information or attempted discussions (see exhibit 10). The majority of the informative portfolio papers—53 percent—presented a broad range of information and related this information in a coherent way in at least one section of the paper. Only 4 percent of the eighth grade informative papers were developed and organized discussions of a theme for specific purposes and audiences.

Nearly three-fourths (73 percent) of the informative papers, however, received a rating of 3 or lower. In an example of a 3 paper, taken from the NAEP report, the writer, an eighth grader, has an organizing principle—introducing himself or herself by describing things she or he likes and does not like (see exhibit 11). However, the information is not developed or elaborated upon.

Relatively little persuasive writing is going on in schools. At grade eight, only 9 percent of the portfolio submissions—or about four hundred papers—were classified as persuasive writing. (In addition to the informative papers, 28 percent were narrative, and 15 percent were classified as "other," including poems, letters, and skill sheets.)

—The scoring guide for evaluating the persuasive papers focused on stating an opinion or position, supporting one's opinion with reasons and explanation, and appropriately addressing one's audience.

—Similar to the results for the informative papers, nearly three-fourths of the papers received a rating of level 3 or lower (see exhibit 12). Described as an elaborated opinion, these types of papers contain opinion statements and attempts to develop the opinions with some type of further explanation.

For example, a paper, written by an eighth grader, states an opinion and gives reasons to support this opinion, but the reasons are only briefly elaborated (see exhibit 13).

I hope that these few examples together with the information about mathematics and reading achievement help provide concrete support for a number of the points Stedman made, namely, that students continue to struggle with basic material and that continuing efforts toward fundamental school reform are warranted.

Exhibit 1. Mathematics: National Averages Compared with the United States

National Averages Compared with the U.S.

Eighth Grade		Seventh Grade	
Country	Average Achievement	Country	Average Achievement
Singapore	643	Singapore	601
Korea	607	Korea	577
Japan	605	Japan	571
Hong Kong	588	Hong Kong	564
Belgium (Fl)	565	Belgium (Fl)	558
Czech Republic	564	Czech Republic	523
Slovak Republic	547	Netherlands	516
Switzerland	545	Bulgaria	514
Netherlands	541	Austria	509
Slovenia	541	Slovak Republic	508
Bulgaria	540	Belgium (Fr)	507
Austria	539	Switzerland	506
France	538	Hungary	502
Hungary	537	Russian Federation	501
Russian Federation	535	Ireland	500
Australia	530	Slovenia	498
Ireland	527	Australia	498
Canada	527	Thailand	495
Belgium (Fr)	526	Canada	494
Thailand	522	France	492
Israel	522	Germany	484
Sweden	519	Sweden	477
Germany	509	England	476
New Zealand	508	United States	476
England	506	New Zealand	472
Norway	503	Denmark	465
Denmark	502	Scotland	463
United States	500	Latvia (LSS)	462
Scotland	498	Norway	461
Latvia (LSS)	493	Iceland	459
Spain	487	Romania	454
Iceland	487	Spain	448
Greece	484	Cyprus	446
Romania	482	Greece	440
Lithuania	477	Lithuania	428
Cyprus	474	Portugal	423
Portugal	454	Iran, Islamic Rep.	401
Iran, Islamic Rep.	428	Colombia	369
Kuwait	392	South Africa	348
Colombia	385		
South Africa	354		
International Average	513	International Average	484

Significantly Higher ☐

Significantly Lower ☐

IEA
TIMSS

Source: Beaton, et al., Mathematics in the Middle School Years, TIMSS, 1996

Source: Beaton and others, *Mathematics Achievement in the Middle School Years: IEA's Third International Mathematics and Science Study (TIMSS)* (Boston College, TIMSS International Study Center, 1996).

Exhibit 2. TIMSS Mathematics, Item 1

Mathematics
Eighth Grade

IEA
TIMSS

6

2

2

2

4

How many triangles of the shape and size of the shaded triangle can the trapezoid above be divided into?

A. Three

B. Four

C. Five

D. Six

Item 1

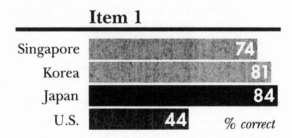

Singapore	74
Korea	81
Japan	84
U.S.	44

% correct

Source: Department of Education, Office of Educational Research and Improvement, *Achieving Excellence: TIMSS as a Starting Point to Examine Student Achievement* (forthcoming).

Exhibit 3. TIMSS Mathematics, Item 2

Mathematics
Eighth Grade

2

Juan has 5 fewer hats than Maria, and Clarissa has 3 times as many hats as Juan. If Maria has n hats, which of these represents the number of hats that Clarissa has?

A. $5 - 3n$

B. $3n$

C. $n - 5$

D. $3n - 5$

E. $3(n - 5)$

Item 2

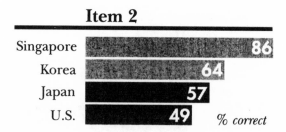

Singapore 86
Korea 64
Japan 57
U.S. 49
% correct

Source: A. Beaton and others, *Mathematics Achievement in the Middle School Years: IEA's Third International Mathematics and Science Study (TIMSS)* (Boston College, TIMSS International Study Center, 1966).

Exhibit 4. TIMSS Mathematics, Item 3

Mathematics
Eighth Grade

> Peter bought 70 items and Sue bought 90 items. Each item cost the same and the items cost $800 altogether.
> How much did Sue pay?
>
>
> Answer: Sue paid _____ $450 _____

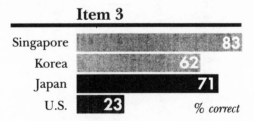

Item 3

	% correct
Singapore	83
Korea	62
Japan	71
U.S.	23

Source: A. Beaton and others, *Mathematics Achievement in the Middle School Years: IEA's Third International Mathematics and Science Study (TIMSS)* (Boston College, TIMSS International Study Center, 1966).

Exhibit 5. NAEP Reading, Grade 8, 1992: Unsatisfactory Response

How the poem "I Am One" helps to understand Anne Frank's Life.

Example: Unsatisfactory response

It talks about how lonely she was when she was little and neary with anyone at all and like to seem to do things on her own.

Source: J. Langer and others, *Reading Assessment Redesigned: Authentic Texts and Innovative Instruments in NAEP's 1992 Survey*, Report No. 23–FR–07 (Washington: National Center for Education Statistics, 1995).

Exhibit 6. NAEP Reading, Grade 8, 1992: Partial

How the poem "I Am One" helps to understand Anne Frank's Life.

Example: Partial

It shows how Anne frank feels that she is only one out of everyone else and though she can't do much she can do something

Source: J. Langer and others, *Reading Assessment Redesigned: Authentic Texts and Innovative Instruments in NAEP's 1992 Survey*. Report No. 23–FR–07 (Washington: National Center for Education Statistics, 1995).

Exhibit 7. NAEP Reading, Grade 8, 1992: Essential

How the poem "I Am One" helps to understand Anne Frank's Life.

Example: Essential

Even though Anne Frank's was one person she still could have an impact on everyone else. Anne cannot not do anything by herself but she can at least do something. Though trying to make a difference will be hard Anne refuses to give up and will try to stop the injustice the Jews have to suffer.

Source: J. Langer and others. *Reading Assessment Redesigned: Authentic Texts and Innovative Instruments in NAEP's 1992 Survey*. Report No. 23–FR–07 (Washington: National Center for Education Statistics, 1995).

Exhibit 8. NAEP Reading, Grade 8, 1992: Top-Rated Response

How the poem "I Am One" helps to understand Anne Frank's Life.

Example: Top-rated response

Anne Frank was there during the time of the Jews being taken by the Nazis. She tell about all of this in her diary so that many generations to come could not it and remember all the horrible things that happened In the poem it says that even though you cannot do everything you should still do everything you possibly can. Anne did this by her diary. She did all she could do and nothing less.

Source: J. Langer and others. *Reading Assessment Redesigned: Authentic Texts and Innovative Instruments in NAEP's 1992 Survey.* Report No. 23-FR-07 (Washington: National Center for Education Statistics, 1995).

Exhibit 9. NAEP Reading, Grade 8, 1992: Percentages

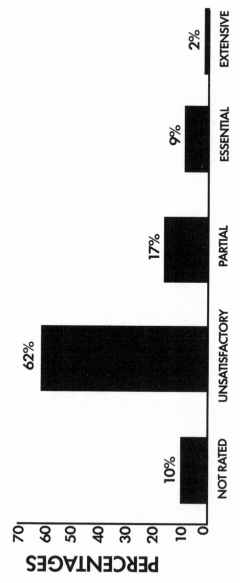

How the poem "I Am One" helps to understand Anne Frank's Life.

Source: J. Langer and others, *Reading Assessment Redesigned: Authentic Texts and Innovative Instruments in NAEP's 1992 Survey*, Report No. 23-FR-07 (Washington: National Center for Education Statistics, 1995).

Exhibit 10. NAEP's 1992 Writing Portfolio Study, Results for Informative Papers

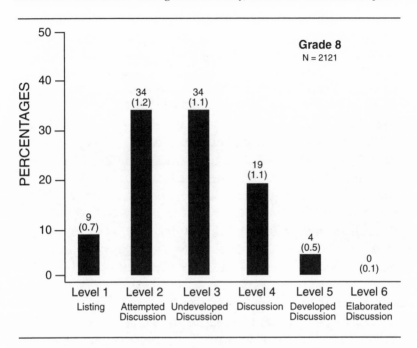

Source: C. Gentile and others, *Windows into the Classroom: NAEP's 1992 Writing Portfolio Study* (Washington: National Center for Education Statistics, 1995).

Note: The standard errors of the estimated percentages appear in parentheses. It can be said with 95 percent confidence for each population of interest that the value for the whole population is within plus or minus two standard errors of the estimate for the sample. In comparing two estimates, one must use the standard error of the difference. Percentages may not total 100 due to rounding error.

Exhibit 11. NAEP's 1992 Writing Portfolio Study, Informative, Undeveloped Discussion, Level 3 Example

An Introduction to Me

I have many favorites. I like to play and watch all kinds of sports. I've played baseball ever since I was seven. I also love to watch it on TV. This year I started football this year. It is my favorite sport to play. I play defensive end on defence and guard on offence. I've also played basketball for three; the position I played was guard + forward. My favorite subjects in school are math and gym because they are the classes I get good grades in. I liked two movies that I saw this summer. One of them is Terminator 2, and the other is Boyz in the Hood.

Some of the music I don't like are classical, opera, and gospil. The sport I really don't like is sorcor is because I've never played it and I probably never will, but I like to watch it on TV or to one of my friends games. At school, I don't like science very well so far or health. And I hate to eat brussel sprouts and spinach. And this paragraph is about all my favorite things, and all the things I hate.

Source: C. Gentile and others, *Windows into the Classroom: NAEP's 1992 Writing Portfolio Study* (Washington: National Center for Education Statistics, 1995).

Exhibit 12. NAEP's 1992 Writing Portfolio Study, Results for Persuasive Papers

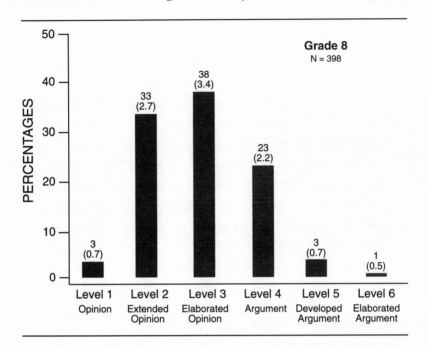

Source: C. Gentile and others, *Windows into the Classroom: NAEP's 1992 Writing Portfolio Study* (Washington: National Center for Education Statistics, 1995).

Note: The standard errors of the estimated percentages appear in parentheses. It can be said with 95 percent confidence for each population of interest that the value for the whole population is within plus or minus two standard errors of the estimate for the sample. In comparing two estimates, one must use the standard error of the difference. Percentages may not total 100 due to rounding.

Exhibit 13. NAEP's 1992 Writing Portfolio Study, Persuasive—Elaborated Opinion, Level 3 Example

NO Homework Please!

It is not a good idea to assign homework every night, especially on the week-ends, because a kid has to have some time to rest his mind from all the homework and studying he or she has done during the week. The week-ends allow a kid to unwind and play and be ready to start another week of school on Monday. My mother would get a rest also because she usually helps me with my homework during the week.

Now that we are getting homework over the week-end, what is next? Will we have to do homework over vacation weeks off from school and over summer vacation? I hope not!

Source: C. Gentile and others, *Windows into the Classroom: NAEP's 1992 Writing Portfolio Study* (Washington: National Center for Education Statistics, 1995).

Comment by Michael Timpane

Lawrence C. Stedman's paper is a model of its kind: a thorough, fair, and accurate review, reducing mountains of diverse, often conflicting, data to an accessible report on the levels, trends, and significance of educational achievement in U.S. schools. It is, in this sense, a sterling example of an important contemporary development in educational policymaking—the eruption of an unprecedentedly sophisticated and empirical debate about these matters. The quality of the discourse should be savored, even at a time when there is a great deal of ideological posturing and interpretive disagreement, and certainly not many settled questions.

This debate has already had an important effect upon policymakers across the range of political persuasions. To put it mildly, no one gets away with many unsubstantiated claims any more. The best way to make an unsubstantiated claim and get away with it used to be to adduce and produce plausible empirical information about it, thereby defeating rivals who had no empirical information whatsoever. Happily, that stage is long past.

Still, care must be taken not to wallow in the debate, high-minded though it may be. To use a metaphor from boxing, there may be a little arm-weariness setting in. Policymakers must begin to seek out areas of agreement and opportunities for common action; otherwise, they may end up in an extended clinch, staggerings around the ring with no effect on the outcome of the struggle. A subtext of many of the conference papers is that they are beginning to discover such common ground.

I wish I could slip away from Stedman's one-word summation—"stagnation"—but I cannot. As I read his paper, I searched for an important counterexample where the situation was better than portrayed, then I would find he had dealt with it. For example, I thought more could be made of his observing the resilience of U.S. schools, their being able to maintain level performance in the face of increasingly daunting problems. However, he then pointed out that during the time that this resilience had taken place the educational level of the adult population, and of the parents of test takers, had risen by two grades. And so it went.

"Stagnation" may be the sort of alarming concept that must be borne in mind, with all of its connotations of lack of change over time, inert components, and resistance to cleanup. How else can the picture he draws so well be characterized? What emerges is unacceptably slow and meager progress despite massive investments and innovations; the end of progress toward more equal performance; and the stunning lack of advanced knowledge or skills in many areas (such as critical reading skills, math beyond arithmetic, or historical and geographic facts). Some comfort can be found in his accompanying lessons concerning the limited significance of much of the achievement evidence; the absence of either a golden age or a current decline in achievement; and the extent to which school performance must take account of broader societal problems and be fostered in conjunction with other realms of social policy and practice. But the comfort may be cold—because the other side of these conclusions is the great difficulty of producing widespread and persistent achievement gains, with the consequent temptation to excuse the schools for their lack of progress.

I agree with Stedman about the serious significance of inequality of outcomes, the meagerness of the progress made, and the end of that meager progress over the past decade. I would hope for further analysis, examining such matters as the relationship of the nation's large social class–based variability in schools to the level of average achievement both among states and localities and among the United States and other nations. Is it too obvious to suggest some ways—such as crusading for improved urban schools—to both reduce the variance and raise the average?

In a different view, the time has come to explore the puzzles of prosperity. *A Nation at Risk,* issued in 1983, reflected a sense that the United States was fading by standards of international economic performance and that the historic annual rate of worker-productivity growth that had existed throughout the past half-century had mysteriously disappeared. The schools took it on the chin for these developments. My plea is for a symmetrical world. The U.S. economy today is the envy of the world. The combined unemployment and inflation index is extremely low by historical or comparative standards. Schools must either escape the blame for what happened in the 1980s or begin getting credit for what has happened in the 1990s.

Similarly, some explanation is needed for the mysterious process by which, notwithstanding schools' unsatisfying performance and progress, U.S. colleges and universities remain the envy of the world. Even with major problems of persistence and performance, more than half of U.S. high school graduates go to college and more than half of those graduate, a staggering accomplishment.

This wasteful and inefficient process, building on supposedly flawed schools, produces a work force that is outstripping most of the world, notwithstanding corporate education and training programs that are hit-or-miss, by any international standard. How does this transformation occur? Does it occur in spite of or because of what happens in schools?

The most fundamental question is: Can the public schools improve and change to the extent needed? If the schools as currently constituted cannot improve much, then policymakers must search for alternatives to them, either in new institutions, in different governance and finance, or in technology. But, if the knowledge and experience exist that can help the public schools perform better and more effectively, then a very different route will be traveled, one of investment in school improvement and professional development.

How much are Americans willing to do to improve education? The public appetite for many of the measures under discussion here is by no means demonstrated. One of the principal benefits of the standards movement is that it has started to change the public's expectations for the better and to make the public, the education profession, and the political world face up to these issues: How much change is needed? And how much are people willing to pay for?

The most significant deliberation on these issues must occur within the education profession. The profession is beginning to change its perspective, but it is not yet ready to comprehend the kinds of changes that might be necessary to improve the schools. In the end, though, the delicate political balance of any policy or program will be how to maintain the willing and eager participation of the almost three million American schoolteachers.

Notes

1. See, for example, Chester E. Finn, *We Must Take Charge* (Free Press, 1991); Seymour W. Itzkoff, *The Decline of Intelligence in America: A Strategy for National Renewal* (Westport, Conn.: Praeger, 1994); Christopher Jencks, "Declining Test Scores: An Assessment of Six Alternative Explanations," *Sociological Spectrum*, vol. 1, no. 1 (1980), pp. 1–15; Diane Ravitch, *National Standards in American Education: A Citizen's Guide* (Brookings, 1995); Albert Shanker, "Making Standards Count," *American Educator*, vol. 18, no. 3 (1994), pp. 14, 16–19; Charles Sykes, *Dumbing Down Our Kids* (St. Martin's Press, 1995); and P. Welsh, "It Takes Two to Tango," *American Educator*, vol. 16, no. 1 (1992), pp. 18–23, 46.

2. William J. Bennett, *To Reclaim a Legacy* (National Endowment for the Humanities, 1984); Lynne V. Cheney, *American Memory: A Report on the Humanities in the Nation's Public Schools* (Government Printing Office, n.d.); and Eric D. Hirsch, Jr., *Cultural Literacy: What Every American Needs to Know* (Boston: Houghton Mifflin, 1987).

3. Itzkoff, *The Decline of Intelligence in America*; Sykes, *Dumbing Down Our Kids*; and Ravitch, *National Standards in American Education*. Charles Murray and Richard J. Herrnstein offer a less well known and more complex formulation that the average student experienced a decline and complete recovery but that academic track students have yet to recover from a large decline on verbal measures. Charles Murray and Richard J. Herrnstein, "What's Really Behind the SAT-Score Decline?," *Public Interest* (Winter 1992), pp. 32–56.

4. Gerald W. Bracey, "Why Can't They Be Like We Were?," *Phi Delta Kappan*, vol. 73, no. 2 (1991), pp. 105–17; Gerald W. Bracey, "U.S. Students: Better than Ever," *Washington Post*, December 22, 1995, p. A19; David C. Berliner and Bruce J. Biddle, *The Manufactured Crisis: Myths, Fraud, and the Attack on America's Public Schools* (Addison-Wesley, 1995); and D. Tanner, "A Nation Truly at Risk," *Phi Delta Kappan*, vol. 75, no. 4 (1993), pp. 288–97.

5. C. Carson, R. Huelskamp, and R. Woodall, "Perspectives on Education in America," *Journal of Educational Research*, vol. 86 (1993), pp. 259–310. For an appraisal of this report, see Lawrence C. Stedman, "The Sandia Report and U.S. Achievement," *Journal of Educational Research*, vol. 87 (1994), pp. 133–46; and Lawrence C. Stedman, "Respecting the Evidence: The Achievement Crisis Remains Real," *Education Policy Analysis Archives*, vol. 4, no. 7 (1996), available via the World Wide Web at http://olam.ed.asu.edu/epaa/.

6. National Commission on Excellence in Education, *A Nation at Risk: The Imperative for Educational Reform* (Government Printing Office, 1983).

7. Sykes, *Dumbing Down Our Kids*.

8. Allan D. Bloom, *The Closing of the American Mind* (Simon and Schuster, 1987); Frank E. Armbruster, *Our Children's Crippled Future: How American Education Has Failed* (New York: Quadrangle Books, 1977); and Paul Copperman, *The Literacy Hoax: The Decline of Reading, Writing, and Learning in the Public Schools and What We Can Do About It* (William Morrow, 1978).

9. Gerald Bracey, "The Second Bracey Report on the Condition of Public Education," *Phi Delta Kappan*, vol. 74, no. 2 (1992), pp. 104–17, especially p. 107; and Bracey, "U.S. Students."

10. National Council of Teachers of English, *Standards for the English Language Arts* (Urbana, Ill., 1996), p. 5.

11. Berliner and Biddle, *The Manufactured Crisis.*

12. International achievement evidence is reviewed elsewhere in this volume, so I do not cover it in this review. A vigorous dispute has taken place over how well the United States has done internationally. Lawrence C. Stedman, "International Achievement Differences: An Assessment of a New Perspective," *Educational Researcher,* vol. 26, no. 3 (1997), pp. 4–15. School critics have portrayed U.S. performance as poor whereas the revisionists argue that this is an illusion created by sampling biases and curricular differences. The evidence supports a middle ground. U.S. performance has not been consistently poor—the youngest students often have done well, even in science, and reading achievement has been among the world's best. In contrast, U.S. math and high school science performances typically have been poor, while geography performance has been mixed. Contrary to the revisionists' claims, the assessments do not compare the broad mass of U.S. students with small elites in other countries. U.S. performance also has been poor even on U.S. curriculum material, suggesting that real deficiencies exist in teaching and learning.

13. Irwin S. Kirsch and others, *Adult Literacy in America* (Washington: National Center for Education Statistics, 1993); and Lawrence C. Stedman and Carl F. Kaestle, "Literacy and Reading Perfomance in the United States from 1880 to the Present," in Carl F. Kaestle and others, eds., *Literacy in the United States* (Yale University Press, 1991), pp. 75–128.

14. The National Assessment of Educational Progress (NAEP) scale is normed at 250 with a standard deviation of 50. The scale mean of 250 is derived from the performance of students at all three ages tested: nine, thirteen, and seventeen. Most students score from 150 to 350. NAEP results show few students scoring below 150. Although the 150–350 levels were set up in the mid-1980s, results from the earlier years (which had been expressed as percentage correct on different types of problems) were placed on the same scale to provide two decades of trend data.

15. Arthur N. Applebee and others, *The Writing Report Card, 1984–88: Findings from the Nation's Report Card* (Department of Education, Office of Educational Research and Improvement, 1990), p. 6; National Assessment of Educational Progress, *Writing Achievement, 1969–1979,* Report No. 10–W–01 (Denver, Colo.: Education Commission of the States, 1980); National Assessment of Educational Progress, *Writing Achievement, 1969–1979,* Report No. 10–W–35 (Denver, Colo.: Education Commission of the States, 1982); and National Center for Education Statistics, *The Condition of Education 1995* (Department of Education, 1995), p. 56. Writing trends are tenuous, however, because they were based on only a few tasks.

16. Bracey, "U.S. Students"; and National Council of Teachers of English, *Standards for the English Language Arts,* p. 5.

17. Jay R. Campbell and others, *NAEP 1994 Trends in Academic Progress* (Department of Education, 1996). For a critique of such "all-time" high claims, see Lawrence C. Stedman, "The New Mythology about the Status of U.S. Schools," *Educational Leadership,* vol. 52, no. 5 (1995), pp. 80–85.

18. National Center for Education Statistics, *The Condition of Education 1987* (Department of Education, 1987), pp. 14–15.

19. National Center for Education Statistics, *The Condition of Education 1995,* p. 234. The causes of this decline at the top are complex and undetermined. Some have interpreted it as a loss of excellence among the best U.S. students. Others have linked

it to changes in college entrance requirements. Selective liberal arts colleges began dropping the SAT requirement or permitting the substitution of the ACT during the late 1960s and 1970s. The proportion of score reports going to liberal arts colleges dropped between 1967 and 1974. Community colleges, specialized schools, and nonselective universities started adding the SAT during the period. See William B. Schrader, "Distribution of SAT Scores to Colleges as an Indicator of Changes in the SAT Candidate Population," in Advisory Panel on the Scholastic Aptitude Test Score Decline, *On Further Examination,* appendix (New York: College Entrance Examination Board, 1977). Hunter M. Breland mentions the additional possibility of an attitudinal shift by test takers as college admissions became less competitive. See Hunter M. Breland, "The SAT Score Decline: A Summary of Related Research," in Advisory Panel on the Scholastic Aptitude Test Score Decline, *On Further Examination,* appendix (New York: College Entrance Examination Board, 1977). Together these changes reduced the number and proportion of high-scorers. Other minor factors that may have contributed to lower scores at the top included fewer test repeaters and a small decline in the overall number of test takers in the early 1970s.

20. Ravitch, *National Standards*, pp. 64–65.

21. Leo A. Munday, *Declining Admissions Test Scores,* ACT Research Report No. 71 (Iowa City, Iowa: American College Testing Program, 1976), p. 9; and National Center for Education Statistics, *Digest of Education Statistics 1996* (Department of Education, 1996). In the 1990s, top scorers on the ACT were redefined as those scoring 27 or above.

22. Campbell and others, *NAEP 1994 Trends in Academic Progress.* The proportions at the 350 level in reading, math, and science dropped 1 to 2 percentage points in the 1970s and have risen 1 to 3 points since. The proportions at the top in the late 1990s are equal to or higher than those of the 1970s. Since the mid-1980s, the proportions reaching the next highest level (300) have been stable in reading and rising in math and science.

23. Clyde M. Reese and others, *NAEP 1996 Mathematics Report Card for the Nation and the States* (Department of Education, 1997), p. 47.

24. National Center for Education Statistics, *The Condition of Education 1995,* pp. 80–81. Some gradual improvement has occurred in math on the NAEP trend assessments since the late 1980s at ages nine and thirteen. See Campbell and others, *NAEP 1994 Trends in Academic Progress.* The grade-level assessments show that fourth, eighth, and twelfth grade students improved their math scores by 9 to 11 scale points between 1990 and 1996. See Reese and others, *NAEP 1996 Mathematics Report Card for the Nation and the States,* p. 26.

25. Bracey, "Why Can't They Be Like We Were?" p. 108.

26. Carson, Huelskamp, and Woodall, "Perspectives on Education in America," p. 272.

27. Itzkoff, *The Decline of Intelligence in America*; and Sykes, *Dumbing Down Our Kids.*

28. The revisionists' own evidence also suggests that the demographic impact was not total. G. Bracey found that contemporary students who had a background similar to the 1941 test takers—white students with a college-educated parent—still only scored around 454 on the verbal section. They scored comparably on the math, however. Bracey, "Why Can't They Be Like We Were?"

29. College Board, *College-Bound Seniors National Report: 1994 Profile of SAT and Achievement Test Takers* (New York, 1994), p. 6; National Center for Education

Statistics, *The Condition of Education 1995*, p. 234; National Center for Education Statistics, *The Condition of Education 1992*, p. 225; and Advisory Panel on the Scholastic Aptitude Test Score Decline, *On Further Examination*, p. 15.

30. Murray and Herrnstein, "What's Really Behind the SAT-Score Decline?" Murray and Herrnstein argued that the white students' composition did not change and thus most of the decline was real. But they presented income data only on the bottom 10 percent, parental education data for the 1980s and not the period of the decline, and no data on academic ability such as changes in class rank, area of study, or type of institution being applied to, all factors that played a role in the decline.

31. Even in the 1970s, changing composition accounted for a substantial portion of test score decline. A greater proportion of students from characteristically lower-scoring groups took the college entrance tests, including women (who score lower on average and whose verbal decline was greater), those intending to pursue "career" majors as opposed to "arts and sciences" majors (verbal scores declined only slightly for these groups; it was the mix that changed), minority students, those of lower socioeconomic background, and students going to two-year community colleges and four-year public universities as opposed to highly selective liberal arts colleges.

32. Advisory Panel on the Scholastic Aptitude Test Score Decline, *On Further Examination*. See also Daniel M. Koretz, *Educational Achievement: Explanations and Implications of Recent Trends* (Congressional Budget Office, 1987), pp. 19, 31, 33. Koretz concludes that self-selection "contributed appreciably" to the overall decline on college admission tests but suggests that the demographic impact on the SAT was limited in the 1970s. He bases this on a decline in proportion of graduates taking the SAT but does not consider changes in the social composition of those test takers. His data also show that the proportion taking the SAT rose steadily from the mid-1970s on, which likely contributed to a continued decline in that decade and, as he notes, likely impeded progress on the SAT in the 1980s.

33. Lawrence C. Stedman and Carl F. Kaestle, "The Great Test Score Decline: A Closer Look," in Kaestle and others, eds., *Literacy in the United States* (Yale University Press, 1991), p. 132. On average, first- or second-born children outperform later-born children, so the trend toward larger families may have contributed to a lowering of SAT scores. In a background report for the Advisory Panel, Hunter M. Breland estimated that changes in birth order accounted for about 16 percent of the verbal SAT decline between 1964 and 1976. Breland, "The SAT Score Decline." A study of the period from 1971 to 1977 produced a 4 to 9.4 percent estimate, although the impact may have been higher. R. Zajonc and J. Bargh, "Birth Order, Family Size, and Decline of SAT Scores," *American Psychologist*, vol. 35 (1980), pp. 662–68.

34. Raleigh Morgan, *Cohort Differences Associated with Trends in SAT Score Averages*, ERIC Document Reproduction No. ED 336 409 (New York: College Entrance Examination Board, 1991). The demographic effects might have been even greater, but the study lacked data on socioeconomic status.

35. J. McMillan and S. Schumacher, *Research in Education* (New York: Longman, 1997), p. 283.

36. Carson, Huelskamp, and Woodall, "Perspectives on Education in America," p. 268.

37. Berliner and Biddle, *The Manufactured Crisis*, pp. 20–21; Bracey, "Why Can't They Be Like We Were?" pp. 108–09; and Richard M. Jaeger, "World Class Standards, Choice, and Privatization: Weak Measurement Serving Presumptive Policy," *Phi Delta Kappan*, vol. 74, no. 2 (1992), pp. 118–28, especially p. 120.

38. Stedman, "The Sandia Report and U.S. Achievement."

39. Berliner and Biddle, *The Manufactured Crisis,* pp. 16–17; Roger Farr and Leo Fay, "Reading Trend Data in the United States: A Mandate for Caveats and Caution," in Gilbert R. Austin and Herbert Garber, eds., *The Rise and Fall of National Test Scores* (New York: Academic Press, 1982), pp. 83–141; Jaeger, "World Class Standards, Choice, and Privatization," p. 120; and Carson, Huelskamp, and Woodall, "Perspectives on Education in America," p. 267.

40. Advisory Panel on the Scholastic Aptitude Test Score Decline, *On Further Examination,* p. 5 (emphasis in original).

41. Berliner and Biddle, *The Manufactured Crisis,* p. 16; and Farr and Fay, "Reading Trend Data in the United States," p. 122.

42. Most of the SAT decline occurred during a tumultuous period in U.S. history—the Vietnam War, assassinations, student protests, and Watergate. Labeling it a "Decade of Distraction," the Advisory Panel felt that it had profoundly affected student performance. Nearly half the decline occurred in a three-year period between 1972 and 1975. The Advisory Panel reached a strong conclusion:

It is hard to understand the suddenness and concentration of these changes—except for the realization that the students entering college during that period had gone through five or six years of national disillusionment, especially for young people, virtually unparalleled in American history.

It was a time of extraordinary distraction, when it would have been hard for students to put the best that was in them into getting high marks on a college entrance examination. This probably made quite a difference.

Quoted matter in Advisory Panel on the Scholastic Aptitude Test Score Decline, *On Further Examination,* pp. 37–38.

Although the evidence was limited, Daniel Koretz felt that the decline was a period rather than a cohort effect, which reinforces the Advisory Panel's conclusion about political upheavals. Daniel Koretz, *Trends in Educational Achievement* (Congressional Budget Office, 1986), p. 33. One problem with the Advisory Panel's explanation, however, is that scores did not recover greatly once the political disruptions ceased. Nevertheless, the disruptions could have had a longer-lasting impact, and eventually the demographic changes in SAT test takers became solidified and kept scores down. Few other explanations can account for the concentration of much of the decline in a few short years. Although concerned about school standards, the Advisory Panel strongly rejected educational uniformity and the elimination of electives and suggested improving the educational value of TV and new media instead of limiting their use. Advisory Panel on the Scholastic Aptitude Test Score Decline, *On Further Examination,* pp. 46–47.

43. D. Hayes, L. Wolfer, and M. Wolfe, "Schoolbook Simplification and Its Relation to the Decline in SAT-Verbal Scores," *American Educational Research Journal,* vol. 33, no. 2 (1996), pp. 489–508; Copperman, *The Literacy Hoax*; W. Turnbull, *Change in SAT Scores: What Can They Teach Us?* (Princeton, N.J.: Educational Testing Service, 1985); and D. Singal, "The Other Crisis in American Education," *Atlantic Monthly* (November 1991), pp. 59–74.

44. Christopher Jencks, "What's Behind the Drop in Test Scores?" *Working Papers for a New Society* (July/August 1978), pp. 29–41.

45. G. Echternacht, "A Comparative Study of Secondary Schools with Different Score Patterns," in Advisory Panel on the Scholastic Aptitude Test Score Decline, *On*

Further Examination, appendix (New York: College Entrance Examination Board, 1977).

46. The Echternacht study was limited, however, in that it was based on principal reports and not researchers' observations of the high schools. The Jackson study was limited to a small set of high schools, sixteen traditional and twelve experimental. R. Jackson, "Comparison of SAT Score Trends in Selected Schools Judged to Have Traditional or Experimental Orientations," in Advisory Panel on the Scholastic Aptitude Test Score Decline, *On Further Examination,* appendix (New York: College Entrance Examination Board, 1977).

47. Advisory Panel on the Scholastic Aptitude Test Score Decline, *On Further Examination,* p. 5; and Turnbull, *Changes in SAT Scores,* p. 1.

48. Cheney, *American Memory*; and Jencks, "What's Behind the Drop in Test Scores?" Cheney (p. 8) described the SAT as follows: "Looming over our educational landscape is an examination that, in its verbal component, carefully avoids assessing substantive knowledge gained from course work. Whether test-takers have studied the Civil War, learned about *Magna Carta*, or read *Macbeth* are matters to which the SAT is studiously indifferent." Jencks (pp. 31–32) noted that "many of the SAT questions measure relatively useless skills that schools do not try to teach" and argued that "a test of this kind is not a very suitable device for assessing how well schools are doing their job, since it measures a great many things they do not and should not teach."

49. This includes problems in two unidentified experimental sections. The composition of the SAT test has varied over time; the new version introduced in the 1990s made some modest changes—including some open-ended math questions and permitting calculators. Some SATs from the late 1980s and early 1990s had eighty-five verbal questions in two sections that counted—twenty-five antonyms, twenty analogies, fifteen sentence completions, and twenty-five reading comprehension questions. The two math sections that counted consisted of sixty questions—twenty quantitative comparisons and forty dealing with arithmetic, basic algebra, and geometry. The experimental sections had either forty or forty-five verbal questions and either twenty-five or thirty-five math problems. See College Entrance Examination Board, *10 SATs* (New York, 1988), pp. 12, 19; and A. Robinson and J. Katzman, *Cracking the SAT and PSAT: 1993 Edition* (Villard Books, 1992), pp. 31, 105–06.

50. Part of the SAT decline could have been caused by changes in students' test-taking skills, ability to work quickly, or motivation to do well instead of a measurable weakening of their academic achievement. The SAT's validity has been seriously questioned. See David Owen, *None of the Above: Behind the Myth of Scholastic Aptitude* (Boston: Houghton Mifflin, 1985); and James Crouse, *The Case against the SAT* (University of Chicago Press, 1988).

51. Like the SATs, the achievement tests are constructed to ensure that their difficulty levels remain constant over time, so that should not have been a factor. During the 1967–76 period, a minor decline was evident on the American history test and a larger one on the Math II test. Literature performance changed little. Although a smaller group of students takes achievement tests than takes the SAT, their performance is directly relevant to concerns about performance at the top and as a barometer of achievement for the college-bound. During the entire 1970s and later decades, performance on most achievement tests was generally stable or improving. Although this may be partly explained by a decline in the numbers of achievement test takers in the 1970s, suggesting a higher-performing group of students was involved, these students' verbal SAT scores

did not change much or, as the Advisory Panel noted for the 1967–76 period, declined in several cases. Since the early 1980s, both the number of achievement test takers and their scores have gone up, suggesting real improvement. See Paul Barton, *Performance at the Top: From Elementary through Graduate School* (Princeton, N.J.: Educational Testing Service, 1991), pp. 61–62; College Board, *College-Bound Seniors: Eleven Years of National Data from the College Board's Admissions Testing Program, 1973–83* (New York, 1984); and J. Stern, "Table of SAT and Achievement Test Scores for Samples of Candidates Taking Achievement Tests, 1966–67 to 1975–76," in Advisory Panel on the Scholastic Aptitude Test Score Decline, *On Further Examination*, appendix (New York: College Entrance Examination Board, 1977).

52. Advisory Panel on the Scholastic Aptitude Test Score Decline, *On Further Examination*, pp. 22–23.

53. Munday, *Declining Admissions Test Scores*, p. 9; National Center for Education Statistics, *The Condition of Education 1991* (Department of Education, 1991); and National Center for Education Statistics, *Digest of Educational Statistics 1996*.

54. Math PSAT scores declined in the 1950s and 1960s, while verbal scores rose. The reverse trends took place between 1966 and 1974. The 1983 PSAT verbal score was about the same as the 1966 peak, while the math score was about the 1960 level, though below the mid-1950s. See Murray and Herrnstein, "What's Really Behind the SAT-Score Decline?" p. 37. C. Murray and R. J. Herrnstein's data differ, however, from that presented by H. Breland for the Advisory Panel, which showed much smaller changes in verbal and math PSAT scores for the 1960, 1966, and 1974 renormings. See Breland, "The SAT Score Decline," p. 25. Scores for 1974 were comparable to those of 1960. Berliner and Biddle were wrong when they state that annual PSAT data are based on representative samples and not volunteers. See Berliner and Biddle, *The Manufactured Crisis*, p. 24.

55. Berliner and Biddle, *The Manufactured Crisis*, p. 35.

56. Copperman, *The Literacy Hoax*; and Stedman and Kaestle, "The Great Test Score Decline." In contrast, substantial evidence exists that national test scores remained stable or declined only slightly in the 1960s, particularly at the high school level. See Lawrence C. Stedman and Carl F. Kaestle, *An Investigation of Crude Literacy, Reading Performance, and Functional Literacy in the United States, 1880 to 1980,* Program Report 86–23 (University of Wisconsin at Madison, Wisconsin Center for Education Research, 1986); and Lawrence C. Stedman and Carl F. Kaestle, "Literacy and Reading Performance in the United States from 1880 to the Present," *Reading Research Quarterly*, vol. 22, no. 1 (1987), pp. 8–46, especially pp. 19–20.

57. Scores at specific grades and subjects typically declined a total of about .2 to .3 of a standard deviation—not just for the 1970s, but throughout; a few, such as the verbal SAT and ACT math, declined .4 to .5 of a standard deviation. See Koretz, *Trends in Educational Achievement*, pp. 125–26. Although such drops in standard deviations have been considered alarming, leading authorities describe such "effect size" differences in more measured terms. Jacob Cohen describes effect sizes of .2 as "small" and .5 as "medium," while Howard Bowen describes effect sizes of .1 to .19 as "small" and .2 to .39 as "moderate." See Roger E. Kirk, *Introductory Statistics* (Belmont, Calif.: Wadsworth Publishing Co., 1978), p. 231; and National Center for Education Statistics, *The Condition of Education 1995*, p. 239. Given that up to half of the declines were related to demographic changes, the total declines were relatively small. Such effect sizes, in any case, do not directly measure how much students are learning. Standard

deviations reflect relative standing among individuals instead of the actual amount that performance has changed. The real drops in achievement amounted to only a few percentage points, not a worrisome result.

58. Paul Copperman, "The Achievement Decline of the 1970s," *Phi Delta Kappan,* vol. 60, no. 10 (1975), p. 738. Like many school critics, Copperman assumed that virtually all the test score decline was real and thus ignored a large compositional effect. He also presumed that the skill decline began in the mid-1960s and continued steadily thereafter, which exaggerated the size of the decline. His claim of a drop to the 39th percentile was based on an estimated 2.5 percent standard deviation drop per year from 1965 to 1978. Thirteen years of such a drop yielded an overall 32 percent drop, or 11 percentile points. Because this figure was unadjusted for compositional effects, and because the real skill decline occurred primarily in the 1970s, the overall decline was much less than Copperman claimed. Figuring 1.3 to 1.8 percent of a standard deviation per year for seven years (the 1970s decline minus the estimated 30 to 50 percent compositional effect) produces a total decline of 9.1 to 12.6 percent of a standard deviation for achievement tests during the 1970s. This amounts to a drop of only 4 to 6 percentile points, to the 44th or 46th percentile level. Koretz reported the 1970s percentile decline to be around 5 to 9 percentiles on several tests of high school seniors; subtracting demographic effects yields a similar 3 to 6 percentile decline. Koretz, *Educational Achievement,* p. 54.

59. Stedman and Kaestle, *An Investigation of Crude Literacy,* appendix.

60. Koretz, *Educational Achievement,* especially pp. 32–33, 36; and Stedman and Kaestle, "Literacy and Reading Performance in the United States from 1880 to the Present." Independently, Koretz reached a similar estimate of the impact of these factors, though he felt the high side was less likely. He estimated that changes in ethnic composition may have produced one-tenth to one-fifth of the decline and that changes in family size produced from 4 to 25 percent. Other societal factors also may have contributed smaller amounts.

61. Roughly every seven years, test publishers redesign tests. So that school districts can compare results on the new tests with those on the old ones, the publishers conduct renorming or "equating" studies in which samples of students are given both the new and the old tests. Researchers have used the data from such studies to determine national trends, but this was not their original purpose and problems abound. See Stedman and Kaestle, *An Investigation of Crude Literacy, Reading Performance, and Functional Literacy in the United States.*

62. Munday, *Declining Admissions Test Scores,* p. 23; and Stedman and Kaestle, *An Investigation of Crude Literacy.*

63. National Center for Education Statistics, *Digest of Education Statistics 1991* (Department of Education, 1991), p. 17.

64. In the past, some commentators argued that NAEP reading tests showed different trends because they were easier than the standardized commercial tests and tested lower-level skills. The percentage of questions answered correctly by seventeen-year-olds on NAEP, however, was comparable to that on other achievement tests, and the proportion of the test devoted to inferential skills was similar. See Stedman and Kaestle, *An Investigation of Crude Literacy,* appendix.

65. National Council of Teachers of English, *Standards for the English Language Arts,* p. 5.

66. R. L. Linn, M. E. Graue, and N. M. Sanders, "Comparing State and District

Results to National Norms: The Validity of Claims That Everyone Is Above Average,'' *Educational Measurement: Issues and Practice* (Fall 1990), pp. 5–14.

67. Berliner and Biddle, *The Manufactured Crisis*, p. 33; and Stedman, ''Respecting the Evidence.''

68. Stedman and Kaestle, ''Literacy and Reading Performance in the United States from 1880 to the Present,'' in Kaestle and others, *Literacy in the United States.*

69. Linn, Graue, and Sanders, ''Comparing State and District Results to National Norms.''

70. Arthur E. Beston, *Educational Wastelands: The Retreat from Learning in Our Public Schools*, 2d ed. (University of Illinois Press, 1985); Hirsch, *Cultural Literacy*; and Richard Hofstadter, *Anti-Intellectualism in American Life* (Random House, 1962).

71. Hirsch, *Cultural Literacy*; and Rudolph Flesch, *Why Johnny Still Can't Read: A New Look at the Scandal of Our Schools* (Harper and Row, 1981).

72. Copperman, *The Literacy Hoax*, p. 39.

73. David C. Berliner and Bruce J. Biddle, ''Making Molehills out of Molehills: Reply to Lawrence Stedman's Review of *The Manufactured Crisis*,'' *Education Policy Analysis Archives*, vol. 4, no. 3 (1996), available via the World Wide Web at http://olam.ed.asu.edu/epaa/; and Bracey, ''The Second Bracey Report on the Condition of Public Education.''

74. Roger Farr, Leo Fay, and H. Negley, *Then and Now: Reading Achievement in Indiana, 1944–45 and 1976* ERIC Document Reproduction No. ED 158 262 (Indiana University, 1978).

75. R. Farr, J. Tuinman, and M. Rowls, *Reading Achievement in the United States: Then and Now*, ERIC Document Reproduction No. ED 109 595 (Indiana University, 1974), especially p. 140.

76. Stedman and Kaestle, ''Literacy and Reading Performance in the United States from 1880 to the Present,'' in Kaestle and others, *Literacy in the United States.*

77. Berliner and Biddle, ''Making Molehills out of Molehills.''

78. National Council of Teachers of English, *Standards for the English Language Arts*, p. 5.

79. Both studies were flawed by sampling problems, however. A. Eurich and G. Kraetsch found that 1928 University of Minnesota first-year students outperformed their 1978 counterparts on a standardized reading test, but the fifty-year gap had produced a major difference in the type of student entering the university. J. Elligett and T. Tocco used an equating study involving only one school district. The Indiana results were more credible coming from an entire state and a better executed study. For a table of then-and-now studies see Stedman and Kaestle, ''Literacy and Reading Performance in the United States from 1880 to the Present,'' in Kaestle and others, *Literacy in the United States*, pp. 81–85.

80. Stedman and Kaestle, ''Literacy and Reading Performance in the United States from 1880 to the Present,'' in Kaestle and others, *Literacy in the United States*, p. 89.

81. My preliminary investigations suggest that academic performance has been weak for much of the twentieth century, even before the impact of progressive education, the shift from an academic elite to a mass social high school, and the 1918 Cardinal Principles report—a national high school reform report that promoted social efficiency and that critics blamed for weakening academic standards.

82. National Center for Education Statistics, *Youth Indicators 1996: Trends in the Well-Being of American Youth* (Department of Education, 1996), pp. 34, 54, 68; and

William J. Bennett, *The Index of Leading Cultural Indicators* (Simon and Shuster, 1994), pp. 29, 78.

83. Campbell and others, *NAEP 1994 Trends in Academic Progress,* pp. A–72, A–140.

84. Bennett, *The Index of Leading Cultural Indicators,* pp. 38, 40. Data were through 1991. Reports of having ever used marijuana and hallucinogens were down by almost half and cocaine by almost two-thirds from their peaks. The data, however, come from annual surveys and are based on self-reported usage—the downward trend thus could reflect an increasing reluctance to admit drug use instead of a decline in actual use. But the survey is anonymous and one would assume that much of the peer pressure to hide such behavior would have decreased, not increased, during the time. (The Nancy Reagan campaign to "Just Say No" might have had the opposite effect, however.)

85. D. Viadero, "Report on the 10th Graders Torpedoes Perceptions," *Education Week,* August 3, 1994, p. 10.

86. National Center for Education Statistics, *Youth Indicators 1991: Trends in the Well-Being of American Youth* (Department of Education, 1991), p. 20; and National Center for Education Statistics, *Youth Indicators 1996: Trends in the Well–Being of American Youth* (Department of Education, 1996), p. 24.

87. National Center for Education Statistics, *Youth Indicators 1996,* p. 74.

88. Andrew J. Coulson, "Schooling and Literacy over Time: The Rising Cost of Stagnation and Decline," *Research in the Teaching of English,* vol. 30 (October 1996), pp. 311–27; and Herbert J. Walberg, "U.S. Schools Teach Reading Least Productively," *Research in the Teaching of English,* vol. 30, no. 3 (1996), pp. 328–43. The expenditure issue is complex, however, with questions about appropriate inflation adjustments for schooling costs, the increasing portion of expenditures going to special education, and the connection between spending and achievement. On this last point, see the exchange in the April/May 1994 issues of *Educational Researcher* between Eric Hanushek and Larry Hedges, Richard Laine, and Rob Greenwald.

89. Fourth and eighth graders' progress also slowed considerably—from an annual rate of 3 to 4 scale points between 1990 and 1992 to a rate of only 1 point between 1992 and 1996. Reese and others, *NAEP 1996 Mathematics Report Card for the Nation and the States,* p. 26.

90. Campbell and others, *NAEP 1994 Trends in Academic Progress.* Science scores at all three ages were flat between 1992 and 1994.

91. Campbell and others, *NAEP 1994 Trends in Academic Progress;* and T. Smith, *The Educational Progress of Black Students: Findings from the Condition of Education 1994* (Department of Education, 1995).

92. Such conclusions can be overdrawn—year equivalents often exaggerate differences in actual performance. Students' academic growth can be small from year to year, such that students in adjacent grades do not differ greatly in percentage correct or their mastery of material. Also, the more removed a given standardized test is from current school curricula, the less sensitive to growth that test will be. Nevertheless, a four-year difference in performance is substantial and is troubling.

93. Latino students made much less progress than black students did during this past generation. The gap in reading, for example, is larger in the late 1990s than it was in 1980 at all three ages and larger than it was in 1975 for ages nine and thirteen. Black students did make progress in writing during the 1970s. National Assessment of Educational Progress, *Writing Achievement.*

94. Smith, *The Educational Progress of Black Students,* p. 1.

95. Arthur N. Applebee, Judith A. Langer, and Ina V. Mullis, *Crossroads in American Education* (Princeton, N.J.: Educational Testing Service, 1989), pp. 22–23.

96. Campbell and others, *NAEP 1994 Trends in Academic Progress.*

97. Reese and others, *NAEP 1996 Mathematics Report Card for the Nation and the States,* p. 42.

98. L. McLean and H. Goldstein, "The U.S. National Assessment in Reading: Reading Too Much into the Findings," *Phi Delta Kappan* (January 1988), pp. 369–72; Stedman, "The Condition of Education"; and R. Forsyth, "Do NAEP Scales Yield Criterion-Referenced Interpretations?," *Educational Measurement: Issues and Practice,* vol. 10, no. 3 (1991), pp. 3–9, 16.

99. E. Chelimsky, *National Assessment Governing Board (NAGB) Achievement Levels,* interim letter report, ERIC Document Reproduction FO 3YZ821 (General Accounting Office, 1992), p. 4; and Jaeger, "World Class Standards, Choice, and Privatization," pp. 120–21.

100. J. Carroll, "The NAEP Reading Proficiency Scale Is Not a Fiction: A Reply to McLean and Goldstein," *Phi Delta Kappan* (June 1988), pp. 761–64; G. Cizek, *Reactions to National Academy of Education Report Setting Performance Standards for Student Achievement* (Washington: National Assessment Governing Board, 1993); and Reese and others, *NAEP 1996 Mathematics Report Card for the Nation and the States.* Cizek's critique of the National Academy of Education (NAE) report was pointed: "My review finds the NAE Report to be written almost without recognition of the large body of relevant standard setting literature that currently exists" and that "the result of this error is that the evaluators used subjective, unrecognized, and professionally unaccepted standards of evidence in the evaluation" (p. 4). Even supporters of the NAEP proficiency scales, however, have advocated that NAEP report its findings in criterion-referenced terms. See A. Stenner and others, "Most Comprehensive Tests Do Measure Reading Comprehension: A Reply to McLean and Goldstein," *Phi Delta Kappan* (June 1988), pp. 765–67. Such an approach would identify which books students can read and understand, how well students can do specific types of math problems, what historical and civics knowledge students have or do not have, and so on. In NAEP's first decade, many items were publicly released and the reports included interpretive judgments by curriculum specialists. One could readily and concretely see what students nationally knew and could do, which proved useful to teachers, district officials, and the public. (See, for example, National Assessment of Educational Progress, *The Third National Mathematics Assessment,* Report No. 13–MA–01 (Denver, Colo.: Education Commission of the States, 1983); T. Carpenter and others, "Student Performance in Algebra: Results from the National Assessment," *School Science and Mathematics* [October 1982], pp. 514–31; and T. Carpenter and others, "Results of the Fourth NAEP Assessment of Mathematics," *Arithmetic Teacher* [December 1988], pp. 38–41.) The current practice of releasing only a few exercises (along with a unidimensional scaling process that reduces student performance to a single number or a level) hampers such educationally useful analyses. It also obscures the tests' content and curriculum validity.

101. Reese and others, *NAEP 1996 Mathematics Report Card for the Nation and the States,* p. ii.

102. Ina V. Mullis and others, *Trends in Academic Progress,* ERIC Document Reproduction No. ED 338 720 (Government Printing Office, 1991), p. 76.

103. Math educators found that "there are serious gaps in students' knowledge, and they are learning a number of concepts and skills at a superficial level." They concluded

that "student achievement at all age levels shows serious deficiencies." Carpenter and others, "Results of the Fourth NAEP Assessment of Mathematics," pp. 40–41. NAEP analysts also reported that only 5 percent "attained a level of performance characterized by algebra and geometry—when most have had some coursework in these subjects." Ina V. Mullis and others, *The State of Mathematics Achievement* (Department of Education, 1991), p. 80.

104. Only 37 percent recognized Upton Sinclair, Lincoln Steffens, and Ida Tarbell as muckrakers and that Scopes dealt with evolution. D. Ravitch and C. Finn, *What Do Our 17-Year-Olds Know?* (Harper and Row, 1987), p. 268. Only 32 percent knew that U.S. post–World War I foreign policy was isolationist. Fifty-one percent knew the Monroe Doctrine; by the 1994 history assessment, this had dropped to 41 percent. Ravitch and Finn, *What Do Our 17-Year-Olds Know?*, p. 267; and Beatty and others, *NAEP 1994 U.S. History Report Card*, p. 119. In 1990, NAEP analysts concluded that "students are familiar with the events that have shaped American history, but they do not appear to understand the significance and connection of those events." I. Mullis, E. Owen, and G. Phillips, *America's Challenge: Accelerating Academic Achievement*, Report No. OV–01 (Princeton, N.J.: Educational Testing Service, 1990), p. 10. They also reported that students "demonstrate an uneven understanding of the Constitution and American government and politics; their knowledge of the Bill of Rights is limited."

105. Ina V. Mullis, Jay R. Campbell, and Alan E. Farstrup, *NAEP 1992 Reading Report Card for the Nation and the States* (Department of Education, 1993), p. 166; Ravitch and Finn, *What Do Our 17-Year-Olds Know?*; and Lawrence C. Stedman, "An Assessment of Literacy Trends, Past and Present," *Research in the Teaching of English*, vol. 30, no. 3 (1996), pp. 283–302.

106. Applebee and others, *The Writing Report Card*, p. 7. In the 1990 writing assessment, 68 to 79 percent of eleventh graders' persuasive papers were rated unsatisfactory or minimal; informative writing was better, but 31 to 80 percent of the papers were still rated inadequate depending on the task. Mullis and others, *Trends in Academic Progress*, pp. 163, 171, 362; and Stedman, "An Assessment of Literacy Trends."

107. R. Allen and others, *The Geography Learning of High School Seniors* (Princeton, N.J.: National Assessment of Educational Progress, 1990), pp. 26, 73.

108. P. Williams and others, *NAEP 1994 Geography: A First Look* (Department of Education, 1995), pp. 58, 63.

109. Gallup Organization, *A Survey of College Seniors: Knowledge of History and Literature* (Princeton, N.J., 1989), pp. 1, 4, 7, 14.

110. Applebee and others, *The Writing Report Card*, pp. 54, 58. Nevertheless, about one-fourth of seniors' sentences in 1988 were awkward as were more than a third of eighth graders' sentences.

111. Mullis, Owen, and Phillips, *America's Challenge*, p. 10.

112. Berliner and Biddle, "Making Molehills out of Molehills."

113. Berliner and Biddle, "Making Molehills out of Molehills"; and G. Bracey, "On Comparing the Incomparable: A Response to Baker and Stedman," *Educational Researcher*, vol. 26, no. 3 (1997), pp. 19–26.

114. Bracey, "On Comparing the Incomparable."

115. Bracey, "On Comparing the Incomparable." C. Reese and others found that only about a third of seniors felt that doing well on the NAEP math assessment was "important" or "very important," while about a third felt it was "not very important." Curiously, those who felt it was not very important had the highest averages. As Reese and others point out, "these data further cloud the relationship between motivation and

performance on NAEP,'' Reese and others, *NAEP 1996 Mathematics Report Card for the Nation and the States*, p. 108.

116. Mullis and others, *Trends in Academic Progress*, p. 218. The new NAGB levels provide similar latitude. M. Bourque and H. Garrison, *The Levels of Mathematics Achievement*, ERIC Document Reproduction No. ED 342 685 (Washington: National Assessment Governing Board, 1991), pp. 13, 28–32. The most recent NAEP reports indicate that performance can be as low as 65 percent on multiple-choice items and 74 percent on constructed response ones. H. Persky, *NAEP 1994 Geography Report Card* (Department of Education, 1996), p. 97. An 80 percent level of competence was rejected as being too ''stringent.''

117. Claudia A. Gentile, James Martin-Rehrmann, and John Kennedy, *Windows into the Classroom: NAEP's 1992 Writing Portfolio Study* (Department of Education, 1995), pp. 31, 49. The portfolio assessment methodology needs to be systematically and independently evaluated. No doubt, problems will be found that will require some adjustments to the results, but these could lower results as well as raise them.

118. M. Wang, G. Haertel, and H. Walberg, ''Toward a Knowledge Base: Why, How, for Whom?,'' *Review of Educational Research*, vol. 62, no. 3 (1993), pp. 365–76, especially p. 371. In a possible exception, students' performance on NAEP's set writing tasks did not mirror well that on their classroom writing portfolios. Gentile, Martin-Rehrmann, and Kennedy, *Windows into the Classroom*, pp. 128, 130. Low correlations were expected, however, as a result of differences in assessment conditions—the portfolios were made up of students' three best pieces of writing drawn from their classrooms, where they ''are able to choose their own topics, consult with their peers and their teachers, and rewrite their papers several times.'' Gentile, Martin-Rehrmann, and Kennedy, *Windows into the Classroom*, p. 126.

119. B. Bridgeman, ''A Comparison of Quantitative Questions in Open-Ended and Multiple-Choice Formats,'' *Journal of Educational Measurement* (Fall 1992), p. 269ff; M. Martinez, ''A Comparison of Multiple-Choice and Constructed Figural Response Items,'' *Journal of Educational Measurement* (Summer 1991), pp. 131–45; National Assessment of Educational Progress, *The Third National Mathematics Assessment*, p. 32; and V. Rogers and C. Stevenson, ''How Do We Know What Kids Are Learning in School?,'' *Educational Leadership* (February 1988), pp. 68–75.

120. J. Langer and others, *Reading Assessment Redesigned: Authentic Texts and Innovative Instruments in NAEP's 1992 Survey*, Report No. 23–FR–07 (Washington: National Center for Education Statistics, 1995).

121. ''Ignorance of U.S. History Shown by College Freshmen,'' *New York Times*, April 4, 1943, p. 1. Only 6 percent of those in their late twenties even had college degrees and only 29 percent of eighteen- and nineteen-year-olds were in school in 1940. National Center for Education Statistics, *Digest of Education Statistics 1991*, pp. 15, 17.

122. Edgar B. Wesley, *American History in Schools and Colleges* (Macmillan, 1944) pp. 4–6, 10–12. The committee conducting the study was not alarmed by the low level, arguing that history is learned slowly and forgotten quickly. It rejected the notion that history instruction was ''meager or ineffective,'' although, strikingly, students who had taken a high school history course did only marginally better than those who had not.

123. Gallup Organization, *The Gallup Public Opinion Poll 1988* (Wilmington, Del.: Scholarly Resources, 1989), p. 162.

124. Herbert H. Hyman, Charles R. Wright, and John S. Reed, *The Enduring Effects of Education* (University of Chicago Press, 1975), p. 133 and table 2.5. College grad-

uates did much better, 62 to 89 percent, but few adults were college graduates. Only 11 percent of twenty-five- to twenty-nine-year-olds were college graduates in April 1960. National Center for Education Statistics, *Digest of Education Statistics 1991*, p. 17.

125. M. Delli Carpini and S. Keeter, "Stability and Change in the U.S. Public's Knowledge of Politics," *Public Opinion Quarterly* (Winter 1991), pp. 583–612; and Samuel L. Popkin, *The Reasoning Voter* (University of Chicago Press, 1991), pp. 34–35. Limited civic literacy does not necessarily mean the electorate is ignorant or blind. Popkin argues that voters use many information shortcuts to reason about issues and candidates.

126. Berliner and Biddle, "Making Molehills out of Molehills."

127. These findings have direct implications for the collapse of standards argument. U.S. students' poor performance in the pre-decline, pre-1965 period implicates a persistent anti-intellectualism in the culture and the deep structure of schooling—the factory model organization of schools, the assembly-line nature of U.S. curriculum and teaching, and the differentiated curriculum. It suggests that simply restoring old standards (credits, homework, and exams) will not be enough; long-standing institutional forms and social practices also must be changed. These include tracking, diplomas being awarded for seat-time or an accumulation of Carnegie units instead of demonstrated academic performance, low academic expectations, low-level multiple-choice testing, impersonal large-scale bureaucratic schools, fragmented worksheet pedagogy, 120–140 student workloads and forty-five to fifty minute periods that sustain such pedagogy, and so on. In short, attention must be paid to what David Tyack calls the grammar of schooling and what Ted Sizer calls personalization and these need to be combined with high standards of excellence.

128. The *Nation at Risk* report made too much of a high-skilled, high-tech future economy as a rationale for reforming education. L. C. Stedman and M. S. Smith, "Recent Reform Proposals for American Education," *Contemporary Education Review*, vol. 2, no. 2 (1983), pp. 85–104.

129. M. Schudson, "The Informed Citizen in Historical Context," *Research in the Teaching of English*, vol. 30, no. 3 (1996), pp. 361–69.

130. Stedman, "The Condition of Education."

The Effects of Upgrading Policies on High School Mathematics and Science

ANDREW C. PORTER

F ROM THE MID-1980s through the early 1990s, two aspects of the output of high school mathematics and science
instruction were targeted for improvement by state and district education policies. First, states and districts sought to increase the number
of students completing science and mathematics credits, especially
credits in college preparatory courses. A great deal of attention was
paid to increasing the number of students of color and from low-income
families completing such coursework. Second, states and districts
sought to make the instruction in mathematics and science courses more
effective, so that more students would learn more ambitious content.

While the policy initiatives were stimulated in large part by the 1983
A Nation at Risk, their purpose was captured in the *National Goals for
Education,* as published in 1991.[1] In particular, Goal 3 states, ''American students will leave grades 4, 8, and 12 having demonstrated competence in challenging subject matter, including English, mathematics,
science, history, and geography; and every school in America will

The research in this report was supported by the Consortium for Policy Research in
Education through a grant from the National Science Foundation (Grant No. SPA–
8953446), a grant from the Office of Educational Research and Improvement, Department of Education (Grant No. OERI–R–117–G10007), and by the Wisconsin Center
for Education Research, School of Education, University of Wisconsin at Madison. The
opinions expressed in this paper are those of the author and do not necessarily reflect
the views of the National Science Foundation; the Office of Educational Research and
Improvement, Department of Education; the institutional partners of the Consortium for
Policy Research in Education; or the Wisconsin Center for Education Research.

123

ensure that all students learn to use their minds well, so that they may be prepared for responsible citizenship, further learning, and productive employment in our modern economy."[2] In those national goals, science and mathematics were singled out for special attention: "U.S. students will be first in the world in science and mathematics achievement."[3]

Many specific policy initiatives fit under the label of upgrading high school mathematics and science. The two examined here are (1) policies that increase the number of credits of mathematics and science required to graduate from high school and (2) transition courses, primarily in mathematics, designed to assist low-achieving students to take and successfully complete college preparatory courses. Results are taken primarily from two studies, each conducted as a part of the Consortium for Policy Research in Education. The first study, funded by the National Science Foundation (NSF), involved data collection in the 1989–90 and 1990–91 academic years and focused upon effects of increases in high school graduation requirements. The second study, funded by the U.S. Department of Education, Office of Educational Research and Improvement (OERI), involved classroom-level data collection in the 1992–93 academic year and transcript data from each of four consecutive years, beginning with the 1988–89 academic year.

The curriculum reforms of the late 1980s, which have been characterized as hard content for all students, represent a combination of two previous curriculum reforms in the United States.[4] In the late 1950s and early 1960s, the United States undertook a curriculum reform designed to strengthen the curriculum for college-bound high school students. Some attribute the reform to the Soviet launching of *Sputnik* and a race to the moon against the Russians. The goal was to produce more and better scientists and mathematicians; the strategy was upgrading the high school mathematics and science college preparation tracks. In the late 1960s and 1970s, this curriculum reform gave way to a basic skills reform, having as its goal an assurance that all students master at least the minimum basic skills necessary for successful life chances. The curriculum reform of the 1980s combined the ambitious college preparatory content of the first reform with the equity goals of the second.

In response to *A Nation at Risk,* many states and school districts increased the number of credits in mathematics and science required for high school graduation. These reforms were silent on the nature of mathematics and science, although some did specify certain courses that must be taken. In 1989, both the National Council of Teachers of Mathematics (NCTM) and the American Association for the Advancement of Science published content standards that specified the nature of mathematics and science that was deemed most useful for students to master. One year later, the first set of national education goals was published, following the historic education summit in Charlottesville, Virginia, attended by governors and President George Bush. Since the time of the two studies, the National Research Council published its *National Science Education Standards,* and the National Council of Teachers of Mathematics added to its content standards, standards for teaching, and standards for assessment.[5] All of these initiatives are complementary, with each successive policy adding specificity to the preceding policies.

States and districts have been the most active in upgrading policy initiatives, but they have been joined by the federal government and professional societies. While considerable room remained for discretion at the school and classroom levels, much guidance and some requirements were put in place that, if effective, would result in substantial change in what and how teachers teach and in which courses students take. Because these content policies are consistent (or at least not inconsistent) with each other, a national consensus appeared to be emerging. But calls for dramatic shifts in what students are to study and teachers are to teach may stimulate controversy.

Historically, controversy concerning the content of academic instruction in the United States has been on the margins. An occasional book has been banned from the curriculum. Tensions arose between religion and science (for example, the appropriateness of Darwinian versus Creationist interpretations of the origins of man). The curriculum reforms of the 1980s, however, made the core curriculum in mathematics and science an increasingly contentious issue. Perhaps because the NCTM's content standards received high visibility almost immediately, and because they were among the first standards to present major challenges concerning what is taught, they have served as a lightning rod for controversy. By the mid–1990s, hardly a week went by without fundamental differences of opinion being aired in the press about what is most appropriate to teach in mathematics. California has been a site of particularly heated debate, especially as that state undertook revisions of its highly visible and nationally known mathematics curriculum framework.[6] Similar acrimonious debates have taken place in Iowa, Montana, Texas, and elsewhere. On one side of the debate about content are those who advocate the NCTM *Standards*. In California, the NCTM *Standards* advocates controlled the 1992 mathematics framework. California frameworks were headed in the direction of the NCTM *Standards,* even before the NCTM *Standards* had been published. On the other side are those who view the NCTM *Standards* as too soft and vague in their push for greater emphasis upon conceptual understanding and application. These people want traditional mathematics instruction that places primary emphasis upon acquiring skill with algorithms from whole number computation to solving systems of simultaneous linear equations. Mathematicians can be found on both sides of the debate.[7]

Conceptual Framework

In the midst of the heated debates about mathematics content and, to some extent, science content, state and district policies continue to increase high school graduation requirements and transition courses for high school mathematics.

Defining Mathematics and Science Content

Content can be defined at varying levels of precision. For example, mathematics can be subdivided into general areas such as geometry or algebra. Within an algebra course, some topics may be given greater emphasis than other topics; some topics may not be included in the curriculum at all. In teaching linear equations, different forms of a linear equation may be given greater or lesser emphasis. For any particular mathematical topic, teachers may stress different cognitive demands as the intended outcomes from their instruction. Students may be expected to memorize the equation for the point slope form of a line. From the equation, students may be expected to state what is the slope and the intercept of a line. Students may be expected to learn how to analyze a plotted line to determine its intercept and slope. Students may be expected to know how to collect data and fit a line to the data points. Students may be given a problem, where the procedures necessary to solve the problem are not stated explicitly, but where understanding the concept of the point slope form of a line is an efficient and effective way to solve the problem. Thus, the content of instruction may be defined by topics, by cognitive demand, and by the intersection of topics and cognitive demand.

In both the NSF and OERI studies, a language was invented that enumerates the topics and the cognitive demands for high school mathematics and science. Topics are defined by two levels, one nested within the other. In mathematics, distinctions are made among number and number relations; arithmetic; measurement; algebra; geometry; trigonometry; statistics; probability; advanced algebra, precalculus, and calculus; and finite and discrete mathematics. In science, distinctions are made among biology of the cell, human biology, biology of other organisms, biology of populations, chemistry, physics, earth and space science, and general science. Within each of these relatively large areas of content, finer distinctions are made. For example, within statistics are subtopics of distributional shapes, central tendency, variability, correlation or regression, sampling, point estimates of parameters, confidence interval estimates of parameters, and hypothesis testing. For cognitive demand, the distinctions are memorize facts, definitions, and equations; understand concepts; collect data; order, compare, estimate, and approximate; perform procedures; solve routine problems, replicate experiments, replicate proofs; interpret data, recognize patterns; recognize, formulate, and solve novel problems and design experiments; and build and revise theories and develop proofs. In mathematics, at the intersection between topics and cognitive demand, 846 distinct types of content are specified; in science, 612.

Teachers as Political Brokers of Content

Teachers can be thought of as political brokers who understand and interpret the various policies and practices that bear upon their content decisions and, at the same time, take into account their own repertoire of content knowledge and pedagogical strategies as well as their own predilections as to what is most important and appropriate for their students. Thus, in designing and implementing the curriculum for a particular course, a teacher makes decisions about how much time to spend, covering what types of content, with what students, and to what standards of achievement. Collectively, these facets of teacher content decisions define students' opportunities to learn in a particular course. This view of teachers as political brokers making content decisions, and this approach to defining content, grows out of a line of research on teacher content decisionmaking undertaken by a research team at the Institute for Research on Teaching.[8]

Effects of Content on Student Achievement

The policy of increasing the number of credits in mathematics and science required for high school graduation and the policy of introducing transition math courses in high school are both predicated upon the belief that what students study is a powerful predictor of what students learn. At a macro level, this is relatively obvious, especially for the school-based subjects of mathematics and science. Students who study algebra learn more algebra than those who do not, although the amount of algebra learned will be a function of both student motivation and the quality of the pedagogical strategies employed. But at a micro level, content is an important predictor of student achievement as well.

What is the evidence that the content of instruction affects student achievement? At the level of courses taken, research has found consistent and strong relationships between content and student achievement. Adam Gamoran has shown that intermediate-level courses in high school make substantial contributions to student achievement on tests.[9] Other researchers have found similar achievement benefits. Among College Board test takers in New York and California, Penny A. Sebring found that higher test scores were associated with time spent in coursework and that this relationship held for relatively low-achieving students as well as high-achieving students.[10] William H. Schmidt used data from the National Longitudinal Study of the Class of 1972, and Herbert J. Walberg and Timothy Shanahan used data from High School and Beyond to find similar results.[11] All of these analyses statistically controlled for student background variables in reaching the conclusion that high school coursework leads to increased student achievement. Similarly, research on tracking has found that the achievement gap between students in high-level classes and those in low-level classes grows over time.[12] These achievement differences result from differences in pace, complexity, and challenge of instruction between high and low track classes; all are content differences.[13]

At the micro level, establishing strong relationships between the content of instruction and gains in student achievement has not been so easy. Recently, however, surprisingly large correlations have been found between the content of instruction, as defined by the intersection of cognitive demands and topics, and gains on student achievement in first-year high school mathematics classrooms.[14] For this result, the predictor of student achievement gains was alignment between classroom instruction and a student achievement test based on National Assessment of Educational Progress (NAEP) public release items. Two aspects of alignment were defined. Level indicated the percentage of instructional time allocated to tested content. Configuration reflected the degree to which the relative emphasis of types of content in instruction paralleled the relative emphasis of types of content on the test. Alignment was defined as the interaction of these two dimensions. For classroom-level gains, correlation between the alignment of instruction to the test and gains in student achievement on the test was .45. At the student level, correlation between degree of alignment and achievement gains was .26. From these results, it is possible to conclude that the content of instruction may be the single most powerful predictor of gains in student achievement under the direct control of schools.

When the Third International Mathematics and Science Survey (TIMSS) results were released at the eighth grade level, U.S. students once again did not achieve at the levels hoped.[15] Performance in mathematics was below the international average (with forty-one participating countries). Performance in science was slightly above the international average, although still well below top-performing countries. From curriculum analyses, differences were noted between the content of U.S. mathematics and science curricula and content in other countries with higher levels of achievement.[16] The pattern of content for the United States, in contrast with other countries, was to cover many more topics each for less time while keeping topics in the curriculum across grades for longer periods of time. In mathematics, some content on the international achievement test was underemphasized in the United States, especially geometry, metric measurement, and algebra. While causal modeling with TIMSS data has not yet been done (and may prove too difficult), many hypothesize that the unimpressive showing of American students, relative to those in other nations, may be explained largely by the differences in content covered, as described in the curriculum analyses.

A Theory for Describing Policy Strength

Out of the earlier work on teacher content decisionmaking emerged a theory for describing attributes that give content policies influence.[17] Policies are hypothesized to have greater influence to the extent that they are prescriptive. A policy is prescriptive when it is explicit in describing what content decisions are desired. For example, an achievement test identifies, to some extent, what types of content (that is, topics and cognitive demand combinations) are most important. Any particular form of a test does not do this perfectly, because a test is only a sample of the domain of content desired. Thus, the framework on which a test is based may be more prescriptive, in the sense of being comprehensive in its description of what content is desired. But typically a framework is more vague than a test in indicating in detail what students are to know and be able to do. Requirements about who must take the test also have implications for prescriptiveness by indicating which students are to study what content. A demanding test suggests that substantial amounts of time should be spent on instruction aligned to the test.

Consistency is a second policy characteristic. When policies are consistent, one with another, the policies are hypothesized to reinforce each other. Thus, to the extent that content policies of achievement tests, textbooks, curriculum frameworks, and professional development are all aligned as to their content messages, the greater the likelihood of influence upon what is taught and what students study.

To the characteristics of prescriptiveness and consistency can be added the characteristics of authority and power. Policies designed by experts are more authoritative than those that are not. Similarly, policies that have the force of law, are consistent with common practice (that is, norms), and are promoted by charismatic individuals may be more authoritative than policies that do not have these attributes. In contrast, power derives from rewards and sanctions tied to compliance.

When judged against these four attributes, curriculum policies in the United States tend to be weak. Most curriculum policies are not particularly prescriptive, leaving large zones of discretion to schools, teachers, and students. Similarly, curriculum policies tend to be adopted over time, with each new policy being added to those that came before, resulting, for example, in new curriculum frameworks that are inconsistent with continuing student achievement tests. While accountability in education is an issue of considerable discussion and concern, most forms of accountability are mild. When stakes are high, standards tend to be low. For most policies, no formal and explicit rewards or sanctions are tied to compliance. In contrast, numerous efforts are made to build policies that are authoritative. From a theoretical point of view, this is desirable, because policies that are authoritative operate through persuasion. Teachers are persuaded by an authoritative policy that what is wanted is appropriate and in the best interest of both the teacher and the students. Authoritative policies change teachers' conceptions as to the content decisions they should make. Once that occurs, teachers operate on their own beliefs. In that sense, the authoritative policy becomes no longer relevant. In contrast, policies that seek to have their effects through power force compliance without changing teachers' conceptions. This may create dissonance within the teacher and cannot be expected to have a continuing effect, should the powerful policy be discontinued.

Reform Up Close Study

The Reform Up Close Study was conducted to assess the effects of state increases in the number of mathematics and science credits required for high school graduation.[18] By themselves, increases in credits required for high school graduation are not particularly prescriptive. They do specify that students are to take mathematics and science but are silent as to what mathematics and science is required. The policies are both authoritative and powerful in that they are mandated by state law and have serious consequences for compliance.

Some states and districts have added policies that are consistent with the increased credit requirements while adding degrees of prescriptiveness. Florida and South Carolina each initiated a special diploma for students seeking to attend state colleges and universities. These diplomas not only required more mathematics and science, but they also stipulated particular mathematics and science courses to be taken in meeting the requirements. For example, in Florida the regular diploma requires three years of mathematics, while the academic diploma requires four years of mathematics that must include algebra, geometry, and trigonometry. In all states, colleges and universities were also increasing their entrance requirements, requiring more science and mathematics and specifying particular math and science courses.

Some states (for example, California) and several districts (especially large urban districts) were pushing for more students to take more advanced courses in all academic subjects, especially mathematics and science. These district and state initiatives were more informal than formal, sometimes captured in curriculum framework language but other times transmitted through word of mouth. Nevertheless, the push for more students to take more advanced courses was felt at the school level. In some schools and districts, summer programs were used to enable students to complete basic and remedial work in time to take more advanced work in subsequent years. Advanced Placement (AP) course taking also received increased attention. The number of AP courses taught and the number of students receiving AP credit have become indicators of school success nationally and especially in certain states.

Some districts and several schools began to eliminate basic courses in mathematics and science or to require all students to take first-year college prep courses in math and science or both. In addition, Florida and South Carolina placed requirements on the amount of lab time that a science course must include for that science course to count toward graduation, although these state lab requirements were not met in practice.

Those who expressed reservations about increasing high school graduation requirements in mathematics and science hypothesized that, as a result of increased standards, high school graduation rates would decrease, dropout rates would increase, and that these negative results would inflict the greatest harm on minority and poor students. To date, that hypothesis has not proved true. Statistics for the years 1971 through 1995 show no signs of decrease in student persistence. Over that two-and-one-half-decade period, student persistence gradually improved for white, black, and Hispanic students, with the largest increase for black students.[19] In 1990, the percentage of high school students in grades ten through twelve enrolled the previous October who were enrolled again the following October was 96 percent for the total sample, with 96.7 percent for white students, 95 percent for black students, and 92.1 percent for Hispanic students. Taking 1983 as a baseline, the year that *A Nation at Risk* was published, no evidence exists of a rise in student dropout rates. For whites, blacks, and Hispanics, the percentage of students enrolled the previous October who enrolled again the following October was slightly higher in 1990 than it was in 1983.[20] In short, no evidence is available to support a hypothesis that increases in standards during the 1980s led to decreases in high school completion rates and increases in dropouts.

When the hypothesized retention problem did not materialize, a second hypothesis emerged. Was it possible that schools were accommodating students by allowing them to meet the new standards through remedial and basic courses? To address this possibility, William H. Clune and Paula A. White analyzed transcript data on changes in course-taking patterns among graduates of high schools enrolling mostly low-achieving students in four states that had increased their high school graduation requirements.[21] They found that credits completed in academic subjects did increase by a substantial one-half year of instruction on average; the increases in academic credits completed were accomplished through an overall increase in total credits instead of a substitution of academic work for other work; and the largest increases in academic credit completion were in science, but substantial increases were also found in mathematics. Especially important to the argument here, the additional academic credits completed were in courses of varying levels of difficulty, not just in remedial and basic-level courses. In science, many more students completed biology 1, for example, while in mathematics, courses in pre-algebra and algebra 1 were frequent additions to the transcripts of graduating seniors.

For those who doubted the benefits of increased standard setting, a third hypothesis remained. What if, after standards were increased, instruction in courses was weakened? What if the increases in numbers of students taking algebra, for example, resulted in a watered-down algebra curriculum to accommodate the weaker and less motivated students? If such watering down of courses occurred, then the relationship between course taking and student achievement would disappear. The same curriculum that students had studied but not learned before high school would be taught all over again in high school and perhaps still not learned. This third hypothesis served as the primary motivation for the Reform Up Close study of high school mathematics and science.

Sample Selection

States were selected that had made, relative to other states, major increases in the number of math and science credits required to graduate from high school. Florida increased its graduation requirements in math by three credits and in science by three credits, both effective in 1987. California and Pennsylvania increased math and science requirements by two credits each, with California's new requirements taking effect in 1987 and Pennsylvania's in 1989. Missouri increased math and science requirements by one credit each, effective in 1988. South Carolina required three credits of math and two of science, representing a one-credit increase in each subject, effective in 1987. Arizona required two credits in each subject, representing a one-credit increase in each subject, effective in 1987.

In each state, two districts were studied, one a large urban district with enrollment of approximately 200,000 or more and one a small suburban or rural school district with enrollment of approximately ten thousand students or fewer. State initiatives, when mediated by district bureaucracies, could have effects at the school and classroom level that depend, in part, on the size and nature of the district bureaucracy.

All high schools were comprehensive—grade nine through twelve— with a stable grade-level organization and stable population. Each high school was below average in student achievement and served high concentrations of low-income and minority students.

The study focused on courses in which enrollment gains had been substantial following increases in state requirements for graduation. Two math and two science target courses were selected in each school. Where courses that satisfied the big enrollment gain criterion could not be identified, big enrollment was a substitute criterion. For example, general biology might be selected as a course because, while enrollment might have gained only 10 percentage points from 1985 to 1988, enrollment in 1988 was near 100 percent. Preference was given to basic courses, not only because they were typically the ones with biggest enrollment gains, but also because in some cases they represented special courses created to bridge low-achieving students into college preparatory courses. Where possible, multiple sections of the same course were selected across schools for purposes of comparison. The average enrollment gain was 28 percent, and the average percentage of all students in the school completing the course was 61 percent.

Experienced teachers were selected who would be in the building the next year and likely teaching the target course. The average number of years of teaching experience for the total sample was 13.9. Class size was, on average, 25.1 students. The largest school had twenty-eight math teachers and twenty-three science teachers. The smallest school had only four math and four science teachers. Data were collected during 1990 and 1991. The primary methods for describing instruction were teacher logs for the target courses and teacher questionnaires for all math and science teachers and courses in each school.

Teacher Logs

Each school day for a year, each target teacher indicated up to five types of content (topic by cognitive demand) covered in that class period. For each type of content, three pieces of information were required. First, the teacher gave an example or brief description. Next, the teacher wrote a four-digit code, positioning the content within the content taxonomy. The third piece of information was the amount of emphasis given to the content. A ''3'' indicated that either the content was the only content emphasized in the period or received at least 50 percent of the time for that class. A ''2'' indicated the content was one of two to four types of content that day, all of which were emphasized. A ''1'' indicated the content was important content, but not strongly emphasized in that class. During site visits, teachers were trained in the procedures for keeping daily logs. Following training, teachers began immediately to keep daily logs.

Teachers were instructed to complete a log for a particular day's instruction as soon after the class meeting as possible. At the beginning, when teachers were still familiarizing themselves with the procedures, completing the daily log proved difficult for some. Once the taxonomies were better known and the format of the log familiar, completion time typically ranged from five to ten minutes. Because logs were mailed to the University of Wisconsin at Madison on a weekly basis, teachers who were getting behind and teachers who noted problems in the logs could be contacted. Each teacher received $250 per semester for keeping daily logs on their target course section.

Log data were not analyzed unless they described the majority of instruction for two full semesters of a course section. The number of daily logs completed for each teacher and section in the analysis file ranged from a low of 109 to a high of 177, with a median of 165 log days per target section. Sixty-two of the seventy-two target courses, or 86 percent, met this criterion, as did thirty-two math courses and thirty science courses.

From teacher logs, emphasis codes were converted to time by assigning a proportional multiplier to each emphasis code in each combination of logically possible emphasis codes for a given class session. For each teacher, a data file was created describing the percentage of total instructional time allocated to each type of content in the taxonomy for the subject taught. These data files can be thought of as describing the percentage of time over the course of a full year of instruction allocated to a specific type of content; for example, understanding the concept of a variable. From these analysis files, marginal distributions of time can be constructed. For example, what percentage of instruction for the year was devoted to learning about statistics? Or what percentage of instructional time involved interpreting data and recognizing patterns?

Teacher Questionnaire

All math and science teachers in each high school characterized a specific section of a specific course they taught through completion of a questionnaire. The course and section to be described was identified by the research team in advance and indicated on the questionnaire. The intention was to obtain one questionnaire for each math or science course offered in the school. Each teacher received $10 for completing the questionnaire. Repeated followups resulted in an overall 75 percent response rate, 74 percent for mathematics teachers and 77 percent for science teachers. There were 168 completed questionnaires by mathematics teachers and 144 completed questionnaires by science teachers, for a questionnaire analysis file of 312 teachers. On the questionnaire, teachers described the topics and cognitive demands of their instruction, indicating for each the amount of time allocated (four levels from 0 for "not taught" to 3 for "ten or more hours").

From questionnaire data, one variable was created for each general content area (for example, algebra). These variables were formed by summing the weights indicating amount of time devoted to a topic across all topics within each content area and then dividing by the sum of weights for all topics taught. The metric is like percentage of instructional time. Cognitive demand variables were also created. For the topics taught at least to some extent, one variable was the percentage of time topics were taught that required students to memorize (that is, the sum of 4-point scale weights across topics where "memorize" was circled, divided by the sum of weights across all topics). Other cognitive demand variables were the percentage of time topics were taught that required students to solve routine problems, solve novel problems, or build and revise theory and develop proofs. These four cognitive demand categories were ordered, with the respondents asked to indicate the highest level reached for each topic covered. Thus, cognitive demand scales underestimate the amount of emphasis on memorize and routine problems and overestimate the amount of emphasis upon novel problems and develop proofs.

Course Descriptors

Two variables were used to describe the courses studied both in the questionnaire data and in the target sample (where logs were kept). One variable was course level: advanced (1), middle (0), and basic (− 1). Course level was defined in the same way as by Clune and White.[22] They, in turn, drew from the Secondary Schools Taxonomy (SST) and the Council of Chief State School Officers' State Science and Mathematics Indicator Project.[23] Essentially, Clune and White compressed the SST grading of difficulties into three levels, but not in a way that necessarily gives the same meaning to level of difficulty across subject matter areas. For example, the middle level of difficulty for math contains pre-algebra, which seems somewhat easier than the middle level of science, which includes biology, chemistry, and physics 1. Courses were also described by type, which in some cases was synonymous with course title but in other cases represented a grouping of different course titles. For example, in mathematics, a basic math course type was created that included general math as well as consumer and business math. In science, all physics courses were listed as one type even though under that type was included regular physics as well as honors physics.

In the questionnaire sample and especially for the target sample, the percentage of high-level courses was higher in mathematics (53 and 59 percent, respectively) than in science (21 and 7 percent, respectively).

The Influence of Increased Enrollment on Student Opportunity to Learn

Three separate analyses were used to explore the influence of increased enrollment on student opportunity to learn. First, log sample data were compared with questionnaire sample data, because the log sample focused on courses with big enrollment increases, while the questionnaire sample represented all courses. Second, in two schools, some courses were required of all students. Data for these courses could be compared with courses of the same type but which not all students were required to take. Third, regression analyses allowed exploration as to whether course level or class ability was the stronger predictor of course content.

COMPARING LOG COURSES WITH QUESTIONNAIRE COURSES. For each type of math and science course, comparisons of the questionnaire sample with the log sample uncovered only minor differences in what was taught. Thus, the more heavily subscribed log sample courses showed few, if any, signs of being weaker than the questionnaire courses taken by fewer students. For example, the content of algebra 1 looked much the same, regardless of whether or not the algebra 1 section was in a school where algebra 1 had experienced large increases in enrollment. Biology looked much like biology regardless of the percentage of the student body taking the course. For math, a slightly greater emphasis was found in the questionnaire sample on solving novel problems and developing proofs than in the log sample, but this can be dismissed as an artifact of the differences in the data collection strategies. For science, log sample courses put a relatively lower emphasis on general science topics (for example, the nature of scientific inquiry) than did the questionnaire sample. This difference, while valid, is not suggestive of any watering down in log sample courses. Some might say just the opposite, that the more serious science courses would place greater emphasis on topics of biology, chemistry, and physics than on general science topics such as the nature and structure of science or the nature of scientific inquiry.

REQUIRED COURSES. Of the thirty-two mathematics target courses, two of the algebra 1 courses were in schools where algebra 1 was required of all students. One school was in the Arizona urban district, and the other was in the Pennsylvania small town district. These two courses, then, represented excellent instances for studying whether or not such standard setting results in a watered-down curriculum. In comparison with the average for all algebra 1 courses, the Arizona course put less emphasis on algebra (.61) while the Pennsylvania course was just above the average in its emphasis upon algebra (.87). In the Arizona course, the lower emphasis on algebra was replaced by a higher emphasis on number and number relations (.15) and arithmetic (.23). The data in table 1 provide a breakdown for the two courses in the particular types of algebra each emphasized. For comparative purposes, means and standard deviations are presented across all eleven algebra 1 courses. In the case of the Arizona course, the topics of exponents and radicals and functions were less emphasized than for the average of all algebra courses. At the same time, nearly twice as much instructional time was devoted to work with systems of equations than was true for the eleven-course sample of algebra 1 courses (.12 versus .06), a difference of more than 2 standard deviations. Content emphases for the other topics are essentially identical between the Arizona course and the means of the eleven-course sample. The Pennsylvania course is a clear example of standards being held despite the requirement that all students take the course. Functions did not receive as much attention as in the general sample (.02 versus .08), but nonlinear equations received substantially more attention (.12 versus .05), as did expressions (.36 versus .24). Collectively these data are supportive of curriculum upgrading efforts that require all students to take at least beginning-level college prepa-ratory coursework in mathematics. Even the Arizona course, with its lower emphasis on algebra than for the general algebra 1 sample, looks more like an algebra 1 course than a pre-algebra course.

The two required algebra 1 courses had profiles on cognitive demand that stand in contrast to the algebra 1 average profile (see table 2). Both courses put a substantially lower emphasis on computation (routine

Table 1. Algebra 1 Courses Required of All Students: Topic Emphasis Comparisons

Course	N		Algebra	Variable	Expressions	Linear equations or inequalities	Nonlinear equations or inequalities	Systems of equations or inequalities	Exponents and radicals	Series	Function	Matrices
Arizona course	1		.61	.03	.20	.22	.03	.12	.02	.00	.00	.00
Pennsylvania course	1		.87	.03	.36	.24	.12	.02	.07	.00	.02	.00
Algebra 1	11	$\bar{x}$	.83	.02	.24	.25	.05	.06	.12	.00	.08	.00
		s	.107	.037	.148	.099	.047	.039	.101	.002	.159	.001

Source: A. C. Porter and others. *Reform Up Close: An Analysis of High School Mathematics and Science Classrooms*, final report to the National Science Foundation. Grant No. SPA–8953446 (University of Wisconsin at Madison. Wisconsin Center for Education Research, 1993).
Note: $\bar{x}$ = mean; s = standard deviation.

Table 2. Cognitive Demand Variations within and between Course Titles

Course	N		Memorize facts	Understand concepts	Collect data	Order compare estimate approximate	Perform routine procedures	Solve routine problems	Interpret data	Solve novel problems	Theory/ proof
Arizona course	1		.14	.43	.02	.00	.25	.12	.03	.01	.00
Pennsylvania course	1		.00	.18	.10	.02	.23	.47	.00	.01	.00
Algebra 1	11	$\bar{x}$	.05	.22	.02	.01	.46	.18	.03	.02	.00
		s	.069	.140	.029	.015	.187	.138	.027	.027	.002

Source: A. C. Porter and others. *Reform Up Close: An Analysis of High School Mathematics and Science Classrooms*, final report to the National Science Foundation. Grant No. SPA–8953446 (University of Wisconsin at Madison. Wisconsin Center for Education Research, 1993).
Note: $\bar{x}$ = mean; s = standard deviation.

procedures). The algebra 1 mean was .46, with a standard deviation of .187, while the value for the Arizona course was .25 and the value for the Pennsylvania course was .23. The Arizona course made up for its lack of emphasis on computation by putting considerably more emphasis on memorization and understanding, a combined emphasis of .57 in comparison with the algebra 1 courses' combined mean of .27. The Pennsylvania course put substantially more emphasis on ''solve routine problems, replicate experiments/replicate proofs'' than was true for the average of algebra 1 courses (.47 versus .18). This is consistent with earlier findings that the Pennsylvania course seemed, if anything, to be more rigid and to have higher standards than other algebra 1 courses.

Of the thirty science target courses, only one was in a school where the course was required of all students. Freshman chemistry and physics was a required course of study for all students in one of the two Arizona urban high schools. The most similar course type in the target sample was physical science. Within that sample of physical science courses is also a college preparatory physical science course to which the required chemistry and physics course can be compared.

Freshman chemistry and physics in the Arizona high school gave equal coverage to chemistry and physics content (.37 for each content area) and slightly less coverage to general science (.24). The five other general content areas received no content coverage at all in the course. This profile is similar to the college prep physical science course offered in one of the two South Carolina urban high schools. In the college prep physical science course, somewhat less emphasis was given to general science (.16) and somewhat more emphasis was given to chemistry (.52). The required Arizona chemistry and physics course fell within 1 standard deviation of the mean for all physical science courses in the log sample on seven of the eight general content areas. The only exception was for general science content, which was emphasized more in the Arizona course.

Regarding topics within the general content areas, several additional features of the required chemistry and physics course are revealed. In contrast to both the South Carolina college prep physical science course and the average of all physical science courses, the required chemistry and physics course placed a much greater emphasis in chemistry on atomic and molecular structure (.14) and energy (.05) (see table 3). Both of these differences are about 2 standard deviations more than either the college prep physical science course or the mean of all physical science courses. In contrast, the required chemistry and physics course gave less coverage to chemical properties and processes (.02), organic chemistry (.00), and nuclear chemistry (.00).

For physics content, more similarities than differences emerged on topics among the required chemistry and physics course, the college prep physical science course, and the average of all physical science courses (see table 4). The required chemistry and physics course placed more emphasis on properties and structures of matter (.17) in comparison with physical science courses (.08, .061).[24] The required chemistry and physics course gave no attention to the topics of static and current electricity and magnetism, and neither did the college prep physical science course. On average across all physical science courses, however, these topics received modest coverage (static and current electricity (.06, .085); magnetism (.04, .069)).

Within general science content, the greater amount of emphasis on general science found for the required chemistry and physics course was divided fairly equally between the two topics—nature and structure of science and nature of scientific inquiry (see table 5). For nature and structure of science, instructional emphasis was .10, much greater than in the college prep physical science course (.03) and the sample of physical science courses (.02, .034). For the nature of scientific inquiry, coverage was also .10, which compares with .05 for the college prep physical science course and .06 for all physical science courses.

In sum, some differences are evident among the required freshman chemistry and physics course, the college prep physical science course, and the average of all physical science courses, but none of the differences seems particularly remarkable. Nothing suggests that the course is either easier or more challenging than other physical science courses.

The required freshman chemistry and physics course looks like physical science courses on cognitive demand and also like the college prep physical science course in the South Carolina urban school (see table 6). On the one hand, little to no attention is given in any of these courses to novel problems or building and revising theory. On the other hand, all of these courses are dominated by an emphasis on memorizing facts and understanding concepts. Nevertheless, the required course stands out in two ways, in terms of cognitive demand. First, the course placed less emphasis on memorizing facts than did physical science

Table 3. Freshman Chemistry and Physics Course Required of All Students: Chemistry

Course	N	Total	Periodic system	Bonding	Properties and processes	Atomic and molecular structure	Energy	Relations	Equilibrium	Organic	Nuclear	Environmental
Chemistry and physics	1	.37	.05	.02	.02	.14	.05	.09	.00	.00	.00	.00
College prep physical science	1	.52	.06	.01	.14	.05	.01	.11	.00	.08	.06	.00
Physical science courses	8 $\bar{x}$	.35	.03	.03	.07	.07	.01	.10	.00	.02	.01	.00
	s	.122	.024	.022	.058	.045	.016	.051	.001	.035	.021	.011

Source: A. C. Porter and others, *Reform Up Close: An Analysis of High School Mathematics and Science Classrooms*, final report to the National Science Foundation. Grant No. SPA–8953446 (University of Wisconsin at Madison, Wisconsin Center for Education Research, 1993).
Note: $\bar{x}$ = mean; s = standard deviation.

Table 4. Freshman Chemistry and Physics Course Required of All Students: Physics

Course	Total	Energy: Sources and conservation	Heat	Static and current electricity	Magnetism	Sound	Light and spectra	Machines and mechanics	Properties and structures of matter	Molecular and nuclear physics
Chemistry and physics	.37	.09	.00	.00	.00	.04	.01	.06	.17	.00
College prep physical science	.32	.14	.03	.00	.00	.07	.00	.03	.04	.00
Physical science courses	.46 $\bar{x}$	.11	.03	.06	.04	.04	.03	.07	.08	.00
	.104 s	.046	.023	.085	.069	.024	.040	.055	.061	.002

Source: A. C. Porter and others, *Reform Up Close: An Analysis of High School Mathematics and Science Classrooms*, final report to the National Science Foundation. Grant No. SPA–8953446 (University of Wisconsin at Madison, Wisconsin Center for Education Research, 1993).
Note: $\bar{x}$ = mean; s = standard deviation.

Source: A. C. Porter and others, *Reform Up Close: An Analysis of High School Mathematics and Science Classrooms*, final report to the National Science Foundation, Grant No. SPA–8953446 (University of Wisconsin at Madison, Wisconsin Center for Education Research, 1993).
Note: $\bar{x}$ = mean; s = standard deviation.

Table 5. Freshman Chemistry and Physics Course Required of All Students: General Science

Course		Total	Nature and structure	Scientific inquiry	History	Ethical	International system of units	Science/ technology
Chemistry and physics		.24	.10	.10	.00	.00	.04	.00
College prep physical science		.16	.03	.05	.02	.00	.04	.01
Physical science courses	$\bar{x}$	.15	.02	.06	.00	.00	.05	.02
	s	.069	.034	.069	.008	.002	.027	.014

Table 6. Chemistry and Physics Course Required of All Students: Cognitive Demand

Course	N		Memorize facts	Understand concepts	Collect data	Order compare estimate approximate	Perform routine procedures	Solve routine problems	Interpret data	Solve novel problems	Theory/ proof
Chemistry and physics	1		.20	.37	.08	.05	.06	.14	.07	.02	.00
College prep physical science	1		.59	.21	.08	.02	.02	.03	.03	.02	.00
Physical science courses	8	$\bar{x}$	.31	.37	.08	.04	.03	.08	.06	.02	.01
		s	.254	.117	.049	.036	.033	.053	.071	.013	.014

Source: A. C. Porter and others, *Reform Up Close: An Analysis of High School Mathematics and Science Classrooms*, final report to the National Science Foundation, Grant No. SPA–8953446 (University of Wisconsin at Madison, Wisconsin Center for Education Research, 1993).
Note: $\bar{x}$ = mean; s = standard deviation.

courses in general, .20 for the required course versus .31 for the physical science course sample (with a standard deviation of .254). The required course also put much less emphasis on memorization of facts than did the college prep course (.59). With the freed up time from a relatively lower emphasis upon memorization of facts, the required freshman chemistry and physics course put substantially more time on solving routine problems and replicating experiments, .14 for the required course versus .03 for the college prep physical science course, and .08 for the sample of physical science courses. These differences make the required course look more in line with what current curriculum reform is calling for than other physical science courses.

COURSE LEVEL VERSUS CLASS ABILITY AS A PREDICTOR OF COURSE CONTENT. Regression analyses provided yet a third look at the question of whether or not increased enrollments in math and science courses, brought on by increased high school graduation requirements, resulted in a watering down of the curriculum. In regressions to predict classroom content and pedagogy, if increased enrollments had served to compromise the curriculum, then Class Ability should be a stronger predictor of course content and pedagogy than Course Level. If, in contrast, the course curricula had not been compromised, Course Level should be the stronger predictor. In either case, both Class Ability and Course Level could be expected to predict content and pedagogy; the comparison of their strengths of prediction is most important here.

Several multiple regression equations were fit to both questionnaire and log data to explain the variance among class sections studied in the content taught and, to some extent, pedagogical strategies employed. The questionnaire sample affords the best data set for estimating regression equation parameters because of the relatively large sample size.

A Group policy variable was defined as a linear contrast among the six states. Arizona and California were coded 1; Missouri and Pennsylvania, 0; and Florida and South Carolina, −1. This Group variable contrasts states with the greatest emphasis on encouraging higher-order thinking, problem solving, and reasoning (that is, Arizona and California) with states that have the greatest focus on basic skills (that is, Florida and South Carolina). The two states having the fewest state-level curriculum policy initiatives in math and science were in between the two extremes (Missouri and Pennsylvania). The Subject variable was 1 for science and 0 for mathematics.

Because the information available differed between the questionnaire and log samples, and because the log sample was too small to include all of the variables of interest, several differences resulted between regression equations estimated for the two sets of data. Control and climate variables were defined by scales created from teacher questionnaire data. For the questionnaire sample, the control variables were: School Ability (two items, α = .36); School Behavior (eleven items, α = .87); Class Ability (four items, α = .62); Subject; and Course Level. The climate variables fall into three sets: (1) School: Leadership (four items, α = .63); Resources (ten items, α = .78); Institutional Support (five items, α = .59); Shared Beliefs (three items, α = .44); and Teacher Control (eighteen items, α = .56); (2) Class: Percent Female; Percent White; and Class Size; and (3) Teacher: Gender; Ethnicity; Level of Education (four items, α = .44); Years of Experience; Load (three items, α = .49); Responsibility (three items, α = .57); Collegiality (four items, α = .55); and Satisfaction (three items, α = .56).

For the log sample, a similar but not identical set of regression equations was estimated. The sets of control and climate variables were reduced. The control variables were: Class Ability; Course Level; and Subject. The climate variables were: Percent of Female Students in the Class; Percent of White Students in the Class; Teacher Years of Experience; Teacher Level of Education; and Teacher Control.

Four additional dependent variables were defined from the teacher questionnaire data: Change, indicating the frequency and types of changes that occurred in the last three years that might have bearing on teachers' instructional practices (for example, changes in textbooks, changes in length of school day); Teacher Demands on Students (for example, amount of homework assigned and taken seriously); Active Learning (for example, extent to which students are engaged in discussion, report writing, lab or field work, observation, measurement, interpreting data, designing experiments, and other forms of active learning); and Higher-Order Thinking (for example, extent to which instruction in the course being described on the questionnaire involves problem solving and applications).

For predicting emphasis on mathematics topics, Course Level was a much stronger predictor than Class Ability (see tables 7 and 8). (In the tables, only Regressions with significant R^2s at .05 are shown. All regression coefficients are standardized.) These results held for both

Table 7. Math Questionnaire Sample Regressions: Group, Control, and Climate Variables to Predict Content

Independent variable	Number		Arithmetic		Measurement		Algebra		Geometry		Trigonometry		Precalculus		Theory/proof	
	B	p	B	p	B	p	B	p	B	p	B	p	B	p	B	p
Group	.09	.347	.06	.546	-.19	.058	-.04	.652	.03	.730	-.10	.318	.06	.555	.07	.489
School Ability	-.03	.830	-.08	.535	-.16	.194	.12	.315	-.25	.049	.17	.167	.23	.054	-.13	.294
School Behavior	.09	.425	-.01	.896	-.06	.569	-.03	.820	-.10	.407	.07	.521	.14	.201	.16	.167
Class Ability	-.22	.017	-.10	.292	.06	.503	-.05	.609	.04	.685	.18	.060	.21	.021	.21	.024
Course Level	-.38	.000	-.46	.000	-.37	.000	.47	.000	.13	.161	.27	.005	.35	.000	.17	.066
Leadership	.20	.076	.08	.469	-.17	.170	-.09	.448	-.18	.148	.04	.766	.09	.444	.11	.372
Resources	-.01	.928	.10	.355	.13	.252	-.08	.468	.04	.705	-.06	.572	-.12	.264	-.14	.218
Institutional Support	.05	.679	.00	.987	.03	.816	.15	.230	-.02	.872	-.17	.192	-.11	.360	-.16	.198
Shared Beliefs	-.10	.333	-.03	.798	-.01	.895	-.07	.466	.20	.056	.16	.118	-.06	.556	.12	.257
Teacher Control	-.18	.043	-.02	.811	.05	.621	-.00	.973	.18	.053	.01	.931	-.12	.164	.12	.180
Percent Female	.08	.343	.05	.582	-.11	.241	-.08	.357	.01	.875	-.04	.677	.05	.605	-.14	.132
Percent White	.05	.645	.01	.934	.12	.290	-.16	.149	.34	.004	.05	.661	-.35	.002	-.16	.157
Class Size	.01	.932	.02	.821	.16	.089	-.01	.943	.11	.230	-.08	.445	-.25	.006	-.04	.698
Teacher Gender	-.03	.754	.06	.484	-.01	.905	.09	.307	-.05	.562	-.01	.873	-.15	.089	-.10	.265
Teacher Ethnicity	.02	.786	.03	.705	-.00	.970	.12	.198	-.34	.001	.03	.737	.14	.129	-.09	.333
Teacher Education	.07	.408	-.03	.758	-.15	.094	.13	.141	-.01	.897	-.04	.632	.05	.582	.18	.045
Teacher Experience	-.14	.118	-.14	.127	.12	.211	.06	.518	-.03	.784	-.11	.237	.12	.167	.08	.391
Teacher Load	-.04	.701	.03	.773	.03	.778	.03	.786	.06	.570	-.24	.023	.08	.416	-.04	.679
Teacher Responsibility	-.05	.633	-.16	.118	.09	.402	.15	.149	-.04	.678	-.16	.124	.04	.733	.03	.758
Teacher Collegiality	-.00	.992	-.10	.372	-.07	.526	.09	.413	.02	.883	.02	.822	-.04	.732	-.03	.778
Teacher Satisfaction	-.10	.339	.09	.395	-.01	.902	.01	.929	.01	.932	-.04	.737	.10	.327	-.11	.317
R^2	.321		.298		.256		.272		.234		.264		.304		.271	
p	.001		.002		.016		.007		.040		.011		.001		.008	
Residual df	117		117		117		117		117		117		117		117	

Source: A. C. Porter and others. *Reform Up Close: An Analysis of High School Mathematics and Science Classrooms*, final report to the National Science Foundation. Grant No. SPA–8953446 (University of Wisconsin at Madison. Wisconsin Center for Education Research. 1993).

Table 8. Math and Science Log Sample Regressions: Group, Control, and Climate Variables to Predict Pedagogy and Content

| | Mathematics | | | | | | Science | |
| | Arithmetic | | Measurement | | Algebra | | Physics | |
Independent variable	B	p	B	p	B	p	B	p
Group	.18	.099	.03	.842	-.14	.340	-.31	.086
Class Ability	.07	.652	-.10	.641	-.12	.585	-.02	.902
Course Level	-.83	.000	-.68	.000	.74	.000	-.65	.002
Percent Female	-.24	.048	-.01	.971	-.04	.807	.13	.445
Percent White	-.08	.552	-.12	.491	.01	.975	.05	.775
Teacher Education	-.12	.259	-.00	.984	.15	.322	-.28	.126
Teacher Experience	.04	.746	.14	.407	-.05	.787	-.18	.262
Teacher Control	-.20	.164	.23	.227	-.29	.139	.38	.029
R^2	.793		.615		.597		.575	
p	.000		.006		.008		.018	
Residual df	20		20		20		19	

Source: A. C. Porter and others. *Reform Up Close: An Analysis of High School Mathematics and Science Classrooms*, final report to the National Science Foundation. Grant No. SPA-8953446 (University of Wisconsin at Madison. Wisconsin Center for Education Research. 1993).

questionnaire and log data and were especially true for topics of number, arithmetic, and measurement, all of which were emphasized more in low-level courses, and for algebra, trigonometry, and precalculus, all of which were emphasized more in high-level courses. The one exception to this strong pattern is geometry, which was not predicted by either Course Level or Class Ability but had a significant negative relationship with School Ability; schools serving student bodies judged to be of relatively low ability have math courses that put a greater emphasis on geometry than do schools serving student bodies of higher ability.

Science topics were less well predicted by either Course Level or Class Ability than were math topics. For log data, physics had a strong negative relationship with Course Level. Low-level physical science courses were the courses in the log sample containing physics; no physics courses were in the log sample. In the questionnaire sample, biology of other organisms and biology of populations both had significant positive relationships with Course Level and significant negative relationships with Class Ability (see table 9). Thus, these two topic areas tend to be taught to relatively low-ability classes taking relatively high-level courses.

Three pedagogical variables were predicted by Course Level, but not Class Ability, in the questionnaire total sample. Teacher Demands on Students ($B = .14, p = .035$) and Breadth of Coverage ($B = .20, p = .006$) both had positive relationships with Course Level. Class Ability was not a significant predictor. (In the science sample, however, Breadth of Coverage also had a negative relation with Class Ability, $B = -.33, p = .004$.) Higher-level courses were more demanding and had a greater breadth of coverage. In contrast, an emphasis upon Active Student Learning had a significant negative relationship with Course Level ($B = -.21, p = .000$), and Class Ability was not a significant predictor. Lower-level courses placed a greater emphasis upon active learning, probably reflecting greater innovation in lower-level courses including bridge courses and freshman college prep required courses. For the mathematics sample, Active Learning had a significant negative relationship with School Ability ($B = -.32, p = .007$), in addition to its negative relationship with Course Level ($B = -.32, p = .000$). For log data, emphasis on Graphs ($B = .42, p = .005$) was positively predicted by Course Level, but not Class Ability. Also, Demonstration

Table 9. Science Questionnaire Sample Regressions: Group, Control, and Climate Variables to Predict Pedagogy and Content

Independent variable	Biology organism		Biology population	
	B	p	B	p
Group	.01	.895	.14	.169
School Ability	− .03	.766	− .02	.832
School Behavior	− .04	.721	− .05	.645
Class Ability	− .33	.003	− .42	.000
Course Level	.37	.000	.45	.000
Leadership	− .00	.991	.12	.337
Resources	− .08	.451	− .07	.560
Institutional Support	− .05	.683	.13	.252
Shared Beliefs	.08	.471	− .14	.236
Teacher Control	.40	.000	.00	.989
Percent Female	− .05	.596	− .05	.574
Percent White	− .12	.223	− .03	.752
Class Size	.07	.438	.06	.557
Teacher Gender	− .09	.295	− .03	.738
Teacher Ethnicity	− .13	.171	− .18	.064
Teacher Education	− .12	.221	− .05	.593
Teacher Experience	.06	.524	− .01	.878
Teacher Load	.06	.558	− .05	.636
Teacher Responsibility	.05	.583	.15	.143
Teacher Collegiality	− .03	.752	− .14	.177
Teacher Satisfaction	− .09	.397	− .10	.384
R^2	.343		.307	
p	.002		.008	
Residual *df*	99		99	

Source: A. C. Porter and others, *Reform Up Close: An Analysis of High School Mathematics and Science Classrooms*, final report to the National Science Foundation, Grant No. SPA–8953446 (University of Wisconsin at Madison, Wisconsin Center for Education Research, 1993).

was positively related to Course Level ($B = .38$, $p = .005$), and Student Reports was negatively related to Course Level ($B = − .31$, $p = .040$). In neither regression was Class Ability a significant predictor.

Emphasis on Routine Problems had significant negative relationships with both Course Level ($B = − .17$, $p = .013$) and Class Ability ($B = − .20$, $p = .003$). This student outcome was emphasized more in lower-level and lower-ability classrooms. In contrast, emphasis on Theory/proofs had significant positive relationships with both Course Level ($B = .16$, $p = .019$) and Class Ability ($B = .22$, $p = .002$).

Computer use had a negative relationship with Course Level ($B = − .21$, $p = .002$) and a positive relationship with Class Ability ($B = .14$, $p = .034$). Computer use is more emphasized in lower-level courses, reflecting the use of computers for delivering drill-and-practice instruction. Holding Course Level constant, however, computers were used more frequently with higher-ability classes. Lower-level courses also put greater emphasis on student report writing, a result similar to that seen for active learning. But holding Course Level constant, higher-ability classrooms participated more in student report writing.

For the log sample, the amount of class time not devoted to academic instruction was predicted significantly and negatively by Course Level ($B = -.44, p = .020$) in the math sample and significantly negatively by Class Ability ($B = -.44, p = .031$) in the science sample. In mathematics, lower-level courses are more likely than higher-level courses to use a larger fraction of instructional time for noninstructional purposes. In science, however, the lower-ability classes are more likely to have a relatively large fraction of instructional time used for non-instructional purposes.

While the above results suggest that increased enrollments did not bring about a watered-down curriculum, a few other results were less consistent with that conclusion. Emphasis on Higher-Order Thinking and problem solving had a significant positive relationship with Class Ability ($B = .18, p = .005$) but was not predicted by Course Level. Higher-ability classes received greater emphasis on higher-order thinking, problem solving, and reasoning, regardless of the course level. From the log data, use of concrete models as a pedagogical strategy was positively predicted by Class Ability ($B = .43, p = .035$) but not Course Level in the science sample. Also from the log data, but in the math sample, the extent to which teachers worked with other teachers in planning their instruction was positively predicted by Class Ability ($B = .64, p = .014$). Finally, use of calculators was positively predicted by Class Ability ($B = .21, p = .002$) but not predicted by Course Level in the questionnaire data.

SCIENCE LAB REQUIREMENTS. As an additional upgrading strategy, two of the six states required that a minimum amount of lab time must be included in science courses for courses to count toward graduation. In Florida, at least 40 percent of instructional time in science courses was to be spent on lab work; in South Carolina, 20 percent. The log sample science courses provide a good test of the impact of these state science lab requirements.

Of the ten Florida and South Carolina science courses for which a full year of log data were available, not one met the state requirement for lab work. In Florida, the percentages of instructional time for lab work for the five science classes were .03, .21, .21, .00, and .07. For South Carolina, the percentages of instructional time for lab work were .05, .07, .09, .11, and .11. The log sample science course mean for lab work was .10, with a standard deviation of .067. The Florida mean matched the total sample mean of .10, while the South Carolina mean was only slightly less, .09. State requirements for lab work had no effect on instructional practice, even though, for example, in Florida schools were required to send forms certifying that the lab requirement was being met; and some funding was conditioned upon these assurances.

The lack of intended effect of the state requirements for lab work in science stands in sharp contrast to the positive findings concerning efforts to increase student enrollments in math and science. The lab work requirement meant changes in what schools and teachers do. The graduation requirement and course requirement strategies forced students to change but not schools and teachers.

The findings of these analyses are largely positive on the effects of increased standards for high school course taking in mathematics and science. As states raised their graduation requirements in mathematics and science, students responded by taking more mathematics and science courses, including more college preparatory mathematics and science courses. At the same time, the probabilities of high school graduation remained unchanged, with students just as likely to graduate from high school after the implementation of the new standards as before that time. Furthermore, essentially no evidence exists that the influx of increased numbers of students into mathematics and science courses resulted in a watering down of those courses.

In addition, few indications suggest that teachers had augmented their pedagogical strategies to accommodate the new students. Essentially, the courses remained unchanged by the influx of new students, either as to the content covered or as to the pedagogical strategies employed by teachers. Students changed their behaviors by taking more math and science, while teachers maintained their behaviors by essentially offering the same courses in the same ways as they had done previously (or at least as they were doing for courses that experienced less significant new enrollment pressures).

Transition Math Course Study

The transition math course study flowed conceptually from the Reform Up Close Study and shared many design features.[25] In Reform Up Close, the most innovative and promising strategy for upgrading high school mathematics was a math transition course, Math A, designed and implemented by California teachers but with state support. Math A was serving a variety of purposes; primary among them was as an alternative to the dead-end general math course. Students successful in Math A were expected to pursue college preparatory mathematics courses. Thus, this second study was designed to look closely at transition courses not only in California but also wherever else they might be found. In particular, the study sought to document the nature and effects of the transition math innovation.

Study Design

The study involved two districts in each of two states and two high schools in each district. Of all the states identified as leaders in high school mathematics upgrading (California, Connecticut, Florida, Illinois, Iowa, Kentucky, Louisiana, Montana, New York, North Carolina, Oregon, South Carolina, Texas, Vermont, Washington, and Wisconsin), California and New York were judged to be the two furthest along with a serious transition course effort. California was selected because of its creation and implementation of Math A. New York was selected because, in some districts, Stretch Regents was introduced as an alternative to general mathematics and, in other districts, the University of Chicago School Mathematics Project (UCSMP) was used as an alternative to general math.

Because transition courses are most important for students of relatively low achievement, districts were selected that served high concentrations of such students. In each state, districts selected were urban, had large percentages of low-achieving students, and had initiated transition math courses sufficiently early that they were mature for study. The process of selection involved interviewing state department officials, district and school administrators, and math teachers.

In all but one district, two high schools were studied. As in the Reform Up Close Study, the focus was on comprehensive high schools serving grades nine through twelve, with a stable grade-level organization and a stable student body. Also, the average student achievement was in the lowest quartile of schools within the district and state, and schools were serving high concentrations of low-income students.

District enrollment ranged in size from thirty-three thousand to more than 100,000. High schools ranged in size from one thousand to twenty-five hundred. In one district, the use of transition courses had begun twenty years before the study; but in another district, use of transition courses was only two years old. Percentage of minority students ranged from a low of 35 to a high of 98, while percentage of students from families in poverty ranged from 17 to 80.

The Transition Courses

Math A in California and Stretch Regents in New York are two transition courses.

CALIFORNIA MATH A. By 1992–93, the time of the study, more than 75 percent of California's high schools offered Math A. Originally conceptualized in the 1985 California math framework, Math A was designed to serve as an intermediate step for students who might otherwise have taken ninth grade general mathematics and still might not be ready for algebra. Math A has thirteen units, emphasizing group work, use of manipulatives, student participation, open-ended questions, student portfolios, and assessments that require written responses. It is not a state requirement, but an option that some districts, some schools, and some individual teachers have chosen to adopt. Before a teacher can teach Math A, a five-day inservice session is required. Some districts and schools have added to this minimum inservice requirement, sometimes substantially.

An emphasis upon cooperative learning moves the teacher away from whole-group instruction and helps place students in situations where they must learn to communicate their understanding of math to their peers. To complement the instructional methodology, one- to four-week cohesive units help bring mathematical concepts together around a theme. This high-intensity curriculum strives to cover fewer topics in greater depth.

Teaching strategies include the use of manipulatives and concrete experiences, calculators, drawing visual representations, mathematical modeling, and problem solving that support understanding of mathematics. A course guide provides teachers with the overall course perspective and mathematical ideas, but it is not a textbook package with tear-out fill-in-the-blank answer sheets. An annotated reference guide helps teachers locate appropriate materials. The course emphasizes mathematics embedded in real-world problems, data collection and interpretation, and mathematical modeling.

Math A was studied in San Francisco and San Diego.

STRETCH REGENTS. Stretch Regents covers the same material as regular Regents, but at a slower pace. In some implementations of Stretch Regents, the Regents textbook material is covered in the same order as in the book, but in twice the time. In other schools, the sections of the Regents text perceived to be easiest are covered in a first year, Stretch Regents 1A, and the rest of the material (that is, the more difficult material) is covered in a second year, Stretch Regents 1B.

Regents Math is an alternative to traditional college preparatory mathematics in that the three-year math sequence integrates algebra, geometry, trigonometry, probability, statistics, and problem solving. This integrated Regents approach was required statewide in 1988 for Regents 1, 1989 for Regents 2, and 1990 for Regents 3. However, many districts had implemented the sequence a decade or more earlier. Students in Stretch Regents are considered to be taking college preparatory mathematics and earn Regents credits. Rochester was the New York district where Stretch Regents was studied.

THE UNIVERSITY OF CHICAGO SCHOOL MATHEMATICS PROJECT. In Buffalo, instead of using a Stretch Regents approach to transition math, the UCSMP curriculum was adopted. Students could take UCSMP as an alternative to Regents or general math. The first course in the UCSMP sequence served as the transition course.

The designers of UCSMP intended to create an alternative sequence to traditional college prep mathematics. The sequence was to begin in seventh grade and last for six years. UCSMP, like Math A, puts an emphasis on problem solving, word problems, and real-world applications. Like the Regents curriculum, it integrates algebra, geometry, trigonometry, statistics, and problem solving; but unlike the Regents, it also integrates science, history, and language arts.

Data Collected

At each of the seven high schools in the study, interviews were conducted with the principal, a counselor, and teachers of transition math courses, upper-level math courses, and nontransition basic math courses. To determine the consequences of transition math courses for completing college preparatory mathematics, transcript data were collected. In a Buffalo high school, three years of transcript data were collected on one ninth grade cohort, beginning in 1990–91. In both Rochester high schools, four years of transcript data were collected on one ninth grade cohort, beginning in 1988–89. In both San Diego high schools, a four-year cohort of data was collected on ninth graders, beginning in 1990–91. In San Francisco, one four-year cohort of data for freshmen beginning in 1989–90 and one three-year cohort of data for freshmen beginning in 1990–91 were collected.

Because all high schools studied were serving high concentrations of low-income, low-achieving students, student mobility presented a serious challenge. For example, in one San Francisco high school, the cohort began with 502 students; four years later, there were 334 students, for a one-third attrition rate. Beginning cohort sample sizes across the nine cohorts of data ranged from 988 to 248. Attrition across four years ranged from 67 percent to 19 percent. Attrition from the sample does not necessarily mean that students dropped out of school. Many transferred to another school.

To determine the effects of transition math on the content of instruction and student achievement, teacher and student questionnaire data and student achievement data were collected from a sample of high school mathematics classes. In each school, courses selected for study included transition courses, at least one traditional low-level course (for example, general math or pre-algebra), and at least one college preparatory course (for example, Regents 1 or algebra). San Francisco was an exception, in that all low-level math courses had been eliminated. Initially, the sample included fifty-six classes across the seven schools and slightly in excess of sixteen hundred students. A student achievement test was administered in the fall, winter, and spring of the 1992–93 academic year. Teacher and student questionnaires were administered in the winter and spring.

The student achievement test was created from NAEP public release items. Fifteen percent of the items on the test were arithmetic, 20 percent measurement, 15 percent algebra, 20 percent geometry, 20 percent probability, and 10 percent numbers and sets. As to cognitive demand, 30 percent of the items tested concepts, 15 percent procedures, 20 percent data interpretation, 27 percent routine word problems, and 8 percent novel word problems. Thus, the test was assembled to be as consistent as possible with the National Council of Teachers of Mathematics *Content Standards'* call for rigorous mathematics content that promotes understanding and emphasizes problem solving. The total number of students tested was 1,678, with a total number of tests completed of 3,399, for an average of just in excess of two tests per student. Of the students enrolled in the courses studied, the response rate was 80 percent in the fall, 83 percent in winter, and 75 percent in spring. Of the total sample of students, there were three data points for 620 students, and there were winter and spring data points for an additional 287 students.

Of the original fifty-six classes selected for study, six were ultimately dropped from the sample because they were bilingual classes with questionable data; and two were dropped because they used a special approach, the Interactive Math Program, which made them atypical, both in terms of the nature of instruction and the nature of student achievement. Of the forty-eight-class sample resulting, sufficiently complete data were available on 498 students, who were tested three times and an additional 384 who were tested twice, for a total student sample of 882.

The content of instruction was defined in a way nearly identical to that in the Reform Up Close Study. The definition of topics was identical. The cognitive demand dimension included the following categories: memorize facts, understand concepts, perform procedures and solve equations; collect and interpret data; solve word problems; and solve novel problems. In winter and spring, teachers described the content of instruction for the prior semester of work. For each math topic, teachers indicated the amount of time taught, from not taught to taught in excess of ten hours; and for those topics taught at least some amount of time, teachers indicated the degree of emphasis on each of the six categories of cognitive demand, from 0 to 3 levels of emphasis.

A key variable in the analyses was the extent to which classroom instruction was aligned to the content of the achievement test. The alignment variable was defined by the product of the level and the configuration of alignment between classroom instruction and the achievement test.

Findings about Transition Courses

If transition courses are successful in meeting their purpose, students who participate in them should complete more college prep mathematics credits, and they should learn more mathematics. Transcript data address the issue of math credits completed; student achievement data address the question of how much students learn.

TRANSCRIPT FINDINGS. The distribution of ninth grade students into general, transition, and college prep math courses varied considerably among San Diego and the other districts. In San Diego, approximately two-thirds of the students enrolled in college prep courses; in San Francisco and Rochester, only 20 to 30 percent of the students enrolled in college prep courses. In San Francisco, nearly 50 percent of the students enrolled in transition courses; in San Diego and Rochester, approximately 25 percent of the students enrolled in transition courses.

Placement of students into high school math courses, at least in the urban high schools with highly mobile student populations, is not an entirely rational process. As Brian DeLany found, student placement appears to be based more on satisfying the practical demands of school scheduling than on the basis of student accomplishment and interest.[26] In the California and New York schools studied, nearly 40 percent of the students were not placed according to the schools' reported criteria. In Rochester, all of the students receiving an A or a B in eighth grade mathematics were supposed to take Regents Math. However, only 50 percent of those students took Regents Math. Conversely, several of the students with C + or less in eighth grade ended up in Regents Math. In a similar vein, the plan to reserve transition math for freshmen was not always followed. In San Francisco, nearly half of the students taking Math A were upperclassmen.

Two criteria were set for judging whether or not students completed appropriate amounts of mathematics. One criterion was whether students completed three credits or more of mathematics, as was required for high school graduation in Rochester and San Diego. (Only two years of mathematics were required for graduation in the other districts.) The other criterion was whether students completed two years or more of college prep mathematics credits, as might be expected, for college-bound students.

Against the criterion of completing three or more years of mathematics, of those students starting out in general math, 60 percent met the criterion; of those starting out in transition math, 61 percent; and of those starting out in college prep math, 84 percent. Thus, placing students in the more challenging transition math had no negative effect upon their meeting high school graduation requirements in mathematics, in comparison with being placed in general math. Not surprisingly, those starting out in college prep math were the most likely to complete three math credits.

Fifteen percent of the students starting out in general math met the criterion of completing two or more years of college prep mathematics; as did 50 percent of those starting out in transition math, and 88 percent of those starting out in college prep math. Considerable variability was found among schools. In Rochester, less than 5 percent of the students starting out in general math completed two or more years of college prep mathematics; in San Diego, 30 to 35 percent of the general math students ultimately completed at least two credits of college prep mathematics. Similarly, for students enrolled in transition courses, Rochester students had only a 13 percent likelihood of completing two or more college prep credits; nearly two-thirds of San Diego transition course students completed two or more college prep math credits. Using a logistic regression analysis, differences among course types were significant at the .01 level.

To some extent, these results showing the value of transition math over general math may be a function of higher-achieving students taking transition math than those taking general math. In Rochester, analyses were done using a logistic regression analysis with grades in eighth grade as a control variable. For students with a C in eighth grade mathematics, of those enrolling initially in general math, only 1 percent completed two or more credits of mathematics. Of those initially enrolling in transition math, 18 percent met the criterion; and of those initially enrolling in college prep, 88 percent met the criterion. Similar results were found when conditioned on students' having received a C + in eighth grade. In San Diego, eighth grade standardized test results in math and reading were available for control variables. Again using a logistic regression model, students scoring average on the standardized tests and who initially enrolled in general math were 51 percent likely to complete two or more college prep math credits. Those enrolled in Math A were 63 percent likely, and those who started in college prep math were 88 percent likely. Similar differences were found when conditioned on low standardized test results. These differences were statistically significant at the .01 level.

Transition courses had no negative effect on percentages of students who completed high school graduation requirements in mathematics, while having positive effects on the percentage who completed two or more credits in college prep mathematics. However, students who started out in college prep mathematics did significantly better on both criteria than did students in the transition courses, even when controlling for past math grades or past standardized achievement test results.

ACHIEVEMENT FINDINGS. In addition to completing more and more worthwhile courses in mathematics, knowing whether students learned more mathematics is important. The achievement test was administered in the fall, winter, and spring of the 1992–93 school year. In winter and spring, teachers were surveyed to report on the content of their mathematics instruction. Control variables were gender, race, final math grade in the previous year, and, at the classroom level, socioeconomic background of the students. Analyses of achievement gains were done using a three-level hierarchical linear regression model.[27] The first level of analysis assumed a linear growth in achievement for each student over the school year. The second level measured differences between students within classes, and the third level was for between-class differences. For purposes of analysis, general math and pre-algebra math were collapsed into a single low track category. Transition math was Math A, Math B, Stretch Regents, and UCSMP. College prep math was algebra or Regents 1. Of the forty-eight classes for which sufficiently complete data were available, eight were in the low track, twenty-six were in transition math, and fourteen were in college prep math. Analyses were based on 882 students across these forty-eight classrooms.

With control variables in the model, the low track math course students gained significantly less over the course of the year than did students in college prep math. Gains for students in transition math were approximately midway between the low track math and college prep track math students, though not significantly different from either.

When the indicator of content coverage was added to the analyses, the significant differences among course types on student achievement gains disappeared. In short, the key difference between college prep math, transition math, and general math in promoting student achievement was in the alignment of the content of instruction to the test.

Conclusion

Stimulated by the report *A Nation at Risk,* states and districts across the nation sought to upgrade high school mathematics and science experiences, especially for low-achieving students. Starting in the mid-to-late 1980s, the primary policy approach was to increase the number of credits of mathematics and science required for high school graduation. From the point of view of teacher content decisionmaking, this policy strategy is distinctive. Teachers are to continue doing what they have been doing; the students' practices are to change. Increasing the number of credits in mathematics and science that the students must complete to graduate from high school is not a particularly prescriptive policy. Only the time students are to spend studying mathematics and science is specified. The policy is silent as to the nature of the mathematics and science that students are to study. The requirement might be satisfied by taking challenging college preparatory mathematics and science courses. Alternatively, the requirement might be met by taking the least challenging remedial courses available. The policy is powerful, in the sense that students are rewarded for compliance and punished for lack of compliance. The policy also has the authority of state law.

States and districts adopted a number of additional policies to add prescriptiveness to the policy of increased credits required for graduation. One measure to add prescriptiveness was to eliminate low-level courses so that the only way to meet the credit requirements was to take challenging mathematics and science courses. A more direct approach was to require all students to take college preparatory courses. Some states and districts created optional special diplomas requiring completion of more challenging mathematics and science courses. Some states promoted Advanced Placement courses by using the numbers of students completing these AP courses as an indicator of the health of the education system. Public universities in some states increased their college entrance requirements in mathematics and science. All of these initiatives can be seen as pushing students to take particular mathematics and science courses in meeting the required minimum number of credits.

Minimum competency testing, however, represented an important inconsistent policy. In Florida, where students were required to pass a minimum competency test in mathematics to graduate from high school, students struggling to meet the requirement tended to take remedial mathematics courses. Because no minimum competency test was required in science, students met the increased credit requirements through taking a variety of courses. Thus, to some extent, the Florida graduation test in mathematics dampened the positive effects of the increased credits requirement.

In contrast, the transition math courses represented a highly prescriptive policy. UCSMP mathematics was a complete replacement curriculum. The desired content is laid out in detail for both teachers and students. Stretch Regents, like UCSMP, was a complete curriculum with aligned textbook materials. Math A in California is also prescriptive, though the Math A course is defined by a syllabus, not by detailed curriculum materials, making it somewhat less prescriptive. The lack of consistency between the Math A syllabus and available curriculum materials was the single most common complaint. Teachers found they had to work especially hard in teaching Math A, because of the lack of text materials on which they could rely. All three transition math courses gained authority through having been developed by experts. UCSMP and Math A, however, offered distinctive alternative curricula to that of traditional mathematics. Thus, they lacked the authority of agreement with norms. This was not true for Stretch Regents, which was the same curriculum as regular Regents. None of the three transition math courses represented an official state requirement. They were alternatives that schools, teachers, and students could elect. To some extent, all three transition math approaches are consistent with national professional standards, as represented in the NCTM *Content Standards*. This is especially true for Math A and UCSMP.

The policy to increase high school mathematics and science credits required for graduation proved to be effective. On the one hand, no negative effect was found on the percentages of students graduating from high school. On the other hand, teachers did not water down the curriculum to accommodate the large influx of students, who were, on average, low-achieving. Similarly, the transition courses represented a policy initiative that had its intended effect. Through enrollment in transition courses, more low-achieving students completed more challenging mathematics. In the case of Math A and UCSMP, these results are especially noteworthy, in that both courses required teachers to change in fundamental ways how they taught and what they taught. Typically, education innovations that require teachers to change in fundamental ways have been less successful. Among the many possible explanations for the success of the transition courses, one stands out. Instead of attempting to change something ongoing and traditional, such as the ways in which algebra is taught, the transition courses represented a replacement strategy. Teachers had no history of experience with Math A or UCSMP. To implement these courses, teachers did not have to confront discrepancies between how they had been teaching the course and how they were now being asked to teach the new course. In contrast, when Florida and South Carolina sought to have more lab time inserted into their ongoing science courses, the effects were negligible. Perhaps something like the law of inertia applies.

The policies investigated in the two studies reported here continue in the late 1990s.[28] To the early policy initiatives, policies that increase prescriptiveness kept being added. For example, the Florida class of 2000 will be required to have a C average and must have a passing grade in algebra.[29] New York City has initiated a policy that requires all students to take Regents mathematics.[30] Based on the results reported here, these more recent high school upgrading policies in mathematics and science can be expected to have positive effects. Furthermore, the results clearly suggest that low-level math courses should be eliminated. What the work reported here does not address in any conclusive way is whether all students are best served by being required to take college preparatory mathematics, or whether transition courses are a useful alternative. On the one hand, students taking transition math courses completed their graduation requirements and took more college preparatory mathematics in greater percentages than did students taking general math. Transition math students also learned more mathematics than those taking general math. On the other hand, even when results are controlled for past student achievement, students who started out in college preparatory mathematics completed the most college prep credits and had the biggest gains in mathematics achievement. But in the studies reported here, only small percentages of students who were seen by traditional criteria as underqualified took college preparatory mathematics classes. If all students were to take college preparatory courses in mathematics, the Reform Up Close results predict that the curriculum will remain intact (that is, not be watered down). But what percentage of students would pass the courses, and how much would they learn in the process? Students who take and fail college preparatory courses could learn more mathematics than students who take and pass transition math courses. Clearly, the transition math courses, especially in the form of Math A, represent an alternative where the pedagogical strategies are more consistent with today's professional standards than are the pedagogical strategies employed in either general math or college preparatory math. If these pedagogical strategies are effective, especially with low-achieving students, then transition math courses are a good alternative for low-achieving students.

Comment by Robert Floden

Andrew C. Porter reports on the effects of a simple idea—changing course requirements. The requirements for high school graduation can be changed with the stroke of a pen. Moreover, implementation of the policy can be easily monitored by examining transcripts.

The slightly less simple underlying idea is that the content students encounter in these different courses will make a big difference in what they learn. Prior research has demonstrated connections between content coverage and achievement at a gross level; the studies reported today show that the relationship holds up in a more fine-grained analysis.

Additional support is given by the Third International Mathematics and Science Study (TIMSS), which concluded that the U.S. students' lackluster performance is partly the result of a diffuse U.S. curriculum. If U.S. students spent more time on a smaller set of topics, they might perform better on these international tests.

As a manipulable correlate of achievement, course content is an attractive policy lever. Strategies such as altering graduation requirements or requiring students to take transition courses instead of general mathematics are comparatively easy to carry out. Students are required to change courses, and teachers need only teach content already in their repertoire to a new set of students. High school teachers are, for example, asked to teach algebra concepts to students who used to take general mathematics.

Ironically, these curriculum shifts make a virtue out of what seemed to be a vice. High school teachers have often been criticized for emphasizing subject matter more than students and for being unwilling to change what they teach. That fits Porter's finding that when high school graduation requirements were changed, teachers maintained the content in their advanced courses, even though they now had many students who were previously seen as unprepared or uninterested. Although this might be seen as insensitivity to the needs of these students, it can also be seen as a resistance of the temptation to water down the content. In other words, the change in graduation requirements takes advantage of the teachers' commitment to course content to alter students' opportunity to be exposed to advanced mathematics and science.

One might say that this represents holding high expectations for all students. Or one might simply say that the teachers have strong views about what they ought to teach, whether or not the students are able to learn it. The connection between content taught and content learned suggests that it is to the students' advantage to be in these advanced courses, whether or not the teachers expect all the students to master the material.

This is not to say that what the teacher expects or how the teacher presents the material is unimportant. It is simply a reminder that the exposure to the content is essential to learning. The uniformity of teaching methods in secondary school mathematics and science classes makes differences in the content students study even more important. Most U.S. secondary school mathematics teachers follow a common model for teaching a course, though the instruction may vary across courses. Porter, for example, found that patterns of instruction were different for the transition courses than for the college prep math courses. The variation across courses demonstrates that teachers have some capacity to alter their pedagogy. Perhaps students would learn even more if teachers adopted some of the teaching methods being developed in the college-level calculus reform.

Given the current stability of teaching methods, the benefits of the association between content coverage and learning should not, however, be exaggerated. As Porter cautions, thinking that all students would profit from being thrust into college prep courses is overly optimistic. Some students who are pushed into such courses may learn new content, but not much and not well. Perhaps one thing they also come to believe is that they should not attempt to learn such mathematics. Teachers' focus on the content may sometimes be accompanied by a lack of concern about whether students learn. Mathematics courses are sometimes used for gate keeping, with teachers taking pride in the number of students who fail. Surely the failure of a large number of students should instead be a motivation to see whether some changes in instruction could help more students reach the standard, without watering down the content.

My comments so far, like Porter's paper, have focused on secondary school. Does the simple idea of changing course requirements seem equally attractive for elementary school? Many secondary teachers enter teaching because of their love for the subject matter; elementary teachers are more often motivated by an interest in children. Elementary teachers in the United States often have little interest or preparation in mathematics and science. They sometimes even have anxiety about their own ability to learn these subjects.

Considering this difference, what might be expected if the simple policy strategy were applied in elementary school mathematics or science? Using a policy similar to moving students to higher level high school courses, for example, suppose fourth grade teachers were asked to teach fifth grade mathematics to their students or to teach the content in a different textbook.

Several factors point toward a less favorable influence on student learning. First, the content impact is less clear, because the elementary school curriculum is less standardized and more redundant. Because the content of fifth grade math is less well defined than, for example, first-year algebra, the policy change would be less prescriptive. The overlap in content between fourth and fifth grade would add to the uncertainty about what teachers were being asked to do. Second, the request to teach the content of a different textbook may not have a clear content prescription, because elementary mathematics texts typically cannot be covered in their entirety and teachers vary in their choices about what parts of the book to use. Third, if the content called for is challenging, elementary teachers may lack the mathematical understanding needed to include it in their instruction.

I recently interviewed elementary school teachers in an urban district moving toward standards-based reform, where the district was using standards and assessments to give prescriptive advice about mathematics content. Teachers often said that they were happy to have greater clarity about the goals of instruction. They said, however, that they were not sure what to do to get the students to learn the more challenging content. For these teachers, the situation was different from that of secondary teachers asked either to continue teaching a familiar course to a new set of students or to teach familiar content in the context of a new transition course. Unlike the secondary teachers, the elementary teachers, to be effective, felt a need for their own learning; they needed to learn how to teach a new set of topics and in some cases to learn to understand the topics themselves. Although the simple changes of requirements and course structure have been beneficial for the secondary schools, the effectiveness of secondary teachers could also benefit from their learning—learning about how to represent content to a different set of students, about how to engage those students' interest, perhaps even about the content. Such learning is important if they are to help their students master more advanced mathematics and science, instead of simply being exposed to it.

In summary, the simple idea of getting students to learn more by changing course requirements has great appeal and some demonstrated efficacy. As with most simple ideas, close examination reveals hidden complexity, in this case, around differences between elementary and secondary school and between expecting all students to study the same content and expecting them all to master it. This simple idea is one to be pursued, but with thoughtful attention to the particular circumstances of application.

Comment by Susan Fuhrman

Commenting on the paper by Andrew C. Porter and on the two studies conducted as part of the Consortium for Policy Research in Education that he examines is a pleasure.

I would like to speak to three lessons. The first has to do with teacher change. Porter makes clear that what teachers do is important and that teachers find doing some things easier than others. I could quibble with Porter about what is easy and what is hard. For example, students could accept greater graduation requirements when states required them. But, given the debate over general cultural issues and anti-intellectualism in the United States, the question of student change is more complex.

Furthermore, some of teachers' reluctance may also have to do with the inability of policies to provide adequate resources. For example, the failure to incorporate laboratory experiences in many science courses that gained in enrollment in the 1980s had something to do with facilities as much as it may have had to do with teachers' beliefs about the importance of laboratory experiences.

Teachers do need to change, and change is difficult. One lesson from the research is that they can change when properly supported. Some transition courses were associated with serious professional development, which was more sustained than usual and was focused on the curriculum.

David Cohen has conducted a survey of one thousand California elementary school teachers who were using replacement units in mathematics, like Math A but at the elementary level. New units were constructed to correspond better to the California math frameworks than textbooks did at the time. When teachers took professional development in those units—in the subjects that the students were studying—for a sustained period of time, their practice changed in ways that the National Council of Teachers of Mathematics would approve. These results were self-reported and supported by observational studies.

And their students did better on the 1994 California Learning Assessment System test than did the students of teachers who were taking other kinds of professional development opportunities. As worthy as these opportunities might be and as widespread as these opportunities are—workshops on diversity or workshops on collaborative learning—

they are divorced from the specific content of the curriculum. These other experiences had no effect on practice or on student achievement compared with the experiences that were solidly grounded in, and focused on, the subject that the students were studying and that also involved sufficient time and opportunity to learn. The focus needs to be on what would help teachers make the changes that are expected of them.

The second lesson has to do with methodology. The studies Porter analyzes were lengthy, costly, complex, large-scale, serious, and involved. And fortunately, the consortium could allow for the second study, which followed from the first. That is, one set of research questions could lead to another.

Not enough large-scale, longitudinal, sustained research is done in education. The premium is always on newness, on new research studies. More effort should be made to replicate and to do sustained research. Every research project need not embark on a new direction. The faddism that pervades American education certainly has something to do with the faddism that pervades American educational research. Sustained multiyear research, in which certain questions lead to other questions and all questions can be investigated, is required.

Important to note, however, is how costly and complex the consortium-sponsored studies were. The researchers were stuck in basements of schools doing transcript analyses on handwritten records that had been water-logged and destroyed by other elements while their car was being stolen outside. The more optimistic news about the methodology of these studies is that they were more cost-efficient than expected and they allowed researchers to get inside the classroom to find out exactly what is being taught.

Porter's questionnaires, developed through these two studies, are now widely cited, used, and emulated, and they add to an understanding of teacher practice. A high correlation exists in the Reform Up Close Study between the logs that were kept daily by teachers in the courses with the biggest enrollment gains and the questionnaires teachers were given as well as the observations that were used to validate the other two instruments.

Cost-efficient questionnaires can be developed that assess teaching practice, the content covered, and the cognitive demands of that content. Understanding what is going on inside the classroom is crucial for those interested in reform and looking for improvements in student achievement. Changes must take place in the classroom if achievement changes are going to happen.

The third lesson is the value of the standards-based reform approach. In a number of states, evidence is slowly and incrementally being gathered as standards-based reform takes its deliberate and politically difficult course. This research says that, when directives are clear and explicit about the content and skills expected of students, students of all abilities will perform well. This research also says that multiple policy levers can encourage this kind of ambitious instruction and ambitious content. For various states and cities, Porter looked at not only formal graduation requirements but also tests; special diplomas; college admission requirements; the existence of Advanced Placement (AP) courses, which create a climate of expectations within a school; and other things that can be influenced by policy.

Most important, all the policy levers have to speak in the same direction. They have to be consistent if the effect is going to be achieved; if they are not consistent, trouble results. For example, Florida gave the minimum competency test at the same time it required more units in math. As a result, students took remedial math and not college preparatory math. Meanwhile, no science test was administered, so students took more ambitious classes.

Notes

1. National Commission on Excellence in Education, *A Nation at Risk: The Imperative for Educational Reform* (Government Printing Office, 1983).

2. Department of Education, *National Goals for Education* (1991), p. 3.

3. Department of Education, *National Goals for Education* (1990), p. 3.

4. Andrew C. Porter, Douglas A. Archbald, and Alexander K. Tyree Jr., "Reforming the Curriculum: Will Empowerment Policies Replace Control?," in Susan H. Fuhrman and Betty Malen, eds., *The Politics of Curriculum and Testing: The 1990 Yearbook of the Politics of Education Association* (London: Taylor and Francis, 1990), pp. 11–36.

5. National Research Council, *National Science Education Standards* (National Academy Press, 1996); National Council of Teachers of Mathematics, *Curriculum and Evaluation Standards* (1989); National Council of Teachers of Mathematics, *Professional Standards for Teaching Mathematics* (1991); National Council of Teachers of

Mathematics, *Assessment Standards for School Mathematics* (1995); and American Association for the Advancement of Science, *Science for All Americans* (1989).

6. Millicent Lawton, "Facing Deadline, California Is Locked in Battle over How to Teach Math," *Education Week*, March 12, 1997, pp. 1, 25.

7. Deborah T. Haimo, "Are the NCTM *Standards* Suitable for Systemic Adoption?" in Occasional Paper No. 3 (Madison, Wis.: National Institute for Science Education, 1997); and Judy Roitman, "A Mathematician Looks at National Standards," in Occasional Paper No. 3 (Madison, Wis.: National Institute for Science Education, 1997).

8. Andrew C. Porter and others, "Content Determinants in Elementary School Mathematics," in Douglas A. Grouws and Thomas J. Cooney, eds., *Perspectives on Research on Effective Mathematics Teaching* (Hillsdale, N.J.: Erlbaum, 1988), pp. 96–113.

9. Adam Gamoran, "The Stratification of High School Learning Opportunities," *Sociology of Education*, vol. 60, no. 3 (1987), pp. 135–55.

10. Penny A. Sebring, "Consequences of Differential Amounts of High School Coursework: Will the New Graduation Requirements Help?," *Educational Evaluation and Policy Analysis*, vol. 9, no. 3 (1987), pp. 257–73.

11. William H. Schmidt, "High School Course-Taking: A Study of Variation," *Journal of Curriculum Studies*, vol. 15, no. 2 (1983), pp. 167–82; William H. Schmidt, "High School Course-Taking: Its Relationship to Achievement," *Journal of Curriculum Studies*, vol. 15, no. 3 (1983), pp. 311–32; and Herbert J. Walberg and Timothy Shanahan, "High School Effects on Individual Students," *Educational Researcher*, vol. 12, no. 7 (1983), pp. 4–9.

12. Jeannie Oakes, Adam Gamoran, and Reba Page, "Curriculum Differentiation: Opportunities, Outcomes, and Meanings," in Philip W. Jackson, ed., *Handbook of Research on Curriculum* (Macmillan, 1992), pp. 507–608.

13. Thomas Hoffer and Adam Gamoran, "Effects of Instructional Differences among Ability Groups on Student Achievement in Middle-School Science and Mathematics," paper presented at the 1993 annual meeting of the American Sociological Association; Adam Gamoran, "Alternative Uses of Ability Grouping in Secondary Schools: Can We Bring High–Quality Instruction to Low-Achieving Classes?," *American Journal of Education*, vol. 102, no. 1 (1993), pp. 1–22; and Adam Gamoran and others, "An Organizational Analysis of the Effects of Ability Grouping," *American Educational Research Journal*, vol. 32, no. 4 (1995), pp. 687–715.

14. Adam Gamoran and others, *Upgrading High School Mathematics Instruction: Improving Learning Opportunities for Low-Achieving, Low-Income Youth* (Madison, Wis.: Wisconsin Center for Education Research, 1996).

15. Department of Education, *Pursuing Excellence* (National Center for Education Statistics, 1996).

16. William H. Schmidt, Curtis C. McKnight, and Senta A. Raizen, *A Splintered Vision: An Investigation of U.S. Science and Mathematics Education* (Norwell, Mass.: Kluwer, 1997).

17. John Schwille and others, "Teachers as Policy Brokers in the Content of Elementary School Mathematics," in Lee Shulman and Gary Sykes, eds., *Handbook on Teaching and Policy* (New York: Longman, 1983), pp. 370–91.

18. Andrew C. Porter and others, *Reform Up Close: An Analysis of High School Mathematics and Science Classrooms*, final report to the National Science Foundation, Grant No. SPA–8953446 (University of Wisconsin at Madison, Wisconsin Center for Education Research, 1993).

19. Department of Education, "The Condition of Education, 1996" (National Center for Education Statistics, 1996), p. 9.

20. Department of Education, "The Condition of Education, 1992" (National Center for Education Statistics, 1992), p. 24.

21. William H. Clune and Paula A. White, "Education Reform in the Trenches: Increased Academic Course Taking in High Schools with Lower Achieving Students in States with Higher Graduation Requirements," *Educational Evaluation and Policy Analysis*, vol. 14, no. 1 (1992), pp. 2–20.

22. Clune and White, "Education Reform in the Trenches."

23. Cynthia Brown and others, *The Secondary Schools Taxonomy* (Department of Education, National Assessment of Vocational Education, 1989); and Rolf Blank and Melanie Dalkilic, *State Indicators of Science and Mathematics Education 1990* (Council of Chief State School Officers, 1990).

24. The second number in parentheses is the standard deviation.

25. Paula A. White and others, "Upgrading the High School Math Curriculum: Math Course-Taking Patterns in Seven High Schools in California and New York," *Educational Evaluation and Policy Analysis*, vol. 18, no. 4 (1996), pp. 285–307; and Adam Gamoran and others, "Upgrading High School Mathematics Instruction: Improving Learning Opportunities for Low-Achieving, Low-Income Youth," *Educational Evaluation and Policy Analysis* (forthcoming).

26. Brian DeLany, "Allocation, Choice, and Stratification within High Schools: How the Sorting Machine Copes," *American Journal of Education*, vol. 99, no. 2 (1991), pp. 181–207.

27. Anthony Bryk and Stephen Raudenbush, *Hierarchical Linear Models: Applications and Data Analysis Methods* (Newbury Park, Calif.: Sage, 1992).

28. Diane Massell, Michael Kirst, and Margaret Hoppe, *Persistence and Change: Standards-Based Reform in Nine States* (Consortium for Policy Research in Education, 1997).

29. Kerry A. White, "Graduation-Standards Bill Signed into Law in Florida," *Education Week*, April 9, 1997, p. 16.

30. C. Jones, "New York Stiffens Rules to Graduate," *New York Times*, May 2, 1994, p. A1.

Uncompetitive American Schools: Causes and Cures

HERBERT J. WALBERG

B Y THE STANDARDS of what educated citizens should know, U.S. students perform poorly on examinations in civics, geography, history, and other subjects.[1] Compared with students in other countries, older American students do poorly in mathematics, science, and foreign languages.[2] Yet American students are not behind in the early years of schooling. Their achievement, relative to students in other countries, falls behind when learning is the chief responsibility of schools. In terms of value-added gains in reading, mathematics, and science during the school years, American students do worst among those in affluent countries.

Coming in last in learning gains is attributable to the organization and operation of schools rather than what is spent on them or the quality of entering students. Family conditions for learning have improved substantially in recent decades. Family income has risen, for example, and the number of children per family has declined—both of which are associated with higher ability.[3] Intelligence test scores, a measure of the education industry's quality of raw material, have risen steadily for several decades.

For a half-century, moreover, per-student costs, adjusted for inflation, have risen substantially. Eric A. Hanushek concludes that *"educational productivity is falling at 3.5 percent per year relative to low productivity* [service] *sectors of the economy."*[4] Adjusted for purchasing power, moreover, U.S. school costs have been highest among the countries surveyed by the Organization for Economic Cooperation and Development (OECD) during the past several years. Special reasons may account for such high costs, but additional spending makes little difference, and it appears unlikely that large funding increases will continue.[5]

U.S. schools arguably cost more because they have taken on more responsibilities than those of other countries and have therefore deemphasized academics. However, many elected political leaders, business people, citizens, and parents insist that learning should be the schools' core mission. Congress and state legislatures have called for better progress and passed laws to monitor achievement. The complex system of federal, national, state, and local control also arguably may increase costs, as do large-scale federal programs for poor and handicapped children. If these choices, however, are not accomplishing their purposes, they should be the target for inquiry.

As a result, seven policies that increase efficiency should be examined closely.[6] Four are common sense and are supported by much research: focus schools on their core mission—learning; apply principles of effective instruction; employ uniform curriculum standards; and allow for student differences. After a decade of heroic reports and efforts, however, these steps are still not in place. Therefore, three additional steps are necessary: deregulation, incentives, and privatization.

The School Calamity

By themselves, poor international rankings are flawed indicators of school effectiveness, because learning is a lifelong process begun in infancy. By the time students begin first grade, their high school achievement is partly determined. For this reason, indices of educational effectiveness require analysis of the distinctive value that schools add to learning.

The OECD in 1995 compared country differences in reading literacy of nine- and fourteen-year-olds.[7] Reading is the best single indicator of language skills and predictor of achievement in school subjects. Mainly through reading, students acquire information and ideas in academic subject matter. Even solving mathematics and science problems depends on reading skills.

In the OECD survey, U.S. nine-year-olds ranked well. They should have, because they were much better prepared when they entered school than previous generations. Intelligence test renorming surveys for the last half-century show that American children's language mastery at the time of school entry has steadily and substantially increased.[8] Several social conditions apparently account for increases in children's preschool verbal and other academic skills; namely, preschool and child care programs that teach many children the alphabet and other language skills, increasing family income and years of education associated with children's language mastery, and increased children's exposure to verbal mass media.

Just as social and familial reading encouragement varies across time, so, too, does it vary across countries. Many possible determinants of early childhood reading skills exist—for example, preschool and child care policies, family practices in child rearing (including alphabet teaching), degrees of bilingualism in families and society, age of starting school, family income and wealth, and cultural cohesion. Because countries vary in these respects, the OECD devised a value-added index of progress during school years.

The reading literacy progress index is the (cross-sectional) difference in country scores for the two age groups, nine and fourteen. It is a well-suited index of school progress in several respects. By age nine, all normal children in OECD countries have started primary school; by age fourteen, almost none has dropped out of secondary school. Measuring differences between them adjusts differences in reading readiness, socioeconomic status, and other conditions as much as the state of the art of international research on education policy allows.

Of the sixteen OECD countries surveyed, American schools held last place, according to the international standard of reading progress. They also spent the most money per student served, thus making them least efficient with the least gains and highest costs (see figure 1).

In 1996, the OECD published analogous value-added gains in science and mathematics for students in the seventh and eighth years of schooling.[9] Data on the twenty-four participating OECD countries (and candidates Korea and the Russian Federation) are presented in figure 2. U.S. schools again yielded the least gains in both subjects.

Causes of Inefficiency

Research on improving learning shows that common-sense principles work well. For example, you tend to learn what you are taught, and the more you study and the bigger the incentives, the more you learn.

Figure 1. Reading Progress and Spending

Reading progress (ages 9–14)

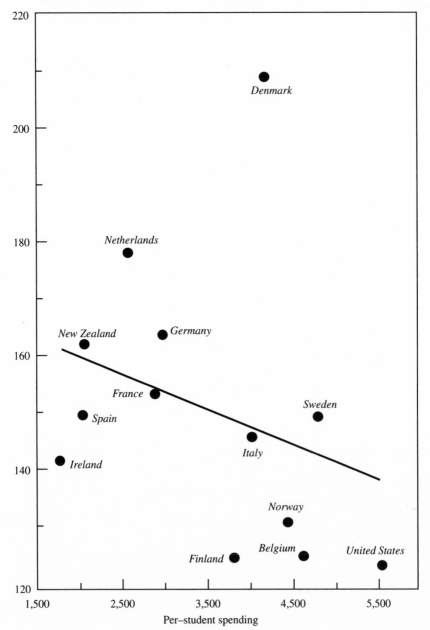

Per–student spending

Figure 2. Seventh to Eighth Grade Learning Gains

Mathematics

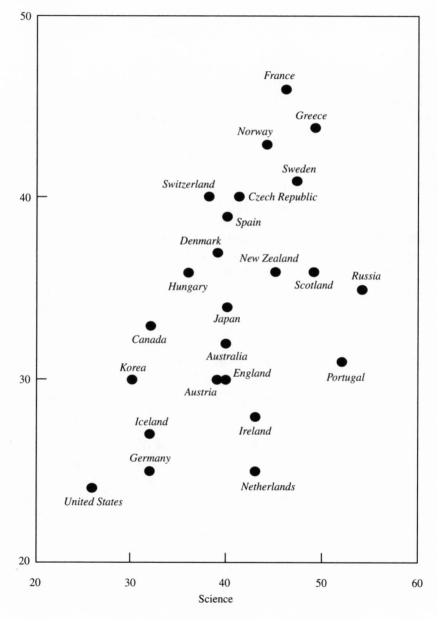

Science

Educators and policymakers, however, have often ignored such research. Other problems also appear to handicap American students.

Lack of Standards and Accountability

Like Australia, Canada, and Germany, the U.S. system has no education ministry, well-defined national goals, curriculum, or testing system. States are constitutionally responsible for providing a system of free schools but leave much discretion to local boards. What is taught in classrooms, in turn, is highly variable even within the same school. Therefore, aside from vague notions, a teacher in any grade may not depend on what the teacher in the previous grade has taught. The lack of coordination across grades and subjects is especially harmful to children who move, particularly if they are also poor.

Lack of standards means that state and local boards can hardly assess progress made by districts, schools, and teachers. To the extent that curriculum and goals vary, comparing schools is difficult, which makes accountability for results nearly impossible.

School boards frequently split into factions, and few members have extensive board and executive or education experience. Often serving limited terms, they seem more interested in personnel and ideological issues than whether the schools are achieving results. Assessing learning progress, moreover, requires some mastery of educational productivity research, psychometrics, and statistics, just as assessing businesses progress requires accounting and other skills.

Given that few educational leaders have mastered such skills, they are often taken in by such fads as whole language, authentic tests, and site-based management, the success of which is undemonstrated in randomized experiments or statistically controlled research. School board members tend to follow what interests them—often personnel, inputs, and processes rather than results. Usually unpaid, their stewardship is often of corresponding value. Administrators are paid, not for results, but according to their advocacy of faddish ideology and the number of their subordinates. Confusion and bureaucracy correspondingly grow.

Centralization

Despite the lack of uniform standards and accountability, the governance and funding of public schools have become more centralized in the last half-century, leading to other kinds of inefficiency. States increasingly centralized education finance and control. They paid increasingly larger shares of school costs, but the higher the state share, the worse the state's achievement even with vast increases in inflation-adjusted per-student spending.[10] Higher state shares make school boards and administrators less accountable to local citizens because they need not justify expenditures as carefully.

Larger state shares also entail increased regulation, reporting, bureaucracy, and distraction from learning. Much energy goes into the question of who governs—the federal government, the state, the local district, the school, or the teacher. Affixing responsibility for results seems impossible.

During the past half-century, schools and school districts, moreover, have increasingly consolidated into larger units that achieve less. Average school enrollments multiplied by a factor of five, although large schools tend to be more bureaucratic, more impersonal, and less humane. Large middle and junior high schools tend to departmentalize and employ specialized teachers and ancillary staff who confine themselves to their specialties instead of imparting a broad view of knowledge. The teachers in large, departmentalized schools tend to know their students much less well than teachers who have the same students for most subjects for nearly the whole day.[11]

About fifty years ago, U.S. school districts numbered 115,000; in the late 1990s, about 15,000, the largest of which tend to be least effective. The reasons for their inefficiency are best seen in New York and other large cities with up to nine hundred schools. In such huge districts, school board members can hardly name the schools let alone hold them accountable.

Meanwhile, small adjacent public school districts and private schools within districts give rise to incentives that cause all schools to compete and raise their productivity.[12] Choice plans that allow students to cross school and district boundaries also increase productivity. As Caroline Minter Hoxby found,

> Areas with greater opportunities for choice among public schools have lower per-pupil spending, larger class sizes, and lower teacher salaries. The same areas have better student performance, as measured by students' educational attainment, [starting] wages, and test scores.[13]

In an analysis of the Massachusetts interdistrict public school choice plan, David Armor found an underlying reason for such productivity improvements: Schools and districts that lost students improved their policies and programs to win them back.[14] With choice and competition, markets apparently work in education as they do in other industries. They lead entrepreneurs to innovate, cut costs, and improve results for citizen consumers.

Unaccountable Management and Labor

Public schools are government subsidized quasi-monopolies. They are unchallenged by entrepreneurial leadership and the incentives, efficiency, and consumer appeal provided by market competition. With legislators and school boards often under their thumbs, teachers' unions and administrators can exploit forced-choice customers in service of their interests in minimizing workload and maximizing pay and perquisites.

Teachers' unions—few call them professional associations—have done splendidly for their members. In college, education majors typically score worst or near worst on ability tests among undergraduate majors. Yet, as teachers, they have a 180-day school year—the shortest among teachers in industrialized countries (and much less than the roughly 235 days most salaried U.S. professionals normally work). In large cities and elsewhere, many teachers are in school only about six hours according to contract. Some grade papers in the evening, but many other professionals also work at home. In addition, teachers have little accountability, nearly inviolable tenure, and early and generous pensions that increasingly threaten city and state budgets.[15]

Teachers are acting rationally in their own interest, as are their unions, in maximizing their benefits while reducing their efforts. School boards and state legislators have been remiss in failing to provide effective management, informed stewardship, and accountability to citizens who pay the bills.

Teachers' unions have done better for themselves than for their members. During the past half-century when membership in private sector unions declined, teachers' unions increased their membership. They contracted for expensive smaller classes, which do little for learning. With fixed budgets, smaller classes mean lower salaries because costs must be spread among more teachers. Smaller classes increase the number of teachers and, indirectly, union members, central coffers, and legislative influence.

In bargaining, school boards have not been a match for nationally organized unions that can bring to bear strong, narrow self-interests, statistical research, and specialized expertise to negotiations. Yet, according to Harvard University and University of Chicago economists Caroline Minter Hoxby and Samuel Peltzman, respectively, teachers' union success was associated with worse results for students. Statistically controlled surveys showed that the sharp rise in teacher union membership and militancy for the period 1971–91 not only increased per-student costs dramatically but also increased dropout rates and adversely affected test scores in forty-eight states surveyed.[16] As teachers' unions grew in membership, income, and power, they gained greater influence over state legislatures, which in turn increasingly usurped local control and left the schools unaccountable to local taxpayers.

Federally Induced Inefficiency

Federal officials further usurped local autonomy and reduced efficiency in directing the spending of more than $175 billion in program dollars for categorical and compensatory programs to remedy various social and individual ills.[17] In theory, these funds paid for small, special classes and services for children categorized as poor, migrant, bilingual, racially segregated, and psychologically impeded. In practice, the federal legislation created special producer interests and huge bureaucracies at the federal, state, and local levels.

These programs had little foundation in research, and subsequent studies showed they were ineffective and, in some cases, harmful. Such stigmatic epithets as "mildly mentally retarded" and "learning disabled" lowered teachers', parents', peers', and children's own expectations for what they can learn. Despite increased costs and administrative complications of categorical programs, evaluations over the last several decades showed that such students are often spuriously categorized. Even those appropriately categorized often learn more in regular than segregated special classes. Yet, spending on such programs increased inexorably; billions of dollars were brought into congressional districts.

Such federal and state categorical programs resulted in increasingly poor productivity (ratios of achievement results to inflation-adjusted per-student costs). Also contributing to poor productivity are complex, conflicting, and often-changing federal and state regulations. They cause educators to serve many masters in central offices, statehouses, and Washington and to neglect their central purpose—the learning of all children. Along with the natural and self-interested proclivities for bureaucracies to expand, such regulations cause the United States to have among the highest percentages of costs for nonteaching staff among OECD countries.[18]

Nonmarket Inefficiency

American schools have largely become a quasi-monopolistic, heavily regulated, status quo system favoring inefficient providers. Unlike leaders of private firms, school board members and administrators are unguided by consumer purchases of their services. Only the rich or those who sacrifice substantial income have recourse to private and the best suburban schools. Generally, those who live in cities, the poor, and minorities and those who most need better schools can least afford them. They are handicapped by special interests, federal regulation, and subsidies for failed programs, even though their schools most need innovation, efficiency, and customer appeal.

To increase effectiveness and efficiency, public schools require competition, as do other industries. From a consumer view, for example, Mazda, Mercedes, and Saab have improved the products of General Motors, Ford, and Chrysler. Competition among producers increases quality, innovation, diversity, and consumer satisfaction while reducing costs.

Similarly, international markets challenge whole countries. The policies they adopt, the efficiency of public services, and the preponderance of private sectors determine the quality of life. Countries that insulate government and private domestic providers from competition deny citizens superior services and goods at lower costs that markets provide.[19] Countries that heavily subsidize public providers and arbitrarily or corruptly regulate private providers fence out investment and innovation. They harm themselves with unemployment and poor economic growth. They hurt other countries by refraining from free international commerce that raises world prosperity. Compare the histories of China with Hong Kong and Taiwan, North Korea with South Korea, or Eastern Europe with Western Europe. Free market forces increasingly challenge countries that heavily subsidize and regulate providers; the time has come for schools to compete.

Steps to Increase Productivity

Given that the United States has the least effective schools among affluent countries, what can policymakers do? Extensive research and common sense reveal the efficacy of seven reforms. The refractory forces of convention and special interests may ensure that such reforms may not be enacted intensively and extensively. Therefore, privatizing schools is required to make them more responsive to national needs and consumer preferences.

Focus Schools on Learning

As enrollments rose in the last half-century, schools took on ever more specialized, often nonacademic, tasks.[20] School boards responded to state mandates and other external pressures to add specialized administrators and separate programs for health, psychological, and other services. These services were added as legislatures, special interests, regulatory agencies, and professional associations built consensus among themselves. They brought pressure to bear on state departments of education and school districts to provide specialized and peripheral programs such as driver education.

If schools are not carrying out their core mission, how can they be expected to assume such additional responsibilities? This is an especially important question today, when "full service" or "collaborative service" schools are proposed that would assume responsibility for family functions and coordinate health, social work, recreation, and other community functions. The usual answer is that when problems are severe, everyone is responsible. However, when many agencies are nominally responsible, no one is responsible, and any agency that claims thirteen goals has none.

Federal initiatives, moreover, further divide the schools' mission and multiply administrative complexities, especially in large urban districts where they are most prevalent.[21] Funding for special education, bilingual, migrant, and vocational programs, for example, promotes special interests but excludes educational generalists, other specialists, and lay citizens. Private schools and public schools in smaller districts often skip such programs, thereby maintaining a cohesive core curriculum of solid academic subjects taken by most students and associated with higher achievement.

Besides districts, schools have become larger. Although bureaucratic growth may have been well intentioned, it has had harmful psychological consequences. A good example is subject matter specialization in elementary schools. In many communities, the last few years of the traditional eight-year elementary school have been replaced by departmentalized middle and junior high schools. In such schools, students may now have five or so specialized teachers, none of whom knows them as well as teachers who have the same class most of the day. Like hospitals that treat diseases instead of patients, such schools are likely to teach subjects instead of students.

Smaller districts and schools, moreover, can adapt to local preferences and conditions as well as strengthen ties among teachers and parents that induce learning. They are likely to do fewer things better and avoid spurious categorization of students, ineffective programs that ill-serve them, and inefficient administrative complexity.

In any case, making learning the school's primary mission seems essential. Big city districts are most handicapped by the complications of serving many masters because greater fractions of their operating funds come from federal and state categorical programs. Even when their costs are reimbursed, such programs often are not only ineffective but also cause administrative nightmares. Thus, federal and state laws have most damaged the schools that contain students with the greatest needs.

Apply Principles of Effective Instruction

Since the late 1940s, scholars have published hundreds of randomized experimental studies of effective instruction. Since the early 1990s, much of this was condensed to eight handbooks of research on instruction in science, mathematics, and the other school subjects, some of them running to nine hundred double-columned pages by dozens of chapter authors. In a project sponsored by twenty-eight influential professional education organizations with more than two million members, Gordon Cawelti invited the editors of these specialized works (and me on generic principles) to describe in a page or two each of ten most effective teaching strategies.[22] This and other synthetic works cannot easily be summarized, but a few pervasive principles can serve as illustrations.[23]

AMOUNT OF INSTRUCTION. The 1983 report of the National Commission on Excellence in Education, *A Nation at Risk,* made clear that U.S. students have the shortest school year among major countries.[24] Data in table 1 present a meta-analysis of estimates of the influence or effect of time on learning outcomes from statistically and experimentally controlled studies.[25] Of 376 estimates, 88 percent were positive—one of the most consistent findings in education research. The sizes of the effects are moderate over a week or a semester; so, time is hardly a short-term panacea. Over many years, however, student engagement in study and practice time yields huge benefits, as is known from Asian schools and from studies of world-class performers in many fields who require well-organized and substantial numbers of hours per week to attain high performance levels.[26]

Supplementing school time is homework. Meta-analysis showed moderate effects of merely assigning homework, but grades and teacher comments tripled homework's effects. A recent economic analysis of a large national sample estimated that an extra half-hour of nightly homework between grades seven and eleven boosts math achievement by almost two grade equivalents.[27] On their own or with the help of school staff, moreover, parents can employ children's time before and during the school years to prepare them for serious academic work. They can foster academically stimulating activities such as museum going and leisure reading, and they can engage themselves in their children's schools.

QUALITY INSTRUCTION. Hundreds of instructional methods studies have been carried out, and thousands of achievement comparisons of classroom groups have been made. Many studies have employed random assignment of alternative methods to experimental and control groups as in agricultural and medical research. Their results have been compiled and compared to discover which work best. Because they work well and can be widely employed, several instructional methods and principles deserve mention.[28]

The most prevalent form of teaching, "direct instruction," can be

Table 1. Time Influences on Learning in Various Types of Research Studies

Area researched	Number of estimates	Percent positive	Correlation mean (N)	Effect mean (N)
Studies in which instructional time was extended	162	83	.27 (34)	.40 (57)
Earlier start in school or extra preschool	49	73	.08 (1)	.27 (32)
Lengthening the school day or week	26	88	.40 (7)	.96 (7)
Lengthening the school year	11	91	.22 (5)	n.a. (0)
Learning extended by homework and study	43	88	.23 (19)	.41 (18)
Extracurricular participation	33	85	.46 (2)	n.a. (0)
Studies of how school time was used	103	96	.43 (50)	.49 (18)
Program length or long-term study	42	93	.57 (21)	.69 (5)
Attendance rate	6	100	.48 (4)	.32 (1)
Efficient time use	55	93	.31 (25)	.42 (12)
Theoretically driven studies	111	90	.35 (53)	1.10 (6)
Less time needed to learn a topic	18	89	.70 (6)	n.a. (0)
Studies of time on task	79	89	.26 (37)	1.10 (3)
Matching time spent to time needed	14	100	.47 (10)	1.10 (3)
All studies	376	88	.37 (137)	.47 (81)

Note: n.a. = not available.

traced to the turn of the twentieth century and is what citizens and parents expect to see in classrooms. It is most effective when exhibiting key features and following systematic steps: (1) daily review, homework check, and, if necessary, reteaching; (2) rapid presentation of new content and skills in small steps; (3) guided student practice with close teacher monitoring; (4) corrective feedback and instructional reinforcement; (5) homework with a high—more than 90 percent—success rate; and (6) weekly and monthly assessments and reviews. The traits of effective teachers employing direct instruction include clarity, task orientation, enthusiasm, and flexibility. Effective direct teachers also clearly organize their presentations and may occasionally use student ideas.

Other methods of teaching also work well and have distinctive features that may be contrasted with direct instruction, which, if aimed at the average student, may be too advanced for slower students and too repetitive for the quick. Consequently, "adaptive instruction" has been employed to make instruction more suitable to individual or groups of children. One traditional form is tutoring one or a few students, thereby tailoring parts of lessons to precisely what they require and closely monitoring their progress.

Another form is "mastery learning," which, for subject matter to be learned in a sequence, requires frequent tests to guarantee that the student has mastered one unit before going on to the next. Because of its emphasis on outcomes and careful monitoring of progress, mastery learning can save learners' time, allowing for remediation and as much as 500 percent more time for students who need attention. It allows faster learners to skip material they already know. In these ways, it is superior to direct teaching in suiting instruction to small groups and individuals rather than to the average class member.

Computer-assisted instruction (CAI) often incorporates mastery principles. Programs require careful analysis of the subject matter and common learner errors that can be quickly diagnosed and corrected. One advantage of CAI is that it can be used anytime, anywhere. Given that courseware does not require the continuous presence of teachers, it could be used at home as a supplement to or a substitute for whole-class instruction. Although development costs are high, hardware costs are declining and programs are growing in scope and efficacy.

Computer and mastery programs require special planning, materials, and procedures. If, because of the National Educational Goals, U.S.

subject matter becomes more uniform, both mastery learning and computer-assisted instruction are likely to become more prevalent because the development costs can be spread over many schools. (For that matter, mass instruction could be provided at home or wherever convenient by television and other forms of "distance education" as it is in many parts of the world with low population density. Done well, such programs have proven highly cost-effective.)

Direct instruction, mastery learning, and computer-assisted instruction are top-down from the teacher's or textbook plan. From these, students may or may not pick up independent or team learning skills. Several methods such as tutoring, "cooperative learning," and "reciprocal teaching" promote these as well as subject matter competence. By teaching one another, for example, students can learn independent research and presentation skills. They may learn how to give and receive criticism and how to work with others as is called for in adult life. To learn something well, it is often good to teach it because such teaching requires organizing one's thoughts logically and anticipating misunderstandings and questions.

No single one of these methods is advisable all day; some variety is necessary to maintain teachers' and students' motivation. Other effective methods of instruction, moreover, could be described. Many such methods that work well, however, are either unchosen or poorly carried out. They are hardly panaceas, but, if well conducted, they make for moderate progress. Combined with more hours of school time and homework, they could raise U.S. achievement levels substantially.

ORGANIZATION OF WORK AND INSTRUCTION. Figure 3 illustrates the parallelism of effective instruction with principles of personnel and work organization—division of labor, quality management, and market-based decentralization.[29] The first panel illustrates Adam Smith's insight about the efficiency of specialized labor: Each worker or work unit, if concentrated on a single task, can be far more efficient in contributing to total value of a product or service; the early production lines of the Ford Motor Company may come to mind. Psychologists later theoretically justified work specialization by showing people's limited capacity to absorb and to consider more than a few chunks of information at a time.[30]

Similarly, independently working professionals and others who group repetitive or similar tasks pay the time price of only one set-up.

Figure 3. Evolution of Work Organization

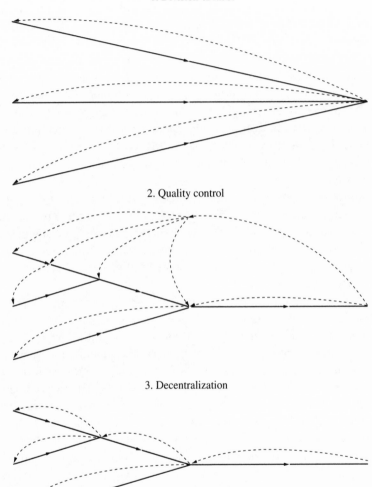

1. Division of labor

2. Quality control

3. Decentralization

Note: Work flows to the right, feedback to the left.

Working on unlike tasks places burdens on memory that requires refreshing or reinvention. Excellent performance in a field requires many hours of concentrated effort on limited tasks as in the case of coronary bypass surgeons who confine themselves to their specialty operation.

As work in organizations increases in scale and specialization, the executive cannot direct, monitor, and provide useful comments for all workers. General Motors acquired or created production units such as Buick and Chevrolet and service units such as finance and advertising, each with its own executive (see second part of figure 3). Coordination of efforts and specialization could further increase. Production units' profits (the difference between sales and costs for each unit) could influence board directors' decisions about bonuses, investment, and expansion.

Still, such organization adds complexity and lengthens the chain of command to as many as a dozen levels of administration between chief executive officers and workers, which increases costs, decisionmaking time, possibilities of confusion, and people serving multiple masters. The service units' contributions to added value, moreover, could not be easily measured.

Stung by foreign competition, progressive industries are adopting a form of work organization first widely put into place by cost- and quality-conscious Japanese firms. It assigns substantial managerial responsibilities to teams of workers that treat other units of the firm as their suppliers and customers (see third part of figure 3). If their internal suppliers of semifinished goods or services do not meet their standards, including just-in-time delivery, they can reject them and contract with external individuals and firms. Similarly, worker-managers risk losing their own internal and external customers if they disappoint them.

Worker-managers are paid in proportion to the value they add; that is, the increase in the value of the outputs over input and production costs. Because raising quality and cutting costs are in their interest, worker-managers can be given considerable voice in purchasing and in the hiring of new workers for their units. In tying rewards to results, this competitive arrangement can release the entrepreneurial potential of efficient individuals and work groups. It can also eliminate uncompetitive groups that impair quality, consumer appeal, and prosperity.

Such radical decentralization to work teams makes for greater competitiveness in internal and external markets. Avoiding long chains of command allows for quick feedback and decisionmaking, especially important at a time when speeds of innovation and delivery are crucial aspects of consumer appeal. The money formerly flowing to middle managers can be used to improve quality and contribute to profits and expansion. Such work calls for people who are competent not only in production but also in executive skills of planning, contracting, monitoring, teamwork, and satisfying internal and external customers. For the well prepared, such work may be challenging, satisfying, and remunerative.

To put such a system into place requires more than a new management organization and competent employees. It requires giving them a kind of ownership stake in the success of their units. If their units prosper, they prosper, and the firm as a whole, its stockholders, and the nation prosper. Because such worker-managers own much of the firm's increasingly valuable human and social capital and directly control the means of production, they constitute the largest category of the firm's ownership. True ownership requires, if not private property rights for employees in this broad sense, then employee stakes in their unit's success.

Educators have an opportunity to prepare students for such work and to use these methods themselves. Effective instructional methods embed some of these principles. Computer-assisted instruction and mastery learning, for example, include quality standards. Tutoring, cooperative learning, and reciprocal teaching delegate some planning and monitoring authority to students as workers. The challenge is to employ such methods more widely. The degree to which this can be accomplished depends on standards in curriculum and assessment. It would also require a precise system of achievement measurement to determine the value added by each work unit; that is, a teacher, team, or school staff.

Employ High Uniform Standards

In *Horace's Compromise,* Theodore Sizer describes the common pattern of a teacher who gains an orderly and familiar relation with his students by telling them the absurdly easy questions he will ask on a test. He gains the admiration of his principal even though his and his students' efforts are at a pathetic minimum.[31] Because solitary teachers cannot raise standards on their own, educational policymakers (legislators and state and local school board members) need to consider how to increase the uniformity, rigor, focus, and coherence of subject matter.

Lest there be doubt about the lack of standards, consider what students think, for they are schools' most direct and immediate customers. Three-fourths of the one thousand high school students randomly sampled by Public Agenda said stiffer graduation requirements and required exit examinations would make students pay more attention to their studies.[32] Three-fourths also said students should not graduate who have not mastered English, and a similar percentage said students should be promoted to the next grade only if they master the material. Almost two-thirds reported they could do much better in school if they tried. Nearly 80 percent said students would learn more if schools made sure they were on time and did their homework. More than 70 percent said schools should require after-school classes for those earning Ds and Fs.

The United States has a decentralized school system, and teachers often select, according to their preferences or district policy, a small fraction of material from voluminous textbooks. Consequently, what students know and can do at the end of the academic year in any state is highly heterogeneous. As a new school year begins, American teachers bore bright students by reviewing and presenting prerequisite material to bring the least able students up to par before proceeding with new content. Especially in need are about one-fifth of the students, and more often those from low-income families who move from other schools, districts, and states.

Countries with national systems of education can prescribe uniform subject matter at each grade level and thereby avoid this inefficiency. Because they can assume students have mastered prerequisite material, teachers in these countries can present new subject matter immediately after a quick review of previous work. By these timesavings, students can forge ahead to more rigorous subject matter. Curricular uniformity has other advantages: Textbooks can be one-fifth the size of American ones designed to cover the diverse subject matter specifications of various states. Computer-assisted instruction, examinations, and other curricular materials can be more sharply focused on what students are expected to learn. Teachers can share ideas about the selected subject matter and how best to teach it. Universities and employers can count on what students have been taught.

A uniform national system can be not only more rigorous and focused, but also more coherent. Teachers of one subject can reinforce learning in other subjects. Mathematics teachers can illustrate their lessons by ideas being taught in physics. Language teachers can refer to what students learned three years earlier in history classes. Teachers and students may more easily converse because they have a common basis of knowledge and skills.

The principle may apply to states and to the nation as a whole. Common core knowledge of American culture, geography, history, and literature may be required for the nation to remain cohesive. Students who are culturally illiterate or ignorant of the national language and heritage may be unable to participate in economic and civic life.[33]

Still, a uniform national curriculum, assessment, and standards imposed by the federal government would be controversial. Federal education programs have often exhibited a pattern of inefficiency and failure. Even if a uniform federal system would yield some efficiency, it would violate principles of states' rights and local control. Many educators, taxpayers, and public officials rightly fear giving power to special interests and a federal bureaucracy out of touch with mainstream values. The excessive influence of national teachers' unions on politicians justifies such fear.

Thus, state departments of education, private groups such as testing agencies, and subject matter groups would be best advised to establish competing standards from which public and private schools could choose. These would be analogous to private industrial and professional standards that have successfully evolved and promoted commerce throughout the world. A few standards groups—the analogs of Apple, Microsoft, and Sun—likely would dominate and compete with one another for customers. The market, however, would leave room for diverse preferences.

Allow for Student Differences

Most children can learn, but they cannot learn at the same rate or to the same level. Students vary enormously in their talents and in the circumstances outside school that comprise about 87 percent of their waking hours in the first eighteen years of life. Some students, generally those from high-income homes, begin school already knowing how to read. They learn at a faster rate, enjoy schooling, and pursue it longer. Less-well-prepared students, more often of lower socioeconomic status, encounter frustration, fall behind, and withdraw. (Despite contrary advocacy, secondary and higher education is regressive or inegalitarian in that children from poor families drop out much more frequently—a reason that egalitarian social democrats in Sweden have proposed fixed-value lifetime vouchers that could be sold at the age of maturity or used for adult sabbaticals.)

Early childhood programs such as Head Start have rarely had success, and the occasional early gains evaporate within three years. The Perry Pre-School Program, often cited as the basis of Head Start, appeared to raise graduation rates, lower rates of placement in special education, and decrease delinquency. These apparent effects, though, were small, disputed, and borderline in significance. The evaluation was conducted by project staff who may have had an interest in continuation and expansion of the project. Ten other such projects studied by the Consortium for Longitudinal Studies showed no such long-term effects.[34]

Studies of the U.S. Department of Education's Chapter 1 compensatory program for low-income school children, on which more than $50 billion has been spent, rarely show significant differences between program and comparable control students. In view of the long history of spending and failure, educators and others should be cautious about promising to compensate for family and neighborhood differences in socioeconomic status and related factors. Similarly, policymakers should be more cautious about the testimony of program advocates, especially those that evaluate their own accomplishments.

MATTHEW EFFECTS. What can be expected are ''Matthew effects''; that is, the notion that the academic rich get richer as they go through school. Ability differences within grades and years become more obvious to teachers, students, and observers. With acquired knowledge and reading skill so important in academic learning, individual differences among students are apparent not only in mathematics and science but also in such verbal subjects as English, civics, history, and geography. Such heterogeneity pressures teachers to set low standards or to track students.

Careful observational studies further illuminate the U.S. achievement problem.[35] They show that the abilities of beginning U.S. students equal those of Japan and Taiwan. With each subsequent year of school, however, U.S. students fall further behind; by fifth grade, the worst Asian class exceeded the best U.S. class. The steady progress of Asian students appears attributable to a fast, unrepetitive curriculum, parental stimulation at home, and cultural beliefs in hard work instead of luck or talent as a chief determinant of success in mathematics. The challenge is to establish schools in the United States that can at least partially create these kinds of incentives, attitudes, and accomplishments.

GROUPING. Despite many studies of programs that failed to compensate educationally for family inequalities, some reformers still promise equality of learning results. Even equality of opportunity, however, may be unrealistic. Having students three or four grade levels apart in achievement makes whole-group teaching inefficient. Teachers, for example, who reasonably aim for students in the middle teach the quick what they already know and the slow what they are yet incapable of learning.

A compromise made in many countries is to provide six years of primary school, three years of lower secondary, and three years of upper secondary school. As in a short foot race, the six years of primary school can be fairly uniform before large differences among students become obvious; special programs, extra study, and summer school may help slower students keep up. By the end of the sixth year of primary school, however, students are likely to be heterogeneous in what they know and can do.

Therefore, lower and upper secondary schools are often differentiated with respect to academic rigor, interests, and specialization. Examinations and counseling can be employed to screen students into programs designed for those who are relatively homogeneous with respect to achievement and interest. Such schools can custom tailor their programs to their students' abilities and preferences.

Market-based management, however, might enhance effective, efficient, and more egalitarian learning. It would require a management system as well as a rigorous system of external examinations that would provide the measure of value added for rewarding results.

EXTERNAL EXAMINATIONS. In Japan, students take competitive achievement examinations that filter them into schools of various gradations of rigor, thereby enabling hard-working children from poor families to attend more rigorous schools. In traditional European education, students are funneled into vocational, technical, and, for the university-bound, academic schools depending on externally set achievement test standards.[36] In both Japan and Europe, examinations serve as inducements for students to work hard at their studies—the chief ingredient in learning. They are also a means of maintaining quality control over lower schools and a way of homogenizing abilities in higher education to make it more efficient.

U.S. students, even before they enter school, are ability segregated according to residence, because large differences in socioeconomic status exist among parts of cities and suburbs. Nearly all American public secondary schools, moreover, track students into courses and programs of various levels of difficulty. Otherwise, teachers would encounter the problems of direct instruction on an even larger scale.

Such differences among students must be frankly considered for several reasons. Many American students are "socially promoted" from grade to grade and eventually graduated as a reward for the "seat time" of attending classes. Coasting through easy courses is rational behavior, especially because employers and most colleges do not review high school transcripts of grades and courses taken. Consequently, those who work immediately upon graduation are less well prepared than they should be, and they lack disciplined work habits. Because they are likely to bounce from one job to another, employers may be unwilling to hire them. Those that pursue a postsecondary education start with remedial work they should have mastered in high school, which costs time and money.

If explicit standards for differentiated diplomas were adopted such as basic, proficient, and advanced (similar to the National Assessment Governing Board standards), employers could base starting pay upon them, thereby providing greater incentives to learn. Colleges might provide tuition allowances for superior high school performance. Mastery of special areas such as foreign languages, mathematics, and computer skills might be similarly employed. U.S. precedents include the Advanced Placement examinations of the College Entrance Examination Board and the New York Regents examination—both of which deserve expansion and which may require additional incentives.[37]

Hold Educators Accountable

Citizens—including parents, educators, legislators, and members of state and local school boards—pay for public schools, so they should know how well they are doing. To determine that, they will need to compare the achievement scores of schools with one another and with standards of performance. James Coleman argued that if standards were externally set and measured, as they are in other countries, students could not pressure teachers to lower them. Teachers could then concentrate on helping their students meet the standards, as do coaches in competitive sports.[38]

In addition, as Coleman emphasized, student heterogeneity needs to be taken into account if there are to be fair standards and accountability. Therefore, student progress or the value added to learning by the teacher or school during the most recent year or other term should be the chief criterion.

The value added by a unit at each step is the basis of accountability (see figure 3). This requires a measure at the end of each step so that the gains made by a student or group of students can be assessed. Such value-added gains largely eliminate socioeconomic and other extraneous differences and provide a fairer basis for evaluating progress.[39] As suggested in the third organizational form, a single unit—teacher, team, or school—can be an unambiguous locus of accountability.

As depicted in the second part of figure 3, the present cumbersome system of administering public schools promotes conflicting and ambiguous reporting relations. Complex regulation at the federal, state, local, and school levels not only slows decisionmaking but also removes the possibility of clear accountability. Present providers would undoubtedly object to such a system, but it might be in their long-term best interests as a profession. It seems likely to increase their effectiveness and efficiency, and it could be used to reward results.

Incorporate Appropriate Incentives

The administration of U.S. education by federal, state, and local government allows too many cooks to spoil the broth, high administrative costs, long chains of reporting, and ambiguous accountability. School boards and educators have many masters—none of which can be well served. Least well served but most important are their customers; namely, clients of their services (students, parents, and employers) and taxpayers who pay the bills. The unprecedented scope and complexity of U.S. school administration allow for much abuse.

In the language of organization theory, "coordination costs" among departments and administrative levels divert money, time, and attention away from avowed purposes.[40] "Information problems" prevent governing boards from getting full information on operations and results. Bureaucracies favor standard operating procedures over more productive and client-satisfying innovations.

"Agency problems" allow staff to work in their own self-interest. Presumably, they should instead be trying to suit board directives, consumer tastes, and client preferences. "Free riders" reap benefits of staff membership while evading costs of full effort. "Rent seekers" impose costs for unneeded or unperformed services, thereby reducing value in relation to costs.

These are old stories in organizations, and they apply fully to school governance and operations. The cure lies in rearranging incentives to benefit intended recipients of education services. Under the leadership of Eric Hanushek, thirteen economists in 1994 discussed a variety of programs that encourage attainment of results. These include performance contracting, charter schools, merit pay for teachers, improved teacher selection and renewal procedures, merit schools (in which the staff as a whole is rewarded for raising achievement), and school-based management.[41]

As Hanushek and his associates point out, incorporating increased incentives tied to results has theoretical appeal and has worked well in many industries and in the public sector.[42] The systematic application of value-added feedback, accountability, measurement, and incentives provides a framework for understanding these innovations. The implementation of such a system, however, would leave the organizational particularities to governing boards and worker-managers.

Still, resistance to change has prevented rigorous field tests of such programs of increased incentives in public school—all the more reason that states should create conditions for experimentation, conduct careful evaluations of their results, and expand programs that work best. Because the history of educational reform suggests that such efforts, however, will be feeble and unevaluated, more radical reforms seem in order.

Abolish or Voucherize Federal Education Programs

Many U.S. education problems can be traced to costly, complex, and voluminous federal and state regulations and programs brought about by special interest groups. In 1991, for example, seventy-seven categorical programs for children and families were each funded at $100 million or more per year.[43] The education programs were to serve one or another category of children such as the poor, migrant, low-achieving, "limited-English proficient," "language disabled," "behaviorally disordered," and "emotionally disturbed." Such programs were to reduce the achievement gaps between students so-categorized and other students, but they often had the effect of injuriously labeling and segregating these students from others.

The biggest and best example is compensatory education (also known as Title I or Chapter 1), which in the late 1990s costs about $7 billion per year. With origins in President Lyndon B. Johnson's "War on Poverty" in 1965, its backers represented "perhaps the widest constellation of interest groups ever assembled on a domestic issue." These included "the Big Six" lobbying groups, such as the National Education Association and the American Association of School Administrators.[44]

To compensate for economic inequalities, Chapter 1 was to raise achievement in poor schools by redistributing taxpayer monies to schools with especially high concentrations of low-achieving children in poverty. However, the poorly targeted funds go to 93 percent of all U.S. school districts; and the program serves many nonpoor students, while leaving many poor students unserved.[45]

To target funds on poor, low-achieving children requires their physical separation or "pull out" from regular classes for part or all of the school day (or, less often, simultaneous and mutually distracting lessons for poor and nonpoor students in the same classroom). Employed in 82 percent of compensatory-funded districts, pull-out programs have many inherent problems: Separated children gain time in remedial reading and mathematics but at the expense of nonremedial work in these subjects as well in other subjects such as history, music, and science. Their less qualified teachers or more often poorly trained aides tend to employ repetitive drilling rather than stimulating lessons; they remain ill informed about the subject matter and lessons in the regular class—thus trivializing and fragmenting subject matter. The children, some of whom are assigned to other federal categories, waste time going from room to room and being shuffled from one teacher or aide to another.

As might be expected, repeated large-scale evaluations of the program have been negative. Notwithstanding the extra funds, services, and thirty years of promises and reforms, students in the program still achieve about as well (or poorly) as comparable students not in the program. The gap between poor and nonpoor children remains unaffected.[46]

The new variant on Title I, Schoolwide Projects, concentrates federal funds in schools with 75 percent or more poor students to avoid categorizing and segregating students within buildings. Four evaluations, however, are mixed, and all four showed instances of nonserved control students achieving more than those in Schoolwide Projects—the latest of many broken promises of Title I advocates.[47]

The other huge federally initiated categorical program, special education, is similarly ill founded and ineffective for many of the same reasons. In 1990–91, 4.8 million students were enrolled, most in new federal categories of "neurological deficit," "language impairment," "mild retardation," "emotional disturbance," and "behavioral disorder" (instead of the long-established, scientifically creditable categories of blindness and deafness). In reviewing the programs, the National Academy of Sciences concluded that children should not be placed in such special education programs unless they demonstrate scientifically reliable systems of student categorization and that so-categorized children benefit from the special programs. Federally sponsored special education programs meet neither criterion. Instead, they encourage spurious and insidious psychopathological stereotyping in which little learning is expected by teachers, parents, peers, and categorized students themselves.[48]

Federal "transitional bilingual education" is another sizable example. It requires children to be taught in their mother tongue until they learn English. This denies them the very thing they most need—practice in English, which brought language mastery to American immigrants over many decades. As in special education, once admitted, children often remain in bilingual programs indefinitely.[49] Program administrators and teachers must chose between students' success and protecting their jobs.

Initiated and maintained by the federal government, compensatory, special, and bilingual programs have created a segregated, "second system" in the United States that isolates poor and low-achieving students. Federal programs create many bureaucratic, professional, and semiprofessional jobs. Though costing many billions of federal and state dollars, they do little good and often cause considerable harm to their nominal beneficiaries—American school children, particularly the most educationally needy.

The 6 or so percent that the federal government contributes to elementary and secondary education costs may cause far greater harm. Aside from the segregation, stereotyping, and waste, it distracts administrative and professional attention, energy, and funds from education's end product—classroom learning. This is best seen in large cities where federal programs are most prevalent and test scores are lowest (lower even than their poverty levels would predict). For example, with a 1996 deficit of $2.5 billion, New York City was spending only one-fifth of the public high school budget from federal, state, and local sources on classroom instruction according to a documented estimate.[50]

Thirty years of failure, unfulfilled reform promises, and several hundred billion dollars call for radical solutions. Abolishing the secretary of education's chair in the president's cabinet and reconstituting the U.S. Department of Education appear insufficient. Federal categorical programs are doing the harm. Ending them would serve the public interest and would be consistent with the traditional and constitutional role of states and local communities in setting education policy. It would reduce the influence of perverse incentives and special interests. It would remove complex regulations, simplify administration, and yield shorter state and local feedback loops for accountability. It would terminate the behavior observed by Jane Hannaway: "The job of the categorical program manager is geared to keeping the funding agencies satisfied rather than managing the educational program."[51] The federal money saved could be better raised and spent by state and local agencies, which would further enhance local decisionmaking and accountability. Short of this, unrestricted block grants of federal funds would allow states and local communities to evaluate plausible solutions to American schools' productivity problems.

Another alternative is to provide vouchers through categorical programs. Consider, for example, the approximate $7 billion Title I compensatory program for poor children. The most direct and efficient way to compensate for poor children's educational disadvantages is to give money—not to bureaucrats and professionals—but to poor families in the form of educational vouchers to purchase educational services from a variety of public schools and private providers. This would have an immediate consumer sovereignty effect of putting the customer, not the producer, in charge. It would provide incentives and rewards for success missing from federal programs and public schools because providers would have to compete for students. The feedback loop between provider and customer would be in place. Under such a system, children would have the benefit of regular classes plus enrollment with vouchers in supplementary evening, Saturday, and summer programs that would not be tied to the usual inefficiency of public schools and special interests.

Privatizing Schools

The largest and most fundamental problem is not categorical programs but the lack of competition among government schools, which, in the absence of incentives to improve, leads to the primacy of producer interests over customer interests. Categorical programs and regulations are bureaucracy's vain attempt to assess consumer needs, prescribe solutions, and create accountability in the absence of market forces. Far better than this are decisions made by citizens themselves. How can governments gainsay their preferences?

Various experiments in privatization and contracting out public services to private (not-for-profit and for-profit) firms suggest that they respond swiftly and accurately to citizens' desires.[52] An economist's version of meta-analysis (analysis of results of many studies) shows that, other things being equal, private organizations on average perform significantly better at lower costs and that they are more satisfying to their staff and their customers. The studies concern airlines, banks, bus service, debt collection, electric utilities, forestry, hospitals, housing, insurance sales and processing, railroads, refuse collection, savings and loans, slaughterhouses, water utilities, and weather forecasting.[53]

Nations that rely on the private sector for goods and services also do better. The lower the share of low-, middle-, and high-income nations' public spending of gross domestic product, the greater the economic growth rate, social welfare, and citizen choice.[54] Compare Hong Kong and Taiwan with Mainland China, South Korea with North Korea, Western Europe with Eastern Europe. With respect to economic growth, compare the Asian Pacific countries with Africa, Europe, and India. Ample evidence shows that finance and operation of services are more efficiently controlled by direct citizen choice than by governments.

New Evidence for Free Market Advantages

Vast amounts of research and common experience suggest that markets and competition work well. Providers of public education, nonetheless, insist that education is an exception. They oppose experimental privatization trials but insist on strong evidence for efficacy. In a country, nonetheless, with the highest or near highest costs and the worst (value-added) achievement gains, Americans have the right to ask where the burden of proof lies. Even so, recent evidence refutes the standard producer contentions.

First, enlarging private school choice may be best for public education because what public schools lack is competition; most are, in economic terms, local monopolies.[55] Recent research supports the value of local private competition in improving public schools. Rather than creaming off the best students, the presence of private schools and public schools of choice in geographical areas is associated with better performance of public school students.[56] Their success is no doubt attributable to greater latitude of consumer choice and unleashed competitive forces.

Studies in ten countries including three in the United States suggest that private (including independent and sectarian) schools achieve more at lower costs.[57] Jane Hannaway suggests that responsiveness to consumer preferences is the key to their success.[58] (Government curtailment of their decisionmaking, however, might negate private schools' superior performance.)[59]

The one U.S. instance of a randomized experiment employing vouchers is Milwaukee, Wisconsin. Applicant minority children were admitted to private schools at random because insufficient spaces were available to meet demand. (Even though the costs of the program were about half that of public schools, the state department of education created many uncertainties and difficulties, and various start-up difficulties ensued.) After several years, the selected students did better on standardized tests, sufficiently well that the usual national minority-majority achievement gap was substantially cut.[60] Perhaps even more important and notwithstanding the start-up difficulties, parents were delighted with the private schools.[61]

Consumer Preferences

Surveys show that citizens increasingly favor choice in education, including private schools. A 1992 Gallup poll showed that 85 percent of African Americans and 84 percent of Hispanics supported vouchers.[62] Inner-city minorities particularly favor privatization, because government schools available to them are most often dominated by federal categorical programs and regulations, which make them unresponsive to parents. In Milwaukee, for example, which has had most experience with privatization, 95 percent of African Americans favored private and public school choice, and 70 percent believed that students get a better education from independent and sectarian schools.[63]

Other recent and strong behavioral indications of private preference can be cited. The growth in privately funded vouchers for poor children has been quiet but meteoric. Funded by individuals, philanthropies, and firms, their numbers in seventeen cities have grown from 744 to 6,572 in four years—further evidence of consumer preference.[64]

Another indication of preference for private over public education is the parents of about 900,000 home-schooled children. They sacrifice their time and money for what they consider is a superior education for their children. Many of them fear the violence and lifestyles taught in public schools. Though they are mostly amateur teachers, their children's average achievement on standardized tests exceeds that of 77 percent of regular school children.[65]

In addition, many parents voluntarily pay for private schools and special tutoring, even though the public schools are free of charge. Aside from the efficiency arguments, this alone is proof enough of the virtues of privatization. Citizens are the arbiters of quality in free societies. They—not government—should make the choices that affect their children's lives.

Reconciling Choice and Standards

Even the most ardent free-market libertarians know that wide-scale voucher programs are unlikely to be implemented tomorrow. Powerful special interests—the teachers' unions and other education lobbying groups—adamantly oppose vouchers and strongly influence legislators. They have severely curtailed the number and nature of charter schools, which are, by comparison, a modest and less threatening reform.

Therefore, education privatization will probably require further evidence. Aside from consumer preference, the best criteria are high standards on achievement tests in the standard school subjects. These may be employed in experiments to evaluate the many variations on choice that have been proposed. Even after experiments have been completed, it seems likely that policymakers and parents would continue to want to know about how well students meet achievement standards.

Conclusion

Privatization might satisfy all but the special interests of public school providers and the defenders of the status quo. Change might best start at the top. Vouchers for federal and state special needs programs, for example, would put money and authority directly in the hands of parents instead of in the current system administered from Washington and statehouses through special interests and administrative hierarchies.

Federal voucher programs would supplement, not supplant, special needs children's regular schooling and allow their parents to make their own program choices. Aside from ensuring safety and civil rights protections, regulations could be minimal. Program funds could be free of the rules that suffocate many public schools. Funding could be concentrated less on administrative overhead and more on increasing the amount and quality of educational services. Markets would compensate providers according to their capacity to attract and maintain student enrollments.

At the state and local levels, deregulation of public schools would allow them greater latitude to compete and to provide diversity reflecting consumer tastes. Allowing students to attend public schools outside their neighborhoods would encourage further competition, choice, and consumer sovereignty. However, the forces of the status quo and special interests may prevent the success of the current round of decentralizing reforms. Union opposition and excessive regulations already threaten the few timid charter schools in the United States.

Some policymakers, moreover, may hesitate to increase choice. Some are beholden to special interests. Others do not want to relinquish power to regulate; they doubt parents' intellectual and moral capacity to choose schools for their children.

Still other policymakers would prefer a greater degree of accountability for results. They want to see schools work efficiently toward high standards. Legislatures and school boards could better achieve this if they evaluate results rather than micromanage operations. They could employ value-added learning measures to reward results. Educators could be compensated for the degree that they increase learning as indicated by external objective examinations.

More generally, though, school vouchers have the greatest likelihood of success. The evidence for private schools' superior achievement suggests enlarging their numbers with publicly subsidized vouchers. This would be worth doing if for no other reason than the better performance private schools elicit from nearby public schools. In a free society, however, consumer sovereignty and parental choice for their children should be primary considerations.

Comment by John Bishop

Herbert J. Walberg provides a comprehensive discussion of the causes and possible cures of low achievement levels in American secondary schools. He begins by pointing out that the intelligence quotient (IQ) of children entering school has been rising for decades and that American nine-year-olds do not lag behind their counterparts abroad. During the next four years of school, however, gains in achievement are just about the lowest in the world. The fault, Walberg concludes, lies with the organization and operation of schools, not what is spent on them or the quality of students.

Achievement deficits at the end of secondary school cannot be blamed on the social and ethnic background of the students who entered first grade twelve years earlier. American parents are better educated than their counterparts in other countries, which should give American students an advantage over students in Asia and Europe.

Holding parents' schooling constant, American students compare poorly with Asian and European students. In figure 1 and figure 2, which present data from thirty-six Third International Mathematics and Science Study (TIMSS) countries, the bars represent the science and mathematics achievement levels, respectively, for thirteen-year-old students whose parents have completed secondary education relative to the achievement of U.S. students of the same age and background. The United States ranks seventeenth in science and thirtieth in mathematics. The gaps between the vertical lines represent one U.S. grade level equivalent (GLE)—the difference between seventh and eighth grade TIMSS U.S. test score means. Achievement differentials across nations are very large. In science, Singapore, Korea, Flemish Belgium, the Czech Republic, and Austria are more than one GLE ahead of the United States, and Colombia, Lithuania, Romania, Portugal, Latvia, and Iran are more than two GLEs behind. In mathematics, Singapore, Korea, Hong Kong, and Flemish Belgium are more than four GLEs ahead of the United States, while Colombia is more than four GLEs behind. Schools in a number of Asian and European nations clearly teach science and mathematics more effectively than American schools.

Walberg concludes that American schools lag behind because they are inefficient and that the inefficiency results from lack of standards and accountability, centralization, unaccountable management and labor, federal government dictates, and the monopoly power of local public school providers.

So, what is to be done? The vast literature on school effectiveness and reform offers eleven reform principles and proposals: (1) focus schools on learning; (2) apply principles of effective instruction; (3) increase instruction and homework time; (4) decentralize the organization of work and instruction; (5) employ uniform standards; (6) allow for student differences; (7) provide external examinations; (8) hold educators accountable; (9) incorporate appropriate incentives; (10) abolish federal education programs or establish voucher programs; and (11) privatize schools. Some of these proposals are well researched and widely supported in education policy circles. Others have not been rigorously evaluated or extensively implemented in school settings. The most controversial proposals are based on market analogies and private sector management lessons that may or may not apply to schools. Given space limitations here, I will focus on two issues: external examinations and the power of teachers.

Figure 1. TIMSS Science Achievement at Age Thirteen, Children of High School Graduates

Note: TIMSS = Third International Mathematics and Science Study.

Figure 2. TIMSS Math Achievement at Age Thirteen, Children of High School Graduates

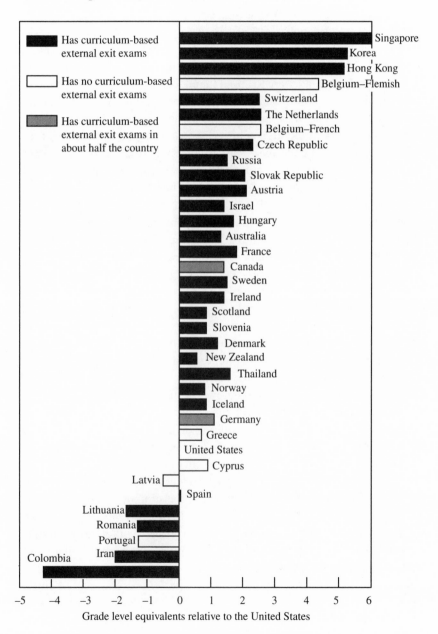

Note: TIMSS = Third International Mathematics and Science Study.

Curriculum-based external exit exams (CBEEEs) should not be viewed as a new untested reform idea. They are used all over the world. Advanced Placement (AP) exams and New York state's Regents exams both fulfill the criteria of a CBEEE. By comparing nations with and without (or with different types of) external external examination systems, a forecast can be made of how teaching and learning would change if a state such as Maryland were to adopt them. The TIMSS data on achievement in science and mathematics provide a preliminary look. The countries with a CBEEE in a subject tend to have higher TIMSS scores; meanwhile, many of the high achievement countries are located in East Asia. An Asian tendency may exist to have CBEEEs, which produces the positive association between CBEEEs and achievement levels. This has been tested in multivariate models. When East Asian nation and gross domestic product (GDP) per capita are controlled, CBEEEs continue to have statistically significant relationships with achievement.[66] The estimated impact is about one U.S. grade level equivalent. Multivariate analyses of achievement differences across Canadian provinces and American states (New York state versus the rest of the nation) yield similar findings. When high school students with similar socioeconomic backgrounds are compared, those living in states or provinces with a CBEEE score significantly higher (about two-thirds of a grade level equivalent higher) on science and mathematics tests.

Little evidence is available to support Walberg's claim that "school boards have not been a match for nationally organized unions that can bring to bear strong, narrow self-interests, statistical research, and specialized expertise to negotiations." American teachers' unions are much weaker than the teachers' unions of the European nations with high-performing students. The pay of American teachers reflects the weakness of their unions. Table 1 presents data on salaries, qualifications, time spent teaching, and pupil-to-teacher ratios in seventeen Organization for Economic Cooperation and Development (OECD) countries.[67] Upper secondary school teachers with fifteen years of experience are paid 60 to 66 percent more than the average worker in Australia, Belgium, Britain, Norway, and France; 73 percent more in Japan; and about twice the average worker in Austria, Germany, the Netherlands, and Switzerland. In the United States, experienced secondary school teachers are paid only 33 percent more than the average worker. Apparently one of the reasons U.S. teachers are poorly paid is the absence of curriculum-based external exit exams. Nations with CBEEEs pay their teachers 21 percent more than nations that lack a CBEEE.

The lower pay in the United States is not compensation for more attractive conditions of work. Pupil-to-teacher ratios are higher in the United States than in many other advanced countries. American upper secondary school teachers are in front of a classroom 825 hours per year, which is considerably more than teachers in Europe and Japan. Dutch upper secondary teachers are the only group that have heavier teaching loads than American teachers.[68] Tenure protections are typically stronger in Europe than in the United States.

If it were true, as Walberg says, that "teachers' unions . . . have done splendidly for their members," then the growth of teachers' unions should have generated an increase in teachers' relative wage and long queues of highly qualified people seeking teaching jobs. However, the growth of teachers' unions coincides with a period of relative decline in the salaries of teachers.[69] Figure 3 presents decennial census data on the ratio of teacher earnings to the wages of other college graduates of the same gender. In 1940, female college graduates in the teaching profession were paid about the same as female college graduates in other occupations. By 1990, teacher salaries had dropped to 80 percent of the wage available to female college graduates outside of teaching. The wage of male teachers dropped from 75 to 65 percent of alternative opportunities between 1940 to 1990. Math and science majors who enter teaching upon graduation are paid 40 percent less than their college lab partners who find work as scientists or computer programmers.[70] The failure of teachers' unions to get their members higher salaries is one of the reasons that the Scholastic Aptitude Test (SAT) scores of freshmen intending to major in education are so low.

While districts with above average salaries and attentive students have their pick of applicants for teacher positions, less favored districts are forced to fill math and science teaching slots with those who lack adequate training. Sixty percent of Texas teachers and one-third of all teachers nationally are teaching outside their field of certification. Many secondary school teachers of mathematics and science have only minimal knowledge of their subject. Calculus is the gateway course for college-level mathematics, physics, and chemistry, yet 46 percent of the 1991 graduates entering math and science teaching jobs did not take calculus in college.[71] Minimum standards for entry into secondary

Table 1. Teacher Pay and Qualifications and Spending per Pupil

Country	Teacher compensation divided by average earnings of all workers[a]		Years of education required to teach[b]		Yearly hours of instruction in upper secondary school[c]	Ratio of secondary school pupils to teachers	Spending per pupil divided by	
	Lower secondary school	Upper secondary school	Lower secondary school	Upper secondary school			Compensation per employee[d]	Per capita GDP[c]
No external exam								
Belgium	1.25	1.61	15	16	637	7.8	.191	.285
Spain	1.40	1.72	15	17	536	16.6	.107	.218
Sweden	1.14	1.32	16	16	593	13.0	.243	.364
United States	1.33	1.33	16	16	825	15.9	.201	.283
Mean (no CBEEEs)	1.28	1.495	15.5	16.3	648	13.3	.1855	.2875
External exam								
Austria	2.01	2.48	15	16	819	9.4	.270	.356
Australia	1.60	1.60	—	—	—	12.9	—	—
Denmark	1.16	1.83	—	—	615	9.7	.226	.280
Finland	1.61	1.67	18	18	556	—	.195	.333
France	1.44	1.66	16	16	532	14.3	.203	.293
Germany	1.82	1.98	19	20	810	16.2	.243	.305
Ireland	1.49	1.49	17	17	801	17.1	.123	.217
Italy	1.31	1.35	17	17	745	8.9	.204	.271
Japan	1.71	1.73	—	—	696	16.6	.182	.202

Netherlands	1.58	2.32	17	17	943	18.8	.149	.195
Norway	1.33	1.65	15	16	586	8.3	.311	.351
Switzerland	1.85	2.13	—	—	716	—	—	.278
United Kingdom	1.63	1.63	17	17	776	15.2	.187	.278
Mean (CBEEEs)	1.58	1.808	16.8	17.1	716	13.4	.2084	.280

Note: GDP = gross domestic product. CBEEEs = curriculum-based external exit exams.

a. Compensation of secondary school teachers was calculated by multiplying their salary after fifteen years of experience by the ratio of compensation to wages for manufacturing workers. This estimate of teacher compensation was then divided by average compensation of all workers. The figure for French upper secondary school teachers is a weighted average of salaries for Agrege (20 percent) and others (80 percent). Howard Nelson and Timothy O'Brien. How U.S. Teachers Measure Up Internationally: A Comparative Study of Teacher Pay, Training, and Conditions of Service (Washington: American Federation of Teachers, 1993), pp. 73, 74, 90, 91.

b. Minimum number of years of education required to be a lower or upper secondary school teacher. Organization for Economic Cooperation and Development. Education at a Glance (Paris, France, 1995), p. 185.

c. Mean number of hours teaching a class per day times the mean number of workdays for teachers. Nelson and O'Brien. How U.S. Teachers Measure Up Internationally, table 11.3, table 11.4.

d. Ratio of the number of full-time-equivalent pupils enrolled in public and private secondary schools to the number of full-time-equivalent secondary school teachers. Organization for Economic Cooperation and Development. Education at a Glance, p. 179.

e. For 1992, spending per secondary school pupil divided by compensation per employee or per capita GDP. Organization for Economic Cooperation and Development. Education at a Glance, p. 90; and Nelson and O'Brien. How U.S. Teachers Measure Up Internationally, p. 91.

Figure 3. Ratio of Teacher to Other College Graduate Earnings, 1940–90

Ratio

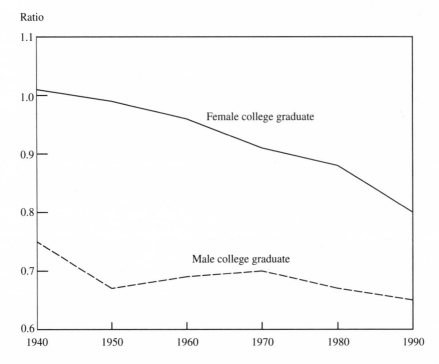

Source: Eric Hanushek and Steven Rivkin, "Understanding the Twentieth Century Growth in U.S. School Spending," *Journal of Human Resources,* vol. 32, no. 1 (Winter 1997), pp. 35–68.

school teaching are higher in Europe and East Asia. In France, for example, secondary school teachers must have a university degree in the subject they teach and must also pass an exam in the subject that typically 69 percent of job candidates fail.

Tenure protects incompetent teachers, but it also protects teachers who set high standards and fail the children of school board members. Adele Jones of Georgetown, Delaware, failed such children and got fired for doing it.[72] If administrators had more power to fire teachers, what guarantees exist that they would not use it to get rid of teachers who use unfashionable teaching strategies such as phonics or who generate parental complaints because homework assignments are too long? Thirty percent of teachers report being pressured ''to reduce the difficulty and amount of work'' and ''to give higher grades than the students work deserves.'' This pressure comes from school administrators and parents, not from their colleagues.

The balance of power between teachers' unions and school administrators and school boards is not the source of or even a major contributor to the low quality of American secondary schools. The fundamental problem is the lack of good signals of student achievement that are comparable across schools; the resulting lack of student, teacher, and school district accountability; and a peer culture that denigrates the studious as nerds, dorks, and suckups.

Comment by Jane Hannaway

Three major areas of discussion in Herbert J. Walberg's paper—specialization, centralization, and competition—raised concerns, and I want to focus my comments on them.

Let me begin, however, by mentioning where the paper made particularly good sense. First, sufficient evidence does exist to suggest that U.S. schools are not on the "efficiency frontier," as economists put it. U.S. schools most certainly can do better, even within current resource constraints. At the same time, the performance of students in many states fares quite well in international comparisons.[73] Second, many factors that Walberg identifies would contribute to greater school productivity:

—Schools that focus on learning as their primary mission are likely to produce more student learning than schools that are diverted to other objectives.

—The more time students spend on learning, ceteris paribus, the more they will learn.

—High-quality instruction will yield greater benefits than low-quality instruction.

—High standards of performance are certainly better than low standards and probably also better than no standards.

—Better information on student performance, in particular value-added measures, would help schools better direct their efforts.

—Educators should be held accountable, to some significant level, for how much students learn.

—The system as a whole would be better off if performance incentives were built into it.

However, Walberg's reasons that the conditions are not prevalent in U.S. schools and his proposed solutions to generate them are not convincing. Both the diagnosis of educational problems and their solutions are important to get right. Reforms have downside risks as well as upside potential, and both sides have to be carefully thought through when instituting new policies.

If the proposed reforms are so commonsensical, why have they not already been undertaken? Are there groups that might be seriously disadvantaged? If so, how can they be compensated or protected? Are there forces (for example, political forces) that have been ignored? If so, how can they be placated? Could the analysis be incomplete, so that what at first blush seems only commonsensical is not at a deeper level of analysis? For instance, if performance is not easy to measure, then introducing performance-based measures may be difficult. If some aspects of performance are easier to measure than others, then performance-based incentives may divert attention toward those areas that are easily measured, thus adversely affecting overall performance.[74] Walberg tends to offer his solutions as no-cost, no-risk panaceas, limiting the usefulness of his paper as a piece of policy analysis.

Specialization

Walberg characterizes specialization as a factor contributing to low productivity in American schools. It comes up in at least two different places in his paper. Both subject matter specialization among teachers in middle and junior high schools and subunit specialization are presumed to limit school efficiency and effectiveness.

Specialization in and of itself is neither good nor bad. It is, however, powerful—partly because it directs the attention and shapes the general frame of reference of individuals in their work. The consequences, both positive and negative, can be significant for an organization. The question is: What is the appropriate type and level of specialization?

Inappropriately defined areas of specialization could depress productivity. If the tasks of an individual or a unit in an organization are defined too generally, the efficiency and expertise with which the tasks are performed are likely to suffer. At the same time, if the tasks of an individual or a unit are defined too narrowly, performance is also likely to suffer for at least two reasons. First, coordination costs might outweigh the benefits of specialization; and, second, matters that are outside the scope of any of the specialized units are likely to be systematically overlooked even though they might affect the effectiveness of the organization. So a position or unit within an organization could be inappropriately defined either because it not specialized enough or because it is too specialized.

Walberg claims schools have become too specialized, but this is questionable. For example, many people contend that too little attention is given to math in schools (Walberg's time factor) or that it is taught too poorly (Walberg's instructional quality factor). Walberg sees specialization as part of the problem. However, it may be part of the solution. That is, specialized math teachers—not only in middle and high school, but perhaps also in elementary school—could be expected to contribute to an increase in instructional time on math, as well as instructional quality. A specialist math teacher would more reliably focus student learning on math for a specified period of time during the school day (the same way a physical education teacher has a defined time, while a generalist teacher would be diverted by other interests. The specialist is also more likely to develop expertise and to be particularly attuned to new developments in math instruction, instructional materials, and the value of different pedagogical approaches, all of which are likely to contribute to instructional quality. Costs also are associated with specialization, which Walberg mentions; for example, a less personal learning environment for students. Determining the costs and benefits of specialization is an empirical issue. Some, but not much, research has been done in the area.

James McPartland and his colleagues investigated some of the effects of specialization in middle schools. Using data on student performance collected by the state of Pennsylvania and data on staffing patterns collected by the Johns Hopkins Center for Research on Elementary and Middle Schools, McPartland found clear evidence of trade-offs in middle schools between specialist teaching and integration of subject matter.[75] Sixth graders in self-contained classrooms reported higher quality relationships with teachers than sixth graders in schools with subject matter departments. Gains in student achievement in schools with subject matter specialists as teachers, however, were higher. Analysis of National Assessment of Educational Progress data also showed higher math and science performance by seventh graders who were taught by subject-matter specialist teachers.[76]

The issues are similar at the district level. Specialized units are not in themselves bad. The question is: Are the specialized units the right ones? For example, if a school district is particularly concerned about accountability, establishing a district office or special position on accountability probably makes good sense. A specialized office or position would help ensure that the district would attend to accountability issues as well as track development in the accountability policies and practices elsewhere.

Walberg's analysis of specialization, while consistent with some popular views, does not fully appreciate the role of specialization in organizations or the benefits it can yield. Before any conclusions can be reached about the relative merits of any particular organizational arrangements in schools, a more balanced and thorough analysis is needed. Questions must be asked about not only the level of specialization but also the type of specialization, and the costs of different organizational arrangements must be weighed against their relative merits.

Centralization

Centralization and decentralization are terms that currently take on a normative cast in popular discussions; centralization is bad and decentralization is good. Walberg's paper reflects this general tone. Some confusion, however, appears in the discussion. For one, centralization at times refers primarily to the size of a school district, not the locus of decisionmaking. The increased size of an organization could be negatively related to centralization. Extensive organizational literature shows that organizational size and centralized decisionmaking are negatively correlated.[77] High School and Beyond data reveal the same relationship in schools. Principals, as well as teachers, in larger school districts report greater autonomy and influence over what goes on in their schools than principals and teachers in smaller school districts.[78]

Because size and centralization are negatively correlated, their effects on productivity must be considered separately. Research shows a systematic effect of district size on performance, but it appears to be conditioned by context factors. For example, N. E. Friedkin and J. Necochea, using data from the California Assessment Program, found that, while school district size has a strong negative effect among low-socioeconomic status (SES) school districts, it has a positive effect among high-SES districts.[79] Joan Talbert and I found a similar pattern of results for urban and suburban school districts with the High School and Beyond data; larger district size benefits suburban districts but hurts urban districts.[80] In other words, conditions—yet to be fully specified—exist under which larger size has negative effects, and conditions exist under which it appears to have beneficial effects. These conditions need to be fully considered before taking policy stands.

Regarding centralization, the locus of decisionmaking, care must be taken to identify the areas and levels of centralization, the areas and levels of decentralization, and how these affect school processes and school outcomes. For example, should accountability be decentralized? Would different schools be held to different standards? Would decentralization lead to greater performance disparities? Are there measures to minimize such effects? Decentralization efforts can have a downside; decentralization does not always lead to beneficial effects. Efforts in New York, for example, have not been successful—possibly because the wrong areas of responsibility were decentralized to the wrong level. And efforts in Chicago have not fulfilled the hopes of reformers.

Centralization cannot be all bad. While Walberg makes much about the poor performance of schools in the United States relative to other countries, he does not try to reconcile these claims with his concerns about centralization. Certainly most, if not all, of these other countries have more centralized systems of education than the United States. What should be made of this? Are there conditions under which centralized systems may be better? If so, they should be identified.

Competition

A mantra about competition and efficiency often passes for argument. Competition generally is a good thing, but it results in efficiency in highly idealized conditions, which is far from justified in schools. Imperfect information is probably the biggest problem—informed, quality-conscious consumers are assumed to be the regulators of an efficient system—but assessing the value of a school, especially for a particular child, is exceedingly difficult. Evidence shows, for example, that parents resort primarily to school location in making their schooling decisions. Imperfect competition also causes problems, as schools define niches, either real or marketing created, or because, once a schooling choice is made, the costs to a child of changing schools is often high. In short, making leaps to policies for education from arguments or evidence based on firms where information about process and product is typically much clearer is very risky, if not misleading. And to be considered is some of the undesired fallout—especially greater social fragmentation—that might emerge from a poorly designed system.

Problems with the economic model, however, do not necessarily mean that no value can be found in a choice system in education. A high level of social division already exists among schools; and while parents may not make the best decisions about schools, their schooling choices may be no worse than the schools their children already attend, especially in inner cities. The real value of education choice may come less from its economic or efficiency consequences than it does from its psychological consequences. A large literature in social psychology claims a strong effect of choice on commitment. And if parents become more committed to their child's school because they chose it, closer school-parent relations, a well-established ingredient of school and student success, may result. Well-designed choice systems—ones, for example, that give preferential treatment to the poor—may help ameliorate some of the problems of social fragmentation in the United States. But attempts must be made to determine why it might work. Only by doing so will systems of school choice be designed that exploit its strengths and minimize its downside risks.

Walberg's paper considers important issues about how organizational and governance factors may contribute to school productivity. These issues should be addressed with careful and full analysis as well as with empirical research—which is sorely lacking right now—and the movement should be away from excessively simplistic formulas for success that drive people into ideological corners instead of into open analysis and discussion.

Notes

1. Diane Ravitch and Chester E. Finn, Jr. *What Do Our 17–Year–Olds Know?: A Report on the First National Assessment of History and Literature* (Harper and Row, 1987); E. D. Hirsch, Jr., *Cultural Literacy: What Every American Needs to Know* (Boston, Mass.: Houghton Mifflin, 1987); and E. D. Hirsch, Jr., *The Schools We Need and Why We Don't Have Them* (Doubleday, 1966).

2. See papers by Howard W. Stevenson and Shinying Lee and Lawrence C. Stedman in this volume.

3. David W. Grissmer and others, *Student Achievement and the Changing American Family* (Santa Monica, Calif.: Rand Corporation, 1994). The *Economist* (February 22, 1997, pp. 27–28) pointed out many positive features of American families and child rearing: U.S. children, for example, start school earlier than previously. When they finish school, young adults increasingly stay on with their families. Large majorities see eye-to-eye with their parents on the value of education, women's roles, religion, racial issues, and how to dress. More and more Americans give kidneys to family members, a greater fraction of elderly live with their families than those in most north European countries, and increasingly greater percentages of mentally retarded Americans live with their families.

4. Erik A. Hanushek, "The Productivity Collapse in Schools," Working Paper No. 8 (Rochester, N.Y.: W. Allen Wallis Institute of Political Economy, December 1996), pp. 10–11.

5. Rob Greenwald, Larry V. Hedges, and Richard D. Laine contend that more money makes a difference in achievement. They showed that excluding much evidence contrary to their contention leaves a remaining body of evidence that on average supports their view even though some studies show negative effects of higher spending. Taking their selective evidence and analysis at face value suggests that raising school expenditures $500 (in 1993–94 dollars) or about 10 percent for per-pupil expenditures, teacher education, experience, and salary, and teacher-to-pupil ratios yields estimated effects of between .04 and .22 standard deviations, or an average of .15. Aside from selective evidential bias, Eric Hanushek has raised persuasive objections to these estimates and their usefulness, such as the lack of description of circumstances of when money makes a difference. In addition, my reservation is that even if these estimates were beyond question, they are tiny—between one-fifth and one-third the size of the effects of effective teaching techniques; for example, assigning and providing feedback on homework. Thus, effective teaching techniques, established through rigorous experimental-control group studies as in agriculture and medicine, yield far larger achievement effects than controversial estimates of expenditures based on passive production-function studies. See Rob Greenwald, Larry V. Hedges, and Richard D. Laine, "The Effect of School Resources on Student Achievement," *Review of Educational Research,* vol. 66 (Fall 1996), pp. 361–96; Eric A. Hanushek, "A More Complete Picture of School Resource Policies," *Review of Educational Research,* vol. 66 (Fall 1996), pp. 397–409; and Herbert J. Walberg, "Improving the Productivity of America's Schools," *Educational Leadership,* vol. 41 (May 1984), pp. 19–27. For the latest compilation of inconsistent expenditure and further answers to criticisms, see Eric A. Hanushek, "Assessing the Effects of School Resources on Student Performance: An Update," *Educational Evaluation and Policy Analysis,* vol. 19 (Summer 1997), pp. 141–64.

6. Economists may think of efficiency or productivity as the ratio of monetary

benefits to costs. These terms are employed differently here as generally referring to value-added learning in relation to costs and student time consumed.

7. Organization for Economic Cooperation and Development, *Education at a Glance: OECD Indicators* (Paris, France, 1995); and John H. Bishop, "Incentives to Study and the Organization of Secondary Instruction," in William Becker and William Baumol, eds., *Assessing Educational Practice: The Contribution of Economics* (Cambridge, Mass.: Russell Sage Foundation, 1996). Bishop proposes deflators for school expenditures.

8. See, for example, James R. Flynn, "The Mean IQ of Americans: Massive Gains 1932 to 1978," *Psychological Bulletin,* vol. 95 (January 1984), pp. 29–51.

9. Organization for Economic Cooperation and Development, *Education at a Glance: OECD Indicators* (Paris, France, 1996), pp. 212–13.

10. Caroline Minter Hoxby, "Is There an Equity-Efficiency Trade-Off in School Finance? Tiebout and a Theory of the Local Public Goods Producer," Working Paper No. 5265 (Harvard University, National Bureau of Economic Research, 1995).

11. Herbert J. Walberg and Herbert J. Walberg III, "Losing Local Control: Is Bigger Better?," *Educational Researcher,* vol. 23 (June/July 1994), pp. 19–26.

12. M. V. Borland and R. M. Howsen, "Competition, Expenditures, and Student Performance in Mathematics: A Comment on Couch et al.," *Public Choice,* vol. 87, no. 3–4 (1996), pp. 395–400.

13. Caroline Minter Hoxby, "Does Competition among Public Schools Benefit Students and Taxpayers? Evidence from Natural Variation in School Districting," Working Paper No. 4979 (Harvard University, National Bureau of Economic Research, 1994).

14. David J. Armor and Brett M. Peiser, *Competition in Education: A Case Study of Interdistrict Choice* (Boston, Mass.: Pioneer Institute for Public Policy Research, 1997).

15. See M. Antonucci, "How Much Do Teachers Really Make?" *Wall Street Journal,* March 11, 1997, p. A22.

16. Caroline Minter Hoxby, "How Teachers' Unions Affect Education Production," *Quarterly Journal of Economics,* vol. III (August 1996), pp. 671–718; and Sam Peltzman, "Political Economy of Public Education: Non-College-Bound Students," *Journal of Law and Economics,* vol. 39 (April 1996), pp. 73–120.

17. Office of Management and Budget, *The 1997 Budget of the United States Government, Historical Tables,* pp. 57–59.

18. See Herbert J. Walberg, "U.S. Schools Teach Reading Least Productively," *Research in the Teaching of English,* vol. 30 (October 1996), pp. 328–43.

19. Charles Wolf, Jr., *Markets or Governments: Choosing between Imperfect Alternatives* (MIT Press, 1988).

20. See Walberg and Walberg, "Losing Local Control."

21. David Strang, "The Administrative Transformation of American Education: School District Consolidation, 1938–1980," *Administrative Science Quarterly,* vol. 43 (September 1987), pp. 352–66.

22. Gordon Cawelti, ed., *Handbook of Research on Improving Student Achievement* (Alexandria, Va.: Educational Research Service, 1996).

23. Many of these conclusions are based on meta-analyses or statistical summaries of a large groups of studies. Though such works may be more familiar as summaries of the efficacy of medical and surgical treatments, meta-analysis originated in education and psychology to summarize the results of many studies. The statistically summarized

results are somewhat analogous to expressing the percentage of games won by a sports team or the average ratio of points won to those lost.

24. National Commission on Excellence in Education, *A Nation at Risk: The Imperative for Educational Reform* (Government Printing Office, 1983).

25. Herbert J. Walberg, Richard P. Niemiec, and Wayne C. Fredrick, "Productive Curriculum Time," *Peabody Journal of Education,* vol. 69, no. 3 (Spring 1994), pp. 86–100.

26. Walberg, "Improving the Productivity of America's Schools."

27. Julian R. Betts, "The Role of Homework in Improving School Quality," UCSD Discussion Paper 96–16 (La Jolla, Calif.: University of California at San Diego, Department of Economics, 1997).

28. See Herbert J. Walberg, "Generic Practices," in Gordon Cawelti, ed., *Handbook of Research on Improving Student Achievement* (Alexandria, Va.: Educational Research Service, 1996).

29. The figure is adapted from James S. Coleman, "Achievement Oriented School Design," paper prepared for the Social Organization of Schools conference at the University of Notre Dame, Center for Continuing Education, March 19, 1994. I am grateful to the late Professor Coleman for the discussion on the principles represented in the diagram and to Joseph Bast for suggestions on adapting it to management principles.

30. H. A. Simon, *The Sciences of the Artificial,* 2d ed. (MIT Press, 1981).

31. Theodore R. Sizer, *Horace's Compromise: The Dilemma of the American High School* (Houghton Mifflin, 1984), p. 156.

32. Ann Bradley, "Survey Reveals Teens Yearn for High Standards," *Education Week,* February 12, 1997, pp. 1, 38–39.

33. See Hirsch, *Cultural Literacy*; and Ravitch and Finn, *What Do Our Seventeen-Year-Olds Know?*

34. Ron Haskins, "Beyond Metaphor: The Efficacy of Early Childhood Education," *American Psychologist,* vol. 44 (February 1989), pp. 274–82.

35. H. W. Stevenson, S. Y. Lee, and J. W. Stigler, "Mathematics Achievement of Chinese, Japanese, and American Children," *Science,* vol. 231 (February 1986), pp. 693–99.

36. John H. Bishop, *The Impact of Curriculum-Based External Examinations on School Priorities and Student Learning* (Cornell University, Center on the Educational Quality of the Workforce and Center for Advanced Human Resource Studies, 1996); and John H. Bishop, "The Effect of National Standards and Curriculum–Based Exams on Achievement," Working Paper No. 96–22 (Cornell University, Center for Advanced Human Resources Studies, January 1997).

37. John Bishop cogently argues that a major problem is the lack of priority given to achievement in U.S. schools. See Bishop, "The Effect of National Standards and Curriculum–Based Exams on Achievement."

38. See Coleman, "Achievement Oriented School Design."

39. Policymakers who value equality of results could differentially reward educators for gains among low achievers.

40. Mancur Olson, *The Logic of Collective Action: Public Goods and the Theory of Groups* (Harvard University Press, 1971); and James M. Buchanan, *The Demand and Supply of Public Goods* (Chicago: Rand-McNally, 1968).

41. Eric A. Hanushek, *Making Schools Work: Improving Performance and Controlling Costs* (Brookings, 1994), pp. 85–124.

42. The *Economist* (November 30–December 6, 1996, p. 80) points out several advantages of profit sharing: By giving workers a stake in the firm or unit, profit sharing can give them an incentive to work harder. It can strengthen employees' loyalty, reduce turnover, and lead to a more experienced and skilled work force. It can allow firms to employ more workers, less often fire them, and take greater risks because wages decline in hard times when profits fall.

43. Maynard C. Reynolds, "Funding," in Margaret C. Wang, Maynard C. Reynolds, and Herbert J. Walberg, eds., *Handbook of Special and Remedial Education*, 2d ed. (Oxford, England: Pergamon, 1995), pp. 345–69, especially p. 346. See also Richard L. Allington and Anne McGill-Franzen, "Individualized Planning," in Margaret C. Wang, Maynard C. Reynolds, and Herbert J. Walberg, eds., *Handbook of Special and Remedial Education*, 2d ed. (Oxford, England: Pergamon, 1995), pp. 5–35.

44. Michael Kirst and Richard Jung, "The Utility of a Longitudinal Approach in Assessing Implementation: A Thirteen–Year View of Title I, ESEA," *Educational Evaluation and Policy Analysis*, vol. 2 (September/October 1980), pp. 17–34, especially p. 20.

45. E. Flaxman, G. Burnett, and C. Ascher, "The Unfilled Mission of Federal Compensatory Education Programs," in E. Flaxman and A. H. Passow, eds., *Changing Populations, Changing Schools* (University of Chicago Press, 1995).

46. Flaxman, Burnett, and Ascher, "The Unfilled Mission of Federal Compensatory Education Programs," pp. 106–07.

47. Kenneth K. Wong and Stephen J. Meyer, *The Effectiveness of Title I Schoolwide Projects: A Synthesis of Findings from the First Years of Evaluation* (University of Chicago Press, June 1997).

48. See Reynolds, "Funding," p. 348.

49. Christine H. Rossell and J. Michael Ross, "The Social Science Evidence on Bilingual Education," *Journal of Law and Education*, vol. 15 (Fall 1986), pp. 385–419.

50. Sheree Speakman and Bruce Cooper, "Bringing Money to the Classroom," in Lawrence O. Picus and James L. Wattenbarger, eds., *Where Does the Money Go?: Resource Allocation in Elementary and Secondary Schools* (Thousand Oaks, Calif.: Corwin Press, 1995), p. 111.

51. Jane Hannaway, "Administrative Costs and Administrative Behavior Associated with Categorical Programs," *Educational Evaluation and Policy Analysis*, vol. 7 (Spring 1985), pp. 57–64.

52. Profit is compensation for risk taking. Those hostile to profits do not seem to realize that beginning a firm requires hard work and capital is often lost because most businesses fail within a year. Even large, dominant firms such as Pan American Airlines go under. Profits also reward risk taking, innovation, efficiency, and competition—exactly what public schools require.

53. Charles Wolf Jr., *Markets or Governments: Choosing between Imperfect Alternatives* (MIT Press, 1988), pp. 137–48.

54. See Wolf, *Markets or Governments*.

55. The forces of failure and convention may suffice to prevent the success of the current round of reforms such as charter schools. Union opposition and excessive regulations already threaten the few timid charter schools.

56. J. F. Couch, W. F. Shughart, and A. L. Williams, "Private School Enrollment, and Public School Performance," *Public Choice*, vol. 76 (August 1993), pp. 301–12.

See also Borland and Howsen, "Competition, Expenditures, and Student Performance in Mathematics."

57. Emmanuel Jimenez, Marlaine E. Lockheed, and Vicente Paqueo, "The Relative Efficiency of Private and Public Schools in Developing Countries," *World Bank Research Observer*, vol. 6 (July 1991), pp. 205–18; Eugenia Froedge Toma, "Public Funding and Private Schooling across Countries," *Journal of Law and Economics*, Vol 39 (April 1996), pp. 121–48; and Emmanuel Gamines and Marlaine E. Lockheed, eds., "Private versus Public Education: An International Perspective," *International Journal of Educational Research*, vol. 15 (1991), pp. 357–97.

58. Jane Hannaway, "The Organization and Management of Public and Catholic Schools: Looking inside the 'Black Box,'" *International Journal of Educational Research*, vol. 15 (1991), pp. 463–81.

59. See Toma, "Public Funding and Private Schooling across Countries," p. 121.

60. Paul E. Peterson, Jay P. Greene, and Chad Noyes, "School Choice in Milwaukee," *Public Interest* (Fall 1996), pp. 38–56.

61. Carried out independently, this random study was contradicted by a previous study (sponsored by the state department of education) that relied on statistical adjustments in analyzing achievement instead of an experimental design, which is all the more reason for far wider and fairer implementation and evaluation.

62. Terry M. Moe, ed., *Private Vouchers* (Stanford, Calif.: Hoover Institution Press, 1995).

63. Nina Shokraii, "Free at Last: Black America Signs Up for School Choice," *Policy Review*, no. 80 (November/December 1996), pp. 20–26.

64. See Moe, *Private Vouchers*, p. 14.

65. See Bridget Murray, "Home Schools: How Do They Affect Children?," *American Psychological Association Monitor*, December 1996, p. 1; Michael P. Ferns, "Solid Evidence to Support Home Schooling," *Wall Street Journal*, March 5, 1997, p. A18; and Debra Viadero, "Home–Schooled Pupils Outscore Counterparts," *Education Week* (March 17, 1997), p. 9.

66. John Bishop, "The Effect of National Standards and Curriculum–Based Exams on Achievement," *American Economic Review*, vol. 87, no. 2 (May 1997), pp. 260–64.

67. Because many countries fund pensions and medical insurance through mandated social security taxes, both voluntary and compulsory contributions for these purposes must be included in the measurement of teacher compensation. Compensation of secondary teachers was calculated by multiplying their salary by the ratio of compensation to wages for manufacturing workers. This estimate of teacher compensation was then divided by average compensation of all workers. Howard Nelson and Timothy O'Brien, *How U.S. Teachers Measure Up Internationally: A Comparative Study of Teacher Pay, Training, and Conditions of Service* (Washington: American Federation of Teachers, 1993), pp. 37, 74, 93.

68. Nelson and O'Brien, *How U.S. Teachers Measure Up Internationally*.

69. Eric Hanushek and Steven Rivkin, "Understanding the Twentieth Century Growth of U.S. School Spending," *Journal of Human Resources*, vol. 32, no. 1 (1997), pp. 35–68.

70. National Center for Education Statistics, *Occupational and Educational Outcomes of Recent College Graduates One Year after Graduation: 1991*, NCES 93–162 (Department of Education, 1993), p. 26.

71. National Center for Education Statistics, *Occupational and Educational Outcomes of Recent College Graduates One Year after Graduation*, pp. 428–29.

72. Ann Bradley, ''Not Making the Grade: Teacher Firing Spurs Debate over Standards and Expectations for Students,'' *Education Week*, September 13, 1993, pp. 1, 19–21.

73. National Center for Education Statistics, *Education in States and Nations: Indicators Comparing U.S. States with the OECD Countries in 1988*, NCES 93–237 (Department of Education, 1993).

74. Bengt Holmstrom and Paul Milgrom, *Economics, Organization, and Management* (Englewood Cliffs, N.J.: Prentice–Hall, 1992); Jane Hannaway, ''Higher Order Skills, Job Design, and Incentives: An Analysis and Proposal,'' *American Educational Research Journal*, vol. 29 (1992), 3–21; and Helen F. Ladd, ed., *Holding Schools Accountable: Performance-Based Reform in Education* (Brookings, 1996).

75. James M. McPartland, ''Staffing Decisions in the Middle Grades: Balancing Quality Instruction and Teacher/Student Relations,'' *Phi Delta Kappan* (1990), pp. 465–68.

76. James M. McPartland and S. Wu, ''Instructional Practices in the Middle Grades: National Variations and Effects.'' Occasional Paper, Johns Hopkins Center for Research on Elementary and Middle Schools, 1988.

77. For reviews, see Jeffrey Pfeffer, *Organizations and Organizational Theory* (Boston: Pitman, 1982); and W. Richard Scott, *Organizations: Rational, Natural, and Open Systems* (Englewood Cliffs, N.J.: Prentice-Hall, 1993).

78. Jane Hannaway, ''Political Pressure and Decentralization in Institutional Organizations: The Case of School Districts,'' *Sociology of Education*, vol. 66 (1992), pp. 147–63.

79. N. E. Friedkin and J. Necochea, ''School System Size and Performance: A Contingency Perspective,'' *Educational Evaluation and Policy Analysis*, vol. 10 (1988), pp. 237–49.

80. Jane Hannaway and Joan Talbert, ''Bringing Context into Effective Schools Research: Urban-Suburban Differences,'' *Educational Administration Quarterly*, vol. 29 (1993), pp. 164–86.

Radical Constructivism and Cognitive Psychology

JOHN R. ANDERSON, LYNNE M. REDER,
and HERBERT A. SIMON

THOSE WHO BELIEVE that education needs a foundation in the modern science of cognitive psychology sometimes feel that they are jousting with windmills. Virtually every educational movement, whatever its merits, claims to have a scientific basis. However, this is often not the case.

Unfortunately, a science of human learning has never had a large influence upon the practice of education. Until recently, such a science has not been sufficiently mature to offer much help to educational practitioners and policymakers. However, in recent decades, a body of theory and knowledge within cognitive psychology has been created that offers important opportunities for improving education. On the whole, education does not give the findings of cognitive science a large role but continues instead to struggle between two prescientific views on learning that date to philosophies of centuries past.

These two prescientific views can be characterized, at the risk of slight caricature, as follows:

The associationist philosophy holds that learning is just a matter of forming associations. Therefore, nothing problematic arises about education. All one needs to do is to teach students the associations they need to learn.

We wish to thank Sharon Carver, Susan Chipman, Albert Corbett, Ellen Gagné, David Klahr, Ken Koedinger, Rich Lehrer, Marsha Lovett, Melvin Reder, and Steve Ritter for their comments on this paper. This is not to imply, however, that any of these individuals agree with the assertions made. Preparation of this paper was supported by grant MDR–92–53161 from the National Science Foundation Directorate for Education and Human Resources.

227

The rationalist philosophy maintains that knowledge is to be found by looking within one's self. Therefore, nothing problematic arises about education. All one needs to do is to allow students to discover what they need to learn.

These two schools have waxed and waned in their centrality to educational practice. During periods of waxing, they acquire additional features from the current intellectual climate. The most recent waxing of the associationist school occurred during the heyday of behaviorism, under the influence of Edward Thorndike and John B. Watson, and the later influence of B. F. Skinner. At its height, this school of thought was connected to such features as programmed instruction and behavioral objectives.[1] Behaviorism has now definitely waned and has become the standard whipping boy for new reform movements in education.

One of the salient features of the behaviorist movement as a psychological theory was to reject the idea of mental structures and to assert that one could understand human thinking wholly in terms of external behavior. Behaviorism in psychology was subsequently replaced by the "cognitive revolution," which demonstrated in many ways that one could understand behavior only by postulating mental structures and processes. However, the phrase "cognitive revolution" is something of an exaggeration, for many of the paradigms and methodologies from the behaviorist era have been carried over, often much modified and augmented, to modern cognitive psychology. Thus, with major theoretical change has come cumulative progress in the science, as is typical in other sciences when they experience "revolutions."

Behaviorism, in its purest form, is applied to education by prescribing the behavior that a student should manifest and ignoring the student's thought patterns. Some educational applications in the behaviorist era maintained this theoretical purity, but often the applications were much looser and simply amounted to emphasizing immediate feedback and careful measurement of educational progress. As this approach sometimes worked well, one example of a successful behaviorist program is worth describing.

D. Porter reports on an experiment with "teaching machines" that tried faithfully to follow Skinner's principles of immediate reinforcement through knowledge of results: Teaching students to spell by means of a series of successive approximations (first the student reads the word, then spells part of it with the other parts provided, and then spells all of it), minimizing errors, and bringing the learning situation close to the transfer situation.[2] In year-long training programs for the second, fourth, and sixth grades, students in the experimental groups (teaching machines) and the control groups (standard instruction) both showed about one grade-level improvement. However, students in the teaching machine groups only required one-third the class time needed by the controls to achieve this. The Skinnerian program emphasized such learning efficiency gains.

While empirical and theoretical problems with behaviorism caused it to be rejected within the science of psychology, it never was rebutted definitively as an educational program. Some projects succeeded, others failed. One approach loosely based on behaviorism was mastery-based instruction. In this approach, students were given as much time as needed to master early material before moving on to later material, to speed up learning of later material and enhance overall learning.[3] Despite its generally positive empirical record, mastery-based instruction is now regarded negatively in educational circles and is not widely practiced.[4]

Behaviorist-oriented education was never a significant presence in the classrooms of America and has all but disappeared. The reasons for its demise are complex and not fully understood. The theoretical and empirical difficulties it encountered within scientific psychology and its replacement by cognitive psychology were probably only minor factors.

Recently the developments in cognitive psychology have been claimed by a new rationalist movement within education called constructivism, whose adherents overlap only slightly with the scientists who provided the experimental and theoretical content for the cognitive revolution. ''Constructivism'' is a vague term that covers a wide range of positions, including some that are mutually contradictory. Some versions are just attempts to bring the new theoretical insights of cognitive psychology into education.

A more extreme version, called ''radical constructivism,'' has taken a particularly strong hold in mathematics education. (We have a particular interest in this movement because our major research concern has been learning of mathematics.) Along with the general rationalist position, it has imported pieces from two other movements that are also strongly represented in modern schools of education—situated learning

and deconstructionist critical theory. Radical constructivism emphasizes discovery learning, learning in complex situations, and learning
in social contexts, while strongly distrusting systematic evaluation of
educational outcomes.

> Learning [in a constructivist classroom] would be viewed as an active,
> constructive process in which students attempt to resolve problems that
> arise as they participate in the mathematical practices of the classroom.
> Such a view emphasizes that the learning-teaching process is interactive
> in nature and involves the implicit and explicit negotiation of mathemat-
> ical meanings. In the course of these negotiations, the teacher and stu-
> dents elaborate the taken-as-shared mathematical reality that constitutes
> the basis for their ongoing communication.[5]

This definition may be difficult to understand, so it is worth describing an instance of a successful mathematical intervention that claims a
basis in radical constructivism, to match the successful intervention just
cited, which claimed a basis in behaviorism. P. Cobb and his colleagues
describe a second grade mathematics curriculum that embodies the
principles of radical constructivism.[6] A good example is their method
for teaching second graders to count by tens. Instead of telling the
students the principle directly, they assigned groups of students the task
of counting objects bundled in sets of ten. Invariably, the groups discover that counting by tens is more efficient than counting by ones.
Building a whole second grade curriculum around such techniques, they
found their students doing as well on traditional skills as students from
traditional classrooms, transferring more and expressing better attitudes
about mathematics. Transfer and better attitudes are measures emphasized by radical constructivists.

It might seem a contradiction that both behaviorist and radical constructivist approaches should produce successful curricula. However,
this points to the difficulty in assessing the connection between educational approaches and learning outcomes. Complex educational interventions involve change on many dimensions, making it hard to assess
what features are responsible for the learning outcomes. Both interventions could have achieved their results independently of the educational
philosophy ostensibly applied. More articulate theory and evaluation
are needed. However, both efforts did seriously try to evaluate their
interventions. Too often interventions are introduced without any real
attempt at objective assessment.

Education has failed to show steady progress because it has shifted back and forth among simplistic positions such as the associationist and rationalist philosophies. Modern cognitive psychology provides a basis for genuine progress by careful scientific analysis that identifies those aspects of theoretical positions that contribute to student learning and those that do not. Radical constructivism serves as the current exemplar of simplistic extremism, and certain of its devotees exhibit an antiscience bias that, should it prevail, would destroy any hope for progress in education.

Theoretical Basis for Radical Constructivism

Frequent references are found to four sources as providing the ''scientific'' foundations for radical constructivism.

Modern Cognitive Psychology

Cognitive psychology is often cited as providing a basis for radical constructivism. For instance, R. Lesh and S. J. Lamon describe mathematics education largely from a radical constructivist approach:

> Behavioral psychology (based on factual and procedural rules) has given way to cognitive psychology (based on models for making sense of real-life experiences), and technology-based tools have radically expanded the kinds of situations in which mathematics is useful, while simultaneously increasing the kinds of mathematics that are useful and the kinds of people who use mathematics on a daily basis. In response to these trends, professional and governmental organizations have reached an unprecedented, theoretically sound, and future-oriented new consensus about the foundations of mathematics in an age of information.[7]

This is typical of the false consensus claims that are rampant in the field. Claims are advanced in the name of modern science that have no basis in the science. In the Lesh and Lamon quote, the distinction between ''factual and procedural rules'' and ''models for making sense of real-life situations'' is not a distinction between behavioral psychology and cognitive psychology. They are both important theoretical components of cognitive psychology, and much current research is concerned with which domains of thoughts are better understood in terms of "mental models" and which in terms of "mental rules."

A consensus exists within cognitive psychology that people do not record experience passively but interpret new information with the help of prior knowledge and experience. The term "constructivism" is used in this sense in psychology, and we have been appropriately referred to as constructivists (in this sense) by mathematics educators.[8] However, denying that information is recorded passively does not imply that students must discover their knowledge by themselves, without explicit instruction, as claimed by radical constructivists. In modern cognitive theories, all acquisition of knowledge, whether by instruction or discovery, requires active interpretation by the learner. The processing of instruction can be elaborate, its extent growing with the amount of relevant knowledge the learner brings to the task.[9]

Modern cognitive psychology does not by any means enjoy agreement on all issues. Agreement has been reached on most of the basic facts of cognition and learning, while substantial controversy remains on certain matters of theoretical interpretation. Enough consensus exists today on matters of fact to support significant educational applications. To mention one in particular, the empirical evidence refutes the radical constructionists' claim that students cannot learn by direct instruction.

We represent an approach to human cognition that is usually described as "information-processing psychology." Precise models of aspects of cognition provide one of its important tools, and these are often used to create computer simulations of the cognitive acts of human subjects in experiments.

Within cognitive psychology, perhaps the most controversial position with which we are associated is the "symbolic" position; that is, the claim that certain aspects of human cognition involve knowledge that is represented symbolically. In contrast, the "connectionist" position maintains that no such symbolic representations exist and that knowledge can only be described in terms of synaptic connections among neural elements.[10] Controversy between the symbolic and connectionist positions has decreased since the late 1980s, and most researchers, including ourselves, have evolved (under the weight of evidence) to "hybrid" positions—recognizing that certain aspects of cognition are best understood in terms of symbolic representations and other aspects in terms of neural connections. The issue today is to decide which aspects of cognition should be modeled in the one mode or the other, and how the symbolic and neural levels can be linked.

Some radical constructivists view themselves as opposing information-processing psychology, particularly in its symbolic form. P. Cobb, E. Yackel, and T. Wood, the most explicit on this issue, present radical constructivism as a rejection of the "representational view of mind." However, we and other cognitive psychologists, who do subscribe to a representational view, find little that is recognizable in the radical constructivists' description of that view.[11] Cobb, Yackel, and Wood quote R. Rorty's mischaracterization of it:

> [According to the representational view of mind,] to know is to represent accurately what is outside the mind; so to understand the possibility and nature of knowledge is to understand the way in which the mind is able to construct such representations.[12]

The representational view of mind, contrary to this claim, takes into account evidence about the relation of the mind to the world and about the accuracy and completeness or incompleteness of the internal representations of the world's features. Representation, in the cognitive framework, is neither a syntactic or logical play with formal symbols lacking reference to the real world nor a literal and mechanical recording of the stimulus.[13] In this framework, forming an internal representation of a problem situation is itself a complex psychological process.

Such radical constructivists often also limit the notion of "symbol" to verbal or logical expressions, then proceed to challenge their adequacy for modeling "nonlinear," "nonlogical," "nonverbal," or "intuitive" forms of thinking. As anyone is aware who uses a computer screen to display diagrams, pictures, or visual arrays of a great variety of kinds, no such limitations exist in the types of symbols that can be employed or in the kinds of "logical" or "nonlogical" processes that can operate on them. Considerable cognitive research recently aimed at exploring the relation of the thinking that is usually called "intuitive" with common, and well-understood, processes of recognizing familiar cues in stimuli.

A symbol (that is, a discriminable pattern) obtains its usefulness from its capacity for denoting (pointing to) objects, relations, and events in the world; but a symbolic mental representation is at best an incomplete and distorted picture of the environment, which correlates thoughts with the information delivered by the senses, and with motor acts and their effects. Our claim is that cognitive competence (in this case, mathematical competence) depends on the availability of symbolic structures (for example, mental patterns or mental images) that are created in response to experience.

In radical constructivist writings, criticisms of the straw-man position typified by the quotation from Rorty are used to discredit the view of the mind employed in cognitive psychology. Modern cognitive theories do not assume that learning is a passive recording of experience.

Misinterpretation of the representational view leads to much confusion about the relation between external mathematical representations (for example, equations, graphs, rules, Dienes blocks, and so on) and the internal representations of these same objects. Radical constructivists, equating the representational point of view with passive recording of stimuli, without transformation, misinterpret inadequacies of the external representations as inadequacies of the notion of internal representation. For instance, if a set of rules in a textbook is incomplete, then the implication is that mental rules cannot capture the concepts. However, cognitive theories postulate (and provide evidence for) complex processes for transforming these external representations to produce internal structures that are not at all isomorphic to the stimuli. For instance, just because a diagram is two-dimensional does not mean that the mental representation of it cannot be three-dimensional.

Little in cognitive psychology supports the more extreme claims of radical constructivism. Indeed, as some radical constructivists recognize, modern cognitive psychology contradicts these claims.

Piaget

One finds frequent reference to Jean Piaget as providing a scientific basis for constructivism. Piaget has had enormous influence on the understanding of cognitive development and was one of the major figures responsible for the emergence of cognitivism from the earlier behaviorist era in psychology. While many of his specific claims have been seriously questioned, the general influence of his theoretical perspective remains. Of key importance to constructivism is Piaget's distinction between the mechanisms of assimilation and accommodation in learning and development. Assimilation incorporates experience passively into a representation already available to the child. However, when the discrepancies between task demands and the child's cognitive structure (representation) become too great, the child must reorganize his or her thoughts. This is called accommodation (recently renamed "re-representation").

Piaget emphasized how the child internalizes knowledge by making changes in mental structure. The constructivists make frequent reference to this analysis, particularly the nonpassive accommodation process. A more careful reading of Piaget indicates that assimilation of knowledge plays a critical role in setting the stage for accommodation, that the accommodation cannot proceed without assimilation. In any event, both accommodation and assimilation are components of the representational view of mind.

Another aspect of Piaget is his stagelike characterization of cognitive development, which has led to the view that large qualitative changes occur as cognition develops. This aspect of Piaget's theory has received the least empirical support. The general view now is that cognitive changes are gradual and cumulative. The best corroborated accounts of Piagetian tasks are information-processing accounts, which identify the various components of knowledge that are being acquired.[14] R. S. Siegler refers to the belief in stages as the "theory of the immaculate transition" and documents its empirical failings.[15]

Situated Learning and Vygotsky

One also finds frequent references to situated learning as providing a basis for radical constructivism, and one finds through situated learning references to L. S. Vygotsky. Vygotsky was a Russian psychologist in the first part of the twentieth century who emphasized the strong social character of human development. The alliance between situated learning and radical constructivism is somewhat peculiar, as situated learning emphasizes that knowledge is maintained in the external, social world; constructivism argues that knowledge resides in an individual's internal state, perhaps unknowable to anyone else. However, both schools share the general philosophical position that knowledge cannot be decomposed or decontextualized for purposes of either research or instruction.

Situated learning has become associated with the view that knowledge does not transfer from the classroom to real-world situations and that instruction must take place in situations that are like the real world and often like job situations. Our critique of this aspect of situated learning led to an exchange that can be read as concluding either that situated learning is wrong in these claims or that it did not assert anything beyond the generally known fact that sometimes learning is somewhat contextualized.[16] To summarize our conclusions in that discussion:

> While important reforms may be needed in American education, the consensus seems to be that these reforms are not in the direction of turning the classroom into a workplace; there is merit in the powerful abstract intellectual tools that have been developed throughout human history.[17]

However, this exchange also converged on the conclusions that important social aspects exist to classroom learning. Beyond this, few implications can be taken from Vygotsky or situated learning for classroom practice. Little connection can be found, one way or another, between the views just discussed and the validity of group instructional methods.

John Dewey

Another figure referred to in both situated and radical constructivist writings is John Dewey. Dewey represents part of an earlier waxing of the rationalist approach to education. While Dewey started as a psychologist, he evolved into a philosopher of education, developing an educational approach loosely based on his earlier criticisms of analytic approaches in psychology before the turn of the twentieth century. Many of the ideas that are espoused in radical constructivism and situated learning are to be found in Dewey's writings, and one has an impression of modern radical constructivist educators reinventing his wheel.

Dewey started a laboratory school at the University of Chicago in 1896, and descriptions of it are enough to make a modern parent envious.[18] The many progressive schools set up in the image of Dewey's Laboratory School in the first part of the twentieth century varied widely but were generally characterized by less directive instruction and more project-oriented learning. Dewey himself was less than enthused by more radical efforts to eliminate a set curriculum from school in the name of progressive education.[19]

Dewey's Laboratory School is a distant memory, and many of the progressive schools based on it had almost entirely disappeared in a swirl of controversy over ''life-adjustment'' education.[20] However, each generation seems to create its own progressive schools, which emphasize many of the same features.

One of the efforts to assess the consequence of this earlier generation of progressive education for college performance found basically no differences between graduates of progressive and traditional schools in terms of their academic performance in college.[21] A sobering notion is that radically different approaches to education resulted in few or no differences in the students who graduated.

This points to the fundamental lack of cumulative progress in education and the need to understand in more detail what is happening under banners of different educational philosophies. What aspects of the Laboratory School or other progressive schools were sound and what aspects were just fanciful anecdotes have not been determined. It was not apparent then and is not apparent now how one goes about replicating the Laboratory School in another environment. What is needed more than a philosophy of education is a science of education. Modern attempts at educational improvement point back to theorists (Piaget, Vygotsky, and Dewey) whose theories are vague by current psychological standards and lack the strong connection to empirical evidence that has become standard in the field.

Major Characteristics of the Radical Constructivist Approach

The most conspicuous characteristics of the radical constructivist approach to mathematics education are reliance on discovery learning, learning in complex ''authentic'' situations, learning in social contexts, and a distrust of empirical evaluations. While more than a grain of truth can be found in the suppositions motivating these approaches, they can be and sometimes are pursued to unproductive extremes.

Discovery Learning

The defining feature of radical constructivism is the view that one cannot teach students but must allow them to create the knowledge that they need. This is sometimes described as a contrast between "instructivism" and "constructivism." One can readily agree that learning must be an active process, for learning requires a change in the learner, which can only be brought about by what the learner does—what he or she attends to, what activities he or she engages in. The activity of a teacher is relevant to the extent that it causes students to engage in tasks they would not otherwise undertake, including, but not limited to, acquiring knowledge provided by the teacher or by books. A teacher may also engage students in tasks, some of which may involve acquisition of skills by working examples. Other tasks include practicing skills to bring them to effective levels, interacting with fellow students, and interacting with the teacher.

The problem posed to psychology and education is to design a series of experiences for students that will enable them to learn effectively and to motivate them to engage in the corresponding activities. On both of these points, disagreement between radical contructivists and other cognitive psychologists would be hard to find. The more difficult problem is determining the desirable learning goals and the experiences that, if incorporated in the instructional design, will best enable students to achieve these goals. Arriving at good designs is not a matter for philosophical debate; it requires empirical evidence about how people, and children in particular, learn, and what they learn from different educational experiences.

A great deal of research shows that, under some circumstances, people are better at remembering information that they create for themselves than information they receive passively.[22] The early study of N. J. Slamecka and P. Graf is typical of research on generative learning. They had subjects try to remember lists of words. There were four conditions:

1. Subjects generated a synonym for each word. For instance, they might be asked to generate a synonym for *ocean* that begins with *s*.

2. Subjects studied a synonym that was provided. Thus, they might study *sea* as a synonym of *ocean*.

3. Subjects generated a rhyme. For instance, they might be asked to generate a word beginning with *s* that rhymed with *tea*.

Figure 1. Probability of Recognition as a Function of Type of Elaboration, Whether Generated or Read

Probability of recognition

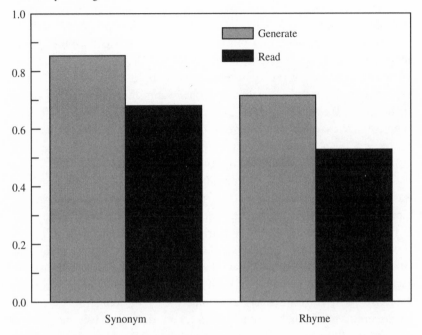

Source: N. J. Slamecka and P. Graf, "The Generation Effect: Delineation of a Phenomenon," *Journal of Experimental Psychology: Learning, Memory, and Cognition,* vol. 4 (1978), experiment 2.

4. Subjects studied a rhyme. For instance, they might study that a rhyme of *tea* is *sea*.

In all cases, subjects were subsequently tested for their recognition of the critical word *sea*.

Subjects learn the material more effectively in conditions where they process the meaning (synonym conditions 1 and 2) and where they generate the material (conditions 1 and 3) rather than study it passively (see figure 1). Comparing extremes, a very substantial effect emerges of 50 percent versus 85 percent recall. Cognitive psychologists debate whether this effect reflects fundamental cognitive factors or factors of motivation and selective attention.[23] However, from an educational perspective, these debates are in a certain sense irrelevant. Such effects are robust and clearly something one wants to take advantage of in instruction.

However, a number of caveats need to be made about such generation effects. First, subjects can learn in the worst conditions, and in virtually all studies, memory is not more than twice as good in generative conditions as in passive conditions. Second, experimental psychologists can only guarantee that their subjects will generate the target material by using artificial material. While the generation effect would appear to generalize to more natural material, it is difficult to guarantee that such material, because of its complexity, can be generated.[24] Getting students to generate much of what one wants them to learn is often difficult. In these cases, some sort of guided instruction is desirable, where one tries to induce students to generate knowledge for themselves to the greatest degree possible, but where one also provides direct instruction to maximize learning efficiency.

The argument that knowledge must be constructed is similar to the earlier arguments that discovery learning is superior to direct instruction. However, little positive evidence exists for discovery learning and it is often inferior.[25] Discovery learning, even when successful in enabling the acquisition of the desired construct, may require a great deal of valuable time that could have been spent practicing the construct (which is an active process, too) if it had been learned from instruction. Because most learning only takes place after the construct has been discovered, when the search is lengthy or unsuccessful, motivation commonly flags. As D. P. Ausubel wrote in 1968, summarizing the findings from the research on discovery learning:

> Actual examination of the research literature allegedly supportive of learning by discovery reveals that valid evidence of this nature is virtually nonexistent. It appears that the various enthusiasts of the discovery method have been supporting each other research-wise by taking in each other's laundry, so to speak, that is, by citing each other's opinions and assertions as evidence and by generalizing wildly from equivocal and even negative findings.[26]

Some argue that direct instruction leads to "routinization" of knowledge and drives out understanding:

> The more explicit I am about the behavior I wish my students to display, the more likely it is that they will display the behavior without recourse to the understanding which the behavior is meant to indicate; that is, the more likely they will take the form for the substance.[27]

An extension of this argument is that excessive practice will also drive out understanding. This criticism of practice (called "drill and kill," as if this pejorative slogan provided empirical evaluation) is prominent in radical constructivist writings. Nothing flies more in the face of the last twenty years of research than the assertion that practice is bad. All evidence, from the laboratory and from extensive case studies of professionals, indicates that real competence only comes with extensive practice.[28] By denying the critical role of practice, one is denying children the very thing they need to achieve competence. The instructional problem is not to kill motivation by demanding drill, but to find tasks that provide practice while at the same time sustaining interest.

However, experimental psychologists have shown that, under some conditions, extensive practice of material produces virtually no learning by at least some measures.[29] These conditions invariably exist where the experimental subjects are induced to engage in mindless recitation of the material. These results point out the grain of truth in the drill-and-kill criticisms: Students need to be engaged when they are studying.

Emphasis on Complex Learning Situations

Radical constructivists often write as if knowledge had some magical property that made it impossible to communicate and, for this reason, no simple instructional situation would suffice to convey the knowledge, whatever it might be. For example, radical constructivists recommend that children learn all or nearly all of their mathematics in the context of complex problems.[30] This recommendation is put forward without any evidence as to its educational effectiveness.

Two serious problems arise with this approach, given that a complex task will call upon a large number of competencies. First, a learner who is having difficulty with many of the components can easily be overwhelmed by the processing demands of the complex task. Second, to the extent that many components are well mastered, the student will waste a great deal of time repeating those mastered components to get an opportunity to practice the few components that need additional practice.

A large body of research in psychology shows that part training is often more effective when the part component is independent, or nearly so, of the larger task.[31] In team training, some part-task training of individuals outside the team is standard because getting the whole team together would be expensive and futile when a single member needs training on a new piece of equipment.[32] In team sports, where considerable attention is given to the efficiency of training, the time available is always divided between individual skill training and team training.

There are reasons sometimes to practice skills in their complex setting. Some are motivational and some reflect the special skills that are unique to the complex situation. The student who wishes to play violin in an orchestra would have a hard time making progress if all practice were attempted in the orchestra context. However, if the student never practiced as a member of an orchestra, critical skills of coordinating with the other performers would not be acquired. The same arguments can be made in the sports context, and motivational arguments can also be made for complex practice in both contexts. A child may not see the point of isolated exercises but will when they are embedded in the real-world task. Children are motivated to practice sports skills because of the prospect of playing in full-scale games. However, they often spend much more time practicing component skills than playing games. Practicing one's skills periodically in full context is important both to motivation and to learning to practice, but not a reason to make this the principal mechanism of learning.

While motivational merit may be found to embed mathematical practice in complex situations, D. C. Geary notes that much reason exists to doubt how intrinsically motivating complex mathematics is to most students in any context. The kind of sustained practice required to develop excellence in an advanced domain is not inherently motivating to most individuals and requires substantial family and cultural support.[33] Geary argues, as have others, that this difference in cultural support accounts for the large gap in mathematics achievement between Asian and American children.[34]

One also finds in constructivist writings an advocacy of the use of ''authentic'' problems.[35] ''Authentic'' is typically ill defined but with a strong emphasis on problems that students might encounter in everyday life. A focus on underlying cognitive process would suggest that this is a superficial requirement. Instead, the real goal should be to get students motivated to engage in cognitive processes that will transfer.[36] What cognitive processes a problem evokes is important, not what real-world trappings it might have. Often real-world problems involve a great deal of busy work and offer little opportunity to learn the target competencies. For instance, high school mathematics classrooms where longer, more real-world-like problems were introduced to situate algebra, much student time is spent on such tasks as making tables and graphs, which rapidly become clerical in nature.[37] Relatively little time is spent relating algebraic expressions to the real-world situations they denote.

Reliance on Social Learning Situations

Some of the learning contexts recommended in radical constructivist writings involve tasks that can be solved by a single problem solver, but the movement more and more is to convert these to group learning situations. This undoubtedly stems in part from the influence of the situated learning movement.

The claim that instruction is only effective in a highly social environment is based on the ideas that (1) virtually all jobs are highly social in nature and (2) learning is closely associated with its context. As J. R. Anderson, H. A. Simon, and L. M. Reder have shown, the second claim is overstated.[38] The first claim is also probably somewhat overstated, although any analyses of job surveys that show how much social interaction, and what kind, is involved in various jobs remain unknown. Some jobs are not social in character, and this claim does not hold. Likewise, performance is highly social in other jobs. People with such jobs must learn to deal effectively with the social nature of their work.

While a person must learn to deal with the social aspects of jobs, all skills required for these jobs do not need to be trained in a social context. Consider the skills necessary to become a successful tax accountant. While the accountant must learn how to deal with clients, learning the tax code or how to use a calculator does not have to be done while interacting with a client. Training independent parts of a task separately is preferable, because fewer cognitive resources will be required for performance, thereby reserving adequate capacity for learning. Thus, learning the tax code is better without having to interact with the client simultaneously, and learning how to deal with a client is better after the tax code has been mastered.

Another facet of the claim that instruction is best in a highly social environment comes from those claiming advantages for cooperative learning as an instructional tool.[39] Cooperative learning, also known as "communities of practice" and "group learning," refers to learning environments where people of equal status work together to enhance their individual acquisition of knowledge and skills. These environments are to be contrasted with tutoring (where the tutor and tutee have unequal knowledge and status) and team training (where the desired outcome is concerned with team or group performance). A review by the National Research Council (NRC) Committee on Techniques for the Enhancement of Human Performance noted that research on cooperative learning has frequently not been well controlled (for example, nonrandom assignments to treatments, uncontrolled "teacher" and treatment effects), that relatively few studies "have successfully demonstrated advantages for cooperative versus individual learning," and that a number of detrimental effects arising from cooperative learning have been identified—the "free rider," the "sucker," the "status differential," and "ganging up" effects.[40]

The NRC review of cooperative learning notes a substantial number of reports of no-differences, but, unfortunately, a huge number of practitioner-oriented articles about cooperative learning gloss over difficulties with the approach and treat it as an academic panacea.[41] It is applied too liberally without the requisite structuring or scripting to make it effective. Cooperative learning needs to be structured with incentives (for children at least) that motivate cooperation and a shared goal structure.[42] The costs of this type of instruction, with uncritical application, likely will outweigh the intended benefits.

In colleges, group projects are increasingly popular among instructors, but group learning can become counterproductive. Students sometimes complain that finding meeting times for working together on assignments is difficult and that some students exploit the system by allowing other partners in the group to do all the work (and hence acquire all the knowledge and skills). A reported practice among some students is to divide the labor across classes so that one member of a group does all of the work for a project in one class, while another carries the burden for a different class. Clearly these are not the intended outcomes of cooperative learning but will occur if thoughtful implementation and scripting of the learning situation are not evident. Some of the popularity of this approach with college teachers stems from class-size manageability: Monitoring and advising $N/3$ or $N/4$ projects is easier than N individual projects.

Distrust of Standard Evaluation

The denial of the possibility of objective evaluation is perhaps the most radical and far-reaching of the constructivist claims. How this principle is interpreted by all constructivists is not clear. Some radical constructivists have engaged in standard evaluations of learning interventions.[43] However, others are uncomfortable with the idea of evaluation, reflecting in part the influence of the philosophy of ''deconstruction'' on radical constructivism. D. Charney documents that empiricism has become a four-letter word in deconstructionist writings.[44] D. H. Jonassen describes the issue from the perspective of a radical constructivist:

> If you believe, as radical constructivists do, that no objective reality is uniformly interpretable by all learners, then assessing the acquisition of such a reality is not possible. A less radical view suggests that learners will interpret perspectives differently, so evaluation processes should accommodate a wider variety of response options.[45]

Evaluating any educational hypothesis empirically is impossible because any such test necessarily requires a commitment to some arbitrary, culturally determined, set of values. In the hands of the more moderate constructivists, the claim advocates focusing evaluation on the process of learning more than the product (what is learned), in what are considered ''authentic'' tasks, and involving multiple perspectives in the evaluation.

This milder perspective leads to more subjective and less precisely defined instruments of evaluation. While we share with most educators their instinctive distaste for four-alternative forced-choice questions and we agree that mathematics assessment should go beyond merely testing computational skills, we question whether the open-ended assessment being advocated as the proper alternative will lead to either more accurate or more culture-free assessment. The fundamental problem is a failure to specify precisely the competence being tested for and reliance on subjective judgment instead, with all the openings for social and intellectual bias that this reintroduces.

A number of papers addressed this issue.[46] L. B. Resnick, D. Briars, and S. Lesgold present two examples of objectively equivalent answers (receive equal scores in their objective assessment scheme).[47] However, they are uncomfortable with this equal assessment and feel a subjective component should be added so one answer would receive a higher score because it displayed greater "communication proficiency." Although the "better" answer had neater handwriting, one might well judge it simply more long-winded than the "worse" answer. "Communication proficiency" is in the eyes of the beholder.

J. A. Dossey, in explaining the new National Assessment of Educational Progress open-ended scoring, states that a student will be given 50 percent (two points) for the right answer if the justification for the answer is "not understandable" but will be given 100 percent (four points) for the wrong answer if it "does not reflect misunderstanding of either the problem or how to implement the strategy, but rather seems to be a copying error or computational error."[48] Such subjective judgments will open the door to a great deal of cultural bias in assessment.[49] Anytime the word "seems" appears in an assessment, it should be a red flag that the assessors do not know what they are looking for. The information-processing approach would advocate specifying precisely what one is looking for in terms of a cognitive model and then testing for that.

Another sign of the radical constructivists' discomfort with evaluation manifests itself in the motto that the teacher is the novice and the student the expert.[50] The idea is that every student gathers equal value from every learning experience. The teacher's task is to come to understand and value what the student has learned. As J. Confrey writes:

> Seldom are students' responses careless or capricious. We must seek out their systematic qualities which are typically grounded in the conceptions of the student. . . . [F]requently when students' responses deviate from our expectations, they possess the seeds of alternative approaches which can be compelling, historically supported and legitimate if we are willing to challenge our own assumptions.[51]

Or as Cobb, Wood, and Yackel write:

> The approach respects that students are the best judges of what they find problematical and encourages them to construct solutions that they find acceptable given their current ways of knowing.[52]

If the student is supposed to move, in the course of the learning experiences, from a lower to a higher level of competence, why are the student's judgments of the acceptability of solutions considered valid? While the teacher is valued who can appreciate children's individuality, see their insights, and motivate them to do their best and to value learning, definite educational goals must be set. More generally, if the "student as judge" attitude were to dominate education, when instruction had failed and when it had succeeded, when it was moving forward and when backward, would no longer be clear.

Understanding why the student, at a particular stage, is doing what he or she is doing is one thing. Helping the student understand how to move from processes that are "satisfactory" in a limited range of tasks to processes that are more effective over a wider range is another matter. As L. B. Resnick argues, many concepts that children naturally come to (for example, that motion implies force) are not what the culture expects of education and in these cases "education must follow a different path: still constructivist in the sense that simple telling will not work, but much less dependent on untutored discovery and exploration."[53]

A Cognitive Psychology Alternative

While we cannot claim to possess a philosophy that specifies all the answers to how education should proceed, modern cognitive psychology does contain some pointers about how one should progress in mathematics education.

Cognitive Task Analysis

If a single central theme can be pointed to in research in cognitive psychology, then it is that conceptual power derives from taking a complex cognitive phenomenon and analyzing it into its underlying components; that is, understanding the behavior of the whole from an understanding of the components and their interactions. Debate continues within the field (and research to settle such debate) as to what the components are, but general agreement has been reached that more understanding results from such a task analysis. Often different theoretical proposals for the components turn out to have similar consequences, because these proposals are still analyzing the same task, and the structure of that task is crucial.[54] What is important is to analyze what the task structure means for the mind of the person performing it.

In the context of education, real value is found in identifying the components that a student needs to learn and targeting their instruction. In many cases, this knowledge is not apparent in the surface structure of a problem, and students have difficulty learning as a consequence. A major problem, for example, in the acquisition of geometry proof skills was that students had difficulty identifying the component skills.[55] Typically in geometry, students are shown complete proofs and are left to figure out what problem-solving steps underlie finding these proofs. A similar problem seems to haunt students' attempts to master algebra word problems.[56] Task analysis has played an important role in efforts to teach mathematics in American schools and in Chinese schools.[57]

Task analysis will often reveal prerequisite knowledge required for students to learn a new competence. Often this prerequisite knowledge has not been mastered by significant subsets of the student population. An example is knowledge of the number line and basic operations on it. R. Case and S. Griffin found that many at-risk students lacked this knowledge, which is a prerequisite to mastering early school mathematics.[58] Explicitly teaching this knowledge to the students dramatically increased their success at first grade mathematics.

As knowledge domains become more advanced, their underlying cognitive structure tends to become more obscure. Thus, while providing feedback on the final answer remains easy, providing feedback on the individual mental steps that lead to the answer becomes difficult. Teachers often are unaware, at an explicit level, of what this knowledge is and do not know how to teach it. Attempts to convey some relatively basic skills reveal this problem. A good case in point is reading when one goes beyond the basic word identification skills. A. S. Palinscar and A. L. Brown were able to produce dramatic improvements in students' comprehension skills by introducing to the students and then having them practice the skills of summarizing, clarifying difficulties, asking questions, and so on.[59] These are valuable activities to engage in while reading, but apparently these children had not been taught them, and they were unable to acquire them independently.

Analysis of incorrect performance by students is also valuable for revealing systematic errors or bugs in their thinking. In many cases, not much feedback occurs during the typical conditions of practice, and the student might wind up entrenching the wrong knowledge structures. A well-studied case of this is subtraction, where students can acquire the wrong rules and practice them to a state of perfection.[60] A comparable situation involves naive physics; students may have spent a lifetime of practicing the wrong physics, which is hard to discard when they come into the classroom.[61] Making teachers aware of the systematic confusions that students suffer produces improved educational outcomes.[62]

Role of Deliberate Practice

One unfortunate consequence of the popular slogan "drill and kill" is that it leaves the impression that practice is bad. On the contrary, studies of expertise have thoroughly established that expert skills take a long time to acquire and a great deal of practice. Cognitive task analysis shows why. Underlying any complex competence are a large number of knowledge components, each requiring substantial practice to be mastered. J. R. Anderson has shown that learning a complex competence requires learning its many components.[63]

A conscious effort almost seems at work to discredit the importance of time spent learning. C. C. McKnight and others try to debunk this factor.[64] They report statistics for seventh grade Japanese and eighth grade American students receiving 101 and 144 hours of instruction, respectively. However, this comparison is misleading. The seventh grade is the only year in twelve years of schooling that Japanese students spend so little time in mathematics. They spend 175 hours in most of elementary school (where the class time devoted to mathematics is twice that of American students), 140 hours in the rest of junior high, and more hours again in senior high.[65] In addition to, but not included in, these tallies are the numerous hours many Japanese students spend in after-school classes called juku where they get further intensive tutoring. Moreover, time is spent much more efficiently in the Japanese classroom. Students receive instruction 90 percent of the time in a Japanese classroom but only 46 percent of the time in an American classroom.[66] In the Pittsburgh public schools, despite an official figure of 140 hours, ninth grade students average only about sixty-five hours a year learning mathematics in the classroom.

Psychological studies of learning show repeatedly that the first variable of human learning is time on task. Granted, other factors, such as how one spends that time, matter. Also, one could spend time learning useless things. But amount learned is roughly proportional to amount of time spent learning.[67] The second variable of human learning (that is, forgetting) is time away from task. Thus, the long summer vacation in America becomes suspect, and dropping some important topics such as algebra for a year (typically geometry intervenes between algebra I and algebra II) creates ideal opportunities for forgetting to do its work. Teachers frequently complain about all the reteaching they have to do after summer vacation.

While time on task is critical, rote drill is not advocated. How time is spent is critically important. As constructivists (and others) emphasize, one wants students to be actively involved in the learning process. K. A. Ericsson, R. T. Krampe, and C. Tesch-Römer, in their study of the development of expertise, emphasized "deliberate practice."[68] Deliberate practice is defined as involving motivated subjects receiving informative feedback with careful and continuous coaching and monitoring. Unfortunately, these conditions are often not met in American classrooms. H. W. Stevenson and J. W. Stigler have emphasized the involved and focused explanations and discussions that are part of Asian mathematics classrooms.[69]

As important as practice is for the student, it is important for the teacher to practice, too. Asian teachers spend more time than American teachers preparing and practicing their instruction. Stigler and Stevenson state that Japanese teachers give what amounts to a performance in a mathematics classroom.[70] American teachers teach smaller classes but have fewer preparation periods, while Asian teachers teach larger classes but also receive more preparation periods. One thing that facilitates the development of teaching expertise in Asian schools is that the curriculum is relatively constant and does not change much from year to year. In contrast, in the reform-minded and faddish world of American education, the curriculum never stays constant long enough for teachers to reach a level of mastery.

Transfer, Insight, and Understanding

Radical constructivist writings often recommend that students learn "with understanding" in contrast with the old "behaviorist" approaches of rote learning. Determining what "understanding" might mean in learning and its application to real tasks is vital. Understanding a concept means nothing more nor less than having a rich network of knowledge structures that can be used to solve problems that involve the concept flexibly in many contexts. Each one of the knowledge structures has to be learned separately. Thus, understanding of a domain does not come in one fell swoop of insight but is built up bit by bit over time.

For example, to say that a student has understood a concept such as fractions means that the student can use that knowledge flexibly in many situations. Thus, the student can figure out how much pizza each of three children will get if they have to share half a pizza; the student will recognize that, when thirty-five people must be transported by buses that each hold twenty people, two buses are required, not one-and-three-quarters; the student can explain why one inverts a fraction to divide by it; and so on. A child does not suddenly acquire the ability to do all of this.

The belief in moments of transformation in education is undoubtedly linked to the old belief in developmental psychology that children transit abruptly between stages, which in turn is often linked to Piaget. Instead, as R. S. Siegler documents with great care, development is always gradual and continuous.[71] The same is true of education.

One classic contrast between learning with understanding and rote learning is M. Wertheimer's comparison of students taught to solve problems by rote or "insight."[72] Students given insight into the formula for the area of a parallelogram (by observing a construction) were able to transfer it to other figures for which the formula (base times height) is correct. Children just taught the formula were not able to transfer this knowledge. Children in both conditions learned a set of facts and procedures. However, in the insight condition, they were taught a different and richer set of facts that enabled the transfer. The insight instruction took longer, reflecting the richer knowledge that was learned.

M. K. Singley and J. R. Anderson studied extensively the conditions under which knowledge learned in solving one kind of problem would transfer to solving another kind of problem.[73] They showed that transfer between domains was typically not all-or-none but varied with the amount of knowledge the two domains shared. Understanding how knowledge will transfer between domains depends critically on task analyses that examine the knowledge structures that the learner has acquired in one domain and assess their applicability to another domain. Transfer will occur to the extent of shared cognitive elements.

Writers on education who argue for magical moments of understanding in which knowledge becomes transformed point to the phenomenon of insight. Some experimental research has been done on insight problems.[74] One striking feature of such problems is that subjects do not know that they are close to producing a solution much before they arrive at it. Because insight problems are defined as problems that require a single key insight for their solution, not surprisingly it only takes a little time to encode that one bit of knowledge once it is recognized. In contrast, noninsight problems (such as doing a proof in geometry) require developing multiple pieces of knowledge. In such cases, students can judge when they have solved some, but not all, of a problem.

In a careful analysis of the mutilated checkerboard problem, a famous insight problem, C. A. Kaplan and H. A. Simon studied the relation between the critical insight and the rest of the problem solution.[75] The mutilated checkerboard problem requires deciding whether it is possible to cover a checkerboard with dominos that each cover exactly two squares of the board. When two squares are cut out from opposite corners of the checkerboard, covering the whole board becomes impossible, because each domino covers a black and a white square and two opposite-corner squares of the same color have been removed. This is called the parity insight; and subjects typically spend several hours trying unproductive paths before considering it, but then solve the problem relatively rapidly. However, despite the apparent sudden nature of this solution, steps lay the foundation for the insight, such as choosing to consider invariances in the problem. Moreover, when subjects did think of the insight, they still had to go through the process of working out its implications. Complete proofs of impossibility did not occur instantaneously but had to be developed given the decision to regard parity. So, even in insight problems, bundles of knowledge do not come magically in one fell swoop but have to be worked out piece by piece.

Empirical Assessment

More than anything else, the development of educational methods needs constant assessment. Research programs should not be foisted on the public as educational programs until a careful analysis has been conducted of their learning consequence. A need exists for something analogous to the Food and Drug Administration, which would assess the consequences of educational programs just as the consequences of drugs are assessed before releasing them. Most fad educational movements would not survive such empirical evaluations. Would resistance emerge to empirical validation within the radical constructivist movement if no fear arose of what the evaluations would show? Commitment to a philosophy of education encourages unwillingness to have the philosophy disproved.

Part of the difficulty that radical constructivists, and other educators as well, have with assessment is that no evaluation instrument is perfect. To focus on the deficiencies is to ignore the information that an assessment provides. A classic example was the assessment of Project Follow Through, which found that direct instructional methods were more effective in the early grades with at-risk children of low socioeconomic status than open classroom methods.[76] This report was immediately drowned in criticisms of all of its shortcomings, completely distracting attention from the important information that was contained in the evaluation.[77] Scientists know that they must be sensitive to the limitations of their instruments but that they must not ignore what their instruments are saying.

While knowing which educational perspectives produce positive results is important, also of significance is understanding what aspects of the intervention are producing the various parts of the learning outcome. Within research on educational evaluation, a distinction is made between "summative" evaluations and "formative" evaluations. Summative evaluations try to identify the learning consequences of some fixed educational treatment, while formative evaluations try to identify how a treatment can be improved. More research is needed in cognitive psychology that would perform a formative role and help to determine what works and what does not work in educational applications. Regrettably, much research in cognitive psychology is too abstracted from the real world to be of use to the educator. More laboratory research needs clear connections to educational problems so that it could better inform educational interventions.

Important issues of empirical assessment do exist. A serious one is to define goals. No instructional intervention will optimize everyone's goals. Furthermore, different assessments may reach different conclusions about what a student has learned. Therefore, the goals of education must be discussed and the consequences of different methods of assessment must be considered. However, these legitimate concerns should not cause educators and scholars to ignore gathering those data that can inform their thinking.

Conclusion

The time has come to abandon philosophies of education and turn to a science of education. Consider the analogy of medicine. For thousands of years, before any real knowledge of human physiology existed, remedies for some pathological conditions were known and used, sometimes effectively, by both doctors and others. J. Gleick has provided a vivid description of prescientific medicine:

> Its practitioners wielded the authority granted to healers throughout human history; they spoke a specialized language and wore the mantle of professional schools and societies; but their knowledge was a pastiche of folk wisdom and quasi-scientific fads. Few medical researchers understood the rudiments of controlled statistical experimentation. Authorities argued for or against particular therapies roughly the way theologians argued for or against their theories, by employing a combination of personal experience, abstract reason, and aesthetic judgment.[78]

When medicine began to adopt the methods of science, far more powerful treatments were developed concurrently with the development of modern physiology and biochemistry; treatments are now based squarely on these sciences. To acquire powerful interventions in disease, understanding of the mechanisms of disease—of what was going on in the diseased body—had to be deepened. This is the revolution of twentieth century medicine, and its results speak for themselves.

In the same way, human beings have been learning, and have been teaching their offspring, since the dawn of the species. A reasonably powerful "folk medicine" has evolved, based on lecturing and reading and apprenticeship and tutoring, aided by such technology as paper and the blackboard—a folk medicine that does not demand much knowledge about what goes on in the human head during learning and that has not changed radically since schools first emerged.

To go beyond these traditional techniques, the example of medicine must be followed and (as cognitive psychology has been doing for the past thirty or forty years) a theory of the information processes that underlie skilled performance and skill acquisition must be built. A theory is needed of the ways in which knowledge is represented internally, and the ways in which such internal representations are acquired. Cognitive psychology has now progressed a long way toward such a theory, and much is already known that can be applied, and is beginning to be applied, to improve learning processes.

If progress is made to a more scientific approach, traditional educational philosophies will be found to be like the doctrines of folk medicine: They contain some elements of truth and some elements of misinformation. This is true of the radical constructivist approach. Only when a science of education develops that sorts truth from fancy—as it is beginning to develop now—will dramatic improvements in educational practice be seen.

Comment by K. Anders Ericsson

Important implications of the training of expert performance exist for general education in the schools and for particular educational methods advocated by proponents of radical constructivism.

The greatest scientific advantage of education of expert performers compared with general education is that the final goal for training experts is specified from the start and agreement has been reached on how to assess the attained level of performance for individual subjects and thus to evaluate the outcomes of training. In contrast, the goal of general education in public schools is much broader and needs to include the successful preparation for many different occupations and obligations of citizens. Consequently, beyond the common goals of general education, such as the fostering of independent, creative, and productive members of society, identifying specific educational goals that are uniformly valued and can be objectively assessed has been difficult. A further challenge is that society is going through dramatic structural changes, so determining which specific skills and knowledge that will be essential ten to twenty years from now is hard. Hence, modern educators have trained many generalizable abilities such as creativity, general problem-solving methods, and critical thinking. However, decades of laboratory studies and theoretical analyses of the structure of human cognition have raised doubts about the possibility of training general skills and processes directly, independent of specific knowledge and tasks. For example, research on thinking and problem solving show that successful performance depends on special knowledge and acquired skills, and studies of learning and skill acquisition show that improvements in performance are primarily limited to activities in the specific domain.[79] Some recent theoretical approaches to education can be viewed as direct reactions to the lack of generalizability of traditional education in, for example, mathematics and science.

Proponents of radical constructivism argue that an important reason for the failure of contemporary instruction lies in its implicit encouragement of memorization and mindless drill.[80] Students find memorizing information by rote easier than understanding the studied information and relating it to relevant experiences in their lives. Today's teachers are said to have structured the learning activities so much that students are more successful by guessing what the teachers want to hear than by trying to generate the correct answers by careful thought. The proposals by radical constructivists to remedy this educational failure rely on a return to the learning processes underlying natural cognitive development. Greatly influenced by Jean Piaget's theories of assimilation and accommodation, radical constructivists argue that learning evolves from the necessary adaptations required by successful engagement in activities in the task domain.[81] Genuine learning is self-directed, and many radical constructivists agree with Piaget that "each time one prematurely teaches a child something he could have discovered for himself the child is kept from inventing it and consequently from understanding it completely."[82] Finally, the inherent enjoyment of engaging actively in reasoning and problem solving can be fostered only if the students generate or chose the problem as their own.[83] Based on these considerations, radical constructivists recommend educational settings where students are forced to take the initiative and guide their own learning. Many radical constructivists even discourage the teacher from correcting students when their reasoning and ideas are invalid because such criticism may jeopardize their self-confidence in their independent reasoning and challenge their self-respect.[84] In sum, radical constructivists believe that self-guided learning will lead to genuine understanding and to skills for independent thinking and reasoning.

In their criticism of the educational method of self-guided learning, John R. Anderson, Lynne M. Reder, and Herbert A. Simon argued convincingly that recent advances in cognitive psychology and cognitive science provide educational methods that are superior to self-guided learning.

Experience and Expert Performance

Recent reviews show that extended engagement in activities of a chosen domain is necessary to attain expert performance.[85] First, when performance is assessed with representative measurement criteria in longitudinal studies, no evidence is available for sudden increases in performance from one time to the next. Second, expert performers continue to improve their performance beyond the age of physical maturation (the late teens in industrialized countries) for many years and even decades. The age at which performers typically reach their highest level of performance of their career is in their mid-to-late twenties for many vigorous sports and for arts and science a decade later or in their thirties and forties. The continued, often extended, development past physical maturity shows that experience is an essential factor mediating improved performance. The most compelling evidence for the necessity of vast experience before attaining high levels of performance is that even the most talented need around ten years of intense involvement before they reach an international level.[86] The necessity of active engagement to improve performance in a domain of expertise is well established and consistent with claims by both radical constructivism and the information-processing theories of learning and skill acquisition.

When individuals initiate regular engagement in a domain, whether a type of leisure or work, they go through a limited period of relatively rapid improvements when salient errors are corrected until they reach an acceptable level of performance. However, after that initial improvement, further increases are typically small. More generally, the length of experience in the domain has been found to be at best a weak predictor of current level of performance in a wide range of domains.[87] Hence, mere engagement in activities (experience) does not lead to improvement in performance.

The lack of benefit of additional experience on improved accuracy of performance is consistent with Piagetian notions of accommodation endorsed by radical constructivists and notions of impasse as a condition for changes to the mediating cognitive mechanisms.[88] When individuals' engagement with their environments runs smoothly, no change in the structure of performance would be expected. Even if the activity fails, no opportunities typically arise for corrections. Under these types of conditions, observable improvements of performance would hardly be expected. However, the same performance could easily be improved by special training activities designed to improve performance. The training involves the design and presentation of situations that challenge the trainees sufficiently but that they can master with full concentration and repetitions. The term "deliberate practice" has been used to refer to training activities that were designed by a teacher solely for the purpose of improving an individual's performance.[89] To engage in these training activities is judged to be effortful and less enjoyable than regular recreation, and thus active participants in domains rarely engage in deliberate practice even though they recognize that engaging in it would improve their performance. In sum, active engagement in a domain does not invariably, nor even typically, lead to improvement of performance, once some initial acceptable adaptation has been attained.

In almost every domain, promising individuals are supervised by a teacher who instructs them and designs their practice from a very young age. B. S. Bloom found that many international-level performers had relocated to be close to a desired teacher or an excellent training environment and virtually all of them had sought out a teacher, who either had reached the international level or had prior students who had reached that level.[90]

Several factors make it nearly impossible for individuals to guide themselves to expert levels of performance without the help of excellent teachers. Whereas cognitive development in children is surprisingly invariant across two different environments and cultures—that is, African rural and American suburban communities—large differences can be observed in domains of expertise, such as music, sports, and science, that depend on the historical time and the specific culture.[91] One of the primary reasons is that domains of expertise have over time developed methods for accumulating discovered knowledge, skills, and produced artifacts and hence extracted an externalized body of organized experience that can be transferred from the current to the next generation.[92] Individuals no longer must discover knowledge and methods from scratch, and individuals are not only able to match but also to surpass the level attained by pioneering predecessors. The necessary role of teachers for mastering any of the arts and sciences becomes apparent when one considers that the accumulation of knowledge and achievements is based on specific shared concepts, notational systems, and instruments and that the innovation of new concepts and laws was a prerequisite for the emergence of modern theories and their highly efficiently organized knowledge. The increases in level of expert performance over time are taken for granted in science and sports, but the improvements in instruments and equipment makes inferences about large changes in skill level difficult. However, in domains with fewer changes in instruments, such as performance with the piano and violin, today's performers readily master music that was considered unplayable by the best musicians in the nineteenth century and can match or often surpass the technical virtuosity of legendary musicians of the past.[93] Similarly, in many sports with minimal equipment, such as running, diving, and swimming, the highest level of performance attained early in the twentieth century is now commonplace and matched by a vast number of serious amateurs.[94]

In all major domains, an accumulation of effective methods has occurred for teaching the accumulated knowledge and skills. Over the last couple of centuries, teachers and coaches have gained insights into how sequences of easy training tasks can allow students to eventually master more complex tasks, which may often at first sight appear unattainable to the student. Furthermore, teachers know how and to what degree of mastery the simpler tasks have to be acquired to serve as building blocks of more complex skills. Unlike the beginners themselves, teachers can foresee the future demands and avoid the need for complete relearning of previously attained skills. The core assumption of deliberate practice is that expert performance is acquired gradually and that effective improvement of students' performance depends on the teachers' ability to isolate sequences of simple training tasks that the student can sequentially master by repetition with feedback and instruction.[95] Deliberate practice requires training tasks with a difficulty level such that they lie outside the students' current repertoire, and their mastery requires that the students concentrate on critical aspects and gradually refine their performance through repetition in response to feedback. Hence, the requirement for concentration sets deliberate practice apart from both mindless drill and playful engagement as the latter two types of activities would, if anything, merely strengthen the current structure of the performance rather than change it.

In many domains, promising children start training with teachers at very young ages. Because of the requirement of sustained concentration, the duration of training is initially short—typically no more than fifteen to twenty minutes per day, which leaves room for other activities. Many parents help their children to concentrate during practice, to establish regular practice patterns, and to encourage them by pointing out practice-related improvements in their performance.[96] With increasing age, the involvement of future expert performers increases, and toward the end of adolescence the commitment to the domain-related activities is essentially full time. Furthermore, recent reviews have assembled a broad range of evidence supporting the claim that individual differences in giftedness and talent, especially among children, can be attributed to differences in practice history rather than any innate differences in talent.[97] More talented children improve faster in large part because they spend more time in practice each week.[98]

Cognitive Mediation and Internalization

When individuals try to master an everyday activity, such as driving a car or typing, the goal is typically to achieve effortless performance as rapidly as possible. After some limited period of training and experience, the appropriate responses are elicited by the individuals without the need for effortful attention, and the skill has been automatized.[99] In contrast, the key challenge for aspiring expert performers is to avoid the arrested development associated with automaticity and to acquire skills to support continued learning and improvement.

The superior performance of experts can be reliably reproduced in laboratories by giving them representative tasks that capture the essence of their expertise.[100] This general approach was originally proposed by A. de Groot, who instructed good and world-class chessplayers to think aloud while selecting the best move to the same set of unfamiliar chess positions.[101] He found that the quality of the selected moves was closely associated with chess skill. In a recent review, K. A. Ericsson and A. C. Lehmann found that in a wide range of domains experts' think-aloud protocols revealed how their superior performance is mediated by deliberate preparation, planning, reasoning, and evaluation.[102] At increased levels of performance, individuals have acquired improved mental representations to maintain accessibility to relevant information and to support more extensive and flexible reasoning about an encountered task or situation.[103] In most domains, better performers are able to rapidly encode and store relevant information for representative tasks.[104]

The training of future expert performers is not only a matter of shaping and increasing their performance but also involves the acquisition and refinement of mental representations that allow the student to image desired performance and to monitor concurrent performance. When beginners are initially introduced to practice in a domain, the teacher presents them with simple objectives and tasks and will often explicitly instruct the beginners to pay attention to specific aspects. The assigned goal for the training activity provides the beginners with feedback, which is supplemented by the teachers' instruction to the subjects to make specific changes and corrections. As the complexity of the acquired level of performance increases, so does the complexity of the practice tasks and goals. The teacher will primarily provide higher level instruction that requires that students are able to monitor their performance and are able to engage actively in problem solving to correct errors and improve performance. Hence, in parallel to improvement of performance, students acquire improved representations to image the desired performance, to monitor their performance, and to identify methods to reduce discrepancies.[105]

In many instances, the relevant information that is extracted and encoded changes as a function of attained level of performance. For example, the primary reason that expert racquet players can react rapidly to return a fast serve is not the result of an innate speed advantage but the acquisition of improved perceptual skills to anticipate the path of the ball.[106]

The highly developed representations allow skilled performers to improve by training organized by themselves. One of several general methods consists of the study and analysis of the performance and achievements of masters in the field.[107] Self-study allows for gradual refinement of representations and associated knowledge through attempts to reproduce the achievements of masters in the domain.

Creativity

The popular view of creativity still holds that the creative process is spontaneous and reflects a highly personal contribution from mysterious sources. Within this framework, creativity is believed to be higher during childhood and increasingly stifled by education and the demands for deliberate practice. In contrast, the expert-performance view focuses on providing the students with all the tools that give them the necessary control to image and create their products and achievements. The highest level of achievement in a domain, according to this view, involves the making of a major creative contribution that changes or redefines the boundaries and definition of that domain of expertise. To have a chance to make a major innovation, performers must have assimilated the prior relevant knowledge and be familiar with earlier related achievements. Extended education is, thus, necessary even to recognize a major innovation as such if it were to be generated or encountered accidentally.

The empirical evidence on creative achievement shows that individuals have not, as a rule, been able to make creative contributions to the domain until experiencing a long preparatory period during which they mastered the relevant aspects of that domain. Even in the cases of revolutionary innovation where the creative ideas redefine the domains, the creative individuals have a long history of education during which they studied and mastered the existing techniques, such as Picasso.[108]

In sum, the training of expert performers should not stifle creativity but instead provide the tools and knowledge to empower the experts to be more successful and effective in their daily work and their search for innovative ideas, especially those rare ones that go beyond the current knowledge and practices. Given the unpredictable nature of innovations, their generation must reflect some type of playful exploration of possibilities.[109] Hence, the extended education of expert performers primarily elevates the level of play by providing the appropriate tools and the rich knowledge of other experts' previous achievements.

Conclusion

In many different domains dedicated to optimal development of expert performance, a fairly similar pattern of training has evolved over decades or centuries of experimentation. Consistent with the proposal of radical constructivism, the focus is on keeping the student actively engaged in activities. However, rather than encouraging the students to select their activities by themselves, teachers guide the individual development of students and design their training and monitor progress. The designed training activities help the student focus on selected goals and provide feedback and opportunities for refinement by repetition. Throughout the extended training, the future experts acquire improved representations that allow them to guide and monitor their own learning to prepare for independence as performers and as guides for their future development. When experts have assimilated the accumulated relevant knowledge in their domain and have all the necessary tools, the education is completed and the expert goes on independently to assimilate new knowledge and make individual creative contributions. Hence, the controversy over how much and whether teachers should guide the development of mastery of domains of knowledge is one of determining at which point students have acquired the necessary mental tools to design and monitor their own learning effectively and to reach specific standards of mastery. These assessments must be made on a case-by-case basis, but the general implication from studies of expert performance is that the refinement of representations that support reasoning and understanding continue for many years or even decades of adulthood.

Some more general implications can be drawn for educational practices from studies of expert performance and deliberate practice. They show how mastery is learned and that everyone improves his performance by focused training. The more that is understood of the cognitive representations and complex skills that mediate expert performance and continued improvement of performance, the more that is understood of the educational challenges of facilitating their acquisition. With new methods of assessment, educators should be able to monitor the acquisition of the representations, give feedback of the progress, and propose remedial training activities, if necessary. Most important, the complexity of the mechanisms mediating expert performance shows that these mechanisms would not result from mindless drill with any training tasks. Master teachers and expert performers unanimously claim that during deliberate practice individuals have to maintain full concentration and be actively engaged to modify their performance.[110] Master teachers recommend that the students learn to monitor their level of concentration and, when it cannot be sustained fully, that they stop their practice to recuperate.

The real challenge for educators is that effective improvement of performance requires active engagement and concentration by students. The challenge is similar in domains of expertise where individuals are drawn to the inherent enjoyment of playful social interactions. In contrast, parents and teachers almost invariably have to actively support the engagement in deliberate practice and show its instrumentality in attaining the desired higher level of performance. One possibility would be to try to convert practice into play. However, when educators propose to remove guidance and feedback from learning activities, one might worry that these more playful activities may be more enjoyable but at the direct expense of their effectiveness in improving performance.

The option that emerged through the long history of training of expert performance involves the increase of learning effectiveness with designed training activities that require concentration. With extended experience, knowledge of how to best schedule and motivate practice has been accumulated, but the most important insight concerns the limits on daily deliberate practice and the need for relaxation and recuperation. When individuals start practice, the daily duration of deliberate practice is short (fraction of an hour). Although it increases with the number of years of training, not even full-time professionals appear to be able to sustain more than four to five hours of deliberate practice every day without risking exhaustion and eventual burnout. Designed training activities and deliberate practice provide powerful tools for efficient learning in the schools. However, teachers must help their students to learn to monitor their level of concentration and also arrange a flexible curriculum that mixes deliberate practice with alternative activities that require less concentration and opportunities for relaxation. More generally, these and other insights from the training of experts will contribute information about the constraints and potential for effective learning in the public schools.

Comment by Robert Glaser

Distinguished cognitive psychologists, in an important step for science and society, are now engaged in the application of principles of human cognitive performance and learning to improving education. Not to be neglected is the integration of knowledge of human mentality with professional knowledge and educational practice. The question is: How can what is known about cognition, about the environments in which cognitive processes are nurtured, and about the details of high levels of competence be used to maximize the abilities of U.S. students? Toward this end, appropriate tactics must be learned from the ventures of other sciences in practical developments where the interaction between science and practice has been enormously beneficial for both. For example, the press for the development of transistors, space flight, and health and physical well-being have opened up new fields of science and service. So, too, can educational design reap great benefits from the current engagement of top-notch scientists interested in cognition, culture, and human development.

At the beginning of my interests in this work, two major events stimulated interaction between theory and educational practice. One, mentioned by John R. Anderson, Lynne M. Reder, and Herbert A. Simon, was the movement of B. F. Skinner's behaviorist psychology into the educational scene. Within a decade, hundreds of instructional programs were published, different kinds of teaching machines were for sale, and societies were founded in a dozen countries. The reasons for the demise of this movement are left as a puzzle by Anderson, Reder, and Simon. To my mind, there were two: individualization of the rate of instruction and mastery criteria made the conventional school structure unmanageable, and behavioristic theory did not have the principles for a cognitive analysis of performance and could not go the distance in attending to learning through understanding and reasoning. From the point of view of the interaction between science and practice, in programmed instruction's rush to be put to use, applications were quickly separated from any test of the theory underlying them. A mutually correcting system in which failures and limitations in both practice and theory could be confronted never developed.

The second more powerful event in the interaction of application and theory was that World War II aroused interest in research on complex human performance, much of which focused on the performances involved when individuals controlled complex systems of people and machines, generally concerned with the detection and transfer of information required for decisionmaking. A link was forged between human cognitive capacities and models of performance of these capabilities in terms of information processing systems. Here, practical necessity contributed significantly to modern cognitive theories of human performance.[111]

A modern science of cognition developed that influenced and was influenced by the study of cognitive development in children. L. B. Resnick and I noted in the 1972 *Annual Review of Psychology* that "in increasing numbers, experimental psychologists are turning their enterprise to analyses and investigations of the instructional process."[112] Over the past twenty-five years, renewed study of learning and the interaction of theory and practice has taken place. The opportunity was offered to interpret advances in cognitive psychology in either constructive or unconstrained ways.

Advances in Cognition and New Conceptions of Learning

Some brief examples of areas of study that consider the interaction of learning theory and educational design are: (1) the analyses of functional, proceduralized knowledge, (2) metacognitive self-regulatory abilities, and (3) the access to knowledge afforded by cultural experiences and community practices.

The first area is functional knowledge and skill. The study of memory has moved beyond the behavioristic theories of simple associations to the descriptions of coherent structures that represent knowledge and meaning. The integration of knowledge behind human performance is now represented by larger, more organized constructs that explain the power and speed of mental activities. And modern learning theory is faced with the challenge of delineating the conditions that assist in establishing structure and coherence in acquired knowledge.

Toward this objective, studies of learning and studies of the differences between beginners and competent individuals indicate that a course of knowledge acquisition proceeds from a declarative or propositional form to a compiled, effectively used form.[113] Novices can know a principle, a rule, or a specialized vocabulary without knowing the conditions of effective application. In contrast, when more expert learners access knowledge, it is functional in the sense of being bound to conditions of use. Experts and novices may be equally competent at recalling specific items of information, but with practice and experience experts "chunk" these items in sequences that relate to the goals of problem solution and use this capacity for further action and learning. This progression of developing competence from declarative knowledge to well-tuned functional knowledge is specifically described in John Anderson's well-known learning theory.

The theory has guided the development of instructional programs that have proven successful in several domains where the learning objective is the acquisition of efficient and functional cognitive skill. Computer-based instructional programs have been designed for learning problem solving in algebra, generating proofs in geometry, and teaching computer programming.[114] These programs are unique in their reliance on an explicit learning theory, in the evaluation of their use in high school and university settings, and as a stage for systematically testing hypotheses about mechanisms of learning.[115]

A second area of study influencing conceptions of learning and instruction is cognitive science's increasing understanding of metacognitive processes and self-regulatory capabilities. Studies of the knowledge and skill of experts and cognitive development in children reveal the role that self-regulatory or control strategies play in competent performance. These regulatory activities enable the self-monitoring and executive control of one's performance.[116] They include such strategies as predicting outcomes, planning ahead, apportioning one's time, explaining to one's self to improve understanding, noting failures to comprehend, and activating background knowledge. Individuals use such monitoring skills and evaluate the utility of strategies as they employ them; they also change strategies as required in the course of solving a problem or attempting to comprehend a situation. Although good learners have learned to use such skills, other individuals need to be taught to exercise these capabilities.

Instructional programs in reading, writing, and mathematics designed to foster the development of self-regulatory skills are a major area of research.[117] The program for reading comprehension developed by A. L. Brown and A. S. Palinscar has received sustained analysis, evaluation, and wide use.[118] Students in this program acquire specific content knowledge and also learn a set of strategies for independently comprehending text material. The instructional procedure involves three major components: (1) instruction and practice with strategies that enable students to monitor their understanding of text; (2) provision, initially by a teacher, of an expert model of self-regulatory performance; and (3) a social setting that encourages joint observation and shared responsibility for learning.

A third area of influence on instructional design is the study of cultural experience and community participation. Research in cognitively oriented anthropology on cultural practices has brought attention to the high levels of performance that result from the demands of problem solving in everyday life in a community. Outside of formal schooling, individuals develop competence in solving verbal and quantitative problems that arise in community participation and in specialized work in trade and crafts.[119] Participation in social practice is a fundamental form of learning relevant to learning theory and to the social settings of formal instructional environments. In this context, learning engages resources in the practices of the community.[120]

Environments for instruction influenced by this work have been developed where students are involved in building and using knowledge for meaningful learning. The designers of these environments refer to L. S. Vygotsky's notion of creating a zone of proximal development where learners perform within their range of competence while being supported to realize potential levels of higher performance. In classroom learning communities or "communities for knowledge building," students participate in the transmission of knowledge by seeking, sharing, and acquiring knowledge among themselves with continued teacher guidance.[121] These communities of knowledge building are distinguished by efforts to turn over processes that are usually under the teacher's control to the students. Students are helped to formulate goals, direct their own inquiry, monitor their understanding, and use the resources available to design their own settings for acquiring knowledge. In this participatory environment for learning, teachers and students share the expertise they have or take responsibility for finding out about needed knowledge that they can bring back to the group. Teachers often teach in response to student needs, rather than in a fixed sequence, but the curriculum consists of topics to which students return for deepening knowledge and understanding. A community of discourse exists in which learning through constructive discussion, conjecture, questioning, criticism, and presenting evidence is practiced as the normal thing to do instead of the exception.[122]

Conclusion

The programs have been empirically evaluated, including the assessment of student achievement and other learning outcomes; changes in teachers' concepts; and analysis of the fidelity of the educational environment to the designers' interpretation of theory. The coordination of practice and theory encouraged by Anderson, Reder, and Simon is proceeding in other innovations in educational practice. The combination of modern knowledge of learning and cognition and information about the outcomes and practices of the U.S. education systems should contribute to the improvement of student performance.

Despite the later interpretations of J. Dewey's philosophy, in his presidential address in 1899 before the American Psychological Association, he expressed the importance of developing a generative "linking science" between psychological theory and practical work just like the one in scientific medicine between natural science and the physician. Dewey said:

> The real essence of the problem is found in . . . [a] connection between . . . the theorist and the practical worker—through the medium of the linking science. . . . It is the participation by the practical man in the theory . . . that determines . . . the effectiveness of the work done, and the moral freedom and personal development of the one engaged in it.[123]

Without this, he said, educators are compelled

> to resort to purely arbitrary measures, to fall back upon mere routine traditions of school teaching, or to fly to the latest fad of pedagogical theorists—the latest panacea peddled out in school journals or teachers' institutes—just as the old physician relied upon his magic formula.[124]

Notes

1. A. A. Lumsdaine and R. Glaser, eds., *Teaching Machines and Programmed Learning* (Washington: National Education Association, 1960); R. C. Atkinson and H. A. Wilson, eds., *Computer-Assisted Instruction* (New York: Academic Press, 1969); N. E. Gronlund, *Stating Behavioral Objectives for Classroom Instruction* (Macmillan, 1985); and R. F. Mager, *Preparing Instructional Objectives* (Palo Alto, Calif.: Fearon, 1962).

2. D. Porter, *An Application of Reinforced Principles to Classroom Teaching*, Cooperative Research Project No. 142 (Harvard University, 1961).

3. B. S. Bloom, "Learning for Mastery," *Evaluation Comment*, vol. 1 (1968), p. 2; B. S. Bloom, *Human Characteristics and Social Learning* (McGraw-Hill, 1976); R. Glaser, "Individuals and Learning: The New Aptitudes," *Educational Researcher*, vol. 1 (1972), pp. 5–13; F. S. Keller, "Good-Bye Teacher," *Journal of Applied Behavior Analysis*, vol. 1 (1968), pp. 78–89; and P. Suppes, "Modern Learning Theory and The Elementary School Curriculum," *American Educational Research Journal*, vol. 2 (1964), pp. 79–93.

4. T. R. Guskey and S. Gates, "Synthesis of Research on the Effects of Mastery Learning in Elementary and Secondary Classrooms," *Educational Leadership*, vol. 43 (1986), pp. 73–80; and C. Kulik and R. Bangert-Downs, "Effects of Testing for Mastery on Student Learning," paper presented at the annual meeting of the American Educational Research Association, San Francisco, Calif., 1986.

5. P. Cobb, E. Yackel, and T. Wood, "A Constructivist Alternative to the Representational View of Mind in Mathematics Education," *Journal for Research in Mathematics Education*, vol. 23 (January 1992), pp. 2–33.

6. P. Cobb and others, "Assessment of a Problem–Centered Second Grade Mathematics Project," *Journal for Research in Mathematics Education*, vol. 22 (January 1991), pp. 3–29.

7. R. Lesh and S. J. Lamon, *Assessment of Authentic Performance in School Mathematics* (Washington: AAAS Press, 1992), pp. 18–19.

8. E. A. Silver, "Foundations of Cognitive Theory and Research for Mathematics Problem-Solving," in A. H. Schoenfeld, ed., *Cognitive Science and Mathematics Education* (Hillsdale, N.J.: LEA, 1987).

9. M. T. Chi and others, "Self-Explanations: How Students Study and Use Examples in Learning to Solve Problems," *Cognitive Science*, vol. 13 (April–June 1989), pp. 145–82; K. Bielaczyc, P. Pirolli, and A. L. Brown, "Training in Self-Explanation and Self-Regulation Strategies: Investigating the Effects of Knowledge Acquisition Activities on Problem Solving," *Cognition and Instruction*, vol. 13 (1995), pp. 221–52; J. D. Bransford and M. K. Johnson, "Contextual Prerequisites for Understanding: Some Investigations of Comprehension and Recall," *Journal of Verbal Learning and Verbal Behavior*," vol. 11 (December 1972), pp. 717–26; and D. E. Kieras and S. Bovari, "The Role of a Mental Model in Learning to Operate a Device," *Cognitive Science*, vol. 8 (July–September 1984), pp. 255–73.

10. For example, J. L. McClelland and D. E. Rumelhart, eds., *Parallel Distributed Processing: Explorations in the Microstructure of Cognition*, vol. 2 (MIT Press, Bradford Books, 1986); and D. E. Rumelhart and J. L. McClelland, "On Learning the Past Tenses of English Verbs," in J. L. McClelland and D. E. Rumelhart, eds., *Parallel Distributed Processing: Explorations in the Microstructure of Cognition*, vol. 2 (MIT Press, Bradford Books, 1986).

11. Cobb, Yackel, and Wood, "A Constructivist Alternative to the Representational View of Mind in Mathematics Education."

12. Cobb, Yackel, and Wood, "A Constructivist Alternative to the Representational View of Mind in Mathematics Education," p. 3, from R. Rorty, *Philosophy and the Mirror of Nature* (Princeton University Press, 1979).

13. Much of the research and theory in information processing psychology concerns subjects' misrepresentation of reality.

14. For example, R. S. Siegler, *Children's Thinking: An Information Processing Approach* (Englewood Cliffs, N.J.: Prentice-Hall, 1980).

15. R. S. Siegler, *Emerging Minds: The Process of Change in Children's Thinking* (New York: Oxford University Press, 1996).

16. J. R. Anderson, H. A. Simon, and L. M. Reder, "Situated Learning and Education," *Educational Researcher*, vol. 25 (May 1996), pp. 5–11; J. G. Greeno, "On Claims That Answer the Wrong Questions," *Educational Researcher*, vol. 26 (1997), pp. 5–17; and J. R. Anderson, H. A. Simon, and L. M. Reder, "Rejoinder: Situative versus Cognitive Perspectives: Form versus Substance," *Educational Researcher*, vol. 26 (1997), pp. 18–21.

17. Anderson, Simon, and Reder, "Rejoinder."

18. For example, K. C. Mayhew and A. C. Edwards, *The Dewey School* (New York: Appleton-Century, 1936). These classes had a 4:1 student-to-teacher ratio, where the students were faculty children.

19. J. Dewey, *Experience and Education* (New York: Collier, 1938).

20. D. Ravitch, *The Troubled Crusade: American Education, 1945–1980* (Basic Books, 1983).

21. D. Chamberlin and others, *Did They Succeed in College? The Follow-Up Study of the Graduates of the Thirty Schools* (Harper and Row, 1942).

22. D. G. Bobrow and G. H. Bower, "Comprehension and Recall of Sentences," *Journal of Experimental Psychology*, vol. 80 (1969), pp. 455–61; and N. J. Slamecka and P. Graf, "The Generation Effect: Delineation of a Phenomenon," *Journal of Experimental Psychology: Learning, Memory, and Cognition*, vol. 4 (1978), pp. 592–604.

23. For example, I. Begg and others, "The Generation Effect Is No Artifact: Generation Makes Words Distinctive," *Journal of Experimental Psychology: Learning, Memory, and Cognition*, vol. 15 (1989), pp. 977–89; D. J. Burns, "The Generation Effect: A Test between Single- and Multifactor Theories," *Journal of Experimental Psychology: Learning, Memory, and Cognition*, vol. 16 (1990), pp. 1060–67; E. Hirshman and R. A. Bjork, "The Generation Effect: Support for a Two–Factor Theory," *Journal of Experimental Psychology: Learning, Memory, and Cogniton*, vol. 14 (1988), pp. 484–94; M. A. McDaniel, P. J. Waddill, and G. O. Einstein, "A Contextual Account of the Generation Effect: A Three Factor Theory," *Journal of Memory and Language*, vol. 27 (1988), pp. 521–36; and N. J. Slamecka and L. T. Katsaiti, "The Generation Effect: Delineation of a Phenomenon," *Journal of Memory and Language*, vol. 26 (1987), pp. 589–607.

24. Bransford and Johnson, "Contextual Prerequisites for Understanding."

25. For example, D. H. Charney, L. M. Reder, and G. W. Kusbit, "Goal Setting and Procedure Selection in Acquiring Computer Skills: A Comparison of Tutorials, Problem-Solving, and Learner Exploration," *Cognition and Instruction*, vol. 7, no. 4 (1990), pp. 323–42.

26. D. P. Ausubel, *Educational Psychology: A Cognitive View* (New York: Holt, Rinehart, and Winston, 1968), pp. 497–98.

27. G. Brousseau, "The Crucial Role of the Didactical Contract in the Analysis and Construction of Situations in Teaching and Learning Mathematics," in H.-G. Steiner, ed., *Theory of Mathematics Education*, Occasional Paper No. 54, pp. 110–19 (Bielefeld, Germany: University of Bielefeld, Institut für Didaktik de Mathematik, 1984).

28. For example, J. R. Hayes, "Three Problems in Teaching General Skills," in J. Segal, S. Chipman, and R. Glaser, eds., *Thinking and Learning*, vol. 2 (Hillsdale, N.J.: Erlbaum, 1985); and K. A. Ericsson, R. T. Krampe, and C. Tesch-Römer, "The Role of Deliberate Practice in the Acquisition of Expert Performance," *Psychological Review*, vol. 100 (1993), pp. 363–406.

29. For example, F. I. M. Craik and M. J. Watkins, "The Role of Rehearsal in Short-Term Memory," *Journal of Verbal Learning and Verbal Behavior*, vol. 12 (1973), pp. 599–607; and A. M. Glenberg, S. M. Smith, and C. Green, "Type I Rehearsal: Maintenance and More," *Journal of Verbal Learning and Verbal Behavior*, vol. 16 (1977), pp. 339–52.

30. For example, R. Lesh and J. S. Zawojeski, "Problem Solving," in T. R. Post, ed., *Teaching Mathematics in Grades K–8: Research-Based Methods*, pp. 49–88 (Needham Heights, Mass.: Allyn and Bacon, 1992).

31. For example, C. M. Knerr and others, *Simulation–Based Research in Part–Task Training*, AF HRL–TR–86–12, AP–B107293 (Brooks Air Force Base, Texas: Air Force Human Resources Laboratory, 1987); and J. Patrick, *Training: Research and Practice* (San Diego, Calif.: Academic Press, 1992).

32. E. Salas and others, "Toward an Understanding of Team Performance and Training," in R. W. Swezey and E. Salas, eds., *Teams: Their Training and Performance* (Norwood, N.J.: Ablex, 1993).

33. Ericsson, Krampe, and Tesch-Römer, "The Role of Deliberate Practice in the Acquisition of Expert Performance."

34. For example, H. P. Bahrick and L. K. Hall, "Lifetime Maintenance of High School Mathematics Content," *Journal of Experimental Psychology: General*, vol. 120 (1991), pp. 20–33; and H. W. Stevenson and J. W. Stigler, *The Learning Gap: Why Our Schools Are Failing and What We Can Learn from Japanese and Chinese Education* (New York: Summit Books, 1992).

35. For example, J. S. Brown, A. Collins, and P. Diguid, *Situated Cognition and the Culture of Learning*, Technical Report No. IRL88–0008 (Institute for Research on Learning, 1988); and Lesh and Lamon, *Assessment of Authentic Performance in School Mathematics*.

36. For example, J. Hiebert and others, "Authentic Problem Solving in Mathematics," paper presented at the annual meeting of the American Educational Research Association, New Orleans, La., 1994.

37. K. R. Koedinger and others, "Intelligence Tutoring Goes to School in the Big City," paper prepared for the Seventh World Conference on Artificial Intelligence in Education, Washington, D.C., August 16–19, 1995.

38. Anderson, Simon, and Reder, "Situated Learning and Education."

39. For example, D. W. Johnson and R. T. Johnson, *Cooperation and Competition: Theory and Research* (Edina, Minn.: Interaction Book Co., 1989).

40. National Research Council, *Learning, Remembering, Believing: Enhancing Human Performance*, edited by D. Druckman and R. A. Bjork (Washington: National Academy Press, 1994); and G. Salomon and T. Globerson, "When Teams Do Not Function the Way They Ought To," *International Journal of Educational Research*, vol. 13 (1989), pp. 89–98, especially pp. 94–5.

41. For example, R. E. Slavin, *Cooperative Learning: Theory, Research, and Practice* (Englewood Cliffs, N.J.: Prentice-Hall, 1990).

42. D. F. Dansereau and D. W. Johnson, "Cooperative Learning," in D. Druckman and R. A. Bjork, eds., *Learning, Remembering, Believing: Enhancing Team and Individual Performance* (Washington: National Academy Press, 1994).

43. For example, Cobb and others, "Assessment of a Problem-Centered Second Grade Mathematics Project."

44. D. Charney, "Empiricism Is Not a Four–Letter Word," *College Composition and Communication*, vol. 47, no. 4 (December 1996), pp. 567–93.

45. D. H. Jonassen, "Evaluating Constructivist Learning," in T. M. Duffy and D. H. Jonassen, eds., *Constructivism and the Technology of Instruction*, chapter 12 (Hillsdale, N.J.: Erlbaum, 1992). Quote on p. 144.

46. I. Wirszup and R. Streit, eds., *Developments in School Mathematics Education around the World*, vol. 3, Proceedings of the Third UCSMP International Conference on Mathematics Education (Reston, Va.: National Council of Teachers of Mathematics, 1992).

47. L. B. Resnick, D. Briars, and S. Lesgold, "Certifying Accomplishments in Mathematics: The New Standards Examining System," in I. Wirszup and R. Streit, eds., *Developments in School Mathematics Education around the World*, vol. 3, Proceedings of the Third UCSMP International Conference on Mathematics Education, pp. 189–207 (Reston, Va.: National Council of Teachers of Mathematics, 1992).

48. J. A. Dossen, "Assessing Mathematics: Enhancing Understanding," in I. Wirszup and R. Streit, eds., *Developments in School Mathematics Education around the World*, vol. 3, Proceedings of the Third UCSMP International Conference on Mathematics Education, pp. 208–22 (Reston, Va.: National Council of Teachers of Mathematics, 1992).

49. R. C. Rist, "Student Social Class and Teacher Expectations: The Self–Fulfilling Prophecy in Ghetto Education," *Harvard Educational Review*, vol. 40 (1989), pp. 411–51.

50. For example, see papers in E. von Glaserfeld, ed., *Radical Constructivism in Mathematics Education* (Dordrecht, The Netherlands: Kluwer Academic Publishers, 1991).

51. J. Confrey, "Learning to Listen: A Student's Understanding of Powers of Ten," in E. von Glaserfeld, ed., *Radical Constructivism in Mathematics Education*, pp. 111–38 (Dordrecht, The Netherlands: Kluwer Academic Publishers, 1991). Quote on p. 122.

52. Cobb, Yackel, and Wood, "A Constructivist Alternative to the Representational View of Mind in Mathemathics Education."

53. L. B. Resnick, "Situated Rationalism: Biological and Social Preparation for Learning," in Lawrence A. Hirschfield and Susan Gelman, eds., *Mapping the Mind: Domain Specificity in Cognition and Culture*, pp. 474–93 (Cambridge, N.Y.: Cambridge University Press, 1994). Quote on p. 489.

54. H. B. Richman and H. A. Simon, "Context Effects in Letter Perception: Comparison of Two Theories," *Psychological Review*, vol. 96 (July 1989), pp. 417–32.

55. J. R. Anderson, C. F. Boyle, and G. Yost, "The Geometry Tutor," *Proceedings of IJCAI* (1985), pp. 1–7; J. R. Anderson and others, "Acquisition of Problem Solving Skill," in J. R. Anderson, ed., *Cognitive Skills and Their Acquisition* (Hillsdale, N.J.: Erlbaum, 1981); and K. R. Koedinger and J. R. Anderson, "Abstract Planning and Perpetual Chunks: Elements in Expertise in Geometry," *Cognitive Science*, vol. 14 (1990), pp. 511–50.

56. R. E. Mayer, *Educational Psychology: A Cognitive Approach* (Little, Brown, 1987); J. M. Paige and H. A. Simon, "Cognitive Processes in Solving Algebra Word Problems," in B. Kleinmuntz, ed., *Problem Solving* (John Wiley and Sons, 1966); and M. K. Singley and others, "The Algebra Word Problem Tutor," *Artificial Intelligence and Education* (1989), pp. 267–75.

57. J. R. Anderson and others, "Cognitive Tutors: Lessons Learned," *Journal of Learning Sciences*, vol. 4 (1995), pp. 167–207; and X. Zhu and H. A. Simon, "Learning Mathematics from Examples and by Doing," *Cognition and Instruction*, vol. 4 (1988), pp. 137–66.

58. R. Case and S. Griffin, "Child Cognitive Development: The Role of Control Conceptual Structures in the Development of Scientific Thought," in C. A. Hauert, ed., *Developmental Psychology: Cognitive, Perception-Motor, and Neurophysiological Perspectives* (North Holland, 1990).

59. A. S. Palinscar and A. L. Brown, "Reciprocal Teaching of Comprehension–Fostering and Comprehension–Monitoring Activities," *Cognition and Instruction*, vol. 1 (1984), pp. 117–75.

60. K. Van Lehn, *Mind Bugs: The Origins of Procedural Misconceptions* (MIT Press, 1990); and R. Young and T. O'Shea, "Errors in Children's Subtraction," *Cognition and Science*, vol. 5 (1981), pp. 153–77.

61. A. B. Champagne, L. E. Klopfer, and J. H. Anderson, "Factors Influencing the Learning of Classical Mechanics," *American Journal of Physics*, vol. 48 (1980), pp. 1074–79; and M. McCloskey, "Intuitive Physics," *Scientific American*, vol. 248 (1983), pp. 122–30.

62. T. P. Carpenter and E. Fennema, "Cognitively Guided Instruction: Building on the Knowledge of Students and Teachers," in W. Secada, ed., *Curriculum Reform: The Case of Mathematics in the United States*, pp. 457–70, special issue of *International Journal of Educational Research* (Elmsford, N.Y.: Pergamon Press, 1992).

63. J. R. Anderson, *Rules of the Mind* (Hillsdale, N.J.: Erlbaum, 1993), chapters 7, 8 10.

64. C. C. McKnight and others, *The Underachieving Curriculum: Assessing U.S. School Mathematics from an International Perspective* (Champaign, Ill.: Stipes Publishing Co., 1990).

65. M. White, *The Japanese Education Challenge: A Commitment to Children* (Free Press, 1987).

66. J. W. Stigler and M. Perry, "Mathematics Learning in Japanese, Chinese, and American Classrooms," in J. W. Stigler, R. A. Shweder, and G. Herdt, eds., *Cultural Psychology* (New York: Cambridge University Press, 1990).

67. H. A. Simon, "How Big Is a Chunk?," *Science*, vol. 183 (1974), pp. 482–88.

68. Ericsson, Krampe, and Tesch–Römer, "The Role of Deliberate Practice in the Acquisition of Expert Performance."

69. Stevenson and Stigler, *The Learning Gap*.

70. J. W. Stigler and H. Stevenson, "How Asian Teachers Polish Each Lesson to Perfection," *American Educator*, vol. 15 (1991), pp. 12–47.

71. Siegler, *Emerging Minds*.

72. M. Wertheimer, *Productive Thinking* (Harper and Row, 1945).

73. M. K. Singley and J. R. Anderson, *Transfer of Cognitive Skill* (Harvard University Press, 1989).

74. J. Metcalfe and D. Wiebe, "Intuition in Insight and Noninsight Problem Solving," *Memory and Cognition*, vol. 15 (1987), pp. 238–46.

75. C. A. Kaplan and H. A. Simon, "In Search of Insight," *Cognitive Psychology*, vol. 22 (July 1990), pp. 374–419.

76. L. Stebbins and others, *Education as Experimentation: A Planned Variation Model*, vol. IV-A (Cambridge, Mass.: Abt Associates, 1977).

77. E. House and others, "No Simple Answer: Critique of FT Evaluation," *Harvard Educational Review*, vol. 48 (1978), pp. 128–60; and C. Bereiter and M. Kurland, "A Constructive Look at Follow Through Results," *Interchange*, vol. 12 (1981), pp. 1–22.

78. J. Gleick, *Genius: The Life and Science of Richard Feynman* (New York: Pantheon Books, 1992).

79. A. Newell and H. A. Simon, *Human Problem Solving* (Englewood Cliffs, N.J.: Prentice-Hall, 1972); J. R. Anderson, "Acquisition of Cognitive Skill," *Psychological Review*, vol. 89 (1982), pp. 369–406; J. R. Anderson, *The Architect of Cognition* (Harvard University Press, 1983); J. R. Anderson, "Skill Acquisition: Compilation of Weak-Method Problem Situations," *Psychological Review*, vol. 94, no. 2 (1987), pp. 192–210; W. G. Chase and H. A. Simon, "The Mind's Eye in Chess," in W. G. Chase, ed., *Visual Information Processing*, pp. 215–81 (New York: Academic Press, 1973); P. Fitts and M. I. Posner, *Human Performance* (Belmont, Calif.: Brooks/Cole, 1967); and M. K. Singley and J. R. Anderson, *The Transfer of Cognitive Skill* (Harvard University Press, 1989).

80. L. P. Steffe and J. Gale, eds., *Constructivism in Education* (Hillsdale, N.J.: Erlbaum, 1995).

81. E. von Glasersfeld, "A Constructivist Approach to Teaching," in L. P. Steffe and J. Gale, eds., *Constructivism in Education*, pp. 3–15 (Hillsdale, N.J.: Erlbaum, 1995).

82. J. Becker and M. Varelas, "Assisting Construction: The Role of the Teacher in Assisting the Learners' Construction of Preexisting Cultural Knowledge," in L. P. Steffe and J. Gale, eds., *Constructivism in Education*, pp. 433–46 (Hillsdale, N.J.: Erlbaum, 1995); and J. Piaget, "Piaget's Theory," in P. Mussen, ed., *Carmichaels' Manual of Child Psychology*, vol. 1, pp. 703–32 (Wiley, 1970). Quote on p. 715.

83. von Glasersfeld, "A Constructivist Approach to Teaching."

84. P. Lewin, "The Social Already Inhabits the Epistemic: A Discussion of Driver; Wood, Cobb, and Yackel; and von Glasersfeld," in L. P. Steffe and J. Gale, eds., *Constructivism in Education*, pp. 423–32 (Hillsdale, N.J.: Erlbaum, 1995).

85. K. A. Ericsson, "The Acquisition of Expert Performance: An Introduction to Some of the Issues," in K. A. Ericsson, ed., *The Road to Excellence: The Acquisition of Expert Performance in the Arts and Sciences, Sports, and Games*, pp. 1–50 (Mahwah, N.J.: Erlbaum, 1996); and K. A. Ericsson and A. C. Lehmann, "Expert and Exceptional Performance: Evidence on Maximal Adaptations on Task Constraints," *Annual Review of Psychology*, vol. 47 (1996), pp. 273–305.

86. A. E. Elo, *The Rating of Chessplayers: Past and Present* (London, England: Batsford, 1978); H. A. Simon and W. G. Chase, "Skill in Chess," *American Scientist*, vol. 61 (1973), pp. 394–403; J. R. Hayes, *The Complete Problem Solver* (Philadelphia, Pa.: Franklin Institute Press, 1981); and K. A. Ericsson, R. Krampe, and C. Tesch-Römer, "The Role of Deliberate Practice in the Acquisition of Expert Performance," *Psychological Review*, vol. 100, no. 3 (1993), pp. 363–406.

87. Ericsson and Lehmann, "Expert and Exceptional Performance."

88. von Glasersfeld, "A Constructivist Approach to Teaching"; A. Newell, *Unified Theories of Cognition* (Harvard University Press, 1990); and K. VanLehn, "Rule Ac-

quisition in the Discovery of Problem-Solving Strategies," *Cognitive Science*, vol. 15 (1991), pp. 1–47.

89. Ericsson, Krampe, and Tesch-Römer, "The Role of Deliberate Practice in the Acquisition of Expert Performance."

90. B. S. Bloom, "Generalizations about Talent Development," in B. S. Bloom, ed., *Developing Talent in Young People*, pp. 507–49 (Ballantine Books, 1985).

91. C. M. Super, "Developmental Transitions of Cognitive Functioning in Rural Kenya and Metropolitan America," in K. R. Gibson and A. C. Petersen, eds., *Brain Maturation and Cognitive Development*, pp. 225–51 (New York: A. D. Gruyter, 1991).

92. Ericsson, "The Acquisition of Expert Performance"; and D. H. Feldman, *Beyond Universals in Cognitive Development*, 2d ed. (Norwood, N.J.: Ablex, 1994).

93. A. C. Lehmann and K. A. Ericsson, "The Historical Development of Domains of Expertise: Performance Standards and Innovations in Music," in A. Steptoe, ed., *Genius and the Mind* (Oxford, England: Oxford University Press, forthcoming).

94. K. A. Ericsson, "Deliberate Practice and the Acquisition of Expert Performance: An Overview," in H. Jorgensen and A. C. Lehmann, eds., *Does Practice Make Perfect? Current Theory and Research on Instrumental Music Practice*, NMH–publikasjoner 1997: 1 (Oslo, Norway: Norges Musikkhögskole, 1997).

95. Ericsson, Krampe, and Tesch-Römer, "The Role of Deliberate Practice in the Acquisition of Expert Performance."

96. Bloom, "Generalizations about Talent Development"; and A. C. Lehmann, "Acquisition of Expertise in Music: Efficiency of Deliberate Practice as a Moderating Variable in Accounting for Sub-Expert Performance," in I. Deliege and J. A. Sloboda, eds., *Perception and Cognition of Music*, pp. 165–91 (Hillsdale, N.J.: LEA, 1997).

97. K. A. Ericsson, "Expert Performance: Its Structure and Acquisition," *American Psychologist*, vol. 49, no. 8 (1994), pp. 725– 47; J. A. Sloboda, J. W. Davidson, and M. J. A. Howe, "Is Everyone Musical?," *Psychologist*, vol. 7 (1994), pp. 349–54; and M. J. A. Howe, J. W. Davidson, and J. A. Sloboda, "Innate Talents: Reality or Myth?," *Behavioral and Brain Sciences*. (forthcoming).

98. J. A. Sloboda and others, "The Role of Practice in the Development of Performing Musicians," *British Journal of Psychology*, vol. 87 (1996), pp. 287–309.

99. Anderson, "Acquisition of Cognitive Skill"; and Fitts and Posner, *Human Performance*.

100. K. A. Ericsson and J. Smith, "Prospects and Limits in the Empirical Study of Expertise: An Introduction," in K. A. Ericsson and J. Smith, eds., *Toward a General Theory of Expertise: Prospects and Limits*, pp. 1–38 (Cambridge: Cambridge University Press, 1991).

101. A. de Groot, *Thought and Choice and Chess* (The Hague: Mouton, 1946; reprinted 1978).

102. Ericsson and Lehmann, "Expert and Exceptional Performance."

103. Ericsson 1997; and K. A. Ericsson and W. Kintsch, "Long–Term Working Memory," *Psychological Review*, vol. 102 (1995).

104. Ericsson and Lehmann, "Expert and Exceptional Performance."

105. Ericsson, "The Acquisition of Expert Performance"; and R. Glaser, "Changing the Agency for Learning: Acquiring Expert Performance" in K. A. Ericsson, ed., *The Road to Excellence: The Acquisition of Expert Performance in the Arts and Science, Sports, and Games* (Mahwah, N.J.: Erlbaum, 1996).

106. B. Abernethy, "Selective Attention in Fast Ball Sports II: Expert–Novice

Difference," *Australian Journal of Science and Medicine in Sports*, vol. 19, no. 4 (1987), pp. 7–16.

107. Ericsson, "The Acquisition of Expert Performance."

108. H. Gardner, *Creating Minds* (Basic Books, 1993).

109. D. K. Simonton, "Creative Productivity: A Predictive and Explanatory Model of Career Trajectories and Landmarks," *Psychological Review*, vol. 104 (1997), pp. 66–89.

110. Ericsson, "The Acquisition of Expert Performance"; and Ericsson, Krampe, and Tesch-Römer, "The Role of Deliberate Practice in the Acquisition of Expert Performance."

111. A. Newell and H. A. Simon, *Human Problem Solving*, (Englewood Cliffs, N.J.: Prentice-Hall, 1972).

112. R. Glaser and L. B. Resnick, "Instructional Psychology," in P. H. Mussen and M. R. Rosenzweig, eds., *Annual Review of Psychology*, vol. 23, pp. 207–76 (Palo Alto, Calif.: Annual Reviews, 1972). Quote on p. 207.

113. J. R. Anderson, "ACT: A Simple Theory of Complex Cognition," *American Psychologist*, vol. 51 (January–June 1996), pp. 355–65.

114. M. W. Lewis, R. Milson, and J. R. Anderson, "Designing an Intelligent Authoring System for High School Mathematics ICAI: The Teacher Apprentice Project," in G. Kearsley, ed., *Artificial Intelligence and Instruction: Applications and Methods*, pp. 269–300 (Addison–Wesley, 1987); J. R. Anderson, C. G. Boyle, and G. Yost, "The Geometry Tutor," in *Proceedings of the International Joint Conference on Artificial Intelligence*, pp. 1–7 (Los Angeles, Calif.: International Joint Conference on Artificial Intelligence, 1985); and J. R. Anderson, R. Farrell, and R. Sauers, "Learning to Program in LISP," *Cognitive Science*, vol. 8 (April–June 1984), pp. 87–129.

115. J. R. Anderson and others, "Cognitive Tutors: Lessons Learned," *Journal of Learning Sciences*, vol. 4 (1995), pp. 167–207.

116. A. L. Brown, "Knowing When, Where, and How to Remember: A Problem of Metacognition," in R. Glaser, ed., *Advances in Instructional Psychology*, vol. 1, pp. 77–168 (Hillsdale, N.J.: Lawrence Erlbaum Associates, 1978).

117. A. Collins, J. S. Brown, and S. E. Newman, "Cognitive Apprenticeship: Teaching the Craft of Reading, Writing, and Mathematics," in L. B. Resnick, ed., *Knowing, Learning, and Instruction: Essays in Honor of Robert Glaser*, pp. 453–94 (Hillsdale, N.J.: Erlbaum, 1989).

118. A. L. Brown and A. S. Palinscar, "Reciprocal Teaching of Comprehension-Fostering and Monitoring Activities," *Cognition and Instruction*, vol. 1 (1984), pp. 175–77; and A. L. Brown and A. S. Palinscar, "Guided Cooperative Learning and Individual Knowledge Acquisition," in L. B. Resnick, *Knowing, Learning, and Instruction: Essays in Honor of Robert Glaser*, pp. 393–451 (Hillsdale, N.J.: Erlbaum, 1989).

119. For example, T. N. Carraher, D. W. Carraher, and A. D. Schliemann, "Mathematics in the Street and in School," *British Journal of Developmental Psychology*, vol. 3 (1985), pp. 21–29; J. Lave, *Cognition in Practice: Mind, Mathematics, and Culture in Everyday Life* (Cambridge University Press, 1988); G. B. Saxe, *Culture and Cognitive Development: Studies in Mathematical Understanding* (Hillsdale, N.J.: Erlbaum, 1991); S. Scribner, "Studying Work Intelligence," in B. Rogoff and J. Lave, eds., *Everday Cognition: Its Development in Social Context*, pp. 9–40 (Harvard University Press, 1984); and J. W. Stigler and R. Baranes, "Culture and Mathematics Learning," in E. Z. Rothkopf, ed., *Review of Research in Education*, vol. 15, pp. 253–306 (Washington: American Educational Research Association, 1988).

120. J. G. Greeno, "Number Sense as Situated Knowing in a Conceptual Domain," *Journal for Research in Mathematics Education*, vol. 22 (1991), pp. 1–49; and J. Lave and E. Wenger, *Situated Learning: Legitimate Peripheral Participation* (Cambridge, Mass.: Cambridge University Press, 1991).

121. A. L. Brown, "The Advancement of Learning," *Educational Researcher*, vol. 23, no. 8 (1994), pp. 4–11; A. L. Brown and J. C. Campione, "Communities of Learning and Thinking, or a Context by Any Other Name," in D. Kuhn, ed., *Contributions to Human Development*, vol. 21: *Developmental Perspective on Teaching and Learning Thinking Skills*, pp. 108–26 (Basel, Switzerland: Karger, 1990); Cognition and Technology Group at Vanderbilt, "From Visual Word Problems to Learning Communities: Changing Conceptions of Cognitive Research," in K. McGilly, ed., *Classroom Lessons: Integrating Cognitive Theory and Classroom Practice*, pp. 157–200 (MIT Press/Bradford Books, 1994); and M. Scardamalia and C. Bereiter, "Higher Levels of Agency for Children in Knowledge Building: A Challenge for the Design of New Knowledge Media," *Journal of the Learning Sciences*, vol. 1 (1991), pp. 37–68.

122. A. L. Brown and J. C. Campione, "Guided Discovery in a Community of Learners," in K. McGilly, ed., *Classroom Lessons: Integrating Cognitive Theory and Classroom Practice*, pp. 229–70 (MIT Press/Bradford Books, 1994).

123. J. Dewey, "Psychology and Social Practice," *Psychological Review*, vol. 7 (1900), pp. 105–24. Quote on pp. 110–11.

124. Dewey, "Psychology and Social Practice," pp. 112–13.

The Use and Misuse of Research in Educational Reform

TOM LOVELESS

M OST EDUCATORS and lawmakers still believe that good
research produces good policy and that good policy produces good education in the schools. I suspect even jaundiced observers
hold to this idealization on some level, since when things go wrong
with school reform, when test scores go down or parents and teachers
rebel against some newfangled idea, either policy or research is usually
singled out as the culprit. This paper analyzes research and policy as
well as the problems that occur when research and policy are joined to
promore educational reform. Two recent state-initiated reforms illustrate how research may be distorted as it is absorbed by the educational
system. Such distortions arise from structural flaws in educational governance. Research on practice enters the educational system at bureaucratic levels far removed from the schools and classrooms where practice takes place. This alienation of research from practice negatively
affects education policy, compelling a reconsideration of how educational research, policy, and practice are connected in the current
system.

I wish to thank Adam Gamoran, David Hart, Helen Ladd, Diane Ravitch, Cecilia
Rouse, and Carol Weiss for their helpful comments on earlier drafts. The research
assistance of Greg Dorchak and Tina Choi is also appreciated. The views expressed in
this paper are those of the author and do not necessarily reflect the views of these
individuals.

Educational Research

In the latter half of the nineteenth century, prestige in the academic disciplines became wedded to the scientific advancement of knowledge. As graduate training rose to prominence in Germany and the United States, higher education focused on the production of original research in highly specialized, departmentalized fields.[1] The building blocks of modern academic inquiry were institutionalized—among them, formulating hypotheses based on prior research, gathering data with replicable protocols to rigorously test these hypotheses, and publishing findings after the scrutiny of peer review. The faith in science underpinning these methods ultimately not only dominated the creation of new knowledge in the natural sciences, but also penetrated such applied disciplines as medicine and engineering and eventually influenced, by introducing new modes of logic, disciplines as distant from the natural sciences as law and philosophy.[2]

The twentieth century witnessed the rapid development of complex public school systems and the kindling of scholarly interest in children's learning and the activities of formal schooling. In the United States, a network of researchers evolved that was headed by universities' schools of education and included federal and state departments of education, local school districts, professional educator groups and teachers' unions, philanthropic foundations, think tanks, advocacy groups, and researchers from other academic fields (most notably, psychologists during the first half of the twentieth century and social scientists during the second half). And yet today, notwithstanding a century of work from such an eclectic group, educational research is not considered very scientific. This perception has prevented twentieth century educational research from gaining the full respect of the academic community. On campuses across the country, education research and schools of education suffer from low prestige.[3]

Inherent qualities of educational research hinder its full acceptance as science. Like other social scientists, educational researchers typically cannot randomly assign subjects to treatment and control groups, forcing a reliance on quasi-experimental studies.[4] Research on the teaching of reading, for example, runs the gamut from the least experimental— simply comparing the performance of children in a new reading program with the performance of children in existing programs—to more sophisticated designs that try to equalize experimental and control groups on variables known to influence reading achievement.[5]

This research has fostered a deeper understanding of how to teach children to read, but in the strictest sense, it is weak science. Even the best quasi-experiments contain unavoidable bias. The students and teachers involved in reading experiments are necessarily voluntary, introducing a confounding element into studies. Because teachers who are enthusiastic about a new program probably teach better with it than teachers who object to the program's aims or methods, any subsequent gains that are detected may be illusory. Moreover, determining causality in instruction is extremely difficult because teaching and learning are nearly always bidirectional. Teachers make different strategic choices based on the qualities students bring with them to school. During instruction, as students indicate that they understand or do not understand what is being taught, teachers alter their instruction accordingly.[6]

Even when quasi-experiments conscientiously control the individual characteristics suspected of influencing outcomes (including motivation), context characteristics are frequently omitted from study designs. To continue with the example of reading, it is an elementary school subject where instruction has been traditionally conducted in reading groups. Studies assigning similar children to traditional and experimental classrooms but neglecting to incorporate the characteristics of reading groups into the research design (for example, the ability and behavior of group members, the group's pacing through curriculum, the amount of time group members are allotted for seat work and other activities) are leaving uncontrolled some of the most significant factors in the teaching of reading.[7]

As Rebecca Barr and Robert Dreeben pointed out in their landmark study of first grade reading, this oversight stems from conceptualizing learning how to read as the product of individual-level characteristics (the learner's) interacting with a classroom-level technology (the reading program's). The influence of a middle level of organization—the instructional group—is neglected. The same objection can be raised with studies of school characteristics that leave out classroom-level phenomena (one of the most damning criticisms of the Coleman Report of the 1960s and the effective schools literature of the 1970s) and studies of district- or system-level effects that leave out subsystem levels of educational activity altogether. Recently, this problem crops up in production function studies that elucidate neither the precise elements of the school's production function nor how they operate together to produce learning. Here is the challenge: Learning is never limited to a child's experiences with an educational system, a school, or a reading program but extends to, and is frequently dominated by, interactions with the curriculum, teachers, and fellow students at multiple levels within educational institutions (in the school, classroom, and instructional group) and with interactions outside these institutions (in the community, family, and peer group).[8]

These nodes of influence are not only lodged at different levels of aggregation, but they are also interrelated and in flux. Thus, families and peer groups affect the composition of classrooms, and over a period of time, the families, peer groups, and classrooms change. This makes a shambles of scientific replicability over both space and time. The same program has been found to be fundamentally different at different school sites. And programs found effective after thorough evaluation have been found ineffective—and dramatically altered—when revisited at the same sites only two or three years later.[9]

These limitations are daunting but they do not render educational research a hopeless enterprise. They do mean, however, that findings are inherently contingent. Good researchers are well aware of their works' methodological limitations and qualify their conclusions accordingly. They properly warn that particular conditions must be in place for particular outcomes to occur and that they are unable to account for all of the possible influences on learning. Turning through the pages of the best educational journals, one encounters the obligatory cautions: Findings are ''suggestive'' not definitive and ''more research on the question is needed.''

At its current stage of intellectual history, then, educational research is in a tenuous position, both in terms of its reputation as a disciplinary field within the academy and in terms of its standing as a body of verifiable knowledge. This state of affairs has important ramifications for the use of research findings in the real world. Research can offer only ambiguous direction to policy. The importance of this ambiguity is magnified because, with the traditional routes to academic prestige closed off, educational research must hunt elsewhere for legitimation. Policymaking forums are good places to look. The transaction that is offered to policymakers is research for legitimacy. Researchers' reputations are enhanced when their ideas are realized in legislation or regulation. In return, policymakers are able to claim that their initiatives reflect "what the research says," and they gain a stamp of scientific approval (even if quasi-scientific) for the causes they champion. These transactions are particularly powerful when it comes to educational reform since decisionmakers routinely embrace findings that have not been tested or confirmed by practical application in classrooms. Compounding the error, when such findings are converted into substantive policy proposals, the ambiguities of research may be stripped away and forgotten.

Educational Reform

Reform is born of urgency. Educational reformers seek to change an aspect of education that they believe to be unfair, inefficient, inimical to student achievement, or objectionable on some other grounds. Reformers are apt to wield policy as the instrument of their desired change, appealing to federal, state, district, county, city, or school policymakers to correct deficiencies in the educational system. Such appeals have been remarkably successful. The latter half of the twentieth century probably witnessed the enactment of more education policies—maybe several times more—than the whole prior history of schooling stretching back to the ancient Greeks. When the state of Michigan rewrote its education code in 1996, it was able to eliminate 205 of the 620 sections of the old code. California's code is spread over more than seven thousand pages, occupying eleven of the twenty-six volumes of that state's laws.[10]

And these are only state policies. Some districts' policies number into the thousands, stuffed into stacks of three-ringed binders. Upon close examination, these policy binders are often little more than operations manuals, detailing everything from the color of classroom walls to the proper phone greeting by office personnel.[11] When the policies of the federal government, the fifty states, and the nation's approximately fifteen thousand school districts and eighty thousand public schools are added together, the numbers are staggering.

Besides this quantitative accomplishment, however, policy has not proven a reliable method of effecting change. Two contradictory mind-sets exist on education policy's relationship to reform. One is that policy is intrusive and that it stifles innovation. The steady accretion of policies, added to yesterday's reforms, forms a dense layer of rules and regulations, blocking a flexible response to emergent problems and undermining coherence in the policy system.[12] The other view is that like virga, rain that falls but never reaches the ground, reforms leaving Washington, Albany, or Sacramento evaporate long before they reach the classroom. Even when policies manage to penetrate the system, educators reshape objectives to match local conditions. Other reforms are written into policy but simply ignored by practitioners. Again and again, scholars of educational reform have documented the historical failure of policy to leave a lasting imprint on schools.[13]

Why do reforms fail? The most prevalent explanation is that schools are hidebound institutions, a trait reinforced by education's swollen bureaucracies and the dysfunctions of educational politics. Another view sees resistance to innovation running deep among school people and strengthening during their careers, as if hostility to change is encoded in the DNA of the professional educator.[14]

But there are other plausible explanations. School people might be smart to ignore innovations when so few are of proven merit. An analysis of thirty-four prominent reforms adopted since 1960 estimates that no more than six have been educationally worthy.[15] In a case study conducted by researchers at the University of Utah, teachers resisted a school-based management scheme because, at the same time that the reform increased teachers' workload, its promise to increase the teachers' authority over their own work proved hollow. It may be a good thing that school people generally ignore policies bent on changing education's core operations if such polices entail unacceptable costs or only rarely lead to improvement.[16]

If policies typically are not implemented and if the few that are implemented are generally unproductive, why all the policies? This mystery deepens when the weaknesses of research and policy are considered in tandem. Research is tentative on educational questions, and policy has trouble affecting educational functions. Oddly enough, these limitations are fairly well known to those actors at the intersection of education's research and policy systems—researchers, politicians, bureaucrats, and practitioners—but policy is continually called upon to reform American education. An enormous market exists for research-backed policy, and, ambiguities and all, research and policy continue to rain down on schools. Approximately 100,000 research articles are published in educational journals annually, and in California alone, approximately two thousand education bills are introduced in the legislature each year.[17]

Although educational practitioners—namely, teachers and school principals—are frequently the targets of educational reform, they are not the consumers of educational research. As a result, research's insights on how to make educational practice more productive are never communicated directly to practitioners but are instead interpreted, and sometimes misinterpreted, by officials higher up in the educational system, shorn of their contingencies and qualifiers, and then packaged for selling to teachers and principals. The process sustains an enormous flow of reforms into schools and classrooms, but it may also produce reforms that are disconnected from a base of substantiating evidence, thereby distorting what research actually recommends.

Instructional Reform

Constructivism is a theory of cognition that has been stretched into a pedagogical philosophy by its most ardent followers. Constructivists have been successful in writing two principles into state policy—the elevation of student-centered learning activities over teacher-centered instruction and the devaluation of basic skills in reading and math instruction. Enshrining these two principles in state policy itself constitutes a third effect, the promotion of state prescriptions for teaching under the guise of instructional policy. These themes are not new. They are long-standing doctrines of the progressive education movement, which, having faded away with discovery learning and open classrooms in the 1970s, was revitalized by ideas stirring in the field of cognitive psychology.[18]

The Rosetta stone of constructivism is that students construct their own knowledge. This sounds reasonable enough, but interpreted religiously, a number of traditional schooling practices are called into question. The premise of constructivism implies that the knowledge students construct on their own, for example, is more valuable than the knowledge that is modeled for them; told to them; or shown, demonstrated, or explained to them by a teacher. Echoing the historical mantra of progressive education, constructivists argue that the essence of education—its means, ends, and motivating force—should be generated from within the learner, not decided by an external source. The teacher, the textbook, the curriculum, indeed, the entire school and the external authorities it embodies are recast as facilitators in the student's construction of new knowledge, no longer the sources of it. Without suggesting that constructivism endorses a social order out of *Lord of the Flies,* it is fair to say that authority definitely shifts from the adult to the child in the constructivist classroom.

Research does not confirm the belief that such a shift in authority promotes learning. Studies of discovery learning, the last manifestation of student-centered instruction, suggest that placing youngsters at the helm of their own intellectual development is generally unproductive. Student-centered practices may be defended on ideological grounds— that granting students power, whether it is educationally beneficial or not, is intrinsically good—but empirical support for enhanced leaning is weak.[19]

Constructivism also strives to steer classrooms away from such traditional, facts-oriented learning as knowing the rules of spelling and grammar, knowing the rules of punctuation and capitalization, memorizing the multiplication tables and other basic arithmetical facts, and acquiring basic decoding skills related to sound-symbol relationships. Instead, learning is directed toward problem solving, critical thinking, learning how to work in groups, and developing a healthy self-esteem. Basic skills are recognized as useful, but they are not given top priority in the constructivist classroom, nor is their mastery presumed necessary before higher-order tasks can be tackled.

Research is unable to resolve disputes over the knowledge students should acquire in public schools. That is for political institutions to decide. But the evidence is even murky on the questions research can address—the proper balance of memorization and other activities to become proficient in, say, algebra; the minimal amount of basic facts that must be known before one can move on to higher mathematics; the proportion of time to be shared between learning the rules of composition and crafting written work before one becomes a skilled writer;

the optimum amount of phonics instruction and exposure to literature that leads to capable readers.[20]

California's curriculum frameworks in language arts (1987) and mathematics (1992) are two crowning achievements of progressive doctrine. Both documents embrace constructivism, both lay claim to being based on the latest research, and both ignore the limitations of the research they cite. The documents make clear that student-centered learning is favored over direct instruction by a teacher. The language arts framework embraces an integrated program that is critical of phonics instruction in reading and of any separate, formal instruction in the rules of spelling, grammar, punctuation, or capitalization. Learning to read and express oneself with language, the framework explains, is "so intensely personal and human" that it "cannot be limited to a daily list of ten or 15 skill objectives or to the completion of meaningless worksheets."[21] A good classroom climate is established when "the learner becomes the center of learning rather than the teacher."[22]

Reform is necessary, declares the math framework, because "too few young people leave school mathematically powerful."[23] Accordingly, the first chapter of the framework is devoted to the topic of "Mathematical Power" and the second chapter to "Developing Mathematical Power in the Classroom." What is mathematical power? Astonishingly, the framework has difficulty defining this, the central goal of the mathematics curriculum, in concrete terms, stringing together instead a list of watery phrases. Thus, students should be able to use "mathematical thinking, mathematical ideas, communication, and tools and techniques" with "confidence and enthusiasm," while "appreciating history and society."[24] In "empowering mathematics program[s]" students "are in control of the technology," choosing from among "manipulatives, calculators, and computers."[25] Teachers are "facilitators of learning rather than imparters of information," creating an environment where students "construct their own understanding of mathematics."[26] And a teacher on the framework committee urges, "Our classrooms can be student-oriented, self-directed, and nonauthoritarian. We can drop the role of a figure who passes judgment on what is right and wrong."[27]

As documents called curriculum frameworks, these two publications are curiously devoid of curriculum. One telling clue to the math framework's priorities is that the chapter entitled "The Structure and Content of the Mathematics Program," the heart and soul of prior math frameworks, begins on page 75. In the previous math framework, published in 1985, the chapter entitled "The Content and Structure of the Mathematics Program" began on page 8. From start to finish, the 1985 framework totaled forty-five pages; the 1992 framework totals 217 pages, bloated because regulating instruction had thoroughly usurped defining content as the framework's primary mission.

California has a long history of state involvement with the school curriculum. A constitutional amendment instituting state selection of textbooks was ratified by voters in 1884, and the state continues to adopt the books used in grades K–8 today. The state's first subject area curriculum guide appeared in 1948, *The Social Studies Program for the Public Schools of California.* For the next several decades, curriculum frameworks focused on content, describing the school curriculum in terms broad enough to guide local authorities in developing courses of study. The 1962 social studies framework, for example, consisted of three parts: a brief outline of the K–12 program, a grade-by-grade description of content and learning goals, and the basic concepts that students would encounter from geography, history, political science, and so on. For the most part, instructional methods were conscientiously avoided by the frameworks.[28]

But the math and language arts framework committees assembled by the California State Department of Education in the late 1980s and early 1990s had other ideas. They wanted to use the frameworks to profoundly change how teachers teach, not to articulate a clear set of standards for what students should learn. The irony is that the frameworks pursue their goals by being directive with teachers in ways that they discourage teachers from being with children. The 1992 California math framework, for example, is both lamb and lion, discouraging teachers from telling students "what is right or wrong," but explicitly telling teachers which instructional strategies are right or wrong. A checklist of desired and undesired teaching strategies (arranged in columns labeled "traditional," "alternative," and "desired" practices) are scattered throughout the text and collected together in an appendix. Cooperative learning groups, manipulatives, and expecting students to explain their thinking on "holistic" tasks are desired; instruction focused on specific objectives, assignments featuring drill and practice, and expecting student mastery are "traditional" and presumed bad. And these instructional choices, it is said repeatedly, are supported by research, presented as unqualified findings of what constitutes best practice. This claim is only true if the goals of traditional instruction—and such old-fashioned virtues as accuracy and precision in mathematical computations—are replaced with the process-oriented goals of the new instructional regime.[29]

That regime is now in retreat. Although isolating the effects of state policies from other influences on achievement is extremely difficult, all signs are that California's instructional policies have been nothing less than an educational disaster. When the 1994 National Assessment of Educational Progress (NAEP) scores were released in the spring of 1995, Californians were stunned to find the state's students scoring in the cellar on reading performance, either dead last among the states or just off the bottom. The state's own test results in mathematics were equally dismal. Newspapers up and down the state howled at the results and blasted the frameworks as the cause. And the public fury did not dissipate quickly. One year later, an article in the *Sacramento Bee* headlined "Why California Kids Can't Read" included an admission from former state superintendent Bill Honig, on whose watch the language arts and math frameworks were adopted. Honig confessed that the language arts framework went too far in recommending unsubstantiated teaching strategies and explained, "It is the curse of all progressives that we are anti-research and anti-science, and we never seem to grasp how irrational that attitude is. This is probably our deepest failure."[30]

Again, it cannot be shown unequivocally that the state's instructional reforms are responsible for falling achievement, but they certainly can be placed at the scene of the crime. Although defenders of the frameworks point to factors outside the schools for the falling test scores— that is, immigration and restricted education funding—such explanations are unconvincing. The decline in achievement cuts across all racial and socioeconomic groups in the state. When the children of college graduates are compared from state to state, for instance, a comparison that removes most of the influence of family background, California's school children still score near the bottom of the pack.

Honig's successor as state superintendent, Delaine Eastin, moved quickly to quell the uproar. Eastin appointed two task forces to review the frameworks' role in the achievement decline and ordered their reports completed within four months. Releasing their findings in the fall of 1995, the task forces split on the culpability of state policy. Employing frank language, the reading task force rejected the state framework on the subject, in particular its endorsement of "whole language" techniques in reading instruction. The math report was less willing to criticize the constructivist innovations in the math framework, however, concluding that no one knew if teachers were following the framework's policies and arguing that the reforms had not been given a fair chance if teachers were uncertain how to use them.[31]

Despite the mixed messages, the instructional reforms of the earlier documents had been discredited beyond repair. In the 1995 session of the state legislature, a session otherwise riven by ideological feuding, a coalition spanning the political spectrum passed bills to undo the frameworks' excesses. Phonics instruction, computational skills, and spelling were all mandated; new documents were ordered that would establish substantive content and performance standards; and a new test was scheduled to assess what students learn.[32] The state department of education and the state board of education issued policy advisories in reading and math in 1996 that recommended balanced approaches to math and reading instruction. And in 1997, the release of the 1996 NAEP scores brought a new round of criticism. A widely respected observer of California's political scene, columnist Dan Walters, attributed the state's low math scores to "educational theorists insisting that old-fashioned computational skills be subordinated to touchy-feely concepts." He sadly concluded, "A generation of innocent and helpless children is being educationally crippled and California will feel the effects for decades."[33]

California's failed instructional reforms illustrate the difficulty of converting educational research into educational reform. The issue is not whether progressive instructional practices are good or bad. Teachers should employ progressive methods or traditional methods—or stand on their heads while they teach—whatever promotes student learning. These are failures of governance, not of teaching; the failure of state officials to supply teachers with the whole, unvarnished research on recommended instructional practice, and the failure of state curricular documents, by focusing on methods instead of content, to present a model curriculum for children to learn.

Tracking Reform

Tracking refers to grouping students by ability for the purpose of instruction. In one form or another, tracking has been a mainstay of the twentieth century school. From the first grader's reading group to the high school senior's Advanced Placement (AP) class, schools attempt to match curriculum with the different learning needs of students, and students are assigned learning material of varying levels of difficulty.

Tracking has also been a persistently controversial practice, with debates raging over if, when, and how ability grouping should occur. The controversies surrounding tracking have generated a tremendous amount of research, yet two of the most crucial questions in the debate remain unanswered: Is tracking beneficial or harmful to student achievement? And what happens to achievement when tracking is abolished and students are grouped heterogeneously by ability?

The first question, whether tracking is good or bad, remains unanswered because of mixed findings. Some studies have concluded that ability grouping benefits particular groups of students, especially highly advanced students and students who need intensive remedial instruction.[34] Other studies show ability grouping harmful to students in low groups, with these students experiencing weak, uninteresting curricula and suffering from the stigma of the "low track" label and the low expectations of teachers. Because poor students and students of color are disproportionately represented in these low groups, the charge is levied that tracking is inequitable.[35] Still other studies find the differential effects of tracking a result of students' exposure to different curricular materials and instructional practices, factors that may vary considerably among classes in the same track or among classes presumed to be heterogeneously grouped.[36] Taken as a whole, the evidence suggests that low-achieving students suffer academically from placement in low tracks, but it is silent on whether or how low tracks can be altered to make them more productive or if low-ability students would benefit from placement in high track classes. The evidence also suggests that high-achieving students benefit from ability grouped classes, but only when a challenging curriculum is offered. Neither of these suggestions is etched in stone, however.[37]

The second question, whether untracking—randomly assigning all of a school's students to their classes—is better than tracking remains unanswered for a simple reason: So few untracked schools exist that schoolwide grouping of students heterogeneously by ability has never been adequately evaluated. A number of researchers have tried to draw inferences about heterogeneous grouping from their data, but these conclusions suffer because whether the data include untracked schools is unclear.[38]

The most conspicuous example of drawing such flawed inferences is in *Keeping Track,* Jeannie Oakes's popular 1985 book. Perhaps the most important text of the antitracking movement, Oakes's book claims to show that heterogeneous grouping is a school policy with no losers, only winners. Drawing on data collected at twenty-five schools, Oakes compares seventy-five high track classes, eighty-five average track classes, sixty-four low track classes, and seventy-five classes identified as heterogeneous. She concludes that "*everyone* usually seems to do at least as well (and low and average students usually better) when placed in mixed groups."[39] This statement is based on data showing the heterogeneously grouped classes scoring higher than low and average track classes on indicators of educational quality (for example, teacher enthusiasm, use of instructional time, classroom climate).

But in the book's opening chapters, Oakes presents evidence that nearly all twenty-five schools in the study were tracked.[40] In other words, except for one small junior high school, the schools housing the seventy-five heterogeneously grouped classes employed tracking. They grouped students by ability into some classes and mixed the students who were left into classes labeled "heterogeneous." The problem is that these classes are not heterogeneous at all—heterogeneously grouped classes cannot exist at tracked schools.

Here is a hypothetical example designed to accurately reflect the deficiencies of Oakes's study as well as illustrate the limits of empirically comparing tracking and untracking using most large-scale databases: A high school siphons off its very highest achieving students, about 10 percent of enrollment, into an honors-level English class; its very lowest achieving students, about 5 percent, into a special education class; another 10 percent of students who are of limited English proficiency into a bilingual class; and another 5 percent of low achievers into a special dropout prevention program. The remaining 70 percent of the students are randomly assigned to classes labeled "heterogeneous" in ability.

Along come a group of researchers who draw a sample of students from the school and ask students, teachers, and administrators a series of questions. Students are asked what kind of classes they are in, and most answer that they are in heterogeneous classes. Teachers are asked what kind of classes they teach, and most say they teach heterogeneous classes.[41] The school principal is asked how the classes at the school are formed, and the response is that most are created by random assignment—that is, most are heterogeneous classes. By all accounts, this is an untracked school. In such prominent national databases as High School and Beyond (HSB) and the National Educational Longitudinal Study (NELS), this school will appear as untracked—and, as they did in *Keeping Track*, the classes serving randomly assigned students will appear as heterogeneous classes—although the school and the classes are nothing of the kind. The school is a tracked school with classes that are differentiated by both their curricula and the ability of students enrolled in them—even the classes that are called "heterogeneous."

If the researchers compare the achievement of students at this school with a second school that treats the broad 70 percent of students in the middle differently, assigning them to what are labeled "regular" and "remedial" classes, this second school will probably show up as tracked in HSB and NELS. If the comparison finds the remedial track students of the second school learn less than similar students at the first school—that is, if students below grade level do better in the "untracked" setting than in the "tracked" one—what policy recommendations can be made? That tracking should be abolished? No, although many researchers have endorsed such a recommendation based on murkier evidence than this.

The basic problem is that the recommended policy, detracking, would place all of a school's students—all of them, not just the 70 percent in the middle of the achievement continuum—in the same classes. But nowhere in major national databases can schools practicing this recommended grouping scheme be identified to see how their students are faring.

Surely something has been learned about whether the degree of tracking at schools affects achievement. The first school may not be fully detracked, but it is definitely less tracked than the second school. Can the conclusion at least be reached that grouping average and below average students together is better for low achievers than grouping these students into separate classes?

Perhaps, but this conclusion also has problems. The untracked school in this example provides differentiated classes for special education, limited English, ''at risk,'' and high-achieving students—a menu of specialized programs that is fairly common in the contemporary American high school. The low-achieving students who are left to receive the benefits of ''heterogeneous'' classes are a select bunch; they are unrepresentative of low-achieving students generally and likely constitute a homogeneous group themselves.

But the more pressing problem for interpreting achievement differences between the two schools arises from what is still unknown in the comparison, especially from what is unknown about how the two institutions produce learning. Oakes's study offers no student achievement data, so, readers are never given estimates of the achievement differences resulting from tracking. In addition to inadequate policy variables, national databases have poor measures of the curriculum and instruction that students experience. Although NELS represents an improvement over HSB in this regard, these databases' somewhat crude measures of policy, curriculum, and instruction mean not only that the most commonly proposed reform of tracking, its reduction or elimination, cannot be reliably evaluated, but also that some powerful alternative explanations for achievement differences elude measurement. What if the heterogeneous classes use different textbooks that account for their achievement gains, for example, or cover material on the HSB and NELS tests at faster or slower speeds? The proper policy recommendation might be to change the texts or the pacing of instruction in low tracks to resemble settings—tracked or untracked—where low-achieving students succeed.[42]

For research to guide policy on the tracking issue, then, policymaking must overcome contradictory research findings on tracking's effects, profound limitations on the data that are most frequently collected to investigate tracking, and the lack of good models where tracking has been abandoned.[43]

These are formidable hurdles. Policymakers in a large number of jurisdictions have ignored these handicaps to push for tracking's abolition, and they claim that research backs their actions when they do it. Fueling a powerful reform movement that sprang to life in the 1980s were a litany of books and articles critical of tracking, most notably, *Keeping Track* by Jeannie Oakes and one deeply influenced by Oakes, *Crossing the Tracks* by Anne Wheelock, along with the condemnation of tracking by such powerful groups as the National Governors' Association and the Carnegie Foundation.[44] Spurred by this advocacy, tracking's opponents indicted the practice's social consequences, claiming that it contributes to achievement inequities by channeling poor and minority students disproportionately into low tracks where their achievement is diminished. Responding to this critique, several state departments of education adopted policy advisories urging middle schools to detrack for equity reasons, and numerous local districts and schools followed suit by eliminating honors and remedial classes in favor of grouping students of varying abilities in the same classrooms.

Massachusetts state officials seized upon the social arguments against tracking. The first official salvo against tracking came in 1990 when the Massachusetts Department of Education issued *Structuring Schools for Student Success: A Focus on Ability Grouping*. The indictment was reiterated and made specific to middle school reform in the department's *Magic in the Middle*, published in 1993:

> Research delineating the harm of rigid ability grouping and tracking on student achievement, student self-esteem and self-efficacy, and school climate is now well established. Most critically, as students are grouped, they experience increasingly distinct levels of access to valued knowledge. Because the effects of tracking are cumulative and because ability grouping in the elementary grades is widespread, differences in achievement may appear dramatic by the middle grades and may seem to justify grouping whole classes by perceived ability.[45]

Later the document recites the claim that disparities in racial achievement can be traced to tracking: "The decline in overall achievement and the widening of test score gaps between white students and their African-American and Latino peers suggest that middle grade students are not equally exposed to the enriched, meaningful curriculum and instruction that will develop the knowledge and skills that they need to succeed."[46]

For several years, I have been conducting a study of how tracking reform is implemented in middle schools. A large number of middle schools in Massachusetts have indeed followed the state policy and eliminated many of their ability-grouped classes. But has detracking been good or bad for these schools' students? It is too early to tell. Since my study concentrates on implementation questions, not whether tracking is good or bad, it does not attempt to answer this question. It does, however, pinpoint characteristics of school policies that future studies of tracking's effects should take into account and suggests that it will be just as difficult to gauge the effects of detracking as it has been to gauge the effects of tracking. Of the several hundred schools I have surveyed and the twenty-nine schools I have visited in two states (California is the other state in the study), only a handful are totally untracked, and these schools are atypical in size, enrolling small numbers of students. In addition, tracking policy varies inside schools. Mathematics courses are almost always differentiated by level of difficulty, with the highest achieving eighth graders enrolled in an algebra course (or occasionally geometry), while English departments are more likely to have warmly embraced heterogeneous grouping. And even in schools attempting to detrack, de facto tracking surfaces through the tendency of high-achieving and low-achieving students to enroll in different electives. That is, higher-achieving students enroll more frequently in foreign language and music classes and low-achieving students in shop, home economics, and physical education classes. The constraints of scheduling students into classes then place students with the same electives into many of the same classes during the day. Consequently, teachers at untracked schools may refer to third period as their ''high class'' and to fifth period as their ''low class,'' although both classes are intended to be heterogeneous in composition. Researchers must carefully scrutinize the policies of the schools they are studying because strategies for grouping students are exceedingly complex. Different policies may be found within the same institution, and no two schools exhibit identical policies or practices.[47]

Tracking researchers are not completely in the dark, but those who recommend detracking—and they are by far the dominant camp among researchers writing on the topic—have not yet identified a large number of schools exhibiting the policy they support, let alone produced empirical evidence documenting success with the policy. The literature on detracking is overwhelmingly anecdotal, and most of the schools in this literature are in transit—in the process of detracking or engaged in incremental reform.[48]

With such profound limitations on the research, why have policy-makers decided to act in the face of insufficient evidence? The short answer is found in the dramatic charges that have been lodged against tracking. With tracking portrayed as an institutionalized form of racism, as a vile artifact of education's historical mistreatment of poor students and students of color, policymakers are willing to forgo solid evidence that detracking will produce educational benefits. The question of whether tracking exacerbates inequities is a valid and important question to be investigated, but the mixed evidence heretofore produced on this question is unsatisfying to reformers. And the absence of evidence on detracking's effects—that it will close the racial achievement gap, have no effect, or perhaps widen the gap further—gives tracking reformers no other option than to restate the indictment of tracking again and again, each time in stronger language. Policy advocacy is largely the art of defining problems and proposing solutions. Tracking reformers have emphasized the former and ignored the latter, or more accurately, offered the latter as assumed. Tracking is bad, therefore getting rid of it will be good.

There are consequences when policy is informed by research in this manner. First, an untested solution has been adopted based on the sheer force of a problem's presentation. No one knows the impact of detracking; its adoption into policy is a gamble. There are apparent risks. At least one study has detected an achievement loss when students are grouped into heterogeneous algebra classes, and another study indicates that high-ability students lose more from detracking than low-ability students gain.[49] Second, and this again refers to data from the study I am conducting in Massachusetts middle schools, the risks associated with this policy gamble are being disproportionately shouldered by schools serving poor, low-achieving students. Urban schools are much more likely to have embraced detracking than suburban schools. Schools serving wealthier students and schools with high achievement choose to continue with ability grouping; they are resisting tracking reform.[50]

Schools with students who allegedly have been victimized by tracking have rushed to abolish the condemned practice. If detracking turns out to be a bust, students who are most in need of real solutions to the problems of low achievement will suffer the consequences. Moreover, even if the more likely scenario unfolds where the effects of detracking are ambiguous or difficult to pin down, schools primarily serving urban students will have been further differentiated from their suburban counterparts. The tracked schools of wealthy communities and untracked schools of poor communities will offer a qualitatively different curriculum to their students, without any guarantee that students in the latter schools have been freed of the dead-end curriculum that constrains their learning.

Conclusion

An ideal process of educational reform, in which research is converted into policy and then policy drives productive change, has been undermined by the fundamental limitations of both research and policy. Educational research suffers from methodological constraints and low stature in the academic community, closing off traditional routes to legitimation. And because educational research is inherently contingent—as a result of the fundamentally contingent nature of learning—it strains to inform either practice or policy. Policy's power is also circumscribed. It is notoriously incapable of affecting the activities of the system it governs.

These limitations are evident when scientific evidence is too weak to justify the adoption or mandating of reforms. New policies satisfy the mutual interests of researchers and policymakers. Researchers gain legitimacy when their theories are adopted into policy, and policymakers can claim that their ideas are backed by research. Evidentiary shortfalls may be overlooked or the findings of research exaggerated, therefore, when reforms help researchers and policymakers stamp their preferences on policy. These preferences frequently contain ideological assumptions or administrative ambitions—and they ramify in an ideological or administrative impact on education.

Theodore J. Lowi observed that the form of politics generated by policy proposals is shaped by the proposals' underlying objectives, especially as they affect the distribution or redistribution of resources.[51] I am arguing that a particular species of education policies—those promoting reform—frequently fall short of scientific justification and that these evidentiary shortfalls manifest themselves later in the policymaking process. In the case of California's instructional reforms, the shortfall appears in an unprecedented level of prescriptiveness for the documents in which the reforms were presented. Intuitively, this makes sense. To implement productive reforms (assuming for a moment that agreement can be reached on desired outcomes), such heavy-handedness would be necessary only in the unlikely event that the reforms reaped educational benefits that were somehow mysteriously hidden from practitioners or, in a more likely scenario, if the reforms exacted costs that practitioners were aware of, but policymakers were not.

In the case of Massachusetts's tracking reforms, the impact can be seen in implementation. The pattern of schools complying with and resisting the state's detracking initiative is definitely nonrandom. This indicates that local policymakers have found the political advocacy on the issue persuasive, specifically, the assertion that detracking will help students of low socioeconomic status and students of color—despite the lack of research verifying this claim. The intrusiveness of California's policy is absent here; the primacy of local control is deeply ingrained in Massachusetts's political culture. But the state's clout still matters in terms of local flexibility. After a few years of experimentation, schools discovering that detracking is not helping their students will be forced into repudiating not only the state's position on the issue, but also the local constituencies allied with that position.

How can the entire process—the amalgamation of research, policy, and change—be moved onto firmer ground, closer to the reform ideal? One way is to appeal for the honest appraisal of evidence and the balanced reporting of research in policymaking. This is an excellent recommendation, but the analysis presented here suggests that barriers are set as deeply in the architecture of reform as in the fallibility of people's intentions. I have focused on state reforms, showing how state policies exacerbate the problem of interpreting research fairly and accurately. If I am right about what drives this distortion—the manner in which research is brought into the educational system—then the great machinery of reform itself is in need of reform.

A good start would be to rethink which levels of the system should have responsibility for various educational functions. Although decentralized policymaking is not always preferable to policymaking that is centralized, policies governing teachers' instructional methods and the scheduling of students into specific classes are poor candidates for centralized control. A system where central officials read and interpret the research on these topics so that they may incorporate relevant findings into policy inherently divorces research from the activities that it seeks to improve. Currently, practitioners read neither research nor policy. No wonder, then, that when things go wrong, which they frequently do, the most common explanation by both researchers and policymakers is, "That's not what we meant." Pushing authority over these matters down to schools and classrooms, opening up avenues for principals and teachers to acquire research, and then holding educators accountable for results would not guarantee that the integrity of research is maintained, but it would relieve some of the pressure for its misuse.

Instructional Policy

Teachers' beliefs are contestable; their power over implementing instructional policy is not. Instruction is conducted by teachers, so if you contend that something is wrong with contemporary instruction, then you are contending that something is wrong with contemporary teachers. To correct the teacher problem, the 1992 California math framework cranks up the administrative machinery for regulating classrooms, distorting research in the process.

Invoking a rigorous burden of proof for all state-initiated reforms is sensible, but for instructional reforms, the threshold should be extraordinarily high. A reasonable criterion for state intervention is the presence of demonstrable harm. Unless evidence exists that a current teaching practice is inherently harmful—truly harmful, not just out of fashion—then the state has no business making instructional policy. Decisions about how to teach should be made by those closest to classrooms, where the myriad influences on instruction can be taken into account. Teachers, informed by research and in consultation with parents, school principals, and other local personnel, are in the best position to select the most effective strategies for teaching the children in their classrooms. In the end, teachers are the ones who instruct, not politicians, bureaucrats, or university researchers. If policy intends to help teachers who are incapable of effective instruction, state proclamations will not likely provide much assistance. If inept teachers are the rule, the state's energies would be better directed toward reforming its teacher credentialing system so that it only places people who can make wise instructional choices into classrooms.

So restrained, the state could still perform a valuable function, providing schools with the latest studies on various instructional techniques, serving as a clearinghouse for the latest theories and research on instruction. But state policymakers must guard against bias in disseminating findings. They should not, in other words, sift through the literature and deem some forms of instruction "best practice." The term is misleading in conveying the idea that there is a universal best practice or even a best practice for the majority of teachers and students. In characterizing the problem of aggregation, where remedies at the microlevel do not add up to a single, all-encompassing macrolevel solution, Thomas F. Green makes the point perfectly:

> Public policy is a crude instrument for securing social ideals. We would not use a drop-forge to quarter a pound of butter or an axe to perform heart surgery. Public policy is the drop-forge or the axe of social change. It is not the knife or scalpel.[52]

Changes in instructional regimes may also mask significant changes in educational philosophy, especially in stipulating the ends of education, the knowledge and skills that students will acquire in school. Only a decade before the 1992 math framework's adoption, the dominant instructional program in California was Madeline Hunter's teaching theories, a model stressing tightly organized lessons that favored basic skills instruction. A decade later, basic skills were out and problem solving was in, and a whole new set of teaching techniques became "best practice." What had changed was not the definition of good teaching, but state policymakers' ideas on the desired ends of schooling. Educational ends should be decided by political processes, with competing notions of valued knowledge deliberated in democratic forums, not decided by experts. These ends must be openly stated and subjected to rigorous debate—allowing parents a role in deciding what their children will learn, and the public a voice in the educational enterprise it will finance and support.

Tracking Policy

The tracking debate swarms with ideological charges—the claim that tracking leads to inequities, the pitting of egalitarianism against excellence, the notion that high-achieving or low-achieving students are harmed under different grouping practices. Many of the questions in the debate raise questions of philosophy—is it right or wrong, for instance, to teach children of the same age at the same school a different curriculum—so to be squeamish about ideology in the tracking debate is a bit foolish. Ideological positions can be scrutinized for such things as consistency in logic and the values they endorse, but another century of research will not settle such questions empirically.

A batch of questions sitting at the center of the tracking debate can be investigated empirically, however, and it is deadening to the debate and dangerous for the crafting of public policy when these questions are swept aside by disinformation. Whether students of color achieve more in tracked or untracked schools is an important question, but as of now, the answer is unclear. Whether low-achieving students—high school students who are struggling with basic mathematics or who cannot read simple sentences—will benefit from heterogeneously grouped classes is also unknown. And whether high-achieving students will achieve just as much when AP English classes are abolished and high achievers are placed in heterogeneously grouped classes remains a mystery. The misuse of research occurs when these questions are presented as closed issues in the tracking literature or dismissed cavalierly by policymakers, all in a campaign to sell detracking to local communities.

Here the old admonition to honestly report all of the evidence is emphatically germane. Polls show that teachers and parents overwhelmingly support ability grouping in schools, and in surveys conducted by the Public Agenda Foundation, African American parents are just as supportive as white parents. If researchers or policymakers wish to convince parents and teachers that they are wrong on this issue, they must do so with solid evidence and reasoned argument. They must also separate out genuine issues of belief and ideology from claims that are verifiable—and come clean on the questions that the evidence cannot answer.[53]

The general principle of governance laid out above applies to this issue. State officials have no business getting involved in how schools group their students unless convincing evidence of harm is found—evidence, for instance, that school officials are using tracking for the purpose of segregating students by race, class, gender, or some other educationally irrelevant characteristic. Although the state of Massachusetts should be commended for presenting detracking as a recommendation, not a mandate, the zealotry that inevitably creeps into policy advisories is present in its tracking documents. Unfortunately, the urge to confer the state's blessings on a favored cause frequently smothers the duty to provide schools with fair and accurate information.

A rethinking of the state's advisory role on school policies is in order, with research thought of as a resource that, like any other resource, should be distributed equitably and fairly to schools. Ideally, the state would supply schools with reliable information so that they could make informed decisions about ability grouping, each school adopting policies that make sense for its own teachers and students. The state would not view itself as the arbiter of research nor as the advocate of one side or the other in policy debates, whether about tracking or any other instructional issue that appropriately should be resolved by the school, not the state. Schools would assume responsibility for educational outcomes and seek out the best information to help them attain their goals.

Are local school people intrinsically more truthful than state policymakers or endowed with special powers to smell out faulty research? Of course not. Teachers and school principals are just as human as state policymakers and academic researchers; on occasion, they, too, will read scientific evidence selectively, blindly follow ideological biases, impose dubious policies on constituents, and make a terrible mess of things. It is precisely because education is populated by human beings with human foibles, however, that policymaking must be pushed down to the lowest possible level in the system—to the level at which policy coexists with the activity that accomplishes policy's ends. Instruction takes place in classrooms and the grouping of students in schools. That is where instructional reform and tracking reform should be decided. Here policy can be quickly modified or completely overhauled when mismatches occur, when the wrong policy is put in place for the context it serves.[54]

My recommendations would open up the reform process by restraining state involvement on issues that should be decided at school sites and by breaking up researchers' and policymakers' monopoly over new knowledge. Power and knowledge are intertwined. As schools gain greater control over their teaching and learning activities, they would become, I believe, more discriminating consumers of educational research. Progressive educationists have presented forceful critiques of

teacher-proof curriculum that "deskills" teachers and of school organizational cultures that destroy autonomy through their "contradictions
of control."[55] The reforms examined here show, however, that such
indignities are not solely the product of old-fashioned curricula, tradi-
tionalist instruction, or hierarchical bureaucracies. They can arise just
as surely from progressive reforms. So while putting power to decide
instructional and grouping practices back in the hands of practitioners
will guarantee the triumph of neither progressivism nor traditionalism,
it may take a small step toward attaining the ideal of converting the
discoveries of research into meaningful school reform.

Comment by Helen F. Ladd

Tom Loveless uses examples from California and Massachusetts to
illustrate structural problems in the relationships among educational
research, policy, and practice. By focusing on how policies are implemented, he draws attention to the "alienation of research from practice" and argues for changes in governance to counter the structural
problems inherent in the current relationships. Of interest to me is the
basic structure of his four-part argument.

First, the incentives faced by educational researchers generate a
problem for policy and practice. In light of the low quality of the
research and the inability of educational researchers to gain recognition
and prestige through the normal route of high-quality research, Loveless
argues that they try to legitimate their research by showing that it
influences policy. In the process, they fail to emphasize appropriately
all its qualifications and limitations. Loveless views this situation as a
structural problem that cannot be overcome simply by encouraging
more honest research.

Second, educational policymakers also face inappropriate incentives.
While Loveless's illustrations refer primarily to state policy, his argument would not rule out its applicability to the district level as well.
Policymakers, argues Loveless, often understand the limitations of policy—and the research on which it is based—but become advocates for
various policies largely because of the continuous public pressure to
reform American education.

   Third, the combination of flawed incentives for education researchers and educational policymakers renders potentially harmful state policy that tries to dictate what should go on in the schools. As illustrated by his two examples—the change to child-centered learning in California and the shift to detracking of students in Massachusetts—attempts to do so can be harmful for children.

   Fourth, the solution to the structural flaws related to the interaction between research and policymaking is to keep policymakers from intervening into certain areas of schooling, particularly those related to instructional policy. Loveless argues that, unless a teaching practice is inherently harmful, the state should not be making instructional policy. That is, full authority over instruction should be given to those who provide instruction, namely the principal and teachers in the school.

   While interesting and provocative, the paper also is unsatisfying. In particular, the conclusion about the desirability of decentralized governance—to which I am sympathetic, provided appropriate safeguards are installed—follows not so much from the analysis but rather from Loveless's initial assertion that state policymakers should not try to affect what goes on in the classroom. That is a remarkable assertion given that the only way to change student outcomes is to change what gets taught and how.

   One can imagine models of policymaking structures that would place full responsibility for instructional decisionmaking at the school level. For example, if state policymakers provided clear state standards, guaranteed adequate resources and support to the schools, and held schools accountable for student performance, a strong case could be made for the state to leave the schools free to decide how best to meet the standards. If this model underlies Loveless's discussion, it deserves to be highlighted.

   Implicit in his argument seems to be the view that because states cannot directly influence what goes on in the classroom, they should not try to do so. But that is a strange way to think about policy and I cannot believe he means to say that. The extensive economics literature on the principal-agent problem directly addresses this issue. In that literature, the principals, like the state policymakers, are trying to change outcomes but must work indirectly through the agents—in this case, the schools—to accomplish their goals. Clearly that can sometimes be a challenge, especially when the goals of the agents differ markedly from those of the principals. The bottom line from that literature is the need for appropriate incentive structures. In the case of education, that might mean that state policymakers would try to change educational practice by redefining educational outcomes and, through some mechanism, hold schools accountable for those outcomes. Hence, lack of direct control need not rule out a state interest in trying to affect what goes on in the classroom.

His position appears also to be based on the view that a stable production function for education does not exist. Given that, the best researchers and policymakers can do is to take account of the effect of context on the relationship between inputs and outputs. That these contexts vary so much from school to school renders it inappropriate for state policymakers to determine best practice and to try to impose it everywhere in the state. This argument rests on relatively firm ground and could, with certain qualifications, lead to Loveless's policy recommendation, namely that local schools should be free to determine what instructional practices work best for them.

But at this point the analysis gets fuzzy. Will policy made at the school level on average be better than policy made at the state level? Presumably there are trade-offs. Experience with decentralization in the Chicago school system and elsewhere suggests that one-third of the schools will make good decisions and do better than with more centralized control, one-third will do no better, and one-third will make bad decisions. Is that better or worse than the outcome that would occur with state-level policymaking? It is hard to say without more analysis.

Loveless would probably respond that the flawed relationship between research and policymaking suggests that the outcome in the decentralized form of governance is likely to dominate the outcome with state policymaking. In the decentralized system, state policymakers would have an incentive to promote objective research that was context-specific so that the local schools would have good information on which to base their decisions. While such an argument has some superficial appeal, it requires some strong assumptions about the availability of information to the local schools and their capacity to use it, assumptions that are not addressed in the paper.

Given the limitations of education research, what should its role be in policy formation? It may be instructive to consider a different example of research—that which explores the relationship between class size and student performance. Whether Loveless would include the promulgation of smaller class sizes in the set of proscribed policies for state policymakers is unclear. Ultimately many policies have some impact on what goes on in the classroom. Does that mean all should be eliminated from the state policymaker's tool kit? If the state decision about class sizes were motivated by a desire to change the dynamics in the classroom, then it would seem to fit into his list of policies that the state should delegate to the local schools. However, the argument that the decision about class sizes should be left fully to the schools rings hollow given how little control schools have over the resources available to them.

What, if anything, is known about the effects of class size on student performance and what does this research imply for policy? Some people, including Eric A. Hanushek, would say that little or no evidence indicates that smaller class sizes increase learning.[56] Hence, Hanushek would argue that state policymakers may have wasted significant resources as they decreased student-to-teacher ratios (Hanushek's proxy for class size) significantly over the last twenty-five years. Hanushek would base that conclusion on his various surveys of the empirical literature on educational production functions that generate no clear patterns of effects. Results from the eighth grade Third International Mathematics and Science Study (TIMSS) would seem to confirm his conclusion. Students in countries with high test scores, such as Korea, are often in classes of forty or more students. Moreover, within such countries, students in the larger classes typically do better than the ones in the smaller classes.

However, given the large cultural differences across countries, care must be taken in drawing inferences for the United States from international comparisons. In addition, other researchers would disagree with Hanushek's conclusion from the U.S. studies. For example, using the same data but a more refined technique of meta-analysis, Larry V. Hedges, Richard D. Laine, and Rob Greenwald find more significant effects of class size on student performance.[57] And in our detailed study of Alabama data, Ronald Ferguson and I found that reducing class sizes from the high twenties to the low twenties for fourth graders appears to improve student learning, especially in math.[58] This study differs from many other studies in that it is based on data for one state, it uses a measure of true class size that is more appropriate than the more commonly used student-to-teacher ratio, and we based our conclusions on a value-added model estimated from longitudinally matched student data.

The best research on this topic is based on Tennessee's Student/ Teacher Achievement Ratio (STAR) project, a controlled experiment to determine how class size affects student achievement in grades K–3. Most people conclude that the study shows that small classes positively influence pupil performance in the early grades and that these effects persist over time.[59] However, this may be tempered with Richard J. Murnane and Frank Levy's note in *Does Money Matter?* in which they describe fifteen schools in Austin, Texas, that received additional funding for, among other things, reductions in class size.[60] Of the fifteen, only two of the schools improved their performance. Those two schools not only reduced class sizes but also made other changes, most notably getting parents more involved and changing the mode of instruction in the classroom. That is, while the funding for smaller class sizes was important in that it facilitated these other changes, it did not by itself lead to greater student learning.

So what should policymakers do with these somewhat mixed research results? Loveless likely would conclude that state policymakers should not require all schools to have small class sizes. While the Ferguson and Ladd results suggest that reducing class size in a state such as Alabama might increase average student learning even in the absence of an additional policy thrust to change the mode of instruction, the Levy and Murnane study suggests that some of that money on reduced class size will undoubtedly be wasted.

Does this mean that the state (or district) should simply have no policy with respect to class size and, instead, should let schools decide for themselves how big their classes should be? I think not, because of the resource problem. Smaller class sizes are expensive. For example, reducing class sizes from thirty to twenty students requires a 50 percent increase in the number of teachers, an increase that most schools could not afford.

So what is the bottom line for research and policy on such an issue? Here is one possible answer: State (or district) policymakers should use the research on the relationship between class size and performance as one of the inputs into the decision about the most desirable class size in the state or the district. (Other arguments for smaller class size may be related less to student performance and more to the quality of the environment for children.) For illustrative purposes, assume they decide on a class size of twenty students in elementary schools. The state could then use this class size in determining the basic foundation level of resources needed to educate children in each school. Once the schools have the resources to offer class sizes of twenty students, I would support Loveless's recommendation that the schools be given the authority to allocate their teachers in ways most suitable given their educational goals. In other words, I support Loveless's call for a change in governance that would give more authority to the schools to make decisions about instructional practice, but only with the provision that adequate funding be made available to the individual schools so that their choices are meaningful.

Comment by Cecilia Rouse

Tom Loveless develops a challenging critique of the current relationship among research, policy, and reform that is sure to catch the attention of many people interested in education policy.

Loveless begins from the premise that the current state of educational research is tenuous because it lacks legitimacy. While I would largely agree with him, the question arises as to whether this is inherent or a reflection of the way that research has been conducted up until now. I would argue that education research is not inherently unscientific, but that well-designed randomized experiments in education are about as convincing as they are in other fields, such as medicine.

Consider the prevalence of experiments in medicine and education. In medicine, randomized trials have become the standard (although observational research is still used for questions that could not ethically be answered with experiments). Meanwhile, many fewer trials have been conducted in education, but not because education does not lend itself to experimental evaluation, because of, say, ethical issues. Ethical dilemmas surely exist in medical research.

One important difference between medical and educational researchers is that the medical community has collectively decided (or reluctantly accepted) that, for procedures and drugs to be accepted, they must be rigorously studied. Similar standards could hold in education. The first step would be to accept that many resources are scarce and to take advantage of this fact to learn more about the policy in question. When resources are scarce and must be allocated, why not use randomization as a form of allocation? For example, for many charter and magnet schools, if a school is oversubscribed, students are currently randomly selected. This provides an opportunity to generate credible estimates of the effectiveness of the program. The analysis must be conducted carefully, but these naturally occurring situations provide fertile ground to provide lessons about charter schools, magnet schools, and other educational reforms.

A second important difference between medical and educational research is that the United States has not put the resources behind educational research endeavors. For example, the annual budget of the National Institutes of Health (NIH) is approximately $12 billion, compared with the $600 million annual budget of the research arm of the Department of Education. While this comparison is not entirely fair because the NIH budget covers more than research, the annual budget for acquired immune deficiency syndrome (AIDS) research alone is $1.5 billion.[61] For a fraction of the money spent on medical trials, educational trials could be run that would generate more compelling results than those currently available. The best evidence of the achievement effects of smaller class sizes comes from the Tennessee class size experiment, which cost approximately $12 million over four years.[62] Similarly, some of the best evidence on labor market training programs has come from randomized demonstration projects.

Another complaint may be that many other factors affect student learning, not just the treatment being studied; that is, the effectiveness of the policy is case-specific. This is true, so large numbers of participating students and teachers are needed to detect if, on average, the policy can make a difference. Even the best policies may not help all students. This is certainly true in medicine. Take the example of protein inhibitors, which have miraculous results for some patients who tested positive for HIV (human immunodeficiency virus), which causes AIDS, and does nothing for others. This does not stop policy from being developed in medicine. Instead, the caveats are understood.

A recent re-analysis of the Tennessee class size experiment shows that not all students gained from being in the smaller classes. Some of this is the result of sampling variability and some of heterogeneous treatment effects. And yet, on average, students in the smaller classes in Tennessee performed better. Would this result hold in other settings? The answer is unknown, which is why conducting other such experiments is important. Future research could also address why smaller classes make a difference. Do teachers pay more attention to students? Or, do teachers teach differently with a small class? The important point is that educational research is not inherently unscientific if the political will exists to fund credible evaluations. That a reform may not affect all children similarly underscores the importance of allowing teachers and parents to have the final say (or at least significant influence) as to which reforms their school or district should adopt.

A second point that Loveless highlights is that policy, such as untracking schools, is being made based on mixed evidence. This makes educational policy just like all other policies. For example, many would argue that the minimum wage is an ineffective way to increase the earnings of low-wage workers, and yet Congress raised the minimum wage in 1996. Similar policies regarding welfare, health care, social security, and immigration are also made. Policies banning smoking in enclosed public places were in place before conclusive evidence on the health effects of secondhand smoke had been established. Sometimes policies have to be made more on faith rather than waiting for conclusive evidence. It is useful to consider whether education policy is unique or if this critique holds up in all policy arenas.

Neither case study Loveless presented was entirely convincing and to-the-point. He seems to argue that the curriculum frameworks adopted by California in 1987 and 1992 caused the relative decline in National Assessment of Educational Progress (NAEP) scores. This assertion suggests that conclusive evidence is available on the effectiveness (or ineffectiveness) of the curriculum frameworks, which he previously argued rarely exists with educational research. Pinning the decline in NAEP scores on the curricular changes seems particularly premature for two reasons. First, he alludes to the possibility that not all teachers and schools implemented the curricular changes. If the curricular changes were not implemented, then they cannot be responsible for the decline in NAEP scores. Second, California had major changes in school financing during the same time period that would make it difficult to separately assess which school policy was at fault without a careful empirical investigation.

In Massachusetts's rejection of tracking students, Loveless argues that detracking is harmful to students. However, the best evidence on tracking suggests that students in heterogeneous classes learn about as much as those in tracked classes. Loveless argues that only traditional policies that have been shown to be downright harmful should be replaced as state-initiated reforms. However, this standard places far too much faith in the status quo. For example, he writes that in the inner-city schools, which have attempted to abolish all tracking, the students could end up the big losers. However, many would argue that the status quo is not working with these students, so a new educational approach should be tried. This argument becomes more compelling when combined with other reasons, such as equity.

Finally, I agree with Loveless's assessment that policies designed to control what teachers do in the classroom are destined to fail in the United States. Given that the United States has one of the most decentralized educational systems in the world and that many families choose where to live based on the schools and therefore believe and desire to have direct influence over their children's education, attempting to control what happens in the classroom is futile. More important, top-down initiatives may not be appropriate for every school, every classroom. At the same time, an international comparison of state control over curriculum, and so on, would be of interest. I have the impression that, in most other countries, the (federal) government has even more control over the classroom than does the state in the United States. And yet, whenever the performance of the American educational system is negatively compared with other (primarily) Western countries and the need is expressed for national standards and the like, a call is not heard for more centralization. Can state control over the classroom not work inherently or merely in the U.S. context?

Notes

1. Joseph Ben–David, *The Scientist's Role in Society: A Comparative Study* (Englewood Cliffs, N.J.: Prentice-Hall, 1971).

2. Daniel J. Wilson, *Science, Community, and the Transformation of American Philosophy, 1860–1930* (University of Chicago Press, 1990); and Andrew D. Abbott, *The System of Professions: An Essay on the Division of Expert Labor* (University of Chicago Press, 1988).

3. Geraldine Joncich Clifford and James W. Guthrie, *Ed School: A Brief for Professional Education* (University of Chicago Press, 1988); and Ellen Condliffe Lagemann, *Contested Terrain: A History of Education Research in the United States, 1890–1990* (Chicago: Spencer Foundation, October 1996).

4. Experimental research is conducted in education, but it constitutes a minuscule amount of the published research in the field. F. Mosteller, R. J. Light, and J. A. Sachs found only ten experimental studies of between-class ability grouping and three of within-class ability grouping in their review of the research, out of several hundred scholarly publications on tracking in the last century. See F. Mosteller, R. J. Light, and J. A. Sachs, "Sustained Inquiry in Education: Lessons from Skill Grouping and Class Size," *Harvard Educational Review*, vol. 66 (Winter 1996), pp. 797–842.

5. Implications of social science's methodological limitations for policy are discussed in Lee Sechrest, "Social Science and Social Policy: Will Our Numbers Ever Be Good Enough," in R. Lance Shotland and Melvin M. Mark, eds., *Social Science and Social Policy* (Beverly Hills, Calif.: Sage Publications, 1985), pp. 69–95. How policymakers incorporate research findings into their decisions is explored in Carol H. Weiss, *Social Science Research and Decision-Making* (Columbia University Press, 1980). Pertaining to research on reading curriculum, Judith A. Langer and Richard Allington conclude: "We know a good deal about reading and writing in general, but the paucity of curriculum research in these domains is astounding. The kinds of studies that address what needs to be taught to whom, under what conditions, and in response to what impetus or sequence have yet to be undertaken. Such studies will need to be complex, taking into account all we know about the social and contextual and cognitive factors that interact with curriculum." Judith A. Langer and Richard Allington, "Curriculum Research in Writing and Reading," in P. W. Jackson, ed., *Handbook of Research on Curriculum*, pp. 687–725 (Macmillan, 1992).

6. Milbrey W. McLaughlin and Joan E. Talbert, "How the World of Students and Teachers Challenges Policy Coherence," in Susan H. Fuhrman, ed., *Designing Coherent Education Policy: Improving the System* (Jossey-Bass, 1993), pp. 220–50.

7. Rebecca Barr and Robert Dreeben, *How Schools Work* (University of Chicago Press, 1983).

8. See Ernest R. House, "A Framework for Appraising Educational Reform," *Educational Researcher*, vol. 25 (October 1996), pp. 6–14. House presents transaction-cost economics as an alternative to the production function perspective that better captures school processes.

9. Richard F. Elmore, "Organizational Models of Social Program Implementation," *Public Policy*, vol. 26 (Spring 1978), 185–228; and Milbrey Wallin McLaughlin, "Implementation Realities and Evaluation Design," in R. Lance Shotland and Melvin M. Mark, eds., *Social Science and Social Policy* (Beverly Hills, Calif.: Sage Publications, 1985), pp. 96–120.

10. Drew Lindsay, "States Take Aim at Regulatory Beast: School Codes," *Education Week*, February 8, 1995, p. 1; and Lonnie Harp, "Michigan Education Code Overhaul Shifts Power," *Education Week*, January 10, 1996, p. 20. For a general description of the legalization of education, see Arthur E. Wise, *Legislated Learning: The Bureaucratization of the American Classroom*, (University of California Press, 1979).

11. Jacqueline P. Danzberger, Michael Kirst, and Michael D. Usdan, *Governing Public Schools: New Times, New Requirements* (Washington: Institute for Educational Leadership, 1992).

12. Susan H. Fuhrman, "The Politics of Coherence," in Susan H. Fuhrman, ed., *Designing Coherent Education Policy* (Jossey-Bass, 1993), pp. 1–34.

13. David B. Tyack and Larry Cuban, *Tinkering toward Utopia: A Century of Public School Reform* (Harvard University Press, 1995).

14. John E. Chubb and Terry M. Moe, *Politics, Markets, and America's Schools* (Brookings, 1990). The classic study of teaching as an occupation is Dan C. Lortie, *Schoolteacher: A Sociological Study* (University of Chicago Press, 1975).

15. Richard A. Gibboney, *The Stone Trumpet: A Story of Practical School Reform, 1960–1990* (Albany, N.Y.: State University of New York Press, 1994). See also Stanley Pogrow, "Reforming the Wannabe Reformers: Why Education Reforms Almost Always End Up Making Things Worse," *Phi Delta Kappan*, vol. 77 (June 1996), pp. 656–63.

16. Andrew Gitlin and Frank Margonis, "The Political Aspect of Reform: Teacher Resistance as Good Sense," *American Journal of Education*, vol. 103 (August 1995), pp. 377–405. For a lively debate on the costs and benefits of Reading Recovery, an early intervention reading program, see Elfrida H. Hiebert, "Reading Recovery in the United States: What Difference Does It Make to an Age Cohort?," *Educational Researcher*, vol. 23 (December 1994), pp. 15–25; Gay Su Pinnell, Carol Lyons, and Noel Jones, "Response to Hiebert: What Difference Does Reading Recovery Make?," *Educational Researcher*, vol. 25 (October 1996), pp. 23–25; and Elfrida H. Hiebert, "Revisiting the Question: What Difference Does Reading Recovery Make to an Age Cohort?," *Educational Researcher*, vol. 25 (October 1996), pp. 26–28.

17. California's two thousand bills is reported in Lindsay, "States Take Aim at Regulatory Beast." The estimate of 100,000 articles comes from Derek Bok, "The Challenge to Schools of Education," *Harvard Magazine* (May/June 1987), p. 52, cited in Richard A. Gibboney, "The Unscientific Character of Educational Research," *Phi Delta Kappan*, vol. 71, no. 3 (November 1989), pp. 225–27.

18. For an account of the rise and fall of progressivism in the 1960s and 1970s, see Diane Ravitch, *The Troubled Crusade: American Education, 1945–1980* (Basic Books, 1983).

19. How advocacy for progressive education has distorted research findings, including the research on discovery learning, is documented and discussed in E. D. Hirsch, Jr., *The Schools We Need and Why We Don't Have Them* (Doubleday, 1996), chapter 5.

20. Alan H. Schoenfeld, "What Do We Know about Mathematics Curricula?," *Journal of Mathematical Behavior*, vol. 13, (March 1994), pp. 55–80. Schoenfeld served on both the 1992 California Mathematics Framework Committee and the 1995 California Mathematics Task Force. He argues that there may be several routes to becoming proficient at solving complex problems, then adds, "But the question of which skills are necessary, to what degree of competency, and what kinds of problems will be caused if students are weak at them, is very much open." Quote on p. 61.

21. California State Department of Education, *English-Language Arts Framework for California Public Schools: Kindergarten through Grade Twelve* (Sacramento, Calif., 1987), p. 2.

22. Ibid., p. 16

23. California State Department of Education, *Mathematics Framework for California Public Schools: Kindergarten through Grade Twelve* (Sacramento, Calif., 1992), p. 2.

24. Ibid., p. 3.

25. Ibid., pp. 40–41.

26. Ibid., p. 41.

27. Ibid., p. 49.

28. David Tyack, Thomas James, and Aaron Benavot, *Law and the Shaping of Public Education, 1785–1954* (University of Wisconsin Press, 1987); and California State Department of Education, *Social Studies Framework for the Public Schools of California, 1962* (Sacramento, Calif., 1962).

29. California State Department of Education, *Mathematics Framework for California Public Schools*, pp. 198–202.

30. Jill Stewart, "Why California Kids Can't Read," *Sacramento Bee*, March 24, 1996, Forum Section, pp. F1, 2.

31. California Department of Education, *Improving Mathematics Achievement for All California Students: The Report of the California Mathematics Task Force* (Sacramento, Calif., 1995); and California Department of Education, *Every Child a Reader: The Report of the California Reading Task Force* (Sacramento, Calif., 1995). For press accounts of the task force reports, see Richard Lee Colvin, "State's Reading, Math Reforms under Review as Scores Fall," *Los Angeles Times*, March 23, 1995, p. a-1; and Sharon L. Jones, "Reading Approach May Turn New Leaf: Task Force Will Urge Teaching Basic Skills," *San Diego Union-Tribune*, August 21, 1995, p. a-1.

32. Ken Chavez and Deborah Anderluh, "Wilson Approves Back to Basics Teaching Plan: Falling Test Scores Put End to State's Experiment with Newer Methods," *San Francisco Examiner*, October 12, 1995, p. a-6. The bill was dubbed the "ABC Bill," an acronym formed by the first letter of its three authors' last names. For earlier coverage of the bill, see Richard Lee Colvin, "School Goals Spelled Out in ABC Bill," *Los Angeles Times*, July 5, 1995, p. a-3.

33. Dan Walters, "Another Jolt on Education," *Sacramento Bee*, February 28, 1997, p. a-3.

34. For contrasting meta-analyses of tracking's effects, see C. C. Kulik and J. A. Kulik, "Effects of Ability Grouping on Secondary School Students: A Meta-Analysis of Evaluation Findings," *American Educational Research Journal*, vol. 19 (Fall 1982), pp. 415–28; and R. E. Slavin, "Achievement Effects of Ability Grouping in Secondary Schools: A Best Evidence Synthesis," *Review of Educational Research*, vol. 60 (Fall 1990), pp. 471–99.

35. Jeannie Oakes, *Keeping Track: How Schools Structure Inequality* (Yale University Press, 1985); and Claude S. Fischer and others, *Inequality by Design: Cracking the Bell Curve Myth* (Princeton University Press, 1996), pp. 163–67.

36. Adam Gamoran and Mark Berends, "The Effects of Stratification in Secondary Schools: Synthesis of Survey and Ethnographic Research," *Review of Educational Research*, vol. 57 (Winter 1987), pp. 415–35. For the inconclusive findings of experimental research on ability grouping, see Frederick Mosteller, Richard J. Light, and Jason A. Sachs, "Sustained Inquiry in Education: Lessons from Skill Grouping and Class

Size,'' *Harvard Educational Review,* vol. 66 (Winter 1996), pp. 797–842. Adam Gamoran also raises the issue of what tracking research has failed to measure in the way
of curriculum and instruction in ''Organization, Instruction, and the Effects of Ability
Grouping: Comment on Slavin's 'Best Evidence Synthesis,' '' *Review of Educational
Research,* vol. 57 (Fall 1987), pp. 341–45; and in Adam Gamoran, ''Measuring Curriculum Differentiation,'' *American Journal of Education,* vol. 97 (February 1989), pp.
129–43.

37. The benefits of ability grouping for high-achieving students are presented in J.
Kulik and C. C. Kulik, ''Meta-Analytic Findings on Grouping Programs,'' *Gifted Child
Quarterly,* vol. 36 (Spring 1992), pp. 73–77. For a discussion of the possibility that
low tracks can be reformed to ameliorate their harmful effects, see Adam Gamoran,
''Alternative Uses of Ability Grouping in Secondary Schools: Can We Bring High
Quality Instruction to Low–Ability Classes?'' *American Journal of Education,* vol. 102
(November 1993), pp. 1–22.

38. Oakes, *Keeping Track*; and J. L. Epstein and D. J. MacIver, *Opportunities to
Learn: Effects on Eighth Graders of Curriculum Offerings and Instructional Ap-
proaches,* Report No. 34 (Johns Hopkins Univerity, Center for Research on Effective
Schooling for Disadvantaged Students, July 1992).

39. Oakes, *Keeping Track,* p. 194.

40. Oakes, *Keeping Track,* pp. 63–64.

41. See D.-J. Brewer, D.-I. Rees, and L.-M. Argys, ''Detracking America's
Schools: The Reform without Cost?,'' *Phi Delta Kappan,* vol. 77 (November 1995),
pp. 210–15. The teachers in the National Educational Longitudinal Study (NELS) were
asked, ''Which of the following best describes the achievement level of the 8th [10th]
graders in this class compared with the average 8th [10th] grade student in the school?
Higher achievement levels, average achievement levels, lower achievement levels, or
widely differing achievement levels.'' Tenth grade teachers were also asked to identify
the track of their class—academic, advanced or honors, general, vocational/technical/
business, or other.

42. One of the rare tracking studies that includes measures of instruction is Adam
Gamoran and others, ''An Organizational Analysis of the Effects of Ability Grouping,''
American Educational Research Journal, vol. 32, no. 4 (Winter 1995), pp. 687–715.
An intriguing finding is that practices may have a differential impact in different tracks.
Authentic questioning by teachers and class discussion were positively correlated with
achievement in high-ability classes but negatively correlated in low-ability classes.

43. The kind of tracking reforms justified by research are debated by Maureen T.
Hallinan and Jeannie Oakes in ''Exchange,'' *Sociology of Education,* vol. 67 (April
1994), pp. 79–91.

44. Oakes, *Keeping Track*; and Anne Wheelock, *Crossing the Tracks: How Untracking Can Save America's Schools* (New Press, 1992).

45. Massachusetts Department of Education, *Magic in the Middle: A Focus on
Massachusetts Middle Grade Schools* (Boston, Mass., March 1993), pp. 5, 6. See also
Dan French and Sheldon Rothman, *Structuring Schools for Student Success: A Focus
on Ability Grouping* (Massachusetts Department of Education, Bureau of Research,
Planning, and Evaluation, January 1990).

46. Massachusetts Department of Education, *Magic in the Middle,* p. 20.

47. The book in progress is T. Loveless, *The Fate of Reform.* Research from the
California portion of the study is in T. Loveless, ''The Influence of Subject Areas on
Middle School Tracking Policies,'' in A. Pallas, ed., *Research in Sociology of Education*

and Socialization, vol. 10 (Greenwich, Conn.: JAI Press, 1994); and T. Loveless, "Parents, Professionals, and the Politics of Tracking Policy," in K. Wong, ed., *Advances in Educational Policy*, vol. 1, pp. 187–212 (Greenwich, Conn.: JAI Press, 1995).

48. Wheelock, *Crossing the Tracks*, provides dozens of examples of schools reforming their tracking practices.

49. Laura M. Argys, Daniel I. Rees, and Dominic J. Brewer, "Detracking America's Schools: Equity at Zero Cost?" *Journal of Policy Analysis and Management*, vol. 15 (Fall 1996), pp. 623–45. See also Brewer, Rees, and Argys, "Detracking America's Schools"; and Robert E. Slavin's criticisms of the research in R. E. Slavin, "Detracking and Its Detractors: Flawed Evidence, Flawed Values," *Phi Delta Kappan*, vol. 77 (November 1995), pp. 220–21. The study of ability-grouped algebra courses is Epstein and MacIver, *Opportunities to Learn*. Note that these studies use NELS data and possess the problems I have described in comparing tracked and untracked classes.

50. Loveless, *The Fate of Reform*.

51. T. Lowi, "American Business, Public Policy, Case Studies, and Political Theory," *World Politics*, vol. 16 (July 1964), pp. 677–715.

52. Thomas F. Green, "Excellence, Equity, and Equality," in Lee S. Shulman and Gary Sikes, eds., *Handbook of Teaching and Policy* (New York: Longman, 1983), pp. 318–41. Quote on p. 322.

53. Jean Johnson and John Immerwahr, *First Things First: What Americans Expect from the Public Schools* (New York: Public Agenda Foundation, 1994).

54. For an analytical model of school policymaking, see Carol H. Weiss, "The Four 'I's of School Reform: How Interests, Ideology, Information, and Institution Affect Teachers and Principals," *Harvard Educational Review*, vol. 65 (Winter 1995), pp. 571–92.

55. Michael W. Apple, *Teachers and Texts: A Political Economy of Class and Gender Relations in Education* (New York: Routledge and Kegan Paul, 1986); and Linda M. McNeil, *Contradictions of Control: School Structure and School Knowledge* (New York: Routledge and Kegan Paul, 1986).

56. Eric A. Hanushek, "School Resources and Student Performance," in Gary Burtless, ed., *Does Money Matter? The Effect of School Resources on Student Achievement and Adult Success*, pp. 43–73 (Brookings, 1996).

57. Larry V. Hedges, Richard D. Laine, and Rob Greenwald, "Does Money Matter? A Meta-Analysis of Studies of the Effects of Differential School Inputs on Student Outcomes," *Educational Researcher*, vol. 23, no. 3 (1994), pp. 5–14.

58. Helen F. Ladd and Ronald Ferguson, "How and Why Money Matters: An Analysis of Alabama Schools," in Helen F. Ladd, ed., *Holding Schools Accountable: Performance Based Reform in Education*, pp. 265–98 (Brookings, 1996).

59. Frederick Mosteller, "The Tennessee Study of Class Size in the Early School Grades," *Future of Children: Critical Issues for Children and Youths*, vol. 5 (Summer/Fall 1995), pp. 113–27; and Alan B. Krueger, "Experimental Estimates of Education Production Functions," Working Paper No. 379 (Princeton University Industrial Relations Section, 1997).

60. Richard J. Murnane and Frank Levy, "Evidence from Fifteen Schools in Austin, Texas," in Gary Burtless, ed., *Does Money Matter? The Effect of School Resources on Student Achievement and Adult Success*, pp. 93–96 (Brookings, 1996).

61. *Budget of the United States Government, Fiscal Year 1997*.

62. Alan B. Krueger, "Experimental Estimates of Education Production Functions," Working Paper No. 379 (Princeton University Industrial Relations Section, May 1997).

Standards outside the Classroom

LAURENCE STEINBERG

I N SOME CIRCLES, "standards" refers to expectations of student performance—the skills, knowledge, and competencies
students ought to be able to demonstrate once they have completed a
given course of study or a particular portion of their educational career.
In other circles, "standards" refers to expectations of educators—the
content of the curriculum, the quality of the pedagogy, and the nature
of the in- and out-of-class activities. And in still other circles, "standards" refers to expectations of educational institutions—the resources
they provide for students and teachers or what are sometimes called
school-delivery or opportunity to learn standards. Reasonable people
may disagree about which of these sets of standards should be the
centerpiece of standards-based education reform efforts—and on what
the specific standards in each of these domains ought to be—but the
emerging consensus is that well-articulated expectations for students,
teachers, and schools must be in place if the quality of student performance in America is to improve.

The nature and necessity of "classroom standards"—that is, expectations regarding student performance, curricular content, and opportunities to learn—should command the lion's share of attention in discussions of how to raise student achievement. What students achieve
must be determined in large measure by what youngsters are expected
to know and be able to do, what teachers are expected to teach, and
what schools are expected to provide to ensure that students and teachers fulfill these expectations.

A fourth set of standards has received far less attention in the national
debate over the future of American education: standards outside the

classroom. Standards outside the classroom are expectations of individuals and institutions that do not directly shape what takes place in the classroom but that nevertheless profoundly influence the educational process. Focusing on classroom standards in the absence of a concurrent and equally forceful consideration of what takes place beyond the classroom will get society only so far toward the goal of raising student performance.[1]

Emphasis on standards outside the classroom should not be construed as a lack of interest in, or commitment to, the need for rigorous standards inside the classroom as well. However, school practices are reflective of, and responsive to, broader social forces, and asking schools to change without simultaneously examining the social context in which they function is neither sensible nor likely to succeed. American schools and educators are primarily responsible for the state of education today, but they have been willingly aided and abetted in their present condition by parents, employers, and postsecondary institutions.

Student Performance Today

With the exception of a few writers, such as Gerald Bracey or David Berliner, who continue to contend that no real problem exists in American student achievement or that problems are limited to the rural or inner-city poor, most commentators on the education scene have noted that the lackluster performance of American students persists. As both Bracey and Berliner have pointed out, the state of education today is no worse than it was twenty years ago.[2] But the situation was not good then, and a concerted school reform movement has been going on for some fifteen years. What has come from the mounds of money and millions of hours that have been spent on school reform during the past two decades? Although occasional success stories are reported in the media about a school or a program that has turned students' performance around, the competence of American students overall has not improved. Few aspects of educational reform tried since the late 1970s have yielded systematically encouraging or replicable results. Reformers often point to success stories such as Central Park East in New York City or the Comer schools in New Haven. These extraordinary accomplishments are worthy of attention and admiration. But it is time to stop focusing on the victory gardens and start looking at the amber waves of grain.

Most labor force economists believe that the present level of performance of American students—even if comparable to the performance of their counterparts two decades ago—is not going to suffice as the demand for high-skilled employees grows and the options for low-skilled employees wane. As Hugh Price, president of the National Urban League, said in 1997:

> The Big Three [auto makers] expect to hire 173,000 new auto workers over the next seven years. These jobs will pay up to $70,000 with over-time. In other words, these are "good jobs." But to get one of these jobs as an auto worker, applicants must pass a reading test, math test, spatial relations test—and a drug test. . . . And that's merely the beginning of the selection process. Those who pass the initial battery of tests are then assigned to a team with several other survivors. The team is given a description of [a] portion of the assembly line in an auto factory, along with job descriptions of those on that section of the line. The team has several hours to come up with ways of improving the productivity of that segment of the manufacturing process. Those that come up with solid recommendations will be offered jobs. This is what one needs to know and be able to do just in order to land a job as an auto worker. We're not even talking about what's required to become an auto executive, auto dealer, auto salesperson, or auto parts supplier.[3]

Will the majority of American students be able to satisfy the likely demands of the Big Three and other major employers in the years to come? According to a 1996 report from the Education Trust, they will not. The proportion of students who score at or above proficiency on National Assessment of Educational Progress (NAEP) reading and mathematics tests ranges from about 10 percent in California, the District of Columbia, and Louisiana to around 35 percent in Maine, Minnesota, and North Dakota.[4] In other words, even in states where student achievement ranks among the best, well under half of the students are not performing at objective, predetermined levels of age-appropriate proficiency. According to the most recent, and carefully conducted, international comparisons, the Third International Mathematics and Science Study (TIMSS), American students in the eighth grade rank below average in math and barely above average in science. According to the National Education Goals Panel—the bipartisan group created to track progress toward meeting the national education goals—little headway has been made toward these goals and, to quote the panel's executive director, Ken Nelson, ''We are not going to make it.''[5]

Those who teach on college campuses complain regularly about how poor the skill level of high school graduates is.[6] According to a report from the California State University system, which enrolls only the top third of the state's high school graduates, 53 percent of entering freshmen in the fall of 1996 needed remedial education in mathematics (that is, they failed the university's proficiency exam) and 43 percent needed remedial education in English.[7] These figures do not include athletes and other students who were enrolled through special admissions. Despite claims of progress made in recent years, the percentage of Cal State freshmen requiring remedial education has increased steadily since 1989, when the system began monitoring this index.

The notion that things are getting better is not borne out by recent surveys of American employers, either. According to a 1991 Harris poll, about two-thirds of parents (71 percent) and students (63 percent) said that high school graduates were well prepared in reading, writing, and math, but only 21 percent of employers agreed. According to a survey conducted for *Training* magazine, 43 percent of American businesses provided remedial education training for employees in 1995, up from 18 percent in 1984. One-third of the corporations surveyed by the Education Quality of the Workforce policy group reported that they had trouble finding skilled labor. The percentage of small and mid-sized business owners who are worried that a lack of qualified workers will soon hamper their growth doubled from 13 percent in 1993 to 25 percent in 1995.[8]

Beyond the Classroom

Why is it so important that any discussion of school reform reach beyond schools themselves? The answer is simple: If the main goal is improving student performance (and not reforming schools merely for the sake of reforming them or to suit other political aims), then a much better chance of succeeding exists if the problem is approached from multiple vantage points. A sizable part of the variability in student performance is determined by factors outside of school.[9] As Hugh Price said:

[Classroom] standards are only half the story, and the easy half at that. Children have little chance of clearing the higher academic bar if we concentrate only on how high it has been set. The crucial, but as yet unanswered, question is whether the adults in children's lives will do what's necessary to equip them to clear the bar.[10]

Education reformers have, for the most part, been guilty of a sort of myopia that has zeroed in on schools and classrooms and has paid only passing attention to the broader context in which schools and classrooms function. And standards-based reform efforts represent their own brand of near-sightedness. As Albert Shanker warned, "Some danger exists that world class standards will become America's latest education slogan."[11]

A second reason can be stated for focusing on standards outside the classroom. As Shanker wrote, and as John Owen pointed out, standards without stakes are meaningless.[12] The best and brightest educators can devise new and rigorous standards for all subject areas, and the most able psychometricians can develop assessments that are accurate and fair. But if students do not care about doing well on these assessments— if no real consequences for doing poorly and no strong incentives for doing well are imposed—students will not invest much effort in school. Without real stakes, standards-based reform will only have to show lofty expectations, wonderful tests, and more depressing test scores.

Some stakes—the consequences and incentives that are linked to student performance—are determined partly by schools themselves. Schools establish stakes when they set and enforce grade promotion and graduation requirements, for example, or if they have no pass/no play policies governing extracurricular programs. But many important stakes that provide extrinsic rewards and punishments are determined by other people and institutions, including parents, peers, employers, and postsecondary educational institutions. How these people and institutions behave affects the extent to which students believe in the benefits of schooling and, therefore, how much effort they devote to academic pursuits.

Do American students today believe in the benefits of schooling? Yes and no. According to many surveys, students believe in the benefits associated with getting a diploma or a degree, but they are skeptical about the benefits associated with either learning or doing well in class.[13] In other words, students believe that their success in the labor force will depend mainly on the number of years of school they complete. At the same time, however, American students do not associate later success either with doing well in school—in terms of their grades or the evaluations of their teachers—or with learning what schools have to teach. In students' eyes, what matters is only whether a person is promoted to the next level—not how well one does or what one learns along the way.

This view is widely held among American high school students. An extremely large proportion of students—somewhere around 40 percent—are just going through the motions. Between one-third and 40 percent of students say that, when they are in class, they are neither trying very hard nor paying attention. Two-thirds say they have cheated on a test in the past year. Nine out of ten have copied someone else's homework. Only about one-fifth of students disengage from school because they are confused; some students tune out mainly because they cannot keep up. For many more, disengagement is not a reaction to too much pressure or to classes that are too difficult, but a response to having too little demanded of them and to the absence of any consequences for failing to meet even the most minimal demands.[14]

Similar conclusions were reached in a 1997 report from Public Agenda, aptly titled *Getting By: What American Teenagers Really Think about Their Schools*.[15] The report was based on a survey of a national random sample of one thousand teenagers, as well as on twelve focus groups convened in different parts of the country. According to the report,

> Students routinely admitted—some with bravado and some with chagrin—that they calibrate their efforts, often meticulously, to do only as much as it takes to get the grade they can live with. For youngsters aiming for private colleges or elite public universities, this concept of "getting by" implies a certain grade-point average. . . . Other youngsters . . . seem satisfied with any passing grade. . . . [S]tudents from across the country repeatedly said that they could "earn" acceptable grades, pass their courses, and receive a diploma, all while investing minimal effort in their school work. . . . [A]lmost two-thirds of teens across the country (65%) say they could do better in school if they tried harder.[16]

Some educational critics have turned these sorts of findings around and pointed them at schools. They fault teachers for having low standards and minimal expectations, and they see these factors as the causes of low student engagement and poor achievement. To frame the problem this way, however, misses an important part of the story. The minimal demands and low expectations characteristic of most schools today developed in response to low student engagement. True enough, the combination of low engagement and low standards creates a vicious cycle—students disengage from school, schools demand less from disengaged students, students disengage further when little is demanded of them, and so on. But to ask schools to shoulder the full blame for student alienation is to disregard the impact that student disengagement, and the broader context that creates it, has on school practices.

That so many American students coast through school without devoting much energy to their schoolwork is easy to understand. They see little reason to exert themselves any more than is absolutely necessary to avoid failing, being held back, or not graduating. Within a belief system in which all that counts is grade promotion—in which earning good grades is seen as equivalent to earning mediocre ones, or worse yet, in which learning something from school is seen as unimportant—students choose the path of least resistance. And because schools hesitate to give students bad grades, hold them back, or deny them a diploma, students believe, with some accuracy, that no real consequences result from doing poorly in school, as long as their performance is not poor enough to threaten graduation.

Owen reaches similar conclusions in his examination of the economic incentives that influence student behavior: Students do not study hard, because it simply is not worth the effort.[17] Given the pervasive practice of social promotion (that is, promoting students to the next grade level on the basis of their age or the time they have clocked in school, instead of on a genuine assessment of their competence or knowledge); the widespread availability of dumbed-down courses in most schools that qualify for bona fide academic credit; the proliferation of nonselective colleges and universities willing to admit any warm body so that the institution can survive financially; the ambivalence that American adults have about encouraging genuine academic excellence at the cost of well-roundedness; and the overall ignorance of employers about job applicants' academic histories, students not surprisingly take the easy route. This is a rational decision on their part.

This observation is neither an indictment of the American national

character nor an aspersion about the moral core of the country's youth.
The fact that people respond to incentives is a fundamental truth about
human nature, which applies as forcefully to adults as to children and
adolescents. If adult workers received automatic raises, could substitute
easy tasks for demanding ones, were assured of employment opportunities, were never praised for working hard, and knew that future employers would not ask about their work histories, most grown-ups would
be slackers, too. As Shanker wrote:

> If you want someone to behave in a certain way, you connect that be-
> havior with something the person wants. Some people reject this principle
> because they are offended by the view of human nature it implies. This
> is understandable. I, too, would prefer a world in which youngsters
> would open up a play by Shakespeare because they were eager to get into
> it instead of being forced to read the play because it is on the final
> examination. . . . [F]or most kids, unless they have to do it, they will
> not.[18]

Educational progressives, who dominate U.S. graduate schools of
education and, therefore, teacher training programs, do not like this
view of human nature. For them, "intrinsic motivation" is the moral
equivalent of cleanliness and godliness. Progressives' commitment to
the view that the only real way to get students to learn is to motivate
them intrinsically is so strong that many school reformers continue to
call for pedagogic and curricular change exclusively designed to make
school and schoolwork more appealing to students. The fad changes
annually, but the underlying logic (or lack of it) has been a constant on
the American educational landscape for many years. If only classes
could be more fun, relevant, vocational, multicultural, hands-on, high-
tech, holistic, ebonic, and so on, students will work harder and their
performance will improve.

This approach has not served anyone very well. Perhaps the right
formula has not been found for motivating students to work hard out of
intrinsic interest, but this quest does not inspire optimism. However,
intrinsic motivation is not unimportant, and good instruction can com-
bine both intrinsic and extrinsic motivation. During the early years of
schooling, students may be more oriented toward the intrinsic rewards
of learning than extrinsic ones linked to performance.

By the time they are teenagers, however, students, to be committed to doing well in school, must have some sense that what they are doing on a daily basis holds some extrinsic value. More specifically, students will not remain engaged in the classroom or committed to doing well in school unless they think that academic success will have a future payoff, either in terms of success in subsequent school settings, achievement in the workplace, increased earnings, or some combination of all three. If students believe that the academic side of school is merely an unpleasant obligation, and that whether they succeed or fail in school is largely irrelevant to their future, they will invest little time or energy in the educational process.

Students' lack of interest in doing well in school is at the core of the education problem. A 1995 report from the Consortium on Productivity in the Schools concluded that American schools had to find ways of becoming more ''productive''—of increasing student performance without receiving additional resources.[19] The consortium's argument was that the demands of the labor force of the twenty-first century would require graduates to be more skilled (and better at higher-order skills in particular) than they are today and that the public had grown so cynical about the quality of schools that it was not likely to be willing to support substantially increased spending on education.

According to the consortium's analysis, one certain impediment to increasing productivity in schools is the small amount of time that American schools devote to academic instruction in basic subject areas. This is not because the school day or school year is too short. Contrary to popular belief, U.S. students spend more hours in school than most of their European counterparts, at both the elementary and secondary levels (the school year is shorter in the United States than in many countries, but the school day is longer). But compared with these same European schools, American schools spend a much smaller proportion of time on core academic instruction. The National Education Commission on Time and Learning estimates that U.S. high school students receive less than half the number of hours of academic instruction as their counterparts in France and Germany do.[20]

This problem is compounded by a failure on the part of schools to take advantage of students' time outside of school. According to the consortium's report, among high school students in nineteen countries, the United States ranked second in the percentage of students who did no daily homework. It ranked seventh in the percentage of students who reported one hour or less of homework daily and fifteenth in the percentage of students who did two or more hours of homework per day.[21] My own data, from a sample of twenty thousand high school students, corroborate these findings: The majority of secondary school students reported spending four or fewer hours per week on homework. Only one in six was spending ten or more hours each week studying outside of school.[22]

A reasonable suggestion would be to address the issue of poor productivity in schools by increasing the amount of time students spend in basic academic instruction and on homework—this is the "back to basics" argument. At the same time, however, the question arises as to why students' time in and outside school is structured the way it is.

Why Incentives outside of School Matter

Social institutions besides schools structure students' time in and outside of school both directly (by providing different or competing incentives for student performance) and indirectly (by shaping the incentive structure of schools themselves). Thus, for example, postsecondary institutions provide direct incentives for students to perform at a certain level by establishing admissions policies concerning courses taken and minimum grades expected. These incentives are direct, because the admissions policies influence students' decisions about what courses they take in high school and how much effort they devote to them.

But postsecondary institutions also create indirect incentives by influencing what high schools offer and what they require students to take, and by influencing parents' perceptions of whether their children are getting a good education. That is, at least some of what schools and parents do is determined by what they think postsecondary institutions want their applicants to be able to do; parents, especially middle-class parents, will judge a school on the basis of how successful it is in placing its graduates and will see their child's education as having been successful if the child is admitted to a postsecondary institution with which they are happy. For this reason, talking about setting standards in the K–12 system is not possible without discussing how these standards are going to be tied to admissions standards at postsecondary institutions or to the entry-level requirements of employers.

Parental Influences on Student Performance

Parents, as well, create incentives for students directly, by rewarding them when they receive good grades and punishing them when they receive bad ones. In my survey of twenty thousand adolescents, for example, 20 percent of the students reported getting a raise in their allowance when they brought home good grades; 44 percent said their parents relaxed their curfew in return for getting good grades; 45 percent reported getting gifts or presents for good grades; and more than half said that in return for good grades their parents gave them more freedom. In contrast, one-sixth of students had their allowances cut when they received bad grades; 22 percent lost the use of the family car; 38 percent were grounded; 45 percent had their curfews tightened; and more than half had privileges taken away. Nearly 40 percent of students say that their parents usually or sometimes make their life miserable when they get bad grades.

Reasonable people may disagree about whether parents should reward or punish their children's school performance, or about the specific rewards and punishments they ought to use, but the fact that at least two-thirds of all parents do something in response to their children's school performance is important. (Of the remaining one-third, roughly half care about their children's performance but choose not to use rewards or punishments, and the remainder do not care. That more than 15 percent of students say their parents do not care how they do in school is a different, but no less important, issue.)[23] Because of the large proportion of parents who react to their child's school performance in one way or another, changing what parents view as an acceptable or unacceptable level of achievement will be essential to any school reform effort. Parents also create indirect performance incentives by influencing what schools offer, expect, and demand. Any discussion of classroom standards needs to examine parents' perceptions and understanding of these standards, because parents are in a powerful position to undermine any standards-based reform.

Improving student performance also will necessitate increasing parental involvement in education; all other factors being equal, children whose parents are involved in school do better than their peers.[24] The problem for schools and parents, however, is that parents may be involved in their children's education in many different ways, and figuring out which types of involvement work best has proved difficult.

The type of parental involvement that matters most is not the type that parents practice most often—checking over homework, encouraging children to do better, and overseeing the child's academic program from home. These behaviors do not harm children's performance in school, but by themselves they make surprisingly little, if any, positive difference in student performance, especially once a child has reached secondary school. Some studies have shown that these behaviors do have a positive impact at earlier grade levels, however.[25]

What sort of parental involvement is worthwhile during the secondary school years? The type of involvement that makes a real difference draws the parent into the school physically—attending school programs, extracurricular activities, teacher conferences, and "back to school" nights.[26] Why should this type of parental involvement have the greater effect? The answer perhaps has to do with the sorts of messages each type of involvement communicates. Showing up at school programs on a regular basis takes a great deal more effort than helping out at home, and this effort does not go unnoticed by students or by school personnel. When parents take the time to attend a school function—time off from an evening activity or time off from their own jobs—they send a strong message about how important school is to them and, by extension, how important it should be to their child. When this sort of involvement occurs regularly, it reinforces the view in the child's mind that school and home are connected and that school is an integral part of the whole family's life.

Little research supports the claim that a third type of parental involvement—parental involvement in school governance—increases student performance. In the context of an educational system run by lay school boards, no need exists for more nonprofessionals, with no training designing school curricula, meddling in educational policy. Schools should stick to schooling and stop trying to be social service agencies, families, or moral engines, and parents should stick to parenting and stop trying to be educational administrators.

The majority of parents do provide concrete incentives for good performance and sanctions against poor performance. The problem, though, is in how parents define what is good and what is poor. My data suggest that the norm of getting by may be as common among parents as it is among their children. More than half of all students say they could bring home grades of C or worse without their parents getting upset, and one-quarter say they could bring home grades of D or worse without upsetting their parents. Nearly one-third of the students say their parents have no idea how they are doing in school. About one-sixth of all students believe that their parents do not care whether they earn good grades in school. Even if students are underestimating their parents' concern, that so many think their parents have little interest in their schooling is evidence of a problem of tremendous significance.

In light of the special importance of parents attending school functions, my findings on the prevalence of this type of parental involvement are even more distressing. Only about one-fifth of parents consistently attend school programs. More than 40 percent never do. Only one-third of parents regularly attend their child's extracurricular performances, such as athletic events or plays. Membership in the national Parent–Teacher Association (PTA) today is half what it was thirty years ago.[27]

More research is needed on the impact of standards-based reforms on parental behavior and school involvement. In preparation for this paper, my staff contacted a sample of school districts that had implemented the core knowledge curriculum advocated by E. D. Hirsch, Jr., and asked if they had monitored how the implementation had affected parental involvement. None had, formally, but all of the school administrators had anecdotes to tell about the positive impact the curriculum had on parents' behavior and attitudes. One reason appears to be that parents are more likely to become involved when they have specific knowledge about what their child is expected to learn and how this learning will be assessed. In the process of letting parents know what was included in the core curriculum, these schools may have inadvertently stimulated parental involvement.

Peer Influences on Student Performance

Intrinsic motivation is not enough, and neither are involved parents. Standards established by the peer group matter a great deal as well, especially in high school. For a large number of adolescents, peers— not parents—are the chief determinants of how intensely they are invested in school and how much effort they devote to their education.

Peers create direct incentives for students by rewarding them for certain activities and personality traits and by scorning them for others, and they create indirect incentives by fostering a particular sort of culture within the school setting, which in turn affects the way that teachers behave. Unfortunately, not much of a place exists in the contemporary American peer culture for students whose primary concern is academic excellence.[28]

Not only is there little room in most schools for the academically oriented, but there also is substantial peer pressure on students to underachieve. Adults might think that teenagers would rather do well in school than do poorly, but this is not necessarily the case. The prevailing norm among American teenagers is that one ought to avoid failing in school and do what it takes to graduate. But among American teenagers, widespread peer pressure says not to do too well. One out of every six students deliberately hides his or her intelligence and interest in doing well while in class because they are "worried what their friends might think." One in five students say their friends make fun of people who try to do well in school. More than one-half of all students say they almost never discuss their schoolwork with their friends. More than one-quarter say they have never studied with their friends. Only one in five has studied with friends more than five times during the past school year.

The adolescents in my survey were asked to identify which crowd their friends belonged to and which crowd they would most like to be a part of. When asked which crowd they would most like to belong to, five times as many students say the "populars" or "jocks" as say the "brains." Three times as many say they would rather be "partyers" or "druggies" than "brains." And of all of the crowds, the "brains" were least happy with who they are—nearly half wished they were in a different crowd.

Patterns of Activity outside of School

How students spend their time outside of school also reflects the sorts of incentive conditions that exist beyond the classroom. As my colleagues and others, including both Stevenson and Owen, have pointed out, American youngsters spend far more time than students in other countries on nonacademic activities—such as part-time work, extra-curricular activities, and socializing with friends—and far less time on school-related matters, such as homework, studying, and reading.[29]

In other industrialized countries, school comes first, and activities such as part-time work or socializing with friends are relegated to any hours leftover after school and homework have been completed. In the United States, though, the reverse is the norm: American students manage their academic schedules to fit into their work and play schedules. Given the large amounts of time American teenagers devote to their after-school jobs, socializing, extracurricular activities, and watching television, that they have any time for studying at all is a wonder. One reason for the country's achievement problems is not simply that American students see few reasons to work hard; it is also the case that youngsters receive many incentives to spend a disproportionately large amount of their free time in activities that detract from their academic careers. One of the worst offenders in this regard is after-school employment.

Student Employment and Student Performance

Few opportunities are available to regulate student behavior, or the factors that affect it, outside of school. Although parents' behavior and peer group norms may be influenced through any number of possible mechanisms—for example, the imposition of more rigorous standards—efforts to regulate parents' behavior will unlikely meet with much approval, and efforts to regulate peer norms beyond what students wear, what weapons they carry, and whom they kiss on the playground will equally as unlikely meet with much success.

Student employment is something that federal and state governments currently regulate, however, in terms of the hours that students are permitted to work, the jobs they are permitted to hold, and the tasks they are permitted to perform. Because child labor regulations are already in place, one can ask how changes in these laws might affect student achievement.

How prevalent is student employment? The best estimates are these: More than 80 percent of high school students have paying part-time jobs during the school year sometime during their high school career.

Approximately 65 percent of high school students work at some point during any given school year. Approximately 33 percent of high school students—or more than two million American teenagers—are employed at any single moment in time during the school year.[30] Changes in child labor regulations, therefore, have the potential to affect a large number of students.

Variations exist in labor force participation by age, race, and region of residence, although not much by socioeconomic status or by gender. Overall, the social profile of the typical teenage worker is a white, suburban or urban high school junior or senior from a working- or middle-class family. Perhaps the most important element of this demographic portrait concerns the family background of the typical working student. Contrary to popular stereotype, working students are not mainly poor or minority youngsters who are working because their family needs their earnings. Working teenagers in contemporary America are primarily middle-income youth who are working to support their own consumer behavior. Little money earned from school-year student employment is saved for college or is used to defray family expenses.

Numerous studies of student employment and its impact on schooling have been conducted. The emerging consensus among researchers is that the negative effects of employment on academic performance are linked to how much, not whether, a student works. Studies that examine weekly hours of employment generally find an important break-point in school performance at around twenty hours per week, whereas differences among youngsters working various amounts of time below this threshold are less often systematically related to school performance. Thus, the association between hours of work and school grades is negligible up until the twenty-hour mark is reached but more substantial, and linear, thereafter. Some evidence also is available that students who have lower grades before entering the labor force may be more susceptible to the negative impact of working long hours than their higher-achieving peers.

Some commentators have pointed out that the observed impact of intensive employment during the school year on student grades is relatively modest. Based on my study, the academic cost of twenty-hour-per-week employment is about half of a letter grade per school year. This finding provides a twist on a "good news–bad news" scenario.

The good news is that working long hours does not harm American students' school performance all that much. So is the bad news.

Precisely for this reason, Ellen Greenberger and I have argued that studies that focus solely on differences in school performance, without examining other aspects of youngsters' involvement in school, may underestimate the impact of working on schooling, because low scholastic expectations place inherent, institutionalized constraints on the range of youngsters' grades and on the amount of time they are expected to devote to homework.[31] Because the national average for time spent on homework is about four hours per week, employment, in whatever amount, will unlikely markedly diminish youngsters' already modest involvement in homework. Similarly, because teachers adjust grading practices and class requirements, and pupils select easier courses to accommodate job demands, the impact of employment on school performance is almost certainly attenuated.

Because students are not randomly assigned to the labor force, determining precisely how much of the association between long work hours and diminished school performance results from academically poor students who are more likely to choose to work long hours or from any negative consequences of working per se is not possible. Both processes appear to be at work: Students who are less engaged in school are more likely to work long hours; working long hours, in turn, contributes to further disengagement.[32] Neither of these observations is cause for celebration.

Approximately one-fifth of employed sophomores and one-half of employed seniors work at least twenty hours each week. (As one might expect, older students are more likely to be employed for long hours than younger students, but this is at least partly because most state child labor regulations link permissible hours of employment to student age.) Although weekly hours of employment vary as a function of gender, parental education, and adolescents' educational plans, the reported differences among groups are in general modest and probably of small practical significance—group differences are small, on the order of one or two hours weekly. Weekly hours of employment do not vary as a function of family income or parental occupation, however.

Again, the important conclusion to draw from these data is that, even when discussion of adolescent employment is limited to those youngsters who are working long enough hours to harm their engagement and performance in school, no evidence is found that school-year employment is an activity of the poor or even of those of modest means. Devoting many hours each week to a paid job is just as common—if not slightly more so—among middle-class, college-bound youth as it is among their less well-to-do counterparts.

However, the United States is the only country in the industrialized world in which working during high school is commonplace, especially among students who have their sights set on continuing their education beyond high school. Other countries encourage their high-achieving students to devote their free time to studying and preparing for college.[33]

In addition to their tremendous investment of time and energy in part-time jobs, American students, compared with their counterparts abroad, spend a substantial amount of time socializing with their friends. American adolescents spend about twice as much time dating and socializing as do their Asian counterparts, for example. The same American teenager who spends fewer than five hours per week on homework manages to spend between twenty and twenty-five hours per week socializing.[34] This does not even include the large amount of time at school that is spent in social activities.

Cross-cultural differences in how students spend their time out of school do not emerge for the first time in adolescence. School and school-related activities occupy proportionately more time in the daily lives of children in other countries from an early age. Part of this is because of the greater demands placed on children in other countries for homework, studying, and the like—but part seems to be attributable to international differences in parents' values and priorities. American parents are not enthusiastic about their children being assigned great amounts of homework and spend relatively less money on purchases designed to facilitate youngsters' achievement. American parents are also more willing to burden their children with household chores than to insist on their devoting time to more intellectual activities, such as reading.[35]

What is behind the American view that it is perfectly fine—even desirable—for teenagers to spend their afternoons in shopping malls, peddling hamburgers and tacos, and gabbing on the telephone with friends? Part of the explanation relates to the issue of classroom standards and expectations for homework; simply put, American students spend so much of their time in nonacademic activities because they can, and parents are reluctant to impose standards that schools themselves do not apply. If schools were more demanding, in and out of the classroom, students would have less time for work and play.

Part of the explanation for widespread teen employment is also economic. American marketers of consumer products spend an extraordinary amount of money convincing teenagers that $150 sneakers, designer sunglasses, and, by extension, the jobs they need to support this lifestyle of ''premature affluence'' are necessities of modern life.[36] The irony is that the same corporate America that works so hard to draw youngsters' attention away from school and into shopping malls and fast food restaurants complains about the poor quality of the American work force.

The 'Well-Rounded' American

A third factor worthy of consideration is society's view of what constitutes healthy adolescence. Americans worry about their children becoming eggheads, about them not being sufficiently ''well-rounded.'' When Johnny starts getting additional hours of homework or is expected to master trigonometry, world history, or chemistry, Johnny's parents will complain that he does not have enough time for football practice, tennis lessons, or television.

The argument that academic demands take their toll on youngsters' mental health and personal happiness is often used by American adolescents and parents to argue against possible steps to raise students' level of scholastic accomplishment. The argument appears in two forms; one emphasizes the ''miserable'' Japanese teenager, and the other emphasizes the ''hidden strengths'' of the American adolescent. Both versions are laughable.

As for the stereotype of the miserable Japanese overachiever, contrary to popular belief, the adolescent suicide rate in the late 1990s is higher in the United States than in Japan—and it has been higher for twenty years. The suicide rate among Japanese adolescents peaked in 1955 and has declined steadily since then. During this same time period, the suicide rate among American adolescents has more than quadrupled.[37]

As for the argument that judging America's schools by student achievement alone is myopic—that American youngsters have their own particular set of strengths—consider the country's relative ranking on various indicators of social and behavioral problems. How can one explain why the putatively successful American approach to well-roundedness and character education has enabled the country to be among the world leaders in youth violence, teenage pregnancy, adolescent alcohol abuse, and juvenile delinquency, not to mention teen suicide? Schools are not to blame for these problems, but the argument that U.S. schools and students have special strengths that are going undetected by NAEP, Scholastic Aptitude Test (SAT), or TIMSS results is not plausible.

From extensive data collected on youngsters' mental health, I was able to compare the mental health of Asian American students, who, on average, were outperforming other students in school, with that of their peers. Like their counterparts living in Asia, the Asian American students reported significantly less depression and anxiety, fewer psychosomatic problems, less delinquency, and less drug and alcohol use than students from other backgrounds.

The data also allowed a comparison of the performance of minority youngsters who had recently arrived in the United States with their peers whose families had been in America for some time. These comparisons were especially disheartening. Individuals were expected to have an especially tough time when they first arrive in a new country, and that, as a consequence, children who are recent immigrants were expected to exhibit more distress and difficulty than their counterparts whose families have been living in the new country for some time. The opposite proved true. The longer a student's family has lived in the United States, the worse the youngster's school performance and mental health, and this holds true for Asian as well as Hispanic youngsters. Foreign-born students earn higher grades in school than their American-born counterparts, even after family background is taken into account. Students whose families have been in the United States longer are less committed to doing well in school than their immigrant counterparts. In contrast, immigrants spend more time on homework, are more attentive in class, are more oriented to doing well in school, and are more likely to have friends who think academic achievement is important. Immigrant adolescents report less drug use, less delinquency, less misconduct in school, fewer psychosomatic problems, and less psychological distress than American-born youngsters.[38]

The longer a family has lived in the United States, the more its children resemble the typical American teenager. Part of this package of traits is, unfortunately, academic indifference, or even disengagement. Compared with their recently arrived counterparts, Americanized ethnic minority youngsters spend significantly more time hanging out with friends, more time partying, more time dating, more time on nonacademic extracurriculars, and more time with peers who value socializing over academics. In essence, the broader context of what it means to be an American teenager in the contemporary United States pulls students away from school and draws them toward more social and recreational pursuits.

Examining the correlates of positive adolescent mental health, seeing why high-achieving students report fewer psychological problems in spite of their superior academic performance is not difficult. Furthermore, the failures of the well-roundedness argument become apparent. Students who do well in school not only report better mental health and fewer behavioral problems than students who do poorly in school, but academic success is also one of the strongest predictors of psychological adjustment in childhood and adolescence. Research on childhood risk and resilience indicates that academic competence is an enormously powerful protective factor.

Raising student achievement is a valuable enough goal in its own right, but these findings suggest that an added benefit of doing so is that it will likely reduce rates of various social and behavioral pathologies that have been so resistant to intervention. Given the minimal impact of school-based interventions on adolescent behavior, the time and resources invested in school-based drug education, pregnancy prevention, and delinquency prevention programs would have been better spent on strengthening the academic programs of schools and raising the scholastic competence of all students.[39]

Conclusion

Students need schools that provide opportunities to learn, demanding curricula, and rigorous performance standards to live up to, and good schools can and should provide all three. But school is only one of many influences—and probably not the most important one—that affect what students learn and how well they perform on tests of achievement and competence.

Student performance is as much a product of the ways in which children and adolescents arrange and structure their lives—the activities they pursue, the priorities they hold, the endeavors they value—as it is a product of the schools they attend. Schools have some responsibility for shaping students' priorities and influencing their beliefs. By not demanding much of students' time out of the classroom, schools undermine their own cause, because these practices allow youngsters to spend too much time on activities whose goals ultimately clash with the schools' overall mission. A vicious cycle is set in motion: The less schools demand, the more students spend their time earning pocket money and socializing with their friends; the more they engage in these activities, the more their interest in school wanes. Confronted with an increasingly disengaged student populace, schools, like the classic permissive parent, have responded by demanding less, lowering standards, and searching for gimmicks to keep youngsters engaged. Unfortunately, this strategy only exacerbates the larger problem.

But this is only half of the story. The failure of the school reform movement to reverse the decline in achievement results from its emphasis on reforming schools and classrooms and its general disregard of the contributing forces that, while outside the boundaries of the school, are probably more influential. A number of pervasive problems outside of school must be addressed if any efforts at school reform are to succeed.[40]

The first, and most significant, problem is the high prevalence of disengaged parents in contemporary America. Nearly one in three parents in America is seriously disengaged from his or her adolescent's life and, especially, from the adolescent's education.

A second contributor to the problem is a contemporary American peer culture that demeans academic success and scorns students who try to do well in school. The adolescent society in America has never been a strong admirer of academic accomplishment, but widespread parental disengagement has left a large proportion of adolescents far more susceptible to the influence of their friends than in past generations. Today, part of being an American adolescent is adopting a cavalier or derisive attitude toward school. The longer a student's family has lived in the United States, the less committed to doing well in school he or she is likely to be.

These problems—parental disengagement and a peer culture that is scornful of academic excellence—are compounded by a third: An activity schedule that demands little academic energy from students when they are not in the classroom and permits students to devote excessive amounts of time to socializing, part-time employment, and a variety of leisure activities. In terms of how much time is expected of them for school and school-related pursuits, American students are among the least demanded of in the industrialized world.

What can be done to raise standards outside the classroom?

First, raise standards inside the classroom. A system should be adopted of minimum national standards, performance-based examinations for grade promotion and graduation within all American schools, and uniform national standards for school transcripts that give parents, employers, and postsecondary institutions clear and useful information on each student's scholastic and behavioral record.[41] Parents, employers, or postsecondary educational institutions cannot be expected to create incentives for higher performance if schools do not provide them with the means to evaluate how each student is performing.

Second, young people and parents must get the clear message that the primary activity of childhood and adolescence is schooling. If children and teenagers are to value education and strive for achievement, adults must behave as if doing well in school—not just finishing school, but doing well in school—is more important than socializing, more important than organized sports, more important than working at after-school jobs, more important than any other activity in which young people are involved. The national debate over the causes and cures of the achievement problem must be transformed from one about reforming schools to one about changing students' and parents' attitudes and behaviors. To do this, a serious and open discussion must take place about the high rate of parental irresponsibility and the toll it is taking on youngsters' lives.

Third, schools must expand efforts to actively draw parents into school programs. This will require restructuring and rescheduling school programs to meet the needs of working parents and encouraging employers to permit employees to take time off from work to attend school activities. Merely asking parents to help monitor their children's homework assignments and course selection—what constitutes parent involvement in most school districts—is not sufficient. And continuing to schedule school and school programs as if it were still the 1950s makes no sense.

Fourth, school performance must count. Probably little can be done to alter the adolescent peer culture directly, but the prevailing and pervasive peer norm of getting by is in part a consequence of socializing students, and their parents, within an educational system that neither rewards excellence nor punishes failure. The vast majority of students know that the grades they earn in school will, under the present system, have little or no impact on their future educational or occupational success. They know that future employers will never see their high school transcript and that, if they do, they will not be able to understand it. With the exception of the most selective colleges and universities, U.S. postsecondary educational institutions are willing to accept virtually any applicant with a high school diploma, regardless of his or her scholastic record. To matter, performance in school must be tied to real consequences.

Fifth, remedial education at colleges and universities should be abolished; states should refuse to provide funding for such programs. Providing remedial education in such basic academic skills as reading, writing, and mathematics to entering college students has trivialized the significance of the high school diploma, diminished the meaning of college admission, eroded the value of a college degree, and drained resources away from bona fide college-level instruction. Moreover, the price of remediation in postsecondary institutions cannot be tabulated in dollars alone; tremendous psychological costs are inherent in the signals widespread postsecondary remedial education programs send to high school students and their parents. Students who have managed to complete high school but who lack the necessary college entry skills should be required to complete remedial course work before they can apply for admission to institutions of higher education.

Finally, child labor laws must be revised in light of the changing nature of the labor force and the increasing demand for high-skilled, highly educated workers. Little evidence exists that students learn the sorts of skills and competencies they will need to be successful adult workers from the after-school jobs that are widely available, while considerable proof is found that extensive after-school employment has more costs than benefits. In the late 1990s, twenty-nine states have no limits on the numbers of hours that students who are sixteen and older may work each week during the school year, and an additional thirteen states permit forty or more hours of employment per week. Of eight states that have more stringent restrictions on weekly hours of employment during the school year, only two—Maine and Washington—limit school-year employment to a sensible twenty hours weekly or fewer.[42]

The achievement problem facing the United States is not caused by a drop in the intelligence or basic intellectual capability of its children, but to a widespread decline in children's interest in education and in their motivation to achieve in the classroom. It is a problem of attitude and effort, not ability. Two decades ago, a teacher in an average U.S. high school could expect to have three or four difficult students in a class of thirty. Today, teachers in these same schools are expected to teach to classrooms in which nearly half of the students are uninterested and in which only a small proportion of the remaining half strives for real excellence. Getting by, instead of striving to succeed, has become the organizing principle behind student behavior in U.S. schools. Pointing the finger at schools for creating this situation is easy, but parents, employers, and the mass media have been willing participants in this process as well. If society is serious about raising student performance levels, the motivational context that parents, employers, postsecondary educational institutions, and the mass media have helped to create and maintain must be addressed.

Comment by Joyce L. Epstein

"Standards" are like icebergs in the Sea of Educational Reform. Some think that standards are floating in a sea of despair, with public schools the staterooms on the Titanic. Others say the public schools are sailing—some smoothly, some blindly, some rudderless—in and around the icebergs. Should schools steer clear of Standards (with a capital "S") and hope they float toward the Sea of Latest Fad? Or, should educators close in and climb on to study standards in depth?

Most attention has been given to the tips of the icebergs. Content standards define what children should know and be able to do; performance standards identify how knowledge will be gauged; opportunity to learn standards refer to the structures and processes of school and classroom organization that help students meet standards; measurement standards offer multiple ways to learn how well students have mastered content and reached levels of performance; and standards for teaching are used to evaluate teacher quality. These terms are becoming increasingly familiar, but most knowledge about standards is still hidden beneath the surface. More needs to be known about how to design and implement high-quality content standards and fair and useful performance standards that will help more students meet high expectations wherever they attend school. Educators had standards (with a small ''s'') long before the current national movement took shape. National and local standards should be integrated to give structure and personality to school reform.

Laurence Steinberg begins to explore the deeper structure of standards by looking outside the classroom. His paper raises many important issues that need to be addressed to improve schools, assist students, strengthen families, and invigorate communities in ways that increase student learning and success. The strongest section of his paper presents issues and ideas about standards for students' part-time employment. Steinberg studied this important topic for several years, and his knowledge contributes a clear argument for guidelines that would establish closer ties between students' part-time employers, their schools, and their families. The weakest sections of Steinberg's paper make blanket, stereotypic statements about whole groups of students, families, schools, peers, postsecondary institutions, and employers. Readers are likely to recognize the strengths of the paper and the important issues raised, so my comments focus on five topics where my research and explanations differ from or extend Steinberg's.

First is the need to emphasize the connections of important contexts in which students live and learn. Steinberg restates the futile arguments that raged in the 1970s about which is more important—the school or the family, parents or peers, peers or schools, students' lack of interest or schools' low standards? Decades of studies and field work in schools indicate that seeking a single most important influence is unproductive for understanding student growth and development, for assisting families, or for improving schools. Instead, multiple, simultaneous, distinct, and complementary influences determine how students succeed in school and in life.

Based on many studies that identify the importance of families and schools, the question becomes: If families are so important, how can schools be organized to inform, engage, and help all families interact with their children across the grades to benefit children's learning? Similarly, in light of many studies that indicate that parents continue to be important even as peers increase in influence, the questions are: If peers and parents (and even the parents of peers) are important in students' lives, how can schools and communities help students and adults establish connections that enable more students to thrive in school, at home, and in their communities? How can school organization and classroom practices include opportunities for positive peer influence and productive, age-appropriate family involvement?

The most productive questions are about understanding the "overlapping spheres of influence" of home, school, and community and improving activities that help all youngsters take school seriously, identify themselves as students, work to meet their stated high aspirations, and develop their finest talents.[43] In part, then, what is inside and outside the classroom "overlap" to influence student attitudes, behavior, and achievements.

Second is the need to recognize the diversity of students and schools. Steinberg reflects on many important problems but gives the impression that low student achievement and poor schools are norms for the nation. It is true that all schools—as all organizations—must continually improve, but most schools are not sad and failing places. Most schools are working hard to help students succeed, and signs are evident of progress in student achievements. Since 1996, national statistics show that students' scores and international comparisons are improving; graduation rates are up; employment of graduates is up; gaps in achievement and graduation rates for students from different racial and ethnic groups are closing; and Scholastic Aptitude Test (SAT) scores are up. The recent trends suggest some positive results of the national, state, and local investments and efforts in reform.

Yet, some schools and districts do not set high standards for all students and are not helping students to work for success. The diversity of schools and among students needs close attention. National and regional data indicate that about 15 percent to 30 percent of students have serious academic problems in middle and high schools, which is too many. Solving the most serious problems requires focused attention on their nature, extent, and locations.

One of Steinberg's most egregious overgeneralizations is that, the longer a student's family has lived in the United States, the worse the youngster's school performance and mental health. The statement is particularly distressing because it is not based on data from a representative, national sample. The too-general statement ignores the long history of immigration, assimilation, and achievement of many groups over time, and it ignores the current diversity within successful and unsuccessful groups of students. For example, children of recent and long-term Latino and Asian immigrants are both successful and unsuccessful. Studies and field work find many new immigrant families and their children struggling mightily in California, Kansas, Massachusetts, Minnesota, Texas, and many other locations. A 1995 U.S. Department of Education report on school dropouts indicated that new immigrants leave school at higher rates than other students and that many new immigrant students (particularly Latino students) never enter school. Their nonparticipation alters portraits of student populations and estimates of student success. The problems and progress of first, second, and third generations of immigrant children are complex and need sensitive and thorough study.

Third is the need to emphasize developmental patterns. Steinberg omits attention to the developmental nature of student success or failure. High school students' attitudes and achievements are largely determined by the quality of educational experiences in and out of school from kindergarten on, with particularly strong effects of activities in the middle grades. Students who are placed in high ability groups or tracks are, typically, offered high content, challenging assignments, and pertinent homework assignments, while students in low ability groups are offered standard fare. Students in the former group are more likely to find high school relevant, exciting, and life-forming, whereas students in the latter group include many who have serious academic and behavioral problems. The dramatic cumulative impact of inequitable experiences and opportunities, often from first grade on, underlies the current pressure for high content and opportunity to learn standards. Problems identified in high school can be corrected only with innovative and strong interventions; problems in high school can be prevented only by cumulative attention to high academic standards and to school, family, and community partnerships from preschool through high school.

Even problems with homework reveal developmental patterns. By high school, the best and brightest students are assigned and do more homework, and slower students are assigned and do less. By contrast, in the elementary grades, slower students spend more time on their work and seek more help from their parents. By high school, many students and their teachers have given up on homework, which is neither purposefully designed nor pertinent for skill building. Steinberg calls for more homework; I call for better homework. Simply assigning more homework will not be enough. Homework must be designed from the early grades on so that it is purposeful, varied, interesting, appropriate for increasing students' skills, and includes interactions with family, community, peers and friends, and information for parents so that they will continue to monitor and encourage their children's work.

Fourth is the need to attend to the major alterable structures and processes that affect student motivation and achievements. Steinberg emphasizes the importance of family and school incentives—sometimes confusing intrinsic and extrinsic motivators—and ignores other major alterable structures of home, school, and community that affect student success. In a review of two decades of research, I developed the TARGET structures as an integrated framework for school, classroom, family, peer group, and community organization. These include the Task, Authority, Reward, Grouping, Evaluation, and Time structures and their related processes, which activate varied important motivational forces in students.[44] For example, increasing student success necessitates consideration of how tasks are designed in curricula; how students and families are included as participants and decisionmakers in school programs; how incentives, recognition, and rewards are offered; how peers are separated or integrated in learning groups; how evaluation standards and procedures operate; and how students are provided time for learning.

The TARGET structures point to the need for balance in children's opportunities and experiences. No contradiction exists in being a high-achieving student and being what Steinberg disparages as "well rounded." Despite his protestations, Steinberg's text and examples illustrate that being well rounded includes high achievement, good mental health, diverse experiences in school, part-time employment, home responsibilities, friendship, and peer group activities.

Fifth is the need for research-based programs of school, family, and community partnerships. Steinberg discusses the need to improve school, family, and community partnerships at the high school level. However, he offers the opinion that involvement at school is more important than involvement at home, again seeming to search for one best answer. Studies using national and local data identify six major types of involvement that help elementary, middle, and high schools create comprehensive programs of partnerships: parenting, communicating, volunteering, learning at home, decisionmaking, and collaborating with the community.[45] Hundreds of age-appropriate activities may be selected to tailor programs to the needs, interests, and goals of individual schools and their students and families. Particular challenges also set high standards for each type of involvement. These challenges must be met to implement an excellent program that includes all families, and that produces specific results for students, families, and the schools.

A growing body of research, including early studies of high schools conducted by Sanford Dornbusch and his colleagues in the 1980s and many studies and field trials since, can guide high schools to develop comprehensive and productive programs of partnership.[46] Numerous surveys and studies in schools reveal that parents are neither irresponsible nor unresponsive as Steinberg charges, but most have been left to figure out on their own how to remain involved at home and at school as their children proceed through the grades. Data indicate that the strength of school programs determines whether, which, and how families become and stay involved in their children's education.[47]

In sum, content standards currently are being developed in most states, and performance standards and linked assessments are required of all states by the year 2000 in the Improving America's Schools Act. Steinberg's discussion points to the need to think broadly about guidelines that affect students in the varied influential contexts in which they learn. His recommendations vary, however, with some sensible and data-based (for example, the need for monitoring the number of hours students work, and the need for better ways to involve families at the high school level) and other seemingly unconnected opinions (such as eliminating all sex education courses and all remedial education programs in postsecondary institutions).

My comments aim to clarify or extend some of Steinberg's statements. First, instead of seeking which context is more important in students' lives, the overlapping spheres of influence of home, school, and community must be acknowledged. Second, instead of wholesale criticisms, the diversity of strengths and weaknesses in the nation's schools and in the efforts and skills of students must be recognized. Third, instead of focusing only on the failings of some high schools and students, the long-term, developmental effects on students of the qualities of their experiences in school, at home, and in their communities from kindergarten on must be made clear. Fourth, instead of overemphasizing incentives, the full complement of structures and processes in school, family, peer, and community environments that activate student motivation to learn in school must be understood and used. Finally, instead of limiting parent involvement to one best strategy, the growing research base must be applied to enable elementary, middle, and high schools to develop comprehensive programs of school, family, and community partnerships that help boost student success in school.

Steinberg presents problems that require attention to equity. Equal access is needed to provide all students with the existing high content and high support that presently are offered to the best and brightest students. He also presents problems that require attention to excellence. That is, all students should be provided access to new content, subjects, and challenges to reach higher levels of learning. Both kinds of problems require attention to the quality of school, classroom, family, and community contexts and their connections. Steinberg concludes correctly that standards inside and outside the classroom help students arrange and structure their lives. His discussion is useful because it calls attention to many issues that are still hidden below the tip of the standards icebergs.

Comment by John D. Owen

Laurence Steinberg believes that successful educational reform should focus on the key actor in the educational process—the student.[48]

While he agrees that the schools have a role in the reform process, he argues that successful educational reform must also include changing the negative attitudes and habits that students now bring to the classroom. He finds that, though the average student does now care about finishing high school and, in many cases, about going on to college, these goals are not perceived as requiring much student effort. And the average student does not care to perform at more than this minimal level.

Steinberg considers how to change this. He finds that student attitudes are influenced by four major factors: employers, postsecondary educational institutions, parents, and peers. The first two should be positive but have comparatively little effect because most employers of high school graduates do not ask to see their transcripts and the great majority of postsecondary educational institutions, which do look at transcripts, accept most or all students who apply. Parents can influence their children and many do a good job; an alarming number, though, are either disengaged from their children or have a negative influence. The teenager's peers have even more influence than parents; in most cases they simply support the ethic of doing the minimum amount of work needed to survive in school.

Steinberg proposes to:

—Raise the return to study effort by adopting minimum national standards as well as performance-based examinations for grade promotion and graduation; instituting uniform national standards for school transcripts that provide usable information on every student's scholastic and behavioral record to parents, employers, and postsecondary institutions; and eliminating remedial education at colleges and universities.

—Involve parents in their children's education.

—Remove an impediment to good study habits by considering a revision of U.S. child labor laws that would limit paid employment by students when school is in session.

Steinberg's basic premise that education reform is desirable is easy to accept. An enormous amount of money is spent on education with mediocre results. Much better results should be forthcoming from this expenditure. Even those who are satisfied with current levels of achievement would presumably prefer to obtain them with a substantial reduction in the tax burden education now imposes.

Steinberg's policy proposals are mostly both familiar and popular. His most controversial suggestion is that legislation be passed limiting part-time employment by students. Two areas of concern arise.

Steinberg emphasizes effects on cognitive achievement, a worthwhile goal. It is also important, though, to consider impacts on the way young people are socialized for adult life. Some empirical work suggests a possible positive link between student part-time employment and future earnings. More generally, defenders of the status quo see the system as training students to be flexible, open to new cues from the environment. Teenagers who work part time while going to school full time learn something about the world of work. College students stay in school, often on a part-time basis, until well into their twenties (in an increasing number of cases until almost thirty). While in school, they can and often do make frequent changes in their career plans. During the first ten years after their entry into the full-time labor market, they typically change jobs at least a half dozen times. This exposure to a wide variety of courses and job experiences gives them, according to this argument, a good preparation for the modern labor market. They have learned to expect continual change and to take advantage of new information as it becomes available—important skills in an era of rapid organizational and technological change.

I have some reservations about this defense of the status quo. Recent changes in the labor market have improved the relative position of workers with good quantitative, verbal, social, communication, and other basic skills. And much of the flexible behavior of the young results from failures in the flow of information between students, schools, and employers—failures that translate into poor incentives and much uncertainty. In these less than optimal conditions, the behavior of individual students may be rational for them but have unfortunate economic and social consequences. All these ramifications of student part-time employment do, though, deserve full consideration before legislating curbs on it.

A second issue is whether it makes more sense to change the incentives that induce students to work part time instead of simply making such work illegal. When individuals respond to a government program in ways that limit its impact (or have other apparently antisocial consequences), governments often react by imposing new constraints on individual behavior. Better policy outcomes are likely if how the behavior follows from the incentives provided by the program is considered before imposing such new restrictions.

Educational achievement is produced by a combination of student time and effort and educational services (teachers, the use of buildings, and so on). At present, the state gives young people highly subsidized educational services, while the student's own time continues to have a significant opportunity cost. Is it any wonder that students endeavor to substitute the inexpensive (to them) resource for the more expensive? That they continue to press for educational credentials that can be obtained with a minimum of effort, forcing high schools to limit homework assignments and to spend much time in class trying to capture the attention of their charges? Or that young people conserve their energy and time for their part-time jobs and their more enjoyable leisure activities?

The problem does not end with the high school diploma. Many college students now work almost full time and study full time (or work full time and study almost full time) with the expected result that they come to class poorly prepared and rely on the classroom lecture for their education.

Considering the available remedies for this basic incentive problem is beyond the scope of these comments; that discussion should, though, be part of the debate on legislative restriction of student part-time employment.

Steinberg's more familiar proposals—minimum national standards, examinations for promotion and graduation from high schools, and the greater use of school-based information about students by employers and colleges—appeal to many reformers. Some do balk at the notion of a single standard imposed by the federal government. The past failures of so many once-popular educational innovations provide a strong argument for allowing the local school district to choose among several standards, including some provided by the private sector. But the more general notion of improved information flows is popular.

A more complete discussion of such proposals should analyze the underlying factors that support current arrangements. At the very least, this can reveal something of the likely resistances to change and suggest more effective strategies for reform. Take as an example raising the stakes for students by improving the quality and the utilization of in-

formation flows (a goal with which I strongly agree). Today, the failure
of employers to utilize the mountain of good information about young
people that could be supplied by high schools significantly reduces these
stakes. This problem has at least two sources. *The Shopping Mall High
School,* published in 1965, showed that high school principals can have
an incentive to provide student information in what economists would
call an "opportunistic" fashion.[49] According to this argument, the public school principal who seeks a successful career must avoid giving
serious offense to any significant group of parents. Pleasing parents of
children of different levels of ability and industry may be best served
by producing transcripts that do not reveal the weaknesses of the less
able or less industrious (for example by devising courses with similar
names but structured for different levels of difficulty). Such tactics
diminish the interest of employers in transcripts. An obvious corrective
for this behavior is a system of external examinations that provides a
supply of consistent, reliable, and useful information for potential employers. A second difficulty lies on the demand side: the reluctance of
employers to use detailed transcripts to hire and place applicants.[50] This
use of transcripts can put employers in a difficult legal situation if they
cannot justify it in terms of the needs of the business (and if the labor
force does not represent races, genders, and other protected groups in
proportion to their numbers in the relevant labor market). Such validation can be so costly that the employer will prefer to use other means
to hire entrants, such as filling jobs that require a substantial level of
skill with those who have already demonstrated ability in some prior
employment experience. This obstacle could presumably be overcome
by legislative and judicial action.

Improvements in both the supply of good information from schools
and the employer demand for it would likely give students a greater
stake in academic accomplishment. If a free flow of relatively reliable
information about students went to employers, high performers could
walk into good jobs upon leaving high school, while the other graduates
would continue to be confined to positions that were temporary and
required little skill. Such a dramatic increase in the return to study
effort could eventually yield more industrious students. But is this
scenario possible in the present political circumstances? Considerable
opposition exists to using external examinations—especially those that
measure such traditional academic achievements as reading, writing,

arithmetic, and algebra skills—to make important decisions about a teenager's future. And significant support is found for retaining controls on the way employers use school-based data, in part because employers could use this information to discriminate. I do not expect any radical change here, at least in the near-term future.

Some progress has been seen in recent years. Weak curricula have been strengthened in a number of schools, for example. These gains have not been accompanied by an increase in the dropout rate or other negative consequences. Acceptance by students and others appears to have been helped by an increased awareness of the need for better academic achievement to obtain even a good blue-collar job. Moreover, in some of the weakest programs, students are so bored that they welcome a curriculum that has more substance.[51] Further gradual improvement along these lines is likely. It is too early to tell, though, whether the more aggressive reforms proposed by Steinberg and others will come to fruition. Neither the long history of less than successful educational reform efforts in the United States nor the contemporary resistance to truly high academic standards encourages an optimistic forecast.

Notes

1. L. Steinberg, *Beyond the Classroom: Why School Reform Has Failed and What Parents Need to Do* (Simon and Shuster, 1996).

2. Gerald Bracey, "The Second Bracey Report on the Condition of Public Education," *Phi Delta Kappan*, vol. 74 (October 1992), pp. 104–17; and D. Berliner and B. Biddle, *The Manufactured Crisis: Myths, Fraud, and the Attack on America's Public Schools* (Addison-Wesley, 1995).

3. Hugh Price, "The No Excuses Era of Urban School Reform," speech delivered at the National Press Club, Washington, D.C., February 14, 1997, p. 3.

4. Education Trust, *Education Watch: The 1996 Education Trust State and National Data Book* (Washington, 1996).

5. "Nation Lags in Its Drive to Meet Education Goals, Report Finds," *New York Times*, November 19, 1996, p. A17.

6. David W. Breneman estimates that the annual cost of postsecondary remedial education is $1 billion. This surely is an underestimate, because much remedial education takes place as part of regular class instruction and is not reported as remedial per se.

7. Kenneth R. Weiss, "Many Cal State Freshmen Lack Math, English Skills," *Los Angeles Times*, March 20, 1997.

8. American Federation of Teachers, *Reaching the Next Step* (Washington, 1997).

9. Specific estimates of the variability in student achievement attributable to school versus nonschool factors differ from study to study depending on the particular variables used and the statistical models tested. That nonschool factors are, in the aggregate, more potent than school variables, however, has been a widely accepted conclusion for at least thirty years, since the publication of James Coleman and others, *Equality of Educational Opportunity* (Government Printing Office, 1966).

10. Price, "The No Excuses Era of Urban School Reform," p. 3.

11. Albert Shanker, "The Case for High Stakes and Real Consequences," in D. Ravitch, ed., *Debating the Future of American Education: Do We Need National Standards and Assessments?*, pp. 145–53 (Brookings, 1995).

12. John Owen, *Why Our Kids Don't Study* (Johns Hopkins University Press, 1995).

13. See, for example, Steinberg, *Beyond the Classroom*.

14. Steinberg, *Beyond the Classroom*.

15. Public Agenda, *Getting By: What American Teenagers Really Think about Their Schools* (New York, 1997).

16. Public Agenda, *Getting By*, p. 20.

17. Owen, *Why Our Kids Don't Study*.

18. Shanker, "The Case for High Stakes and Real Consequences," p. 149.

19. Columbia University, Teachers College, Institute on Education and the Economy, Consortium on Productivity in the Schools, *Using What We Have to Get the Schools We Need: A Productivity Focus for American Education* (1995).

20. National Education Commission on Time and Learning, *Prisoners of Time* (Government Printing Office, 1994).

21. Columbia University, *Using What We Have to Get the Schools We Need*.

22. Steinberg, *Beyond the Classroom*.

23. Steinberg, *Beyond the Classroom*.

24. Extensive literature is available on the positive impact of parental involvement on school achievement. See, for example, J. Epstein, "Parental Involvement: What Research Says to Administrators," *Education and Urban Society*, vol. 19 (1987), pp. 119–36; W. Grolnick and M. Slowiaczek, "Parents' Involvement in Children's Schooling: A Multidimensional Conceptualization and Motivational Model," *Child Development*, vol. 64 (1994), pp. 237–52; Steinberg, *Beyond the Classroom*; and D. Stevenson and D. Baker, "The Family–School Relation and the Child's School Preformance," *Child Development*, vol. 58 (1987), pp. 1348–57.

25. See Epstein, "Parent Involvement."

26. See R. Rumberger and others, "Family Influences on Dropout Behavior in One California High School," *Sociology of Education*, vol. 63 (1990), pp. 283–99; and Steinberg, *Beyond the Classroom*.

27. M. Tabor, "Comprehensive Study Finds Parents and Peers Are Most Central Influences on Students," *New York Times*, August 7, 1996, p. A15.

28. Steinberg, *Beyond the Classroom*. See also J. Bishop, "Nerd, Harassment, Incentives, School Priorities, and Learning," Working Paper No. 96–10 (Cornell University, Center for Advanced Human Resource Studies, 1996).

29. H. Stevenson and J. Stigler, *The Learning Gap: Why Our Schools Are Failing and What We Can Learn from Japanese and Chinese Education* (Simon and Shuster, 1992); and Owen, *Why Our Kids Don't Study*.

30. This, and subsequent passages on the correlates and consequences of school-year employment, draws heavily on L. Steinberg and B. Cauffman, "The Impact of School-Year Employment on Adolescent Development," in R. Vasta, ed., *Annals of*

Child Development, vol. 11, pp. 131–66 (London, England: Jessica Kingsley Publishers, 1995).

31. E. Greenberger and L. Steinberg, *When Teenagers Work: The Psychological and Social Costs of Adolescent Employment* (Basic Books, 1986).

32. L. Steinberg, S. Foley, and S. Dornbusch, "Negative Impact of Part-Time Work on Adolescent Adjustment: Evidence from a Longitudinal Study," *Developmental Psychology*, vol. 29 (March 1993), pp. 171–80.

33. Greenberger and Steinberg, *When Teenagers Work*.

34. Steinberg, *Beyond the Classroom*.

35. Stevenson and Stigler, *The Learning Gap*.

36. J. Bachman, "Premature Affluence: Do High School Students Earn Too Much?," *Economic Outlook USA* (Summer, 1983), pp. 64–7.

37. D. Crystal and others, "Psychological Maladjustment and Academic Achievement: A Cross-Cultural Study of Japanese, Chinese, and American High School Students," *Child Development*, vol. 65 (1994), pp. 738–53.

38. See also the analysis of data from the National Educational Longitudinal Study (NELS) survey in Kao and Tienda.

39. For many examples of the failure of school-based health and behavior intervention efforts, see S. Millstein, A. Petersen, and E. Nightingale, eds., *Promoting the Health of Adolescents: New Directions for the Twenty–First Century* (New York: Oxford University Press, 1993).

40. For a more detailed discussion, see Steinberg, *Beyond the Classroom*.

41. Many commentators have called for similar reforms. See, for example, D. Ravitch, *National Standards in American Education: A Citizen's Guide* (Brookings, 1995).

42. Information on state regulation of child labor is available from the U.S. Department of Labor Wage and Hour Division.

43. J. L. Epstein, "Toward a Theory of Family–School Connections: Teacher Practices and Parent Involvement across the School Years," in K. Hurrelmann, F. X. Kaufmann, and F. Losel, eds., *Social Intervention: Potential and Constraints*, pp. 121–36 (New York: DeGruyter/Aldine, 1987).

44. J. L. Epstein, "Effective Schools or Effective Students: Dealing with Diversity," in Ron Haskins and Duncan MacRae, eds., *Policies for America's Public Schools: Teachers, Equity, and Indicators*, pp. 89–126 (Norwood, N.J.: Ablex, 1988); and J. L. Epstein, "Family Influence and Student Motivation: A Developmental Perspective," in C. Ames and R. Ames, eds., *Research on Motivation in Education*, vol. 3, pp. 259–95 (New York: Academic Press, 1989).

45. J. L. Epstein, "School/Family/Community Partnerships: Caring for the Children We Share," *Phi Delta Kappan*, vol. 76 (1995), pp. 701–12.

46. J. L. Epstein and others, *School, Family, and Community Partnerships: Your Handbook for Action* (Thousand Oaks, Calif.: Corwin Press, 1997).

47. J. L. Epstein, "Perspectives and Previews on Research and Policy for School, Family, and Community Partnerships," in A. Booth and R. Dunn, eds., *Family–School Links: How Do They Affect Educational Outcomes*, pp. 209–46 (Hillsdale, N.J.: Erlbaum, 1996).

48. For further exposition, see Laurence Steinberg, *Beyond the Classroom: Why School Reform Has Failed and What Parents Need to Do* (Simon and Schuster, 1996).

49. Arthur G. Powell, Eleanor Farrar, and David K. Cohen, *The Shopping Mall*

High School: Winners and Losers in the Educational Marketplace (Houghton Mifflin, 1985).

50. See the argument presented by John Bishop in ''Signaling Academic Achievement to the Labor Market,'' testimony before the House Education and Labor Committee, March 5, 1991.

51. For a formal discussion of standards that might be chosen by students, as opposed to those that would maximize educational achievement, total economic output, or the output available to the rest of society (apart from students), see John D. Owen, ''Optimal Effort Requirements for Students,'' Working Paper, Wayne State University Economics Department, 1996.

Remediation in Higher Education: Its Extent and Cost

DAVID W. BRENEMAN

T HE NATURE, extent, and financial costs of remedial programs conducted in institutions of higher education are
not trivial.[1] In the view of the National Association for Developmental
Education (NADE), currently housed at Appalachian State University,
"developmental education" is an umbrella term that includes remedial
education as a component:

> Developmental education is a field of practice and research within higher
> education with a theoretical foundation in developmental psychology and
> learning theory. It promotes the cognitive and affective growth of all
> postsecondary learners, at all levels of the learning continuum. Devel-
> opmental education is sensitive and responsive to the individual differ-
> ences and special needs among learners. Developmental education pro-
> grams and services commonly address academic preparedness, diagnostic
> assessment and placement, development of general and discipline-
> specific learning strategies, and affective barriers to learning.[2]

Remedial education is often thought of as fourteen-to-sixteen-week
college courses covering material that could (or should) have been
learned in high school. Other interventions under the developmental
rubric include individual tutoring, group tutoring, and short-term counseling or courses. NADE does not limit remediation to particular subjects (for example, reading or mathematics) and it does not assume any
objective definition of instructional level as unambiguously remedial
(for example, what is remedial at the Massachusetts Institute of Tech-

nology may be college level at a two-year college). Given these caveats, such open-ended concepts clearly would be difficult to implement in a national survey.

A related issue involves the many students enrolled in remedial courses who are not recent high school graduates. Included in this category are older adults who enter college after many years away from formal instruction and who often have a need for developmental programs that ease their transition back to the classroom. Similarly, many institutions, particularly community colleges, enroll recent immigrants whose prior education was not in U.S. high schools. While the courses taken by these nontraditional students may be remedial in nature, they are essential if many older students and recent immigrants are to benefit from further training. To the extent that "remedial education" carries with it a pejorative connotation, viewed as a failure of the recent elementary and high school experience, some observers worry that developmental programs enrolling such students will be tarred with that same brush and be punished in the appropriations process. This concern is legitimate; unfortunately, data on the age or immigration status of students in remedial programs are generally not available, and certainly not in the national surveys. Most institutions do not collect such information. As a consequence, the data in this paper, largely drawn from a recent National Center for Education Statistics (NCES) survey, include all students enrolled, regardless of age or prior educational circumstance, and no state or institutional data have been located that would permit an estimate of the age distribution or immigrant status of students in remedial courses. Subsequent research, including site visits to several states, could unearth information that would allow such estimates to be made.

In its 1995 survey on remedial education, NCES used the following definition for its respondents:

> For the purposes of this study, we define remedial education to be courses in reading, writing, or mathematics for college students lacking those skills necessary to perform college-level work *at the level required by your institution.* "Throughout this questionnaire, these courses are referred to as 'remedial'; however, your institution may use other names such as 'compensatory,' 'developmental,' or 'basic skills,' or some other term." Please answer the survey for any courses meeting the definition above, regardless of name; however, do not include English as a second

language (ESL) when taught primarily to foreign students. Do not include remedial courses offered by another institution, even if students at your institution take these courses.[3]

This definition has the merit of narrowing the scope of remediation to three subject areas: the three "r's of reading, 'riting, and 'rithmetic.'' Despite the absence of a national curriculum, agreement does exist that K–12 education should equip all students with basic skills in these three fundamental areas. This definition precludes consideration, for example, of whether introductory economics in college might be considered remedial on the grounds that many students take some elementary economics in high school. This type of exclusion seems proper, because no uniform agreement exists in the United States that all high school students should master the rudiments of economics. The NCES survey also makes no reference to the age of the students enrolled; the NCES staff had found that few institutions could provide such information.

NCES Survey Findings

The 1995 NCES survey is currently the most complete source of information on the scope and nature of remediation. Its principal findings follow:

1) About three-quarters (78 percent) of higher education institutions that enrolled freshmen offered at least one remedial reading, writing, or mathematics course in fall 1995. Remedial courses were especially common at public 2-year institutions (100 percent) and institutions with high minority enrollments (94 percent). Public 4-year institutions also were important providers of remediation, with 81 percent providing at least one remedial reading, writing, or mathematics course [while 63 percent of private 4-year institutions did so].

2) Remedial reading courses were offered by 57 percent and remedial writing and mathematics courses by about three-quarters of higher education institutions that enrolled freshmen. Almost all (99 percent) public 2-year institutions offered remedial courses in each subject area.

3) Most institutions that offered remedial reading, writing, or mathematics courses offered one or two different courses in a subject area in fall 1995. The average (mean) number of courses offered was 2.1 for reading, 2.0 for writing, and 2.5 for mathematics. Public 2-year insti-

tutions offered a much higher average number of courses than other types of institutions.

4) Twenty-nine percent of first-time freshmen enrolled in at least one remedial reading, writing, or mathematics course in fall 1995. Remedial courses in mathematics were taken by more freshmen than were remedial reading and writing courses. There was a general pattern of higher remedial enrollments and lower remedial pass rates at public 2-year and high minority enrollment institutions. In general, about three-quarters of the students enrolled in remedial courses pass or successfully complete those courses.

5) About half (47 percent) of institutions offering remedial courses indicated that the number of students enrolled in remedial courses at their institution had stayed about the same in the last 5 years, 39 percent said enrollments had increased, and 14 percent said they had decreased. A greater percentage of public 2-year than of other types of institutions indicated that remedial enrollments had increased.

6) At most institutions, students do not take remedial courses for long periods of time: two-thirds of institutions indicated that the average time a student takes remedial courses was less than 1 year, 28 percent indicated that the average time was 1 year, and 5 percent indicated that the average time was more than 1 year. Students were more likely to take remedial courses for a longer time at certain types of institutions than at others, with fewer public 2-year and high minority enrollment institutions reporting that students take remedial courses for less than one year.

7) Among the 22 percent of institutions that did not offer remedial reading, writing, or mathematics courses in fall 1995, the most frequent reason given was that remedial courses were not needed by students at the institution (66 percent). About a quarter of the institutions indicated that students at the institution who need remediation take remedial courses offered by another institution (22 percent), and/or that institutional policy does not allow the institution to offer remedial courses (27 percent).

8) Institutional credit (e.g., credit that counts toward financial aid, campus housing, or full-time student status, but does not count toward degree completion) was the most frequent type of credit given for remedial reading, writing, or mathematics courses, with about 70 percent of institutions giving this type of credit in each subject area.

9) The most frequently used approach for selecting students who need remedial coursework was to give all entering students placement tests to determine the need for remedial coursework; about 60 percent of institutions used this approach in each subject area.

10) Remedial education services/courses were provided to local business and industry by 19 percent of institutions that enroll freshmen. However, among these higher education institutions, public 2-year institutions were the primary providers of remedial services/courses to local business and industry; half of public 2-year institutions provided these services, compared with only about 5 percent of other types of institutions.

11) A third of institutions offering remedial courses reported that there were state policies or laws that affected the remedial offerings of their institution, with many more public than private institutions reporting that they were affected (57 percent and 40 percent of public 2-year and 4-year institutions compared with less than 10 percent of private institutions). The major way in which state policies or laws affected the remedial offerings was to require or encourage institutions to offer remedial education.

12) About a quarter of institutions reported that there was a limit on the length of time a student may take remedial courses at their institution. Time limits on remediation were set by institutional policy at 75 percent of the institutions with time limits, and by state policy or law at 21 percent of the institutions.[4]

The key findings of the NCES survey are that remediation takes place in all public community colleges, in four out of five public four-year universities, and in more than six out of ten private four-year institutions. Furthermore, in the fall of 1995, nearly three out of ten first-time freshmen enrolled in at least one remedial course. In short, remedial education is widespread and a significant activity in all sectors of higher education.

The NCES survey is silent, however, on financial costs and on the faculty who teach these courses. Financial and opportunity costs would differ greatly if the faculty are full-time, tenure-track professors or part-time, adjunct faculty, paid by the course. In addition, no information was gathered about the subsequent educational careers of students who have taken remedial courses.[5] Other sources must be consulted for information on these variables.

SREB Survey Findings

The other substantial body of information on remedial education, policy, and practices has been compiled over several years by the Southern Regional Education Board (SREB), located in Atlanta, Georgia. This agency covers higher education in fifteen southeastern states. In a series of three reports dating back to 1988, the agency has tracked the scope of remedial education in its member states, profiled the students involved, and addressed institutional practices in detail.[6] Its findings on students and extent of courses are similar to the national NCES data, but its report on institutional practices does provide information not found in the national survey, particularly on faculty. The report said that, on average, four faculty per institution teach at least one remedial course in reading, six teach writing, and seven teach mathematics. Roughly half of the faculty who teach remedial subjects are part time; about half of the faculty were hired explicitly to teach remedial subjects only, while the remaining teachers were given remediation as part of their load. Seventy percent of the faculty teaching remedial courses had a master's as the highest degree, while 14 percent had a doctorate and the remaining 16 percent had a bachelor's degree. (The small number with doctorates is a function of the high level of remediation in two-year colleges, where the doctorate is generally not required.) Finally, only about one-third of the institutions reported that some form of ongoing training is provided to those who teach remedial courses, indicating that faculty development either is not needed or is not seen as a priority of most colleges.[7]

The SREB studies present virtually no data on financing of remedial instruction, and their conclusion is instructive:

> Funding for remedial studies has been hotly debated among legislators and educators—and taxpayers—in recent years. Some argue that remedial study has no place in higher education. A central theme among these critics is that the basics of reading, writing, and mathematics have already been ''bought and paid for'' by funds appropriated to the K–12 system and should not be paid for again (at what may be a higher cost). Many parents and students see enrollment in remedial courses as an unnecessary delay that prolongs the educational process and increases the cost of a college education. Moreover, many college faculty members and administrators believe that remedial studies should not be part of a college's offering, and others believe that a highly visible program weakens the academic reputation of an institution.
>
> These attitudes help explain why remedial programs often go unacknowledged within institutions—particularly the four-year and graduate colleges and universities—and why it is difficult to identify funding

patterns or to determine costs for remedial services. The funds used to operate remedial programs are often buried in the regular budgeting process and are difficult to trace or analyze. As a result, only a modest amount of well documented funding information is available, and it is not possible to provide truly comprehensive per student or program costs—defined and collected in the same way—for comparison across states or institutions.[8]

The only recourse to this dilemma is to examine reports from a small number of states that have looked at costs.

State Data on Costs of Remediation

The State Higher Education Executive Officers (SHEEO) association in Denver, Colorado, confirmed the lack of any national data on costs of remedial education but did suggest a small number of states to contact, including Maryland and Texas.[9] Calls to those two states produced reports that were helpful, although different approaches were taken to estimate cost in each state. In addition, Florida was able to provide gross numbers on budgetary costs of remedial education. A review of the methods and findings in these states could allow a rough estimate of national costs.

Texas relies upon formula-based funding for its public colleges and universities, and remedial education is one of the categories covered under the formula. In the 1996–97 biennium, general appropriations for remediation totaled $153.4 million, up from $38.6 million in the 1988–89 biennium.[10] (Of that total, $142.0 million was for course-based instruction, and $11.4 million for other forms of remedial academic support.) Community and technical colleges received the lion's share of the money ($132.0 million, or 86 percent), with the four-year universities receiving $21.4 million. For the universities, the appropriation for course-based remedial education was 2.93 percent of the total lower division appropriation, and for the community colleges, the comparable figure was 18.39 percent. For the public system as a whole, the remedial appropriation equaled 11.64 percent of the total lower division appropriation.

Most states report data on total state appropriations for public institutions without reference to lower and upper division or graduate instruction. According to Director of Finance Ken Vickers, the total appropriation for the 1996–97 biennium in Texas was $6.9 billion, making the $153.4 million remedial appropriation equal to 2.25 percent of total state funds for higher education. That figure represents one possible parameter for use in estimating national costs.

The Florida Postsecondary Planning Commission reported a nearly identical percentage: $57.5 million in expenditures for remedial education in 1995–96 in the public sector, out of a total public budget of $2.5 billion, meaning that 2.3 percent of public higher education dollars went to remedial education. Both Florida and Texas are rapidly growing states with large numbers of minority students enrolled, which might suggest that their outlays on remediation may be among the nation's highest.[11]

Maryland followed a different approach in making its cost estimates. A special survey was sent to all Maryland colleges and universities, requesting considerable information on remedial education, including each college's estimate of its cost. No presumption was made that state funds were the only source of support for remediation—other sources identified explicitly in the survey were special fees, federal grants and contracts, and all other sources. Nonetheless, all public two-year and four-year campuses combined reported that 91.9 percent of funding came from general institutional funds, which presumably includes, in addition to state support, tuition, unrestricted giving, and unrestricted endowment income (although this is not clear from the survey or the text). The report's authors express caution about the cost data, noting that the dollar amounts "may be just estimates, and are not consistently reported across institutions."[12] In short, the Maryland data do not appear to be highly accurate or directly comparable to the Texas and Florida data, referring to expenditures instead of revenues.

Given these caveats, Maryland reports expenditures in fiscal 1995 of $17.6 million on remedial programs, or 1.2 percent of total expenditures in all public campuses. The bulk of the outlays are reported in two-year colleges ($16.2 million, 4.1 percent of total expenditures). Public four-year campuses report outlays of only $1.4 million, or 0.1 percent of total expenditures. Thus, two approaches to estimating costs of remedial programs are available: percentage of state appropriations, as in Texas, or percentage of college expenditures, as in Maryland. The results are not radically out of line with each other (although the difference in percentage of community college budgets going to remediation in Texas and Maryland is remarkable). A clear need exists, however, for nationally comparable definitions of costs and measurement before anything approaching a definitive cost estimate can be made.

A Rough Estimate of National Costs of Remediation

Two approaches can be taken to estimate national costs of remediation. One method, using the Texas data, involves applying their share of state appropriations for remedial education to national data on state appropriations for public higher education. The second method, using Maryland data, is to apply their percentage of expenditures on remedial education to national data on public college and university expenditures for higher education. In both cases, Texas and Maryland are treated as if they are representative states in providing remedial programs—a big assumption. The only defense is that the NCES survey shows that remedial programs are widespread throughout the country. Further research clearly will be needed, however, to test the accuracy of these assumptions as well as of the tentative estimate of costs provided here.

According to *Digest of Education Statistics 1996,* state appropriations to public institutions of higher education in 1993–94 totaled $40.5 billion, which is the relevant figure for the estimate based on Texas data.[13] If all states spend 2.25 percent of state funds for remedial education, as does Texas, then the national cost for remedial education in public colleges and universities in 1993–94 would have totaled $911 million.

Regarding the Maryland data, educational and general expenditures of public institutions for 1993–94 were $87.1 billion.[14] If all states spend 1.2 percent of their educational and general funds on remedial education, as does Maryland, then the national cost for remedial education in public colleges and universities in 1993–94 would have totaled $1.05 billion.

Given the caveats, it is remarkable that these two different methods of estimating costs are so close. Based on these two extrapolations, the annual cost of remedial education in public institutions nationally can be estimated at between $900 million and $1 billion. Further work is needed before much faith can be put in these numbers, but the similar estimates produced by these two methods suggest that the figures may be in the right ballpark.[15]

Two biases are evident in this estimate, with effects in opposing directions. For reasons of both politics and prestige, institutions have an incentive to underestimate (or underreport) the amount spent on remedial instruction. The larger the cost reported, the greater the attention drawn to the activity, which most institutional leaders would prefer to keep out of the limelight. Thus, most institutions likely err on the side of underreporting the true costs of remediation. Working in the other direction, the cost estimate includes an unknown, but presumably large, number of older students and recent immigrants, whose need for remediation would continue even if elementary and secondary schools were performing splendidly. Ideally, those nontraditional students would be excluded from an estimate of the cost of remediation directly attributable to inadequate preparation of recent high school graduates. Whether these biases roughly offset each other is something only further research will reveal.

Is $1 billion a big number in the world of elementary, secondary, or higher education finance? In 1993–94, public elementary and secondary schools in the United States received $260 billion in revenue, while public colleges and universities received $113 billion in current-fund revenue.[16] Remedial education thus costs 0.4 percent of the total K–12 budget and 0.9 percent of the public higher education budget. One way to think about this issue is to ask whether there are higher-valued uses for 0.9 percent of the public higher education budget than spending it to help students at risk learn the skills they need to succeed in college, even if they should have learned those skills earlier in their educational careers.

The above estimate is for public institutions only and does not include the costs incurred by the 63 percent of private institutions that reported some remedial instruction. Those costs should be included if the data were available.

Conclusion

One would like to know so much more to evaluate the wisdom of allocating resources for remedial education. How do the students fare in the balance of their higher education studies and in their subsequent careers? How effective are educators at identifying those who need remediation? How effective are the various ways of providing it? And perhaps most important, how can current levels of access to higher education be maintained while K–12 education is simultaneously improved so that remediation is rendered unnecessary?

At a further level of complexity, the hidden costs of such widespread acceptance of remediation in U.S. higher education should be considered. For example, to what extent does easy access to remedial courses in college act as a disincentive to student effort in high school? Perhaps if students knew that their need for remedial work could block their admission to college, high school work would be taken more seriously. One may also wonder about potential hidden costs to institutions, in the form of lowered expectations for student performance and an associated watering down of courses, including those beyond the remedial level. Perhaps these and other hidden costs are inevitable side effects of mass higher education, but they should not be ignored. Students, schools, and society could benefit if the need for remediation is reduced.

Given the slow pace at which most education research progresses, however, state policymakers and institutional leaders must act in the absence of good answers to most of these questions for several years to come. If the cost estimates provided here stand up to further investigation, then the expenditure of $1 billion per year for this purpose seems a reasonable and justifiable expense. In the short run, the only realistic way to reduce outlays on remediation would be to limit access to higher education to those who require this service. Based on the NCES data, that could amount to denying access to as many as three out of ten first-time freshmen. That is not a good trade-off.

Meanwhile, serious concern should be raised by the nearly three out of ten first-time college freshmen who require remedial coursework in the basic skills of reading, writing, or arithmetic. While providing the remedial courses needed may be sound policy, a better plan would be to improve the performance of K–12 schooling so that the need for such courses is substantially reduced. One must also wonder how effective a remedial course can be, particularly in a basic skill such as reading, if the student has not gained that capacity in twelve years of schooling. Any way one views it, the extent of remediation required in the United States is a sad comment on its educational system.

An important data limitation that hinders the development of better policy in this area is the absence of age data for the students enrolled in remedial courses. The approach one might take toward recent high school graduates unable to do college-level work, as opposed to older students starting college after many years out of school, might well be different. In particular, the role of recent high school experience is relevant to the first case, but less so in the second. The National Center for Education Statistics should consider conducting detailed, micro-level studies of age and immigrant status of students enrolled in a sample of remedial courses to enable some estimate to be made of the size of each group. Such information would allow more informed policy proposals.

An important point was made by U.S. Department of Education researcher Clifford Adelman, based on a study of student transcripts collected by NCES as part of the High School and Beyond longitudinal survey. He found that eventual degree completion is inversely related to the extent of a student's need for remediation:

> Thus, we should not worry about students who take only one remedial course. For a majority of them, it is a course in writing; for the rest, it is intermediate algebra. Deficiencies in writing one's native language generally are "fixable." After all, writing is generally the last of the language skills to be mastered when one studies a second language. . . .
>
> The data show that if a student needs remediation only in intermediate algebra, that is not cause for deep concern, either, provided that the student is motivated to learn. For example, the transcripts show that students seeking business degrees tend to conquer their deficiencies in algebra quickly. . . .
>
> Reading, however, is another matter—one that demands very serious attention if we are determined to help students earn bachelor's degrees. Deficiencies in reading skills are indicators of comprehensive literacy problems, and they significantly lower the odds of a student's completing any degree. One out of eight students in the national transcript study took remedial reading. Sixty-five percent of those people found themselves in at least three other remedial courses, including mathematics—where reading skills also count.[17]

Adelman's emphasis on the centrality of reading indicates the highest priority should be put on that skill in K–12 education, if the need for the least promising type of remediation in college is to be eliminated.

The current national priority given to reading, from President Bill Clinton on down, would thus seem to be well placed and worthy of support.

Comment by Ansley A. Abraham Jr.

One inevitable consequence of evaluating performance and responsiveness to society's needs is determining how good the return is on the investment. As a result, questions are being raised against a backdrop of higher educational reform—code for improved quality and standards—and modest or diminished state support for public higher education. The natural consequence is greater competition for existing funds. The history of remedial and developmental education has always been one of not quite belonging, of reluctant acceptance as a legitimate and valued function of the academy. Consequently, legislators and administrators see remedial and developmental education as one area of potential economic savings.

David W. Breneman's paper more than adequately summarizes the base knowledge of how extensive remediation is at the higher education level. His review of findings from the 1996 National Center for Education Statistics (NCES) survey and my own research at the Southern Regional Education Board provide the foundation for his summary. I would add only one other study to this summary—the Exxon Project at the National Center for Developmental Education at Appalachian State University. This study is the most sophisticated and comprehensive national survey of remedial and developmental programs and students with which I am familiar. What makes this study unique is that it ties individual remedial and developmental students to specific remedial and developmental programs on specific college campuses.

The second area of higher education remedial and developmental study that Breneman addresses is cost. His conclusions mirror my own research and inquiries into this topic; that is, no national data exist on remedial and developmental costs and any comparisons using state data must be done with extreme caution. Any meaningful information will need to be obtained and extrapolated from the most reliable states or already collected federal and state data. My own survey on this topic

Table 1. Response to 1995 Southern Regional Education Board Survey of Remedial and Developmental Cost

State	Collects remedial and developmental data	Cost data included
Arizona	No	No
Arkansas	Yes	Yes
California	Yes	Yes
Colorado	Yes	Yes
Delaware	No	No
Florida	Yes	Yes
Georgia	Yes	Yes
Kansas	Yes	Yes
Kentucky	Yes	No
Maryland	Yes	No
Mississippi	Yes	No
Montana	Yes	Yes
New Jersey	Yes	No
Nevada	No	No
North Carolina	Yes	Yes
Ohio	Yes	Yes
Oklahoma	Yes	Yes
Oregon	No	No
Rhode Island	No	No
South Carolina	Yes	Yes
South Dakota	Yes	No
Tennessee	Yes	No
Texas	Yes	Yes
Utah	Yes	Yes
Virginia	Yes	No
Wisconsin	Yes	Yes

Note: Of the twenty-six states responding, twenty-one collect remedial and developmental data, five do not; fourteen include cost data, twelve do not.

covering all fifty states in November 1995 elicited twenty-six state responses (see table 1). Of these responses, fourteen states provided cost data, and of these, eleven provided data that could only generously be called usable. The cost figures obtained ranged from $1.5 million to $76 million per year. As in the Breneman paper, definition and comparative problems arose (for example, data were reported for different years; distinguishing whether the cost reported meant appropriation or expenditure was difficult; and the size of a state is a complicating factor).

Breneman offers two strategies for determining national cost for remedial study. One strategy is based on a state allocation model or formula funding model, such as in Texas and Florida, where 2.3 percent of state higher education funds are allocated for remedial education. In this model, the proportion of funds allocated to remedial and developmental studies is applied to the total funds allocated to higher education in all fifty states. This method yielded national cost estimates of about $911 million. A word of caution: My own experience as a consultant to several states on remedial and developmental education suggests that fund allocation does not necessarily convert or result in spending as originally intended. In other words, allocating funds for, or generating funds from, remedial studies does not necessarily mean spending those funds on remediation.

The second strategy is an expenditure model based on the proportion of educational and general funds expended for remedial and developmental education. In Maryland, 1.2 percent of expenditures for public higher education is spent on remedial and developmental education. Assuming other states spend at or about the same rate, and by applying the same proportion to all states, this method yields a national expenditure calculation of $1.05 billion.

Breneman concludes by posing several questions about remedial and developmental education, most of which deal with the effectiveness and success of these programs. On remedial cost, Breneman states, if his costs estimate of about $1 billion, or about 1 percent of the national expenditure on higher education, holds up to further research, then the expenditure is both reasonable and justifiable.

I calculated national remedial education costs using the same sources and fiscal year data (1993–94) as Breneman but employed alternative sets of assumption bases and extrapolations:[18]

—Cost as a Function of Freshmen Taking Remedial Courses. Based on the fall 1993 data, total public undergraduate enrollment is 10 million students and public first-time freshmen enrollment is 1.7 million. This means first-time freshmen represent 17 percent of undergraduate enrollment.

Assuming 33 percent of first-time freshmen are enrolled in remedial education (1,676,000 times .33), then 553,080 freshmen are taking at least one remedial and developmental course. These 553,080 freshmen represent 6 percent (553,080 divided by 10,011,787) of the total undergraduate enrollment at public institutions.

Educational and general expenditures for fiscal year 1993–94 are reported at $87.1 billion. Therefore, $5.2 billion, 6 percent of $87.1 billion, is the proportion of total education and general expenditures spent on students who are enrolled in at least one remedial course their first year.

Assuming each freshman takes an average of twelve classes their first year, and at least one is a remedial course, then the cost of remedial study is $435.5 million ($5.2 billion divided by 12). If the average number of courses taken is nine, then remedial cost could be as high as $580.7 million ($5.2 billion divided by 9).

—Cost as a Function of Education Funds Committed to Remedial Studies. Another way of determining remedial expenditures is to take total educational and general expenditures, $87.1 billion, and multiply it by the proportion of public first-time undergraduate enrollment (17 percent). This yields a $14.81 billion total expenditure to educate first-time freshmen.

By multiplying $14.81 billion by 33 percent (assumed proportion of students taking remediation), the result is $4.9 billion of education and general funds expended on students taking at least one remedial course.

By dividing total expenditures on remedial students, $4.9 billion, by twelve (the average number of courses taken by first-time freshmen), the result is $407.2 million spent on remedial studies. If using nine as the average number of courses taken in the freshman year, expenditures soar to $542.9 million.

—Cost as a Function of Per Pupil Expenditure. The third approach is based on per student expenditure for fiscal 1993–94 of $14,000. Multiplying 1.7 million first-time freshmen by $14,000, the result is $9.5 billion expended to educate all first-time freshmen.

Assuming a third (553,080) of the freshmen are taking remedial courses, $3.1 billion ($9.5 billion times .33) is the total expended to educate all first-time freshmen who took at least one remedial course.

Therefore, $3.1 billion divided by twelve (the average number of courses taken by first-time freshmen) is $260.3 million, or if divided by nine courses the first year, $347 million.

This exercise shows the dramatic effects of using different methods or making different assumptions in determining expenditures or costs of remedial education. Until the issues of definitions and improved information are resolved, the best that can be done is to extrapolate the numbers and make reasonable assumptions. These methods yield results

Table 2. Estimated Forty–Year Lifetime Earnings and Tax Payments of First–Year College Students, Access Allowed and Denied, 1993–94

College access	Number of students[a]	Lifetime earnings[b]	Federal taxes owed[c]	State taxes owed[d]
Allowed	166,000	$265.6 billion	$74 billion	$13 billion
Denied	166,000	132.8 billion	37 billion	6 billion

a. Assumes 30 percent graduation rate.
b. Data from the U.S. Census Bureau. College access allowed = college graduate; college access denied = high school graduate.
c. Assumes 28 percent tax bracket.
d. Assumes 5 percent state and local taxes.

that vary from $260 million to more than $1 billion. Regardless of which method yields the most accurate results, the most critical concern for researchers, legislators, and policymakers is whether these results represent reasonable and acceptable expenditures or costs. The following hypothetical situation illustrates my point.

Using the 1993–94 estimates for students taking at least one remedial and developmental course (553,080 students), if 30 percent pass these courses and go on to earn bachelor's degrees, each of these 166,000 students has an estimated earning potential of about $1.6 million over a forty-year work life according to the U.S. Census Bureau data (see table 2). These 166,000 remedial college graduates have the potential to generate, collectively, income of about $265.6 billion (166,000 times $1.6 million). Assuming these persons are in the 28 percent tax bracket and paying on average 5 percent state and local taxes, over a lifetime of work they would pay more than $74 billion in federal taxes and $13 billion in state and local taxes. Even if the graduation rate is only 10 percent for these remedial and developmental students, 55,308 students would generate $88.5 billion (55,308 times $1.6 million) in income and pay $24.8 billion in federal taxes and $4 billion in state and local taxes over a lifetime of work. The graduation rate would have to drop to about 1 percent before a reversal of fortune occurs on the investment in remedial and developmental education.

In contrast, what would happen if these same 166,000 graduates who began their college careers in remedial courses were denied access to higher education altogether or were limited in the amount of higher education they could receive? For example, a person who has a high school diploma can expect to earn about $800,000 over a forty-year work life. These 166,000 students would have to find jobs right out of high school and their collective lifetime earnings would be about $132.8 billion. For the 28 percent federal and 5 percent state and local tax rates, this group would pay about $37 billion in federal taxes and $6 billion in state and local taxes.

Breneman's paper and this discussion make several key points. First, states—and the nation—reap great returns on the dollars invested in remedial education. The nation ends up with a more highly trained, skilled, and productive work force and a better class of citizen. Second, more and better data are needed that will enable policymakers and practitioners to make better judgments and decisions. Finally, in statehouses and on campuses around the country, the issues of college-level remedial and developmental education are being strongly contested and defended. The amount of remedial and developmental education on college campuses is too high, should be reduced to its lowest levels, and should be delivered as efficiently as possible. However, the current rate of investment in these students seems paltry in contrast to the economic and social benefits society receives over the students' lifetime.

Comment by Caroline M. Hoxby

The extent and cost of remediation in higher education is an important topic and one about which far too little is known. David W. Breneman ought to be praised for attempting to pull together information and data that do exist on this little-understood topic. I mean to compliment his paper when I predict that it will ultimately generate successors that will improve upon its admittedly preliminary estimate of the cost of remediation. Opening up an important issue and setting up an estimate for others to revise is a courageous task.

Why is it important to know what the cost of remediation is? There are two possible answers. First, taxpayers need to know whether they are getting their money's worth. If remediation is common and costly, then taxpayers may be double or triple paying for the teaching of a given body of scholastic material. They might then like to take steps toward reducing this waste. If remediation costs taxpayers only a small amount, then active policies of waste reduction may cost more than the benefits they generate.

Second, remediation is an attempt to teach students material that they have already been taught, perhaps multiple times, in secondary school. If colleges are able to remediate at a cost that is less than or equal to the money already expended on teaching the material in secondary school, then an attempt should be made to learn why colleges are able to get students to learn information that they previously failed to absorb. If colleges and secondary schools demonstrate different levels of success and efficiency, then there are implications for school finance and school reform policies.

The Responsibility for Remediation

One point about remediation deserves strong emphasis. Remediation is an elementary and secondary school problem; it is not a college problem. In one way, this point is obvious: Remediation is, by definition, an attempt to teach students skills they should have learned by the end of secondary school. In another way, however, it is not obvious: Colleges do the remediation; the cost of remediation appears in college budgets; the information that exists about remediation is per college, not per secondary school. Thus, blame is not attached to the institutions that generate the need for remediation. Ironically, this results in the phenomenon that Breneman discusses: Colleges are ashamed of doing remediation and attempt to conceal it.

For any individual college, concealing remediation is reasonable. No college wants to be known as an alternative high school. Colleges want to teach college-level material and their faculty want to be known as college faculty. So, colleges that teach many secondary-school-level courses do not call all of them remedial. They knowingly give college-level credit for some courses in which students are learning secondary school material. In the short run, this strategy can prop up a college's reputation. In the long run, though, colleges are degraded and can no longer teach material that is truly college level. As a group, colleges need to stop covering up for elementary and secondary schools.

Recently, a few state legislatures have considered proposals that would allow public colleges to charge K–12 school districts for remedial courses that their graduates must take. Such proposals are unlikely to become law in any state in the near future, but they serve as a reminder that an ideal accounting system would allocate costs differently from the way they are currently allocated. Perhaps states could keep notional accounting systems that would, at least, allow researchers and legislators to make approximate cost-benefit calculations. For instance, it would not harm any particular college's reputation if all Virginia colleges were to pool their remedial information and report that the Fairfax County School District owed them a certain amount for the remedial courses that its students had had to take. (Econometricians might worry about sample selection because the worst secondary schools would send a smaller share of students to college.)

The Breneman Estimates

What should be made of the Breneman estimates? I agree with Breneman that they are underestimates. Perhaps they are gross underestimates because numerous pressures force the estimates to be biased downward.

Reputational concerns pressure colleges into concealing the full extent of remediation. In addition, students do not like to admit to taking remedial courses. Their consumer behavior—choosing among colleges and among courses within colleges—tends to pressure colleges to dilute the content of regular courses rather than offer additional remedial courses. State legislatures exacerbate the situation by refusing to fund long-term remediation. The legislatures' goal is to limit the amount of remediation that state colleges provide (a maximum number of credits for any individual student), but these funding policies encourage concealment. Federal policy also encourages concealment. Pell grants and subsidized student loans cannot be used for more than a certain number of remedial courses; after that number, the student must begin taking regular college courses to continue receiving federal aid. The final reason that remediation numbers are likely to be underestimates is that low-quality secondary schools disproportionately send their students to a small share of colleges. These colleges must end up with low expectations for what regular college students can learn—even if they use college-level textbooks.

Thus, many pressures force remediation to be understated. The countervailing pressures are weak. For instance, colleges need not worry much about their worst remedial students cheapening the currency of the college's degree. The students who need the most remediation usually do not attain degrees.

To get a better measure of the extent and cost of remediation, external, absolute measures are needed of curriculum content and students' mastery of curriculum. A mathematics class should be called "remedial" based on its content and what the average student learns, not based on its listing in the college catalog. An English class should properly be labled "remedial" if it is; currently remedial classes are usually restricted by definition to reading and writing classes.

In practice, how might a researcher construct better measures? First, the placement examinations that colleges use to assign students to remedial classes could be employed. For example, suppose that the placement examination is comparable to a Regents examination (or that a norming group of students takes both tests). Then, suppose that college X puts students who would be predicted to fail the Regents mathematics exam in college course Y. Mathematics course Y would be called "remedial" regardless of what the college calls it.

Second, information about what students learn in their courses could be used. Many students use the same college textbooks. A comparison could be made of how much of the textbook material is covered by courses. Even better, some colleges use the standardized tests or problem sets that textbooks include as instructor material. If what problems a course assigned or what a course's passing scores were for the standardized examinations were known, then its degree of remediation could be judged. It would help to have norming groups of students who completed problem sets and examinations from multiple textbooks. However, the real obstacle to constructing external, absolute measures of remediation is not difficulty in comparing course materials. Most college faculty could probably rate textbook difficulty with ease. The obstacle is obtaining sufficiently detailed information from colleges about what their students are required to learn.

The Cost of Remediation

What can be learned from Breneman's paper? First, the cost of remediation is probably less than the cost of an average year of American secondary school. To make this back-of-the-envelope calculation,

I took Breneman's estimate of $1 billion annually. Supposing that colleges practice a great deal of concealment, I multiplied the estimate by four: $4 billion annually. But, only a little more than 60 percent of American high school graduates attempt college. To compare the $4 billion with the cost of secondary schooling, amounts for the same number of students should be compared. If the $4 billion were doubled to $8 billion, then the annual cost of remediation is about 40 percent of the cost of one grade of K–12 education in the United States.

Given this calculation, colleges are reasonably good at remediation. That is, community colleges succeed in teaching material to students that the same students resisted learning for up to four years in secondary school. (For example, most remedial mathematics courses cover nothing more advanced than algebra. Remedial reading courses teach students to grasp the sense of texts frequently read in junior high or high school.) Learning is apparently more efficient in colleges than in secondary schools. Keep in mind that the majority of remedial classes are taught at colleges with stretched resources: community colleges, city colleges, the least selective campuses in a state college system.

What are the differences between colleges and secondary schools that account for this? The difference is not money: Remediation costs only 40 percent of a typical year of secondary school. The typical American community college spends considerably less per pupil per year than the typical American secondary school.

One difference may be that college students are more motivated than high school students because their own funds are being invested in school. The opportunity costs of attending college are greater than those of attending secondary school because high school graduates have better labor market opportunities than people without a high school degree. Also, college students generally pay direct schooling costs (tuition and fees), while secondary school is financed by remote third-party taxpayers. Even a Pell grant recipient who pays none of the direct costs still expends a year of Pell eligibility when attending college. By investing their own money in college, students are forced to ask themselves whether they are getting sufficient benefit from school to justify the cost. This a question that rarely occurs to secondary school students.

Another difference is that colleges do not have a captive group of students. College, particularly community colleges, have to adapt to changing circumstances and compete for students if they wish to survive. They have strong incentives to show that their teaching is effective and useful. As a result, many community colleges have learned to work with local employers so that they can quickly adapt their curricula to the changing needs of the local labor market. Teaching colleges increasingly take teaching seriously, providing their students with course evaluation forms, publishing the results, basing faculty promotion and rewards on teaching success, and offering training courses to faculty whose teaching skills are poor.

Possibly, secondary schooling needs to be more like remediation in college. Both students and secondary schools need to have stronger incentives to perform well. Various forms of school choice (charter schools, vouchers, choice among public schools) could give secondary schools stronger incentives to perform. Plans such as Minnesota's, where a secondary school student can attend college with his secondary school's money (and is therefore implicitly discarding college money with every wasted year of secondary school), can give stronger performance incentives to both secondary school students and secondary schools.

Finally, Breneman's paper suggests that forbidding colleges to do remediation is not the right policy. Such a policy would encourage further concealment. Colleges should be encouraged to think of remediation as a secondary school problem and should be asked to provide information about how much each secondary school owes colleges for remediation. Moreover, because colleges appear to be better than secondary schools at getting resistant students to learn material, secondary schools might reasonably be forbidden to teach a body of material more than once to a given student. Instead, secondary schools could put the money that would have been spent on repeating the material into an adult education or community college fund for the student.

Notes

1. This paper examines only one aspect of the total economic cost of remediation—the part reported by public institutions of higher education. Total economic costs would also include costs borne by students through forgone earnings and diminished labor productivity and by society as a whole through a failure to develop fully the nation's human capital. In that sense, remediation is a second effort to repair earlier damage or failure to learn, which results in lower national wealth and higher transfer payments to those with low lifetime incomes. These more global costs are not included in this first attempt to put a dollar figure on the expenses borne by colleges and universities as well as the taxpayers who support them. With financial support from the Thomas B. Fordham Foundation, I am conducting further research on the financial costs of remediation, including several state case studies.

2. Quote taken from the National Association for Developmental Education's World Wide Web site: http://www.umkc.edu/centers/cad/nade/nadedocs/devgoals.htm.

3. National Center for Education Statistics, *Remedial Education at Higher Education Institutions in Fall 1995*, NCES 97–584 (Department of Education, Office of Educational Research and Improvement, October 1996), p. B–1.

4. National Center for Education Statistics, *Remedial Education at Higher Education Institutions in Fall 1995*, pp. iii–v.

5. One question was asked about retention beyond the freshman year. Of the institutions offering remedial programs, 24 percent reported low retention (less than 49 percent returning), 23 percent reported medium retention (50 to 74 percent returning), and 53 percent reported high retention (75 to 100 percent returning). National Center for Education Statistics, *Remedial Education at Higher Education Institutions in Fall 1995*, p. 14, figure 2.

6. Southern Regional Education Board, *Remedial Education in College: How Widespread Is It?* (Atlanta, Ga., 1988); Southern Regional Education Board, *They Came to College?: A Remedial/Developmental Profile of First–Time Freshmen in SREB States* (Atlanta, Ga., 1991); and Ansley A. Abraham, Jr., *College Remedial Studies: Institutional Practices in the SREB States* (Atlanta, Ga.: Southern Regional Education Board, 1992).

7. Abraham, *College Remedial Studies*, pp. 21–24.

8. Abraham, *College Remedial Studies*, pp. 25–26.

9. The State Higher Education Executive Officers is made up of the heads of state coordinating boards of state systems of higher education.

10. These and subsequent data are from Texas Higher Education Coordinating Board, Division of Research, Planning, and Finance *Appropriations for Remedial Instruction in Texas Public Institutions of Higher Education* (Austin, Texas, July 1996), p. 7.

11. Texas identifies the racial and ethnic identity of students benefiting from remediation—36.4 percent served Hispanic students; 16.3 percent, black students; 8.3 percent Asian and other students; and 39.0 percent, white students. Texas Higher Education Coordinating Board, *Appropriations for Remedial Instruction in Texas Public Institutions of Higher Education*, p. 11. Personal correspondence from Pat Pallet, Florida State Board of Education, Postsecondary Education Planning Commission.

12. Maryland Higher Education Commission, *A Study of Remedial Education at Maryland Public Campuses* (Annapolis, Md., May 1996), pp. 6, 39.

13. Department of Education, National Center for Education Statistics, *Digest of*

Education Statistics 1996, NCES 96–133 (Government Printing Office, 1996). The Texas data are reported on p. 339. The annual data for Texas in the digest are consistent with figures from the state's report on remediation, where the data cover a two-year (biennial) appropriation.

14. Department of Education, *Digest of Education Statistics 1996*, p. 357. The Maryland data from that state's report on remedial education are roughly consistent with the numbers published for Maryland educational expenditures in the digest.

15. The California Community College Association reports an expenditure of $300 million on remedial education, while the California State University System reports outlays of $9.3 million. California community colleges account for 21 percent of national two-year college enrollments, which suggest (by extrapolation) national outlays in this sector of $1.5 billion. California may have a higher than average number of immigrants enrolled in remedial courses, however. California Community College Association, "Community College Issues That Must Be Addressed in the Intersegmental Basic Skills Discussion," testimony on behalf of the Chancellor's Office, California Community Colleges, Oct. 27, 1995.

16. Department of Education, *Digest of Education Statistics 1996*, pp. 152, 334.

17. Clifford Adelman, "The Truth about Remedial Work: It's More Complex than Windy Rhetoric and Simple Solutions Suggest," *Chronicle of Higher Education*, vol. 43, no. 6 (October 4, 1996), p. A56.

18. National Center for Education Statistics, *Digest of Education Statistics*, NCES 96–133 (Government Printing Office, 1996). Calculations based on numbers taken from pages 181, 185, 343, 349.